D1296092

Publications of the
CENTRE FOR REFORMATION AND RENAISSANCE STUDIES

Essays and Studies, 13

SERIES EDITOR   KONRAD EISENBICHLER

Victoria University
in the
University of Toronto

Metamorphosis

The Changing Face of Ovid in Medieval and Early Modern Europe

Edited by
ALISON KEITH *and* STEPHEN RUPP

Toronto
Centre for Reformation and Renaissance Studies
2007

CRRS Publications
Centre for Reformation and Renaissance Studies
Victoria University in the University of Toronto
Toronto, Ontario M5S 1K7
Canada

Tel: 416/585-4465
Fax: 416/585-4430
Email: crrs.publications@utoronto.ca
www.crrs.ca

Library and Archives Canada Cataloguing in Publication

Metamorphosis : the changing face of Ovid in medieval and early modern
Europe / edited by Alison Keith and Stephen Rupp.

(Essays and studies ; 13)
Proceedings of a conference held in Toronto, Mar. 12, 2005.
Includes bibliographical references and index.
ISBN 978-0-7727-2035-1

        1. Ovid, 43 B.C.-17 or 18 A.D.--Criticism and interpretation.
I. Keith, Alison Mary II. Rupp, Stephen James III. Victoria University
(Toronto, Ont.). Centre for Reformation and Renaissance Studies IV. Title.
V. Series: Essays and studies (Victoria University (Toronto, Ont.). Centre
for Reformation and Renaissance Studies) 13

PA6537.M48 2007   871'.01   C2007-903591-4

Cover illustration: Dish with scene from the story of Daphne and Apollo,
Gardiner Museum, Toronto. Accession N° G83.1.0381.

Cover design: Paragraphics

Typesetting and production: Becker Associates

Contents

Acknowledgments

We would like to express our gratitude to Alison McKay and David Fallis for their inception, in 2004-2005, of the Toronto-wide Arts Festival on the theme of "Metamorphosis" and to all of our contributors, who responded to the original call for papers with enthusiasm, participated in the discussions with gusto and collegiality, and both composed their original papers and revised their chapters for the volume with alacrity and acumen. The conference was made possible with a grant from the Social Sciences and Humanities Council of Canada and contributions from the Centre for Comparative Literature; the Departments of Classics, English, Fine Art History, and Spanish and Portuguese; and the Emilio Goggio Chair in Italian Studies. We are grateful to all these institutions for their support. We are particularly grateful to the Centre for Medieval Studies at the University of Toronto and the Centre for Reformation and Renaissance Studies at Victoria University in the University of Toronto for their generosity in co-sponsoring and co-hosting the original conference and for their continuing commitment to the project. Professors Lawrin Armstrong, Konrad Eisenbichler, David Klausner, Andy Orchard, and Jill Ross offered much needed assistance at crucial junctures and we remain grateful to them for their ongoing help. It is a pleasure to record as well our debts of gratitude to Rosemary Beattie, whose financial acumen facilitated both the conference and the resulting volume, and especially to Sarah Sheehan, who has been of invaluable assistance in the preparation of the manuscript. Last but by no means least, we are very grateful to Konrad Eisenbichler in his capacity as Editor of the CRRS Essays and Studies Series for the generous care and attention he has bestowed on the project as it has come to fruition.

ALISON KEITH
STEPHEN RUPP

Illustrations

CONTRIBUTORS

SUZANNE CONKLIN AKBARI is Associate Professor of English and Medieval Studies at the University of Toronto. She has published *Seeing through the Veil: Optical Theory and Medieval Allegory* (Toronto, 2004) and is completing *Idols in the East: European Depictions of Islam and the Orient, 1100-1450*. Her next project is titled *Small Change: Metaphor and Metamorphosis in Late Medieval Literature*.

FRANK T. COULSON is Professor of Classics in the Department of Greek and Latin at the Ohio State University where he serves as Director of Palaeography at the Center for Epigraphical and Palaeographical Studies. He has published extensively on the reception of Ovid in the Middle Ages and is currently writing the article on Ovid for the *Catalogus translationum et commentariorum*.

MARILYN DESMOND is Professor of English at SUNY-Binghamton and the author of *Reading Dido: Gender, Textuality, and the Medieval "Aeneid"* (Minnesota, 1994) and *Ovid's Art and the Wife of Bath: the Ethics of Erotic Violence* (Cornell, 2006). Her research interests focus on Classics and medieval narrative, Chaucer, feminist theory and queer theory.

CORA FOX is Assistant Professor of English at Arizona State University, where she teaches courses on Shakespeare and Renaissance literature. She is currently finishing her first book – *Ovid and the Politics of Emotion in Elizabethan England*, which reads English Renaissance Ovidianism in diverse contemporary textual and cultural sites – while on research leave as a faculty fellow of the Arizona Center for Medieval and Renaissance Studies.

JAMIE C. FUMO is Assistant Professor of English at McGill University. She has published articles on Chaucer and on fifteenth-century Scottish and English poetry in *Chaucer Review, Studies in Philology, Neophilologus, Viator, Mediaevalia*, and in various collections of essays. She is especially interested in medieval mythography and Chaucer's classicism, and is currently completing a book-length study of the figure of Apollo in medieval culture entitled *The Legacy of Apollo: Antiquity, Authority, and Chaucerian Poetics*.

ALISON KEITH is Professor of Classics and Women's Studies, Medieval Studies and Comparative Literature at the University of Toronto. She is the author of *The Play of Fictions: Studies in Ovid's "Metamorphoses"* (Michigan, 1992) and *Engendering Rome: Women in Latin Epic* (Cambridge, 2000), and has written extensively on gender and genre in Latin literature and the construction of gender in Roman culture.

MAGGIE KILGOUR is Professor of English literature at McGill University. She is the author of *From Communion to Cannibalism: An Anatomy of Metaphors of Incorporation* (Princeton, 1990) and *The Rise of the Gothic Novel* (Routledge, 1995) and essays on a range of topics savoury and unsavoury. She is currently working on a book on Milton and Ovid.

R. JOHN MCCAW is Associate Professor in Spanish at the University of Wisconsin, Milwaukee and the author of *The Transforming Text: A Study of Luis de Góngora's "Soledades"* (Scripta Humanistica, 2000). His research interests lie in sixteenth- and seventeenth-century Spanish literature and culture, especially courtly love, ritual and Spanish culture.

KATHRYN MCKINLEY is Associate Professor of English at Florida International University and the author of *Reading the Ovidian Heroine: "Metamorphoses" Commentaries 1100–1618* (Brill, 2001). Her central focus is on the ways poets of the high and later Middle Ages responded to, and appropriated, aspects of classical antiquity, especially Ovid's poetry, in their own works.

SANDA MUNJIC is Assistant Professor of Spanish at the University of Toronto. Her research centres on the representation of love and suffering in late medieval and early modern Spain, particularly in prose romances and lyric poetry.

CYNTHIA NAZARIAN is a Ph.D. candidate in Comparative Literature at Princeton University. Her dissertation explores violence and voice in sixteenth-century French and English imitations of Petrarch and Ovid.

JULIA BRANNA PERLMAN specializes in Italian Renaissance art, theory and historiography and is currently an Associate Lecturer in Art History for the Open University in London. With a research background in neuroscience, she is especially interested in the relations among the verbal and visual arts, and among Renaissance physiological and metaphorical models of love, vision, and cognition.

STEPHEN RUPP is Associate Professor of Spanish and Comparative Literature, and Chair of the Department of Spanish and Portuguese at the

University of Toronto. He is the author of *Allegories of Kingship: Calderón and the Anti-Machiavellian Tradition* (Penn State, 1996) and articles on early modern Spanish drama and Cervantes.

THOMAS WILLARD is Associate Professor of English at the University of Arizona and Book Review Editor of *Cauda Pavonis: Studies in Hermeticism*. His studies of alchemy include an edition of Jean D'Espagnet's *Summary of Physics Restored* (*Enchyridion Physicae Restitutae*) (Garland, 1999).

GUR ZAK is a doctoral candidate at the Centre for Medieval Studies, University of Toronto. His dissertation deals with experiences and models of selfhood in the early Italian Renaissance from Petrarch to Poliziano. He has recently published an article in Hebrew on "Narrative, Fragmentation, and the History of Autobiography."

PATRICIA ZALAMEA is a Ph.D. candidate in Art History at Rutgers University. Following a year of research in France, based at the *École Normale Supérieure – Lettres et Sciences Humaines* in Lyon, she is completing her dissertation, "Diana as an Emblematic Image of the French Renaissance Court."

AFTER OVID:
CLASSICAL, MEDIEVAL, AND EARLY MODERN RECEPTIONS OF THE METAMORPHOSES

ALISON KEITH AND STEPHEN RUPP

The *Metamorphoses* of Publius Ovidius Naso appeared in 8 C.E., the very year its author was abruptly banished from Rome by the Emperor Augustus and relegated to Tomis (modern Costanza in Romania), a superficially Hellenised town on the north-eastern edge of the Roman empire as far away from the imperial centre as could be found. Despite Ovid's exile – and the concomitant removal of an earlier work, the *Ars amatoria* (*Art of Love*), from the public libraries of Rome – the *Metamorphoses*, as far as we can tell, garnered great acclaim, both in its own day and after. The reception history of the poem can be documented from a very early period after its release into circulation because it is cited in the following centuries by numerous authors in a wide range of literary genres – rhetoric, satire, epigram, epic, prose narrative, and technical treatises. Here we consider the varied reception history of the poem from antiquity to the Middle Ages with a particular focus on the parallel development of enthusiastic literary (and artistic) imitation, on the one hand, and trenchant rhetorical, later Christian, criticism, on the other. This survey of the poem's reception is offered as a prelude to the specific essays in this volume on European readings and reworkings of material from the *Metamorphoses*.

Ovid himself tells us something of the contemporary reception of the *Metamorphoses* in his first book of poetry from exile. Claiming that it was unfinished when the blow of exile fell, he reports that, in despair, he consigned it to the flames on his departure from Rome (*Tr.* 1.7.11–26). Despite the *Metamorphoses'* ostensibly unfinished state (cf. *defuit et scriptis ultima lima meis*, *Tr.* 1.7.30),[1] Ovid claims that the poem

---

[1] Latin authors in this chapter are cited from the *Oxford Classical Text* editions, except the elder Seneca, Statius and Martial who are cited from the Loeb editions. Contributors have otherwise cited Ovid's *Metamorphoses* from the Loeb Classical

survived his attempt to burn it precisely because it had already found readers: "I think they had been transcribed in multiple copies" (*pluribus exemplis scripta fuisse reor, Tr.* 1.7.24). In exile the poet views the continuing circulation of the *Metamorphoses* as a means of keeping his name before the Latin reading public.

The elder Seneca bears witness to the early popularity of the *Metamorphoses* in the rhetorical culture of the Augustan age. During Tiberius' reign (14–37 C.E.), Seneca compiled two handbooks on declamation in Augustan Rome for his three sons, whom he wished to educate in the rhetorical culture of an earlier era with higher standards than their own. His first treatise, *Controversiae*, records rhetorical display pieces in which speakers argue for or against a defendant in fictional legal cases. Out of sympathy for his sons' interest in witty turns of phrase (*sententiae*), Seneca pays particular attention to their deployment in declamations. Several vignettes in the *Controversiae* illustrate the popularity of Ovid's *Metamorphoses* as a source of these pointed expressions. The most telling comes from the third book, where Seneca records an exchange about epigrams between the declaimer Alfius Flavus and the orator Cestius (3.7):

> Alfius Flavus spoke this epigram (*hanc sententiam*): "He supplied his own nourishment – and his own loss." Reproving him as if he had spoken in bad taste, Cestius said, "It is clear that you read the poets carefully. This idea of yours belongs to the poet who has filled this age not only with amatory *Arts* but also with amatory epigrams (*qui hoc saeculum amatoriis non artibus tantum sed sententiis impleuit*). For Ovid said this in his *Metamorphoses*: "He himself began to tear away at his own limbs with savage biting and, unhappy man, was nourishing his body by diminishing it."

Both Flavus' adaptation of the Ovidian epigram and Cestius' recognition of its source in the *Metamorphoses* (8.877–878) bear witness to the popular diffusion of Ovid's poetry in general, and the *Metamorphoses* in particular, already in the poet's lifetime. However, a pointed contrast concerning the merit of Ovidian verse also emerges from the anecdote, for Seneca reports Cestius' rebuke of Flavus as if he had spoken in bad taste in adapting a popular poet whom Flavus presumably admired.

Library edition. We have regularized Latin orthography by using lower case "u" for "v" in accordance with classical practice throughout this chapter. All translations in this chapter are our own unless otherwise indicated.

Other passages in the elder Seneca's handbooks attest not only to the popularity of the *Metamorphoses* amongst contemporary readers but also to a less sympathetic critical reception. In the last book of *Controversiae*, Seneca introduces the declaimer Publius Vinicius as a great admirer of Ovidian poetry, especially the *Metamorphoses* (10.5.25):

> Publius Vinicius, a very great enthusiast for Ovid (*summus amator Ouidi*), used to say that this idea had been most eloquently put by Ovid, and that it should be kept in mind for fashioning similar epigrams. At Achilles' death Ovid has this finishing touch: "After the death of Hector, this was all that could cause old Priam to rejoice."

The Elder Seneca records Vinicius' quotation from the *Metamorphoses* (12.607–608) in a context that illustrates not only how well known the poem was in contemporary Roman literary circles, but also how popular it was as a model for aspiring orators. Another anecdote in the *Controversiae*, however, confirms in less flattering terms the immediate success of Ovid's poem (9.5.17):

> The orator Montanus had this fault: he ruined his epigrams by accumulation; not content to say a thing well once, he prevents himself from speaking well. For this reason, and for others that can make an orator seem similar to a poet, Scaurus used to call Montanus an Ovid among orators; for Ovid too didn't know when to leave well enough alone. Not to give too many examples of what Scaurus called Montanisms, I will content myself with this one: when Polyxena had been led away to be sacrificed at Achilles' tomb, Hecuba says: "The very ashes of the dead (Achilles) fight against this family" [*Met.* 13.503–504]. Ovid could have contented himself with this; but he added: "We perceived the enemy even in his grave" [*Met.* 13.504]. Nor was he content with this; he added: "I was fertile – for Aeacus' son (Achilles)" [*Met.* 13.505]. Scaurus, however, used to speak truly when he said: it was no less great a virtue to know how to speak than to know how to leave off speaking.

Seneca defines the essential fault of an otherwise unknown orator, Montanus,[2] as self-indulgence, a vice for which Ovid would be repeatedly criticised in antiquity (and beyond). Indeed in an earlier passage, Seneca draws attention to precisely this fault of Ovidian poetry: "he

---

[2]Unless, as our colleague Michael Dewar suggests to us, he is the same man as the poet Julius Montanus, mocked by the younger Seneca (*Epp.* 122.1 ff., *Apoc.* 2) – which would lend a nice note of family continuity to the criticism.

used language by no means freely except in his poetry, in which far from being unaware of his faults he embraced them" (*uerbis minime licenter usus est nisi in carminibus, in quibus non ignorauit uitia sua sed amauit*, 2.2.12). It is striking, moreover, that Seneca here illustrates Montanus' fault not from the orator's œuvre but from Ovid's *Metamorphoses*. Paradoxically, however, Seneca's very criticisms of Ovid's poetic license vividly document contemporary enthusiasm for the epigrammatic wit on display in the *Metamorphoses*.

It is clear that subsequent generations at Rome shared this enthusiasm for both the *Metamorphoses* and Ovid's epigrammatic wit. The younger Seneca, for example, seems to have absorbed his father's illustration of the *sententiae* of an earlier age, even if he does not always heed his father's warnings about Ovidian excess. In both his prose writings and his tragedies he makes use of a pointed, epigrammatic style that owes a great deal to the example of Ovid, in spite of his father's deprecation of Ovidian epigrammatic self-indulgence. Quintilian, first holder of the Flavian chair of rhetoric at Rome (appointed 78 C.E.), comments on the brilliance of the younger Seneca's epigrams (*multae in eo claraeque sententiae*, *Inst. Or.* 10.1.129) despite an otherwise self-indulgent style that Quintilian censures in language reminiscent of the elder Seneca's criticisms of Ovid: "you could wish he'd spoken in accordance with his own talent but other people's judgement" (*uelles eum suo ingenio dixisse, alieno iudicio*, *Inst. Or.* 10.1.130; cf. Sen. Rhet. *Contr.* 2.2.12, quoted above). Indeed, the younger Seneca is likened to Ovid by both ancient and modern scholars because of his rhetorical and epigrammatic style,[3] and his knowledge of the *Metamorphoses*, in particular, is visible throughout his writings. In his philosophical *Dialogues*, for example, he quotes directly from the *Metamorphoses* (six times; second only to Vergil, quoted nine times) and in his tragedies he not only alludes frequently to the poem but also adapts extensively from it.[4] Most striking of all, however, is a specific reference to the *Metamorphoses* in his satiric *Apocolocyntosis* ("Gourdification"). In the course of a debate among the Gods about the dead emperor Claudius, Hercules proposes not only that he be admitted to their ranks (Sen. *Apoc.* 9.5) but also that he be added as well to Ovid's *Metamorphoses*, where the apotheoses of Romulus (*Met.*

---

[3]Cf., e.g., Tarrant, *Seneca's Thyestes*, 22: "Like Ovid, Seneca was often unable or unwilling to restrain his extraordinary cleverness, but, again like Ovid, he could use his rhetorical skill with greater subtlety than he is usually given credit for."

[4]See, e.g., Tarrant, *Seneca's Thyestes*, "Index II. Subjects" s.v. Ovid.

14.805–828) and Julius Caesar (*Met.* 15.745–761) were recorded and that of Augustus predicted (*Met.* 15.868–870).

Like the elder Seneca, Quintilian balances criticism with praise in his assessment of Ovid's achievement in the *Metamorphoses*: "Ovid is certainly given to frivolity in his epic and too much in love with his own genius, but nevertheless he is to be praised in parts" (*lasciuus quidem in herois quoque Ouidius et nimium amator ingenii sui, laudandus tamen partibus, Inst. Or.* 10.1.88; cf. his assessment of the younger Seneca, quoted above). Elsewhere in his magisterial work on *The Education of the Orator*, however, Quintilian seems somewhat more sympathetic to Ovid's accomplishment. In a discussion of the importance of effecting a natural transition from the procemium of a speech to its body, he cites the example of Ovid's transitions in the *Metamorphoses* which, although contrived, successfully achieve their purpose (*Inst. Or.* 4.1.77):

> But there is a contrived and childish affectation in the schools to have the transition itself effect some epigram and to seek applause for this trick, as Ovid is accustomed to play at in the *Metamorphoses*; whom the requirement of connecting the most diverse matters into the appearance of a single form, however, can excuse...

Certainly Quintilian knew the *Metamorphoses* well, since he draws examples from the poem throughout his treatise in order to illustrate various technical facets of rhetoric. In addition to beginning his discussion of transitions with a reference to the poem, he cites the famous opening hemistich of *Metamorphoses* 13 (*consedere duces*) as evidence that the Latin language has no dual form (*Inst. Or.* 1.5.43); he notes the importance of place to an argument by quoting the opening words of the Ovidian Ajax's speech (*Met.* 13.5–6) in the contest for Achilles' arms (*Inst. Or.* 5.10.41); he illustrates readers' desire to read obscenity into any utterance with a quotation from the first book of the poem (*quaeque latent meliora putant*, "whatever lies hidden they think better," *Met.* 1.502, quoted at *Inst. Or.* 8.3.47); he defines emphasis with an example from *Metamorphoses* 10 (*Inst. Or.* 9.2.64); he illustrates rhetorical figures of addition by quoting from *Metamorphoses* 5 (*Inst. Or.* 9.3.48); and he includes two line-endings from the *Metamorphoses* (2.226, 11.456) in his discussion of "excessively soft" (*praemolle*), i.e., effeminate, epic rhythm (*Inst. Or.* 9.4.65). Quintilian's repeated references to the *Metamorphoses* in the *Institutio Oratoria* are a telling index of Ovid's importance in the period and are particularly noteworthy by comparison with his failure to extend similar treatment to Lucan, Statius, and Valerius Flaccus.

Quintilian's choice of Ovidian examples to illustrate a range of rhetorical features intersects suggestively with adaptations of passages from Ovid's *Metamorphoses* in Neronian and Flavian literature. For example, the Neronian satirist Persius (34–62 C.E.), in his opening satire, attacks four specimens of "soft" or effeminate epic verse – one of the features censured by Quintilian and illustrated with examples from the *Metamorphoses* – which the satirist's interlocutor enthusiastically recites (Pers. 1.93–102):

> But decorous connection has been imparted even to rough measures. Our modern poet has learned to fill out the line thus, with 'Berecynthian Attis' [*Berecyntius Attis*], and 'The dolphin which was cutting its way through dark-blue Nereus' [*qui caeruleum dirimebat Nerea delphin*], and 'We removed a rib from the long Appenines' [*costam longo subduximus Appennino*]. Surely this 'arms and the man' [*arma uirum*] is an overblown piece of swollen bark, like an old branch, dried up with its cork stunted." Then must we read something bland and effeminate? "They filled the savage horns with Maenadic lowing; a Bassarid ready to carry off the head of a proud calf and a Maenad, ready to rein in her lynx with vine shoots, redouble their shout of 'Evoe!' as restoring Echo reverberates [*et raptum uitulo caput ablatura superbo | Bassaris et lyncem Maenas flexura corymbis | euhion ingeminat, reparabilis adsonat Echo*].

The "details of these examples suggest that P[ersius] has in mind the work of *Ovidiani poetae*,"[5] and commentators have documented in these lines pervasive reminiscences of Ovid in general and the *Metamorphoses* in particular.[6] For example, *Berecyntius Attis* (Pers. 1. 93) conflates the Ovidian line-endings *Cybeleius Attis* (*Met.* 10.104) and *Berecyntius heros* (*Met.* 11.106); the Graecism *Nerea* (Pers. 1.94) occurs in the second book of the *Metamorphoses* (2.267) while the phrase *caeruleum ... Nerea* is an Ovidian *junctura* (*Her.* 9.14; cf. *Met.* 13.742–743, *at mihi cui pater est Nereus, quam caerula Doris | enixa est*); the spondaic line-ending of *longo ... Appennino* (Pers. 1.95, specifically deprecated at Quint. *Inst. Or.* 9.4.65) appears in hexameter verse first at *Met.* 2.226; Ovid exploits the future participle (on display in *ablatura* and *flexura*, Pers. 1.100, 101) throughout his œuvre and spurs its development in Latin poetry;[7] and

---

[5] Harvey, *Commentary on Persius*, 43; see also 44–47 for detailed discussion of Ovidian reminiscences in these lines.

[6] See most recently Dewar, "Ovid in the 1st–5th Centuries A.D.," 383–385.

[7] Leumann-Hoffman-Szantyr, *Lateinische Grammatik,* Vol. 2 § 390.

reparabilis adsonat Echo (Pers. 1.102) combines Ovid's description of Echo mourning Narcissus (*plangentibus adsonat Echo, Met.* 3.507) with an adjective that appears first in Ovidian verse (*reparabilis, Met.* 1.379, *Am.* 1.14.55, *Her.* 5.103). Interestingly, the scholiast on this passage identifies the Ovidian hack who is the target of Persius' satire as the Emperor Nero himself.[8] Whether or not Persius' interlocutor is the specific target Nero, or simply a general figure for contemporary poetasters, what is important for this survey of the cultural reception of the *Metamorphoses* is that this *Ovidianus poeta* clearly embraces the very stylistic traits censured by both the elder Seneca and Quintilian and repeatedly ascribed to Ovid in antiquity. The effusive praise of this style by Persius' *Ovidianus poeta* illustrates the enduring popularity of Ovid and his *Metamorphoses* – despite the disdain of the satirist and the discomfort of the rhetorical tradition.

The continuing popular circulation of Ovid's *Metamorphoses* is vividly documented a generation later in the *Apophoreta* of the Flavian poet Martial (ca. 40–104 C.E.), a collection of epigrams that not only commemorates the kinds of holiday gifts appropriate to the Saturnalia but is itself figured, in its entirety, as a Saturnalian gift. Towards the conclusion of the collection, Martial includes a series of couplets commemorating presentation copies of perennially popular works of literature, such as those of Homer and Vergil, Cicero and Livy, Catullus and Propertius. Among them is an epigram written to accompany a codex copy of the *Metamorphoses* (*Ouidi Metamorphosis in membranis*, "Ovid's *Metamorphoses* on parchment"): "This mass which has been constructed in a multilayered tablet bears the fifteen-book poem of Ovid" (*Haec tibi multiplici quae structa est massa tabella,* | *Carmina Nasonis quinque decemque gerit*, Mart. 14.192). Recent criticism has seen in this epigram not only evidence of the popular diffusion of the *Metamorphoses*, but also a metaliterary complement to (and compliment on) the poem's literary sophistication: "It is hard not to wonder … whether the codex structure, described as the gathering of interwoven leaves, might not refer to the multi-layered structuring of Ovid's poem with its inter-woven narratives."[9]

---

[8] Sullivan, *Literature and Politics*, 101.

[9] Roman, "Literary Materiality in Martial's *Epigrams*," 135. On Martial's interest in Ovid, see especially Pitcher, "Martial's Debt to Ovid."

To this point our discussion has emphasized the popular reception of Ovid's playfulness and wit in the *Metamorphoses*, paralleled by a more hostile reception in the Roman critical tradition. But Martial's epigram reveals that the poem also inspired literary reflection on more serious issues. The representation of the Olympian deities in terms of Roman imperial politics throughout the *Metamorphoses*, for example, offered later authors a powerful model for reflecting on the public ceremonial and political tensions of the imperial court. Thus Ovid's depiction of the Council of the Gods in *Met.* 1 on the model of a meeting of the Senate in Augustus' home on the Palatine (*Met.* 1.163–180) supplies a model for the representation by Statius (ca. 45–96 C.E.), at almost the same point in the opening of his epic, of a Council of the Gods on the model of a meeting of the Senate under the Emperor Domitian (*Theb.* 1.197–213). Statius borrows several elements of the Ovidian scene: the designation of Jupiter as *pater* (transposed from the beginning of the Ovidian council, *Met.*1.163, to the end of his divine council, *Theb.* 1.204) and of his subjects as *caelicolae*, "heaven-dwellers" (*Met.* 1.174 ~ *Theb.* 1.204, in the same *sedes*; cf. *semidei*, *Met.* 1.192, and *semideum*, *Theb.* 1.206); the seismic effect of Jupiter's entrance on divine audience and cosmos alike;[10] the respect accorded his authority;[11] and the very Roman cast of the architectural setting of the divine council.[12] Statius exploits the ceremonial language of Ovid's mischievous depiction of the divine council but alters his predecessor's playful tone to underscore rather the gravity of the occasion and its cosmic dimensions. In this way he evokes both the extent of Rome's imperial reach and the majesty of her ruler Domitian, an Augustus *redivivus*.[13]

The subject of transformation itself provoked considerable philosophical, literary and artistic debate in antiquity, and Ovid's poem was central to the discussion. The *Metamorphoses* or *Golden Ass* of the Antonine author Apuleius (ca. 125–170 C.E.), for example, concerns itself with a world "every bit as uncertain and labile as the Heraclitean flux of the Ovidian universe."[14] The manuscripts record the title of the mid-second century C.E. work as *Metamorphoses*, which acknowledges

---

[10] Dominik, *Mythic Voice*, 164.

[11] Dominik, *Mythic Voice*, 7–8; Keith, "Imperial Building Projects."

[12] Keith, "Imperial Building Projects."

[13] On Statius' debt to Ovid see Dewar, "Ovid in the 1st–5th centuries A.D."; and Keith, "Ovidian Personae in Statius' *Thebaid*," "Ovid's Theban Narrative in Statius' *Thebaid*," and "Imperial Building Projects."

[14] Kenney, introduction to Apuleius, *Cupid & Psyche*, 2.

Apuleius' considerable debt to Ovid's poem, though the novel also seems to have circulated in antiquity under the title *The Golden Ass* (cf. Aug. *Civ. Dei* 18.18). The novel's opening sentence reveals Apuleius' preoccupation with Ovid's poem (*Met.* 1.1):

> Now, in this Milesian discourse I propose to string together various stories for you and to soothe your well-disposed ears with an agreeable murmur – always providing you are not too proud to look at Egyptian paper written on with the acuteness of a reed from the Nile – to make you marvel at men's shapes and fortunes changed to other appearances and then changed back again [*figuras fortunasque hominum in alias imagines conuersas et in se rursum mutuo nexu refectas ut mireris*].[15]

The promise of marvellous transformations pointedly recalls the opening lines of Ovid's *Metamorphoses*, in which the poet promises to tell of shapes changed into new bodies (*in noua fert animus mutatas dicere formas | corpora*, *Met.* 1.1–2; cf. *carmina mutatas hominum dicentia formas*, *Tr.* 1.7.13), and scholars have documented the pervasive reminiscences of Ovidian lexical and thematic motifs in this sentence.[16] The embedded tale of Cupid and Psyche (Apul. *Met.* 4.28–6.24) is particularly rich in intertextual relations with Ovid's poem: the exposure of Psyche on a crag to a monster (Apul. *Met.* 4.33–35) recalls the exposure of Andromeda on a cliff to a sea-monster (Ov. *Met.* 4.670–739);[17] Venus' jealous persecution of Psyche (Apul. *Met.* 4.29–31) recalls Juno's jealous persecution of Io (Ov. *Met.* 1.601–739), Callisto (Ov. *Met.* 2.466–530), and Semele (Ov. *Met.* 3.256–309); "Psyche herself, at the crucial moment of decision, is portrayed as an Ovidian heroine, a conflation of Althaea, Byblis ... and Myrrha" (heroines from Ov. *Met.* 8, 9 and 10 respectively);[18] and Apuleius' embedded narrative, one of several, also suggestively recalls "the multi-layered structuring of Ovid's poem with its interwoven narratives."[19]

---

[15] Text and translation from Kenney, introduction to Apuleius, *Cupid & Psyche*, 6–7.

[16] Scotti, "Il proemio delle *Metamorfosi*," 43–55.

[17] The tale was very popular: cf. Manilius 5.540–618 and Valerius Flaccus 2.451–549 (whose Hesione is modelled on Ovid's Andromeda).

[18] Kenney, introduction to Apuleius, *Cupid & Psyche*, 19.

[19] Roman, "Literary Materiality in Martial's *Epigrams*," 135, quoted above 21. On Apuleius' debt to Ovid, see especially Scotti, "Il proemio delle *Metamorfosi*," and Kenney, introduction to Apuleius, *Cupid & Psyche*, 30.

Another fertile area of artistic reception of the *Metamorphoses* in antiquity lay in the plastic arts. Although historians of ancient art debate whether Ovid's poem was the impetus for the proliferation of representations of Narcissus and the other mythological characters from the *Metamorphoses* in early imperial wall painting and sculpture or whether Ovid was himself inspired to mythological composition in the *Metamorphoses* by the ubiquity of mythological themes in early Augustan art,[20] the central importance of the poem to artistic representation of mythology emerges clearly in the literary tradition of ekphrases. Apuleius supplies a particularly vivid example of the influence of Ovid's poem on the literary ekphrasis at the opening of the second book of his *Metamorphoses*, in an elaborate description of a statue group of Diana and Actaeon (Apul. *Met.* 2.4):

> Look, Parian marble fashioned into Diana held in balance the middle of the whole atrium, a perfectly brilliant statue with her cloak blown out in the wind, the goddess actively running forward to meet those entering the hall and awesome in the majesty of her divinity. Dogs guarded the goddess' flank on either side, and the dogs themselves were also of marble. Their eyes were threatening, their ears pointed, their nostrils flared, their mouths were savage, and if barking burst in from the neighbour's place you would think it emanated from their marble throats; and, with the dogs rearing up to their breasts – in which detail that outstanding sculptor betrayed the highest evidence of his artistic craft – their back feet strike the ground and their front feet run. Behind the goddess' back the rock rose in the manner of a cave, with moss, grass, leaves, shrubs, grape-vines here and willows there flowering from the marble. Within the grotto, the shadow of the statue gleams from the splendour of the marble. Under the very edge of the rock hang apples and very artistically polished grapes, such as art, jealous of nature, displayed to resemble reality. You would think that some could be plucked for a meal, when wine-rich Autumn blows ripe colour on them; and if you looked down at the spring that, running by the goddess' footprints, trickles into a gentle wave, you would believe that the grape bunches hanging, as in the country, lacked no quality of motion among all the other qualities of reality. In the midst of the marble leaves Actaeon's likeness could be seen, both in stone and in the spring, leaning forward in the direction of the goddess with a curious gaze, already turning into a stage and waiting for Diana to bathe.

---

[20]See, e.g., Leach, *Rhetoric of Space*, 440–467; Galinsky, *Augustan Culture*, 192–194, 228.

Although Ovid's version of the myth of Diana and Actaeon, recounted in the third book of his *Metamorphoses* (3.143–252), does not imply the deliberate spying that Apuleius' phrasing suggests, Apuleius' debt to the Ovidian passage is visible in a number of specific details. In addition to the prominence of hunting dogs in both authors (cf. Ov. *Met.* 3.206–236) and the role of the goddess' attendants in guarding her flank (cf. Ov. *Met.* 3.180–182), the setting of the encounter between goddess and mortal receives a lengthy description in both authors. Ovid describes the setting in a highly wrought ekphrasis (*Met.* 3.155–162):

> There was a valley sacred to belted Diana, Gargaphie by name, thick with pines and sharp-leaved cypress trees, at the extreme end of which was a forested grotto fashioned by no artistry; nature had simulated art through her own talent, for she had constructed a natural arch of living pumice and light tufa. On the right sounded a spring, utterly clear in its slender stream and with a border for its spreading mouth of grassy banks.

Like Ovid, Apuleius locates the goddess at her bath in a secluded grotto (*pone tergum deae saxum insurgit in speluncae modum*, *Met.* 2.4 ~ *in extremo est antrum nemorale recessu*, Ov. *Met.* 3.157), and he embellishes Ovid's comparatively restrained description of the glade's attractions. Both writers reflect self-consciously on the artistry of their ekphrases by invoking the topos of a contest between art and nature (*arte laboratum nulla; simulauerat artem | ingenio natura suo*, Ov. *Met.* 3.158–159 ~ *sub extrema saxi margine poma et uuae faberrime politae dependent, quas ars aemula naturae ueritati similes explicuit*, Apul. *Met.* 2.4). In both passages, moreover, metaliterary considerations animate authorial deployment of the topos. Ovid mischievously characterises his literary landscape, technically an example of *topographia* ("place-writing"), as a natural, rather than artificially constructed, setting, even as he employs the language of artistry and architecture throughout his description (*arte, laboratum, artem, duxerat arcum*).[21] In pointed contrast to the Ovidian ekphrasis' triumph of nature over art, Apuleius' ekphrasis celebrates the triumph of art over nature. In this way Apuleius both draws attention to his own artistry (and that of his Ovidian model) and also seems to engage

---

[21] Ovid's ekphrasis exemplifies the artistic credo of his character Pygmalion (often read as a figure for the poet in the *Metamorphoses*) that artistry should conceal art (*ars adeo latet arte sua*, "so skilfully does his artistry conceal itself," Ov. *Met.* 10.252).

specifically with another topos of artistic competition, the contest between literature and the plastic arts.[22]

Despite the fact that Ovid's *Metamorphoses* never became a canonical school text in classical antiquity, the poem seems to have received a detailed commentary (or commentaries) in the centuries after its publication.[23] The traces of ancient commentary activity on Ovid's *Metamorphoses* suggest one avenue for the continuing reception of the poem in the political upheaval of the third century C.E. Very little Latin literature remains to us from the period, though it is clear that Ovid must have continued in circulation, for his influence is immediately visible when poetry again appears in large quantities and illustrates the continuing popularity of Ovid's poem among Christian readers in late antiquity. In an epigram concerning sex-changes, for example, the fourth-century Gallo-Roman statesman and poet Ausonius cites several mythological instances from Ovid's poem (*Epigr.* 72):

> Vallebanae (noua res et uix credenda poetis,
>   sed quae de uera promitur historia)
> femineam in speciem conuertit masculus ales
>   pauaque de pauo constitit ante oculos.
> cuncti admirantur monstrum, sed mollior agna
>   ...
> 'quid stolidi ad speciem notae nouitatis hebetis?
>   an uos Nasonis carmina non legitis?
> Caenida conuertit proles Saturnia Consus
>   ambiguoque fuit corpore Tiresias.
> uidit semiuirum fons Salmacis Hermaphroditum,
>   uidit nubentem Plinius androgynum.
> nec satis antiquum, quod Campana in Beneuento
>   unus epheborum uirgo repente fuit.
> nolo tamen ueteris documenta arcessere famae:
>   ecce ego sum factus femina de puero.'

(At Vallebana a male bird changed into a female form (a strange event and scarcely to be believed in the poets, but which is transmitted in a truthful history) and a peahen, rather than a peacock, stood before their eyes. All wondered at the portent, but softer than a lamb ... "Why, stupid people, are you amazed at the sight of a known novelty? Or don't you ever read

---

[22]Cf. Horace, *Ars Poetica* 9–10, *ut pictura poesis*; and see, further, Perlman in this volume.

[23]Otis, "Argumenta"; Hollis "Traces of Ancient Commentaries." This commentary tradition burgeons in the Middle Ages: see Coulson in this volume.

Ovid's poetry? Saturn's child Consus transformed Caenis and Tiresias was also of changeable body. The spring Salmacis saw the half-man Hermaphroditus; Pliny saw a man-woman marry. Nor is it so long ago that one of the youths in Campanian Beneventum suddenly became a maiden. Nevertheless I don't want to summon the evidence of old report: look, I have become a woman from a boy.)

Ausonius' speaker (whose identity eludes us because of the lacunose text) chastizes her audience for not immediately recalling sex-change myths from Ovid's *Metamorphoses*. Her examples include the transformation of the maiden Caenis into the warrior Caeneus by Neptune after her rape at the god's hands (*Met.* 12.174–209); the metamorphosis of Tiresias from man to woman (after he attacked a pair of coupling serpents) and back again seven years later (*Met.* 3.320–331); and the emasculation of Hermaphroditus, transformed from a boy to hermaphrodite as a result of his contact with the contaminating waters of the spring Salmacis (*Met.* 4.285–388).

More interesting than the fact that the speaker draws her literary examples primarily from Ovid, and clearly expects her audience to know them, is Ausonius' deployment of the Ovidian vocabulary of metamorphosis throughout the poem.[24] The strange novelty of the event heralded in the first line of the epigram (*noua res*, Auson. 13.72.1) and in the speaker's first words (*speciem notae nouitatis*, Auson. 13.72.7) recalls not only the new bodies which are the subject of Ovid's poem (*in noua fert animus mutatas dicere formas | corpora*, *Met.*1.1–2) but also the strangeness of their transformations, a feature often remarked upon by characters within the poem. Nestor, for example, piques the interest of the Greek warriors at Troy with his claim that the Lapith hero Caeneus had been born a woman (*monstri nouitate mouentur*, "they are stirred by the strangeness of the portent," *Met.* 12.175) and Ausonius recalls this phrase both in his description of the crowd's wonder (*cuncti admirantur monstrum*, 13.72.5) and in his speaker's reference to the known strangeness of the sight (*speciem notae nouitati*, Auson. 13.72.7). Ovid's description of the metamorphosis of Hermaphroditus also seems to be reflected in Ausonius' poem, not only in the use of *semiuir* (Auson. 13.72.11), which occurs in Hermaphroditus' prayer at the end of Ovid's version of the myth (*quisquis in hos fontes uir uenerit, exeat inde | semiuir et tactis subito mollescat in undis*, "whoever has come into this spring a man, let him go

---

[24]On this vocabulary, see Anderson, "Multiple Change."

forth a half-man, and let him grow suddenly soft at the touch of its waters," *Met.* 4.385–386), but also in the suddenness of the Campanian youth's transformation into a maiden (*repente*, Auson. 13.72.14; cf. *subito*, Ov. *Met.* 4.386). Moreover the conclusion of Ausonius' epigram seems to respond to a second reference to Salmacis in the *Metamorphoses*, where Ovid reflects with metaliterary self-consciousness on the wide diffusion of his own poem. Who has not heard of Salmacis' waters, his Pythagoras asks (*cui non audita est obscenae Salmacis undae?*, *Met.* 15.319), in a long speech summarizing in philosophical form the themes of the *Metamorphoses*. Ausonius attests to the enduring popularity of the myths related in Ovid's *Metamorphoses* even as he implicitly relegates the pagan poem to ancient history (13.72.15).

Ausonius' attitude to Ovid and his poem, at least as expressed in this epigram, is more complimentary than that of many late antique Christian authors, who understandably regarded the author of an *Ars amatoria* with considerable suspicion. For example, Isidore, the seventh-century C.E. bishop of Seville who was an important conduit of classical learning for the Middle Ages, cites Ovid (overwhelmingly from the *Metamorphoses*) twenty times in his works – even though he calls him the one pagan poet who must be avoided. This ambivalent reception of Ovid's poetry is already visible long before the advent of Christianity, of course, as we have seen in the bifurcation of the later Latin critical and literary traditions. Despite such ambivalence in the Christian context of late antiquity, however, the *Metamorphoses* continued to circulate and win new readers, enjoying in the European high Middle Ages and early Renaissance an immense popularity in literary, artistic, and musical culture, when Christian scholars, poets, artists and musicians refigured the pagan myths of the *Metamorphoses* in ways that enhanced and extended the meanings – allegorical, psychological, rhetorical, mytho-graphical – available in the Ovidian masterwork, adapting the myths to new languages and new artistic media.

★   ★   ★

The papers that compose this volume bear witness to the changing fortunes of Ovid and his poem – and the continuity of their reception – in medieval and early modern Europe.

Frank Coulson's account of the circulation of the *Metamorphoses* in medieval France well illustrates the importance of the commentary tradition in bridging the reading cultures of classical antiquity and the Middle Ages. He identifies four strands of commentary activity on the poem in the

Middle Ages: scholastic (primarily philological); ethical (primarily allegorical); philosophical and scientific; and composite (uniting the diverse perspectives of philology, allegory, and literary criticism). The authors of these commentaries were concerned not only to elucidate the sense of the text, but also to draw Christian ethical lessons from the poem through allegorical explanation of the characters and their actions; to unite Christian doctrine and pagan philosophical and scientific theory; and to assess the influence of Ovid's poem on contemporary Christian authors.

Three articles discuss the pervasive importance of the Christian allegorical interpretations of the poem proposed in the *Ovide moralisé*. Marilynn Desmond considers the ethical problems posed by the stories of vindictive and vicious pagan gods in the *Metamorphoses* in a Christian context that assumed divine ethical exemplarity, and examines the way in which the *Ovide moralisé* directs the Christian reader's response to the ethical ambiguities posed by the pagan poem. Taking as her case study the myth of Actaeon, she contrasts the moralizing allegoresis of the textual commentaries of the *Ovide moralisé* with the visual programs in the illustrated manuscripts and concludes that the two modes of reception work against one another, with the former highlighting Christian ethical lessons in Ovid's tales and the latter emphasizing a stark contrast between pagan and Christian codes. Suzanne Conklin Akbari considers Christine de Pizan's mediation of the *Ovide moralisé* in the *Mutacion de Fortune* and proposes that her use of metaphor can be understood in terms of Ovidian metamorphosis. Christine develops an understanding of metamorphosis as the process through which outer form comes to reflect inner form on the basis of her reading of the *Ovide moralisé*, and she relates her account of her own metamorphosis from woman into man in the *Mutacion* to her understanding of metaphor in the sense of figurative language. Patricia Zalamea pursues a reading of Christine de Pizan's *Chemin de lonc estude* that explores the relationship between textual exegesis and the iconography of the illuminated manuscripts of the work prepared under her direction. Like Akbari, Zalamea explores Christine's careful articulation of her authorial identity in *Chemin* in terms of vision, while like Desmond, Zalamea highlights the tensions between text and image in the manuscripts prepared under Christine's supervision.

Four articles on the reception of Ovid's *Metamorphoses* in medieval and early modern England bring to light the authority[25] of Ovidian

---

[25] On Ovid's "authority" in medieval Europe, see Dimmick, "Ovid in the Middle Ages."

modes of characterisation and narrative artistry in diverse genres. Two articles consider the reception of Ovid's *Metamorphoses* in medieval England, in Gower and Chaucer respectively. Kathryn McKinley explores Gower's political appropriation of Ovid's myths of Jason and Medea and Tereus and Procne in the *Confessio amantis* in the framework of the moral education of the prince, King Richard II. Jamie C. Fumo argues that Ovidian techniques of storytelling, on display throughout the *Metamorphoses*, inform the Prologue and Tale of Chaucer's Wife of Bath, focusing especially on two moments in the Wife's tale in which Alison strategically revises the myths of Argus and Midas. Two further chapters examine non-literary texts from medieval and early modern England that adapt Ovidian myth to "scientific" ends. Thomas Willard surveys the reception of Ovid as a philosopher of alchemy in the *Metamorphoses*. He argues that Count Michael Maier, Francis Bacon's contemporary, established alchemy as the key to all mythologies and he explores Maier's readings of Ovidian myths as symbolic of the secrets of alchemy. Cora Fox, in turn, takes up Ovid's importance to the medieval and early modern discourse on witchcraft in a discussion focusing on Reginald Scot's *Discoverie of Witchcraft*. Noting that Ovid's Medea and Circe, among other characters in the *Metamorphoses*, offer prominent models to the early modern demonologists in their description and denunciation of contemporary witches and their crafts, she argues that while Scot values Ovid's literary authority in the *Metamorphoses* he is distinctly troubled by the pagan poet's putative authority regarding transformation and its practitioners, especially witches.

Six articles examine the reception of Ovid's poem in the high literary and artistic culture of Renaissance and Baroque Europe. Three explore the reception of individual characters from the *Metamorphoses* in Italian literature and art. Gur Zak documents Petrarch's fascination with Ovid's Narcissus as a model for the experience of self in the *Secretum*, an imaginary dialogue between Petrarch and Augustine. Zak analyzes the thematic triangulation of reflection, desire and self-awareness in the Ovidian tale as a model for Petrarch's self-representation in the *Secretum*, a work that articulates a thematic nexus of mirroring and selfhood; inner division and (self-)exile; identification, identity and self-alienation. Cynthia Nazarian takes up the Petrarchan theme of self-alienation in an exploration of the reception of Ovid's Actaeon in Petrarch's *Rime* and Maurice Scève's *Délie*. On her reading, Scève remembers and, crucially, re-Ovidianizes Petrarch's dismembered Actaeon. Julia Branna Perlman analyzes Ovid's account of Cupid's wounding of Venus in the bridge passage from the tale of Myrrha to that of Adonis in *Metamorphoses* 10 as a multivalent source for Michelangelo's composition *Venus and Cupid*, a painting designed as the centrepiece for a bedchamber in the home of a prominent Florentine banker and patron of the arts. Of particular interest to Michelangelo, she argues, was the invitation – implicit in Ovid's comparison of Adonis' beauty to that of painted *Amorini* – to read this sequence of amatory tales as a meditation on the sister arts of poetry and painting. She suggests that the potent thematic associations of incestuous passion and amatory deception in Ovid's narrative, in combination with the characters' manipulation of vision, their role-playing and blurred identities, furnished Michelangelo, his patron and his contemporaries, with an artistic model that linked painterly triumph with beguiling artifice and challenged the Italian painter to outdo the Latin poet's narrative artistry in an entirely different medium.

Turning from Renaissance Italy to early modern Iberia, two articles investigate the reception of Ovidian characters and the theme of artistic metamorphosis in Spanish literature. R. John McCaw considers Cervantes' interest in Ovid's *Metamorphoses*, attested in *Don Quijote*'s numerous references to the classical poem and its author, in an analysis of the function of Phaethon's ride in the Sun's chariot as a crucial intertext for Sancho Panza's brief social transformation from squire to governor. More broadly, he proposes that Cervantes' metamorphic play with social and personal identity in *Don Quijote*, in combination with his concomitant experimentation with narrative structure, invites interpretation of the novel as a narrative that explores tales and themes of transformation. Sanda Munjic analyzes the engagement of the Spanish poet Góngora, Cervantes' contemporary, with Ovidian bird imagery in his lyric *Solitudes*, an extended text in high Latinate style that combines the modes of lyric, pastoral and epic. Focusing particularly on the crow and owl of *Metamorphoses* 2 and 11, she identifies a complex of themes that Ovid associates with avian transformations: envy, greed, ingratitude and guilt. In adapting Ovidian imagery, Góngora applies these themes to contemporary Iberian seafaring, an endeavour that offers a misleading semblance of epic but is founded on base motives of trade and commercial gain. Munjic links an Ovidian subtext to recent scholarship on the ideology of the *Solitudes*.[26]

---

[26] Beverley, *Aspects of Góngora's "Soledades."*

The final article in the collection, by Maggie Kilgour, reflects on the challenge posed by the *Metamorphoses* as a poem about change and, in particular, artistic revision, for European artists reworking Ovidian tales from Dante and Petrarch to Spenser and Milton. Focusing especially on Milton's *Paradise Lost*, she explores his interest in the opposing aspects of Ovidian metamorphosis: radical transformation, in which one thing irrevocably becomes something completely different, by contrast with transformation that reveals an essential identity that has been there all along; and change as constant flux, which Christian tradition associated with the fall, by contrast with the transcendence offered by change. Both oppositions, she suggests, inform Milton's refractions of Ovid's *Metamorphoses*, appropriations and revisions that reflect upon the nature of change in a fallen world.

University of Toronto

OVID'S TRANSFORMATIONS IN MEDIEVAL FRANCE (CA. 1100–CA. 1350)

FRANK T. COULSON

As a graduate student at the University of Toronto in the late 1970s, I happened upon a brief note by Luigi Castiglioni in which he described recently discovered manuscripts of Ovidian texts in the Biblioteca Riccardiana in Florence.[1] In reference to a manuscript containing a detailed marginal commentary on the *Metamorphoses*, he suggested that "[w]hoever should study attentively the manuscripts of this commentary would write a page which would not be insignificant both for the history of Latin culture in the West during the Middle Ages and for the circulation of the text of the poem during that period."[2] Further research on the commentary revealed that not only had no one examined the "Vulgate" commentary, but that virtually no work had been done on the manuscript tradition of commentaries on the *Metamorphoses* from 1050–1450. This brief reference by Castiglioni led to a lifetime's work uncovering and documenting no fewer than 600 manuscripts containing Latin commentaries, *accessus* (i.e. standard introductions) and lives of Ovid written from ca. 1050 to 1600, all of which will be discussed and catalogued in a projected fascicle of the *Catalogus translationum et commentariorum*.[3] The present article discusses the medieval Latin commentaries on Ovid's *Metamorphoses* that circulated in France from 1100 to 1350, particularly at the cathedral school of Orléans. Part One traces some of the important manuscript finds that have come to light and underlines why such archival work is so important for interpreting the

---

[1] Castiglioni, "Spogli."

[2] Castiglioni, "Spogli," 165; my translation. Castiglioni identified only two manuscripts of the "Vulgate" commentary, namely Florence, Biblioteca Riccardiana, 624 and Milan, Biblioteca Ambrosiana, P 43 sup.

[3] *Catalogus.* The project was initiated by Paul Oskar Kristeller and is currently edited by Virginia Brown. The material on Ovid will appear in volume 11. A preliminary census of manuscripts related to the study of Ovid in the Middle Ages can be found in Coulson and Roy, *Incipitarium Ovidianum*, now supplemented by Coulson, "Addenda and Corrigenda."

school tradition on Ovid. Part Two analyses the varied approaches that medieval commentators in France adopted to the explication of Ovid's *Metamorphoses*.

Before recent research on the manuscripts, the Latin commentary tradition on Ovid was known and accessible to scholars primarily through the works of Arnulf of Orléans,[4] John of Garland,[5] Pierre Bersuire,[6] and Giovanni del Virgilio[7] (who all wrote allegorical interpretations of the poem), and a smattering of manuscripts mentioned by the indefatigable Italian scholar, Fausto Ghisalberti, whose early research on the tradition conducted in the 1930s and early 1940s did so much to bring to light hitherto unknown texts.[8] However, even when a text, such as the *Allegorie* of Arnulf of Orléans or the *Integumenta* of John of Garland, existed in a usable edition, many manuscripts of textual or cultural significance transmitting that same text remained in European libraries awaiting discovery.[9] Worse, there were few if any editions of commentaries on the Ovidian corpus, with the significant exception of Ralph Hexter's pioneering study and editions of *accessus* and commentaries on the *Ars amatoria*, *Heroides*, and *Epistulae ex Ponto*.[10] Lastly, the complex interrelationships of these various threads of commentary had

---

[4] Arnulf is discussed more fully below, 35–36. The best treatment of Arnulf as a commentator on classical texts is still Ghisalberti, "Arnolfo." See also Barkan, *The Gods Made Flesh*, esp. ch. 3.

[5] Garland's *Integumenta Ovidii* is discussed and edited in *Giovanni di Garlandia, Integumenta Ovidii* and edited and translated in Born, "The *Integumenta*." Born, "The Manuscripts" discusses the affiliations of the manuscripts.

[6] For the text of Bersuire's *Ovidius moralizatus*, see his *Reductorium morale, liber XV, cap. ii–xv* and *De formis figurisque deorum. Reductorium morale, liber XV: Ovidius moralizatus, cap. i.* Hexter, "*Allegari* of Pierre Bersuire" and Reynolds, "*Ovidius moralizatus*," provide insightful discussions of the ways in which the text may have been used. Reynolds, "*Ovidius moralizatus*" translates selected passages, while Coulson and Roy, *Incipitarium Ovidianum*, no. 2, and Coulson, "A Checklist" discuss the manuscripts.

[7] Giovanni's allegorical treatment of Ovid's poem entitled the *Allegorie* is edited in Ghisalberti, "Giovanni del Virgilio."

[8] See his *Integumenta Ovidii* and "Mediaeval Biographies."

[9] A complete list of known manuscripts transmitting the *Allegorie* of Arnulf can be found in Coulson and Roy, *Incipitarium Ovidianum*, no. 419, and Coulson, "Addenda and Corrigenda," 164. Manuscripts for the *Integumenta Ovidii* of John of Garland can be found in Coulson and Roy, *Incipitarium Ovidianum*, no. 333 and Coulson, "Addenda and Corrigenda," 162.

[10] Hexter, *Ovid and Medieval Schooling*.

never been explored. The recently published *Incipitarium Ovidianum,* together with its supplement, has provided an initial step in bringing some order out of the chaos.[11] Here, I discuss four texts that manuscript work has placed on a much surer footing: a philological commentary on the *Metamorphoses* written by master Arnulf of Orléans about the year 1180;[12] the "Vulgate" commentary on the *Metamorphoses,* the most important Latin commentary on the *Metamorphoses* from the high Middle Ages;[13] a commentary that scholars had tentatively placed in the period of the Italian Renaissance but that can be conclusively dated to the late twelfth century;[14] and a hitherto uncatalogued manuscript now in the Fabricius collection in Copenhagen containing abundant new *accessus* and commentary material on the Ovidian corpus.[15]

The Archival Background

Around 1180 Master Arnulf of Orléans wrote a philological commentary on the *Metamorphoses,* short sections of which Fausto Ghisalberti discussed and edited.[16] Ghisalberti's work was hampered, however, by the fact that he knew of only one witness to the commentary (Venice, Marc. lat. XIV. 222 [4007]), a manuscript that had lost a folio from its first gathering and was therefore missing the section on Ovid's creation myth. Since the publication of Ghisalberti's article, eleven copies of Arnulf's commentary have been located that transmit either a verbatim or slightly modified version.[17] These newly discovered manuscripts

---

[11] Coulson and Roy, *Incipitarium Ovidianum,* and Coulson, "Addenda and Corrigenda."

[12] David Gura, a doctoral candidate at the Ohio State University, is producing a critical edition. Ghisalberti transcribes portions from Venice, Biblioteca Nazionale Marciana, Marc. lat. XIV. 222 [4007] in his "Arnolfo," and the glosses to *Met.*1.1–150 are critically edited in Coulson and Nawotka, "The Rediscovery of Arnulf," who also provide detailed descriptions of the manuscripts.

[13] For the "Vulgate" commentary, see in particular Coulson, "A Study," "MSS... A Checklist," "MSS... Addendum," and "The *'Vulgate'* Commentary." Selections from the commentary are edited in Coulson, *The "Vulgate" Commentary,* and its *accessus* is discussed and edited in Coulson, "Hitherto Unedited (I)."

[14] For full bibliography, see below, nn. 26, 27, 28 and 30.

[15] For full bibliography, see below, n. 32. I am grateful to the late Judson Boyce Allen for bringing this manuscript to my attention.

[16] Ghisalberti, "Arnolfo," esp. 176–189.

[17] Complete list of manuscripts in Coulson and Roy, *Incipitarium Ovidianum,* no. 419.

allow us to construct more accurately a critical edition, for not only do they provide text missing from the manuscript Ghisalberti discussed, but one of the new manuscripts (Munich, Bayerische Staatsbibliothek, Clm 7205) is a twelfth-century copy that represents a different branch of the textual tradition. Thus, errors transmitted in Marc. lat. XIV.222 [4007] can now be corrected against an independent, early witness. In addition, certain features of the transmission history of the glosses have become evident with this more complete picture. The glosses in the two earliest manuscripts circulate separately from the text of the *Metamorphoses* as continuous lemmata and gloss, in what John Ward has labelled a "catena" commentary;[18] and, significantly, the philological glosses in these manuscripts are found in tandem with the allegories (*Allegorie*) composed by Arnulf himself. The two earliest witnesses, therefore, furnish the medieval reader with what may be termed a compleat approach to the interpretation of the epic,[19] one that embraces the ethical mode of reading (as represented by the allegories) and the utilitarian mode (as represented by the philological glosses). Sub-sequently, however, the philological glosses became detached from their original setting and were often transmitted as interlinear and marginal glosses accompanying manuscripts of the *Metamorphoses*. In addition, in some of these manuscripts the glosses of Arnulf became embedded within a larger commentary and are only noticed when one begins to transcribe the entire series of glosses.

Our second example, that of the "Vulgate" commentary, provides an even more salutary, even cautionary, instance of the importance of conducting exhaustive manuscript work on these commentary texts. The significance of the "Vulgate" commentary was alluded to as early as 1920 when two copies of the text were identified.[20] However, a comprehensive survey of all known manuscripts of the *Metamorphoses* has turned up no fewer than twenty-two witnesses to the text of the commentary and of its introductory *accessus*.[21] A detailed examination

---

[18] See Ward, "From marginal gloss" and "The Catena commentaries."

[19] Hexter, "Medieval Articulations," esp. 69–70, provides a good summary of how the two texts are organised in Munich, Clm 7205.

[20] See above, n. 2.

[21] Fully listed in Coulson and Roy, *Incipitarium Ovidianum*, no. 421. The manu-scripts of the commentary are catalogued in Coulson, "MSS… Addendum," and "New Manuscripts." Three new manuscripts (or manuscript fragments) surfaced subsequent to the completion of my dissertation. These are Austin, Harry Ransom

of these twenty-two witnesses has produced extremely interesting conclusions both for the circulation of the commentary itself during the Middle Ages and for the principles that can be posited for the editing of the text. The earliest known witnesses (ca. 1250) are all written in a northern French *textualis* book hand and confirm that the commentary originated in a scriptorium around Orléans. Later copies of the "Vulgate," however, show that the text had a wider and more diffuse circulation. At least two of the later copies, Vatican City, Biblioteca Apostolica Vaticana (henceforth, BAV), Pal. lat. 1663 and Ottob. lat. 1294, are written in Italian hands; and while the "Vulgate" commentary was not taken up and printed by humanists, there is evidence for its continued circulation and use as late as 1475, since someone has entered the complete text for Book 1.1–567 of the "Vulgate" commentary into an edition of the *Metamorphoses* printed in that year.[22] No mention of these handwritten marginalia is contained in the printed catalogue to the incunables at the British Library.[23]

In the case of the "Vulgate" commentary (and of those commentary texts that can be attributed to a known master), initial assumptions that commentary texts – given their genesis as teaching tools and their constant use in the classroom – would be extremely fluid and would be subject to revision, alteration, deletion, accretion, and substitution as they were used by each generation of scholar or pupil, were confounded. A detailed collation of the manuscripts transmitting Book One of the "Vulgate" commentary revealed a text that was remarkably uniform and showed little variation among the copies. Further, it seemed possible to apply stemmatic theory to the constitution of the text and to divide the manuscripts into distinct families on the basis of shared variants and of physical evidence such as omissions and transpositions.[24] At least two copies of the text could be clearly demonstrated to be *codices descripti*, that is to say direct copies from another witness, and they could therefore be excluded as important manuscripts for the constitution of the text.

Humanities Research Center, MS. 34; London, Sotheby's Sale Catalogue, 19 June, 1989, lot. No. 3011, present whereabouts unknown; and Los Angeles, University of California at Los Angeles Research Library, 100, Box 178 (fragments of Book One only).

[22] See Coulson, "A Newly Discovered Copy."

[23] See *Catalogue of Books,* 146.

[24] For fuller discussion of the relationship of the manuscripts, see Coulson, "A Study," esp. chapter 2.

Lastly, the newly discovered manuscripts permit a more informed understanding of the circulation, influence, and codicological setting of the "Vulgate" commentary. For example, the earliest witnesses to the text share a remarkable similarity in their page layout and decoration: all are decorated with initials in red and blue with pen flourishes and tendrils, and all have a single column of text with three columns of commentary surrounding the text. Later manuscripts, however, modify this layout, with the commentary sometimes laid out in two columns surrounding the text. Additionally, many of the newly discovered manuscripts of the "Vulgate" commentary show how subsequent generations read and expanded the commentary. In BAV, Vat. lat. 1598, for instance, the text is often extensively modified or corrected by a later hand that seeks to expunge the text of obvious errors, or to comment (sometimes rather critically) on the interpretation proffered by the "Vulgate" commentator. BAV, Ottob. lat. 1294, a manuscript of Italian origin originally written in the early fourteenth century, bears witness to many levels of accretions and corrections, while Austin, Harry Ransom Humanities Research Center, MS 34 shows evidence of at least three later hands that have added material to the original text of the "Vulgate." Finally, the investigation of the circulation and diffusion of the manuscripts has given added weight to the hypothesis advanced by Ghisalberti that the "Vulgate" commentary was the Ovidian commentary on which Dante relied for many nuances of interpretation.[25] The existence of at least two manuscripts of Italian origin (BAV, Pal. lat. 1663 and Ottob. lat. 1294) certainly supports Ghisalberti's conjectures.

Thirdly, I turn to a commentary on the *Metamorphoses* that was discussed by Bernard Peebles.[26] At the time, Peebles knew of only three manuscripts to the text, all humanistic copies, one of which mentioned the name of Giovanni Francesco Picenardi of Cremona, in a colophon to the commentary on the *Metamorphoses*, as the writer of the commentary.[27] Peebles drew no conclusion as to whether Picenardi functioned merely as scribe or as actual author of the commentary.[28] Further

---

[25] This thesis is advanced most forcefully in Ghisalberti, "Il commentario medioevale."

[26] Peebles, "The *Ad Maronis mausoleum*."

[27] Modena, Biblioteca Estense ed Universitaria, Est. lat. 306 (α.W.4.13), Padua, Biblioteca del Seminario Vescovile, 142, and Verona, Biblioteca Capitolare, CCXLVIII [219]. The colophon with the name of Picenardi is to be found on fol. 227r of Modena, Est. lat. 306.

[28] Peebles, "The *Ad Maronis mausoleum*," 189: "I leave unexplored here the

research has now turned up two other copies of the text in the libraries of Berlin and Prague[29] that conclusively demonstrate that the text is a late twelfth-century commentary, probably of northern French origin, containing a stratum of gloss, largely philosophical or scientific in import, that differs significantly from other commentaries circulating during the period.[30] Several conclusions concerning the origin and genesis of this commentary may be drawn from a closer examination of the five principal witnesses: the earliest complete witnesses to the text are Prague, VIII.H.32, fols. 78r–91v and Berlin, Lat. oct. 68, fols. 1–22v, the former written in a twelfth-century French hand, the latter apparently written in a twelfth-century German hand. The three later manuscripts date from the period of the Italian Renaissance. All five witnesses transmit the text as a "catena" commentary, that is to say a continuous thread of lemma and commentary. The continued copying and circulation of the text well into the middle of the fifteenth century indicate that the commentary still held a certain authority even at this late date. The manuscript of the text now in the Biblioteca Estense, Est. lat. 306 (α.W.4.13), transmits several other commentaries on classical authors, including the late antique commentary of Servius on Vergil (fols. 1r–199r); a commentary, possibly by Lorenzo Valla, on the *Bellum Catilinae* of Sallust (fols. 228r–252v);[31] and a humanist commentary on the *Epistulae ad familiares* of Cicero (fols. 253r–309v). This Modena manuscript thus appears to have been written with a view to bringing together important commentaries on major curricular authors, since all of the texts, with the exception of the commentary on Sallust (written in a contemporary hand), are copied by the scribe Giovanni Francesco Picenardi at Cremona.

Lastly, I discuss a newly discovered manuscript in the Fabricius collection in Copenhagen with the shelf mark 29 2°, a manuscript copied in northern France (or perhaps Germany) in the early thirteenth century that contains an important collection of *accessus* and commentaries on classical authors of French origin but which to date has escaped scholarly

---

question whether Picenardi has worked in this codex only as scribe, or – as Arisius seems to have been told by Muratori – also as author (or compiler) of the commentaries on Ovid ...."

[29] Berlin, Staatsbibliothek zu Berlin–Preussischer Kulturbesitz, Lat. oct. 68, fols. 1r–22v and Prague, Národní Knihovna Ceské Republiky, VIII.H.32, fols. 78r–91v.

[30] See Coulson, "Giovanni Francesco Picenardi."

[31] See *Catalogus*, 8:241a–b.

investigation.[32] The uncovering of a collection of texts such as those in Fabricius 29 2° discloses much about the reading practices and interests of masters in the late twelfth and early thirteenth centuries. Fabricius 29 2° was assembled to provide standard introductions (*accessus*) and commentaries to those texts considered essential pedagogical tools and which generally formed part of the *Liber Catonianus*.[33] The manuscript consists of two sections written in two roughly contemporaneous thirteenth-century hands. Part One, which forms the bulk of the manuscript, contains full commentaries on Statius' *Achilleis*, Claudian's *De raptu Proserpinae*, and Avianus' *Fabulae*, in addition to Ovid's *Metamorphoses, Fasti, Heroides* and *Tristia*, while Part Two contains full commentaries on the *Epistulae ex Ponto* and *Amores*.

The Ovidian texts in the first section of the manuscript clearly attest to the primacy of Orléans as a centre for the study of Ovid in twelfth-century France. The commentary on the *Metamorphoses* was composed by William of Orléans and originally formed part of a complete set of glosses on the Ovidian corpus called the *Versus bursarii*; the commentary on the *Fasti* is the work of Arnulf of Orléans,[34] who also wrote commentaries on the *Metamorphoses,* the poetry from exile, as well as Lucan's *Bellum civile*. The remaining two commentaries, one on the *Heroides*, the other on the *Tristia*, survive solely in this manuscript and have not yet been identified with known masters. In addition to the full commentaries to the works of Ovid, Claudian, and Avianus, Part One of the Fabricius manuscript also transmits a collection of introductions (*accessus*) primarily to the works of Ovid. The *accessus* to the *Heroides* is the work of Fulco of Orléans,[35] an Orléanais master working at about the same time as Arnulf (late twelfth century). The *accessus* to the *Amores*

---

[32]Fabricius 29 2° has never been adequately catalogued. The manuscript is known to have been at the Dominican monastery at Soest in the fourteenth century due to the ownership mark of Reynerus de Capella on fol. 1r, and to have belonged to Johann Albert Fabricius and Bernhard Rottendorff. It was housed in the University Library of Copenhagen until 1938 when the Fabricius collection was transferred to the Royal Library.

[33]See Boas, "De librorum Catonianorum," and Pellegrin, "*Remedia amoris.*" The *Liber Catonianus* usually consisted of the *Disticha Catonis*, the *Ecloga Theoduli*, the *Fabulae* of Avianus, the *Elegiae* of Maximianus, the *De raptu Proserpinae* of Claudian, the *Achilleis* of Statius, and the *Ilias latina*.

[34]Now edited in *Arnulfi Aurelianensis glosule Ovidii Fastorum*.

[35]For Fulco, see Shooner, "Les *Bursarii Ovidianorum*," and "*Arnulfi Aurelianensis glosule de Remediis amoris.*"

circulated widely in multiple copies, as did the *accessus* to the *Ars amatoria*, itself a product of the French schools, and the *accessus* to the *Remedia amoris* and the *Tristia*. The remaining three *accessus*, to Ovid's *Fasti*, *Epistulae ex Ponto*, and *Ibis*, represent new texts not attested in the scholarly literature.[36] In Part Two of the manuscript, we find two anonymous commentaries on the *Epistulae ex Ponto* and the *Amores*. The commentary on the *Epistulae ex Ponto* exists in multiple copies and was one of the most popular commentaries on the *ex Ponto* in circulation during the late twelfth and thirteenth centuries; the commentary on the *Amores*, however, exists in this single copy and cannot be attributed to any known master.

This archival work conducted in the manuscript repositories of Europe and North America has significantly enhanced our knowledge and understanding of the study of Ovid in France from 1100 to 1350. First and foremost, many new manuscripts of known commentaries on Ovid have come to light. Such is the case with the philological glosses of Arnulf of Orléans, which previously had been known from a single manuscript witness but which can now be reconstructed from eleven copies. Secondly, this archival work has added many hitherto unknown *accessus* and full commentaries to the known canon, thereby revealing the varied and multiple approaches adopted by school masters to the study of classical poetry in the high Middle Ages. Thirdly, this work has, in certain instances, been able to date and localise commentaries erroneously placed in the period of the Italian Renaissance, as is the case for the commentary on the *Metamorphoses* shown to have been composed in northern France in the late twelfth century. Fourthly, important new witnesses have been discovered that have a bearing on the textual tradition of an attested author. For example, knowledge of the text of the philological glosses of Arnulf of Orléans has been greatly enhanced by the discovery of a second twelfth-century witness (Munich, Clm 7205) that represents a new branch of the manuscript family and supplies text missing from the other twelfth-century witness (Marc. lat. XIV.222 [4007]). Moreover, one's knowledge of the text of the "Vulgate" commentary has been revolutionised by the discovery of twenty-two witnesses to the text. Further, through this archival work, the circulation and diffusion of these texts have been documented more accurately,

---

[36] These three new *accessus* are edited in my forthcoming article "Hitherto Unedited (III)."

thereby augmenting our knowledge of their possible influence on vernacular authors. For example, it has been shown that the "Vulgate" commentary circulated not only in France but also in Italy and may have been the Ovidian commentary known to Dante. Finally, this work has brought to light a certain number of anthologies containing multiple commentaries and *accessus*. Thus MS. Fabricius 29 2° discloses the reading practices of the period, illuminating the choice of texts fundamental to the school curriculum.

Explicating the Text

With this increased knowledge of the diffusion and circulation of the manuscripts, we may turn our investigations to the multi-faceted approaches adopted by French masters to the explication of Ovid's epic. Evidence for the school and commentary tradition on the *Metamorphoses* from late antiquity to the revival of learning in the twelfth-century Renaissance[37] is relatively meagre.[38] The majority of complete manuscripts of the poem itself date from the twelfth century onwards.[39] Moreover, only one early "commentary" on the *Metamorphoses* survives, the pseudo-Lactantian *Narrationes,* tentatively dated to late antiquity.[40] The school tradition on Ovid surfaces only in the early to mid-twelfth

---

[37] Haskins, *Renaissance.*

[38] The best survey of Ovidian influence in the early medieval period remains Munk Olsen, *I Classici.*

[39] The manuscripts are catalogued in Munari, *Catalogue,* "Supplemento" and "Secondo supplemento." Updates to Munari's catalogues can be found in Coulson, "An Update to Munari's Catalogue," "Newly Discovered Manuscripts," "A Bibliographical Update," and "Addenda to Munari's Catalogues," and McKinley, "Manuscripts of Ovid," all of which provide information on ancillary texts circulating with the manuscripts of the text.

[40] Cf. Keith, in this volume. For a survey of published material on the *Narrationes,* see Coulson and Roy, *Incipitarium Ovidianum,* no. 54. Cameron, *Greek Mythography,* 4–32 attempts to redate the *Narrationes* to the second century. The fullest discussion of the manuscript evidence and their relationships is now Tarrant, "The *Narrationes.*" The *Narrationes* consist of a series of titles (*tituli*) and mythographic summaries (*narrationes*) on each of the transformations. They are transmitted particularly in one branch of the manuscript tradition of the *Metamorphoses* (the so-called Lactantian manuscripts). During the Renaissance period, they were often copied separately from the text of the *Metamorphoses* and were described as a mythographic treatise. Annalisa Rossi of the Scuola di Archivistica, Paleografia e Diplomatica of Bari is engaged on a new critical edition of the *Narrationes.* See Rossi, "Ricognizioni sulla tradizione manoscritta."

century in a series of manuscripts, housed mainly in Munich, which preserve continuous scholia on the *Metamorphoses* from German schools.[41] These earliest commentaries have not yet been attributed to known masters, with the possible exception of Munich, Clm 4610, which appears to transmit comments by Manegold of Lautenbach (1035 to ca. 1103).[42]

However, with the advent of the cathedral schools in the Loire valley, and particularly those at Chartres and Orléans in the mid-to late-twelfth century, we find a quickening and flourishing of commentary material on Ovid's epic. This strain of commentary material approaches the elucidation of the epic from several distinct perspectives, examining such modalities of reading as the ethical perspective, represented by the allegorical mode of interpretation; the more purely utilitarian perspective, which through prose paraphrase or grammatical explanation sought to explicate the literal meaning of the text; and finally, a more encompassing perspective that provided the reader with grammatical instruction, an ethical framework in which to read the poem, and a more sophisticated analysis of literary aspects of the *Metamorphoses*.

By the twelfth century, Orléans had become a thriving centre for scholars interested in the study of the Latin texts of classical antiquity, particularly its poetic legacy.[43] The pioneering research of the late Hugues V. Shooner and of Bruno Roy has done much to uncover the turbulent and often quarrelsome world of these scholars.[44] Three scholars, who have recently been identified as influential at Orléans in the late twelfth and the early thirteenth centuries, wrote extensive commentaries on all or part of the Ovidian corpus: Arnulf of Orléans, William of Orléans, and Fulco of Orléans. Since Fulco did not comment on the

---

[41] The relevant manuscripts are Munich, Bayerische Staatsbibliothek, Clm 4610, Clm 14482, and Clm 14809. Other important twelfth-century commentaries on the *Metamorphoses* are transmitted in Freiburg i. Breisgau, Universitätsbibliothek 381, and Salzburg, Stiftsbibliothek St. Peter (Abtei), a.V.4.

[42] Clm 4610 is discussed in Meiser, "Über einen Commentar" and Herren, "Manegold."

[43] For studies which treat early masters and the schools at Orléans, see, in particular, Foulques de Villaret, "L'enseignement des lettres"; Delisle, "Les écoles d'Orléans"; and Cuissard, "Les professeurs orléanais."

[44] See, in particular, Roy and Shooner, "Querelles."

Metamorphoses, I shall limit my discussion in this article to those commentaries written by Arnulf and William.[45]

Arnulf of Orléans' allegorical interpretation of the epic, entitled the *Allegorie,*[46] ushered in a genre that was to be extremely influential in the history of the reception of the poem. His *Allegorie* interprets the stories historically, morally, and allegorically. For example, Arnulf gives an explicitly euhemeristic interpretation to the story of Europa, in which the constituent elements of the fable are reduced to historical figures:

> Iupiter in thaurum mutatus Europam filiam Agenoris raptam devirginavit. Re vera Iupiter rex cretensis Europam Agenoris regis Phenicie filiam adamavit ad quam Mercurium id est facundum[47]misit qui virgini persuasit ut ad litus accederet. Quod cum fecisset, Iupiter eam in litore inventam et navi impositam in Cretam portavit quam ibi tenens devirginavit. Sed quia navis eius thaurum depictum habebat in priori parte ideo dicitur in specie thauri eam rapuisse. Vel quia navis eius thaurus vocabatur quam ipsa ascendit. (*Allegorie* 2.13)

> (Jupiter in the guise of a bull ravished and deflowered Europa, the daughter of Agenor. In reality, Jupiter, a Cretan king, fell in love with Europa, the daughter of Agenor, a king of Phoenicia, and he sent Mercury, an eloquent messenger, to persuade the maiden to approach the shore. And when she had done so, Jupiter found her there, transported her to his ship, and carried her off to Crete where he kept her and deflowered her. But since his ship had a bull depicted on its forward section, he is said to have raped her in the guise of a bull. Or perhaps his ship, which Europa boarded, was called "the Bull.")

Leonard Barkan, in his magisterial study *The Gods Made Flesh,*[48] has written eloquently on Arnulf's place within the larger framework of allegory in the Middle Ages, so I will omit a detailed discussion of the *Allegorie.* The text of Arnulf's allegories was disseminated widely in the margins of the manuscripts of the *Metamorphoses,* often in conjunction with the *Integumenta Ovidii* of John of Garland, and had a preponderant influence on subsequent interpretation.[49]

---

[45] Fulco's commentaries on the amatory works of Ovid are discussed in "*Arnulfi Aurelianensis glosule de Remediis amoris,*" and Shooner, "Les *Bursarii Ovidianorum.*"

[46] Edited in Ghisalberti, "Arnolfo." All quotations are from this edition.

[47] I emend the text from Munich, Clm 7205, fol. 34v. Ghisalberti's text reads *id est facundum misit filium qui…*

[48] See Barkan, *The Gods Made Flesh,* esp. ch. 3.

[49] See Coulson and Roy, *Incipitarium Ovidianum,* nos. 257 and 333. Important

In addition to this allegorical strain of interpretation, there existed a more purely philological level of commentary, one that saw its purpose as strictly utilitarian and that is most clearly represented by the Orléanais commentator William, a near contemporary of Arnulf, who wrote a commentary on the entire Ovidian corpus called the *Versus bursarii*.[50] Though the text itself was discussed as early as 1926 by E.H. Alton,[51] it was not until 1981 that it was securely attributed to William.[52] His commentary appears to be a relatively original piece of twelfth-century scholarship, since a perusal of the extant glosses on the *Metamorphoses* dating from the period before 1200 reveals no verbatim correspondences between them and William. William clearly consulted previous scholarship on the poem, however, because the *Versus bursarii* is replete with such references as *secundum sententiam aliorum*, *dicunt alii*, and the ubiquitous *dicunt quidam*. William's approach to explicating the poem contains no allegorisations, nor does he show much interest in literary matters. Rather, he is strictly a philologist interested in construing the grammar, clarifying word meanings, showing students the connections between loose strands of the story line, discussing problems dealing with textual criticism, and furnishing mythological background. Unlike the philological glosses of Arnulf and the "Vulgate" commentary (see below), William is highly selective in the lines he chooses to comment upon.

He is concerned, in particular, to explicate difficult or unusual words for his readers. Hence the gloss on the text for *Met*. 1.10 **nullus**

---

manuscripts transmitting the works of Arnulf and John in tandem include London, British Library, Royal 12.E.XI; Montpellier, Bibliothèque de la Faculté de Médecine, H. 328; Oxford, Bodleian Library, Hatton 92; and Oxford, Merton College, 299. Giovanni del Virgilio imitated this prosimetric mixture of prose and elegiac verse in his *Allegorie* composed at Bologna in 1323/24. Rotondi has conclusively shown that the elegiac verses are incorporated by Giovanni from another source and were not composed by him; see Rotondi, "Ovidio nel Medioevo."

[50] For complete listing of manuscripts and relevant bibliography, see Coulson and Roy, *Incipitarium Ovidianum*, no. 13, and Coulson, "Addenda and Corrigenda," 156. One new manuscript of William's commentary on the *Metamorphoses* has recently surfaced in Copenhagen, Fabricius 29 2°, fols. 1ra–5vb. The text is now edited in Engelbrecht, *Filologie*, who also provides a comprehensive study of the sources, influences, and approaches employed by William in explicating the text.

[51] Alton, "Mediaeval Commentators." See also Alton and Wormell, "Ovid in the Medieval Schoolroom."

[52] Shooner, "Les *Bursarii Ovidianorum*."

Titan (no Titan) reads: "that is to say no illumination. Or 'no' is used for 'not.' Titan means the sun. The word 'Titan' means one who illuminates" (*id est nulla illuminatio. Vel **nullus** pro non, **Tytan** id est sol. Tytan enim interpretatur illuminator*; Engelbrecht, *Filologie*, 2:124). Similarly, the specific meaning behind the verb *aspirate* (1.3) is explained as *favete* (favour). At other times, William rather pedantically outlines the difference in meaning of certain adjectives, nouns, or verbs. He also shows some interest in matters of a textual import. For example, at *Met.* 1.700, Ovid reports that Mercury stops his story in mid-stream since he realises that Argus has been lulled to sleep.

> **Talia verba refert**: talia quantum ad intellectum. **Restabat verba referre**, illa scilicet que promiserat se dicturum. Quidam interserunt versum qui ficticius est, videlicet: "Tibi nubere nimpha volentis votis cede dei," sed copulata coniunctio que sequitur ostendit quod nichil amplius dixit quia **restabat verba referre** que verba promiserat et ea que sequuntur, scilicet **nympham fugisse per avia spretis precibus** etc. (Engelbrecht, *Filologie*, 2:127)

> (**He is relating to her such words**: such words as we have grasped to that point, and **it remained to speak the words**, those words which he had promised he would speak. Some critics intercalate a verse which is not Ovidian, namely "Nymph, cede to the wishes of the god who wants to marry you," but the accompanying link which follows shows that he said nothing further since **it remained to speak the words**, which he had promised and those which follow, namely **that the nymph had fled through the trackless places spurning his prayers** etc.)

Here, William is cognizant of the much vexed question of non-Ovidian lines interpolated into the text. The bulk of William's glosses, however, seek to explicate the syntax of the poem, a technique well illustrated by the commentator's longer comments on *Met.* 1.78, where he begins with direct quotation from the poem, and then proceeds to lemma-by-lemma exposition.

William's commentary, the *Versus bursarii*, exerted a significant influence on the later Orléanais commentary, the "Vulgate," which incorporates verbatim into its text many of the longer grammatical glosses. The recent research of Wilken Engelbrecht[53] has demonstrated that by the fourteenth century the text of the *Bursarii* circulated widely

---

[53] See Engelbrecht, *Filologie,* 2:328–329.

in Western Europe (into such areas as Oxford, present day Flanders, northern Germany, and Lombardy), and influenced such vernacular writers as Juan Rodriguez, the author of *El Bursario*, a translation into Spanish of the *Heroides*.[54]

In the late twelfth century (ca. 1180), Arnulf of Orléans also composed a philological commentary on the *Metamorphoses* that originally circulated with and complemented his allegorical interpretation of the poem (see above). Arnulf concludes these philological glosses with a colophon that clearly identifies him as the author: "**Without tears**: for indeed the souls of the good are not mourned, and hence the soul of Arnulf, who composed these glosses at Orléans, ought not to be mourned. For if he has done his work well, if the sayings of prophets have any truth, I shall be immortalised along with Ovid" (***Indeflebile****: anime siquidem bonorum non deflentur. Vnde et anima Arnulfi qui has glosulas fecit Aurelianis defleri non debet. Et si eas bene fecit, immo si quid habent ueri uatum presagia, uiuam cum Ouidio, Met.* 15.876). Unlike William of Orléans, Arnulf reveals a much wider interest in explicating various aspects of the text, including treating such aspects as grammar, textual cruces, myth, topography, and geography. Moreover, unlike the *Versus bursarii*, which is extremely selective in the lines it glosses, Arnulf's commentary is much more expansive and comprehensive in scope.

The philological commentary begins with a detailed *accessus*, which treats of the six categories under which a literary work could be introduced: life of the poet (*vita poetae*), title of the work (*titulus operis*), subject matter (*materia*), intention of the author (*intentio auctoris*), the usefulness of the work (*utilitas operis*) and under what rubric of philosophy the work should be placed (*cui parti philosophiae subponatur*).[55] Arnulf's life of Ovid, drawn largely from the poet's own autobiographical writings *Tristia* 2 and 4.10, greatly influenced the later tradition of *vitae* of the poet. Arnulf gives an explicitly moral purpose to the reading of the *Metamorphoses* in his exposition of the subject matter of the poem,

---

[54] See Rodriguez, *Bursario*, for a critical edition of the text.

[55] Literature on the *accessus Ovidiani* is extensive. Ghisalberti, "Mediaeval Biographies" provides the best overview. The following edit new manuscript material: Przychocki, "Accessus Ovidiani"; *Accessus ad auctores*, ed. Huygens; and Coulson, "New Manuscript Evidence," "Hitherto Unedited (I)," and "Hitherto Unedited (II)." Minnis, *Medieval Theory of Authorship*, *Medieval Literary Theory*, and Allen, *The Ethical Poetic*, provide theoretical discussions of the importance of the *accessus* for our understanding of literary criticism during the period.

materia, and of the intention of the author in writing the work, *intentio auctoris* (Ghisalberti, "Arnolfo," 181).

> Intentio est de mutacione dicere, ut non intelligamus de mutacione que fit extrinsecus tantum in rebus corporeis bonis vel malis sed etiam de mutacione que fit intrinsecus ut in anima, ut reducat nos ab errore ad cognitionem veri creatoris ....Vel intencio sua est nos ab amore temporalium immoderato revocare et adhortari ad unicum cultum nostri creatoris, ostendendo stabilitatem celestium et varietatem temporalium.

> (Ovid's intention in writing the work is to speak of transformation, so that we may be aware not only of external transformation which takes place in corporeal things be they good or bad, but also of internal transformation in the soul, so that he might lead us back from error to a recognition of the true creator ... or his intention is to call us back from the intemperate love of worldly things and encourage us to the one worship of our creator by showing the permanence of heavenly things, while emphasising the flux of the temporal.)

In his study of the philological commentary, Ghisalberti stresses the somewhat pedestrian and utilitarian nature of Arnulf's glosses, claiming that though our commentator does not rise to the heights of a true philologist he is nonetheless a competent grammarian.[56] A closer perusal of the glosses to the section dealing with the story of Daphne (*Met.* 1.452–567), however, reveals a commentator of greater ability, who provides for the medieval reader elements essential to his understanding of the poem. Arnulf frequently provides a crib for construing the Latin, as for example at *Met.* 1.507 where the grammar of the *ne* clause is explained: **ne prona cadas** *timeo* ("I fear **lest you fall headlong**", Munich, Clm 7205, fol. 30vb); or at *Met.* 1.547 where the ablative *qua* is explained: *defecit enim prepositio* ("a preposition has been left out", Munich, Clm 7205, fol. 31ra). In other places, unusual words are glossed with synonyms more readily grasped by the reader, such as at *Met.* 1.488 where *obsequitur* is glossed "he agrees and he says 'one understands the words' "I would freely grant this'" (*obedit et ait (subaudit "libenter concederem")*; Munich, Clm 7205, fol. 30vb). At 1.499

---

[56] "Filologo Arnolfo non è, ma è tuttavia sempre un buon grammatico" (Ghisalberti, "Arnolfo," 179). Though Ghisalberti in "Arnolfo" transcribes large sections of the glosses from Books One, Two, and Three, I provide my own transcription from Munich, Clm 7205, since Ghisalberti often mistranscribes the text from Venice, Marc. lat. XIV.222 (4007). A critical edition of Arnulf's commentary is a scholarly desideratum.

the diminutive *oscula* is glossed *parva ora* (Munich, Clm 7205, fol. 30vb), and at 1.472 the patronymic applied to Daphne is explained, "***Peneis*** the daughter of Peneus" (***Peneide*** *filia Penei*; Munich, Clm 7205, fol. 30vb).

In the longer glosses to this section, Arnulf incorporates elements of literary criticism and historical reference into his exposition. For example, at line 1.514, Apollo delivers a long discourse on his suitability as a lover, and Arnulf comments: "**You do not know** speaking rhetorically, Apollo commends himself on account of his wealth, wisdom and nobility" (***Nescis*** *rethorice agens commendat se a divitiis, a sapientia, a nobilitate*; Munich, Clm 7205, fol. 30vb). Elsewhere in the commentary Arnulf illustrates his penchant for treating questions related to myth, geography or topography. Ovid begins the story of Mercury and Argus (*Met.* 1.667–723) with an abstruse reference to Mercury's birth from Pleias (1.670). Arnulf provides the medieval reader with background to the myth largely drawn from Servius' commentary on *Aen.* 2.219 and Hyginus, *Fabulae*, 192 (Munich, Clm 7205, fol. 31rb). Arnulf displays his knowledge of geography in the section of the commentary dealing with *Met.* 2. 217–264, in which various areas of the earth are set ablaze during Phaethon's ill-fated flight (Munich, Clm 7205, fol. 32vb).

> [219] **Hemus nondum Eagrius** mons qui diuidit Macedoniam a Thessalia. Oeagrius dictus est ab Orpheo ibi a mulieribus dilacerato, sed hic nondum contigerat, immo futurum erat. Et bene dictus est Oeagrius quia Oeager pater fuit Orphei putatiuus, Phebus uero uerus.

> (**Haemus not yet Oeagrian** a mountain which divides Macedonia from Thessaly. It takes its name from Orpheus who was torn apart there by the women, but this event had not yet occurred but was destined to take place in the future. And it is appropriately called Oeagrian because Oeagrus was the putative father of Orpheus, but Phoebus Apollo was his true father.)

In the glosses for line 219, moreover, we see Arnulf's sensitivity to Ovid's anticipation of the death of Orpheus at the hands of the Thracian women destined to take place in *Met.* 11.1–66.

Cast in a similar vein is a twelfth-century commentary of northern French origin, the so-called *pseudo-Picenardi*, that in emphasising the philological level of interpretation exhibits a unique penchant for explicating the more philosophical and scientific aspects of the poem, particularly in the opening sequence of transformations in Book One.[57]

---

[57] The manuscripts of the commentary are discussed above, nn. 29–31.

The commentary is prefaced by a long and developed *accessus* that introduces the reader to the poem under six primary headings clearly derived from Arnulf's categories: life of the poet (*vita poetae*), title of the work (*titulus operis*), the subject matter (*materia*), the intention of the author in writing the work (*intentio auctoris*), the ultimate objective of the work (*finalis causa*), and the philosophical category under which the work should be classified (*cui parti philosophiae subponatur*).[58] The life of the poet is an expanded version of the life developed by Arnulf of Orléans, but with important modifications: the list of works attributed to Ovid in this commentary places the *Amores* and the *Heroides* in their correct sequence and, contrary to the received opinion among masters in the Middle Ages, our commentator does not believe that the *Metamorphoses* was written as a work of expiation to regain the favour of Augustus, since he states that the epic was composed before the infamous *Ars amatoria*. The treatment of the subject matter of the poem (*materia*) draws on the earlier version of Arnulf of Orléans, who viewed the subject matter as transformation, which can be divided into three classifications: natural, as occurs when corporeal matter changes its form; magical, as occurs in the transformation of Lycaon or of Io; and spiritual, which involves a shift in mental state as occurs in the transformation of Agave. The subject matter of the poem, the later master argues, also serves to structure the poem, in that the poem moves from a general concept of transformation from chaos to order, as developed in the opening segment of Book One, to a more specific concept of transformation from species to species. Lastly, in the final four books the transformation of locale from Troy to Rome prepares the reader for the ultimate apotheosis of Julius Caesar. The objective of the work is two-fold: it leads readers away from vice to embrace virtue and it shifts their perceptions from earthly concerns to the eternal, while it grants to the author, Ovid, the goodwill of the Emperor and of the Roman people as well as financial gain.

The commentary proper reveals a more developed interest in explicating the philosophical or scientific background to individual passages than that of Arnulf. For example, at *Met.* 1.3, Ovid's boast that he will tell of transformation from the very creation of the world down to his own time leads the commentator to a digression on the views of

---

[58] An edition of the *accessus* to the pseudo-Picenardi commentary is forthcoming in Coulson, "Hitherto Unedited (III)."

various philosophical schools of creation (Prague, VIII H 32, fol. 78vb).[59] The commentator offers a lengthy explanation of the creation of the physical world at the hands of the Creator and the manner in which Ovid's poetic treatment modifies it (Prague, VIII.H.32, fols. 78vb–79ra). At *Met.* 1.78, Ovid alludes to "God and a better nature" (*Deus et melior natura*), who are responsible for separating chaos into its various elements, and our commentator again explicates these lines with reference to the position of ancient philosophers on the divine (Prague, VIII H 32, fol. 79rb).

> **Melior natura**, cooperans opifici. Ipsa enim habilis ad separationem. Philosophi tripliciter deum dixerunt, scilicet tugaton (*sic*), id est summum deum, et protopanton, id est primum deorum qui superabundanti fecunditate maiestatis suae noyn, id est mentem, genuit quae maior anima dicitur. Hanc etiam archetipum mundi [mundum MS.] dixerunt, id est principalem figuram istius mundi sensibilis. Haec ex se animam genuit quae minor mens nuncupatur.

> (**Better nature**, assisting the creator. Nature was prone to separation. Philosophers have called god by a three-fold division, namely tagathon, that it the greatest god, and protopanton, that is the first of the gods, who from the exceeding fecundity of its majesty created Noys, that is to say mind, which is referred to as the greater spirit. They even call this the worldly archetype, that is the principal figure of the physical world. And mind generated spirit from itself, which is called lesser mind.)

Another medieval mode of reading the *Metamorphoses* that stressed the utilitarian perspective is that of the prose paraphrase, best exemplified by manuscript lat. 16238 of the Bibliothèque nationale de France in Paris,[60] containing a commentary on Ovid called the "Constructio Ovidii magni" of Jean Bolent, written in France in 1348. The commentary is highly unusual for two reasons: it provides an extremely detailed prose paraphrase of the poem, evidently intended as a learning tool for the student; and it parses many of the difficult Latin words and phrases with their vernacular equivalents, the only extant commentary that does

---

[59] This gloss is similar to a gloss on Book 4.182 of Walter of Châtillon's *Alexandreis* transmitted in Vienna, Oesterreichische Nationalbibliothek, 568 now edited in *Gualteri de Castellione Alexandreis*, 413. I am grateful to David Townsend for this reference.

[60] See Allen, "Eleven Unpublished Commentaries," 284. Nothing further is known of this Jean Bolent.

this on a regular basis. The prose paraphrase restructures and simplifies the more convoluted syntax of the poetic model in order that the student may grasp the basic import of a given section. At *Met.* 1.240, for example, Bolent recapitulates the story line, and then reports in direct speech what has been reported in indirect speech by the narrator (BnF, lat. 16.238, fol. 9rb–va). After summarising each section of the story, he offers comment in individual lemmata that translate Latin phrases into their French equivalents. The commentator also explicates certain phrases. The word *Erinys* (line 18), for example, is glossed as "fury of the underworld," while the Ovidian antithesis "one house was destroyed though one house alone did not merit such punishment" (*occidit una domus, sed non domus una perire | digna fuit, Met.* 1.240–241) is restated more baldly for the reader: "as though he were to say: Not one house rightfully deserves death but every house deserves to die" (*quasi diceret: una domus non meruit mortem set omnis domus mortem meruit,* 16–17). The commentator therefore sees his purpose as two-fold: first by prose paraphrase to assist the reader through the more complex syntax of the original poem and thereby give the gist of the meaning of the passage; secondly, to provide vernacular equivalents for nouns and verbal forms that might be unfamiliar to the student and to supply background for more abstruse mythological references.

The final strain of commentary discussed in this article is the composite commentary, which attempts to explicate the poem from diverse perspectives, including the philological, the allegorical, and the literary. It is best exemplified by the "Vulgate" commentary, produced in the Loire valley, possibly at Orléans, about the year 1250.[61] The "Vulgate" is the single most important commentary on the *Metamorphoses* from the high Middle Ages. Its multi-faceted approach to the explication of the poem makes it unique, for the commentator not only deals with the most rudimentary questions of grammar and syntax (often, though not exclusively, in the interlinear glosses), but he also grapples with more advanced problems related to mythography, science, and, most interestingly, matters of literary import, where the "Vulgate" commentator shows remarkable insights into Ovidian style, poetic technique, structure, characterisation, and Ovidian influence

---

[61] Selections from the "Vulgate" commentary are edited in Coulson, *The "Vulgate" Commentary.* The manuscripts are catalogued in Coulson, "MSS... A Checklist," "MSS... Addendum," and "New Manuscripts." Discussion of the approaches adopted by the commentary can be found in Coulson, "The *'Vulgate'* Commentary," and McKinley, *Reading the Ovidian Heroine.*

on the poetry of the twelfth-century Renaissance, particularly that of Alan of Lille, Bernard Silvester, and Walter of Châtillon. The commentary may be viewed then as one that serves the master and the student at multiple levels of instruction, from the most basic, in which the master concentrates on units of syntax and meaning, to the most advanced, where the master is concerned with the complexities of Ovidian style and literary effect.

The "Vulgate" commentary synthesises the medieval scholarship on Ovid from the eleventh to the mid-thirteenth century. Many of its glosses and longer comments are drawn directly from a series of commentaries of German origin from the early twelfth century found in manuscripts now housed in the Bayerische Staatsbibliothek in Munich and the Stiftsbibliothek St. Peter in Salzburg.[62] Additionally, the sources for many of the allegorisations are drawn from the *Allegorie* of Arnulf of Orléans, and direct borrowings from the commentary of William of Orléans, labelled the *Versus bursarii,* can be traced.[63]

At its most rudimentary level, the "Vulgate" commentary was intended as a teaching tool to explicate the text of the poem. For example, the interlinear gloss[64] in the commentary provides synonyms or explanations for words in the text that undoubtedly posed problems for the medieval reader. At *Met.* 1.14, the proper noun *Amphitrite,*[65] which by metonymy means "sea," is glossed as *magnum mare*. The allusion to the gate of Taenarus at the opening to Book Ten (*Met.* 10.13), through which Orpheus descends to the Underworld, is explained and parallels cited from Vergil and Statius.[66] In other instances, the interlinear gloss explains the structure and syntax of the text. The letter "o" over proper names and pronouns signals that they are in the vocative case; prepositions over nouns frequently serve to explain the use of various cases; and superscript prefixes denote the commentator's suggestion that a compound verb should be understood for the simple form. Interlinear glosses (at times cued with the marginal gloss that surrounds the text) clarify unusual syntax in the Ovidian text that may have caused

---

[62] See above, n. 41.

[63] See above, n. 50. Engelbrecht, *Filologie,* 1:331–337 traces these borrowings at some length.

[64] Wieland has written profusely on the function and classification of interlinear glosses. See, in particular, his *The Latin glosses* and "Interpreting the Interpretation."

[65] The manuscripts of the "Vulgate" all read *Amphitrites.*

[66] Book 10.1–67 of the "Vulgate" commentary is edited in Coulson, *The "Vulgate" Commentary.*

difficulties for the medieval reader. For example, in the story of Myrrha from Book Ten (10.424), Myrrha responds cryptically to the probing of her nurse "oh mother happy in her husband" (*o felicem coniuge matrem*). The following word *hactenus* ("so much" [she said]) is explicated by the "Vulgate" commentator with the interlinear gloss "Myrrha" in order to underline to the reader that this was the extent of her utterance. Interlinear glosses often also indicate the particular type of ablative: for example, the interlinear gloss *propter* above an ablative will indicate that we are dealing with an ablative of cause. At other times, the interlinear gloss serves to clarify the use of parts of speech such as adverbs. So at *Met.* 10.438 Myrrha's nurse is described by the narrator as *male sedula* ("a busybody up to no good"), the "Vulgate" commentator, realising that the adverbial use of *male* is unusual, glosses it with *ad malum* (for evil).

The marginal commentary that accompanies the text frequently reflects the scholarly concerns of thirteenth-century grammarians. For example, the "Vulgate" commentator relies principally, though not exclusively, upon the *Doctrinale* of Alexander of Villa-Dei and the *Graecismus* of Eberhard of Bethune for mnemonic verse tags to help his students retain essential points of grammar, syntax and meaning. At *Met.* 1.637, Ovid stresses that in supplication to Argus the transformed Io can only moo, and our commentator evokes the *Graecismus* (19.32) to underline the suitability of the sound: "**Mooings:** Cows characteristically make this sound, as those verses that distinguish various animal sounds clearly show: The horse whinnies, the bull moos ..." (*Mugitus: boum proprie est mugire, sicut innuitur in quibusdam versibus quorundam animalium et volucrum proprietatem distinguentibus: Hinnit equus, mugit taurus ...*; Coulson, "A Study," 314–315). Like Arnulf of Orléans and John of Garland, moreover, both of whom wrote works explicating the hidden allegorical meanings behind the *Metamorphoses*, the "Vulgate" commentator provides numerous allegorical interpretations for individual stories that prefigure the fuller Christianising treatment the poem will undergo in the fourteenth century in the *Ovidius moralizatus* of Pierre Bersuire[67] and the French vernacular *Ovide moralisé*.[68] The "Vulgate" commentator tends to extract and rearrange earlier allegorical

---

[67] For the manuscripts of the *Ovidius moralizatus* and a full bibliography, see Coulson and Roy, *Incipitarium Ovidianum*, no. 2.

[68] The *Ovide moralisé* is treated in Demats, *Fabula*; Engels, *Etudes*; and most recently Pairet, *Les mutacions*.

material drawn from the *Allegorie* of Arnulf of Orléans and the *Integumenta Ovidii* of John of Garland, often incorporating allusions to twelfth-century poets. To give the reader the flavour of this type of interpretation, which was to have such a long history, I append the allegorical interpretation of the story of the giants from *Met.* 1.162 (Coulson, "A Study," 176–177):

> This story should be understood allegorically: through those who were born from the blood, one understands that wicked men give rise to wicked men. For a bad tree cannot produce good fruit. Whence Matthew of Vendôme says (*Tobias*, 1164–1165): "the tree reveals itself by its foliage"; and Pamphilus (*de amore*, 351) confirms this statement by saying: "Nature often marks its offspring with clear signs." Or this and the preceding transformation should be read historically: Jupiter, a King of Crete, besieged certain tyrants, yet their offspring did not totally perish.

The two primary allegories, one moral and the other euhemeristic, are taken directly from Arnulf's *Allegorie* (1.5). The veracity of the moral allegory is further emphasised and confirmed by reference to two twelfth-century authors, Matthew of Vendôme and the anonymous author of the *Pamphilus*.

The "Vulgate" commentator also shows a marked interest in identifying for the reader the rhetorical devices employed by Ovid. For example, the commentator remarks on such devices as *antonomasia, chronographia, epexegesis, emphasis, hysteron proteron,* and *synecdoche,* amongst others.[69] Additionally, as was the case with the philological glosses of William and Arnulf of Orléans, the "Vulgate" commentator takes great pains to map the devices by which Ovid unifies a poem whose narrative strands might appear to be only loosely connected. For example, our commentator delineates how Ovid develops the story of Phaethon so that the narrative spans Books One and Two: [*Met.* 1.750] "Ovid here anticipates the first transformation of the next book, just as before the eighth book he says about Achelous: **Why do I linger in stories of others**? But in that section, Ovid truly anticipates whereas here he seems to provide merely an appearance or illusion, and thus he says **there was**" (*Prelibacio est prime mutacionis sequentis libri, sicut ante octauum* (sic) *librum de Acheloo dicit:* **Quid moror externis**? *Set ibi est prelibacio uera, hic non uera set est apparicio uel fictio*[70]

---

[69] See Coulson, *The "Vulgate" Commentary*, 9–10 for further discussion.

[70] The correcting hand in V has erased the original reading of the "Vulgate" (*comparicio*).

et hoc est fuit; BAV, Vat. lat. 1598, fol. 11r). He is similarly sensitive to the way in which the stories of the river god Achelous envelop the narrative line of Books Eight and Nine, commenting thus on *Met.* 8.879: "Here begins the preparation for the next book. For Achelous foreshadows the first transformation of the next book, how he had the power to change himself now into a snake, now into a bull, which he later narrates at the request of Theseus. Hence he says: **Why do I linger in stories of others**?" (*Hic incipit preparacio ad librum qui sequitur. Prelibat enim Achelous primam sequentis libri mutacionem, qualiter habebat mutare se nunc in anguem, nunc in taurum, quod narrando ad peticionem Thesei postea prosequitur. Dicit ergo*: **Quid moror externis?**; Vat. lat. 1598, fol. 80r).

At the beginning of Book Ten, the god of marriage Hymen serves as a structural bridge between Books Nine and Ten, since he appears at the marriage of Iphis and Orpheus. The "Vulgate" lays particular stress on the way in which the adverb *inde* underlines the connection: "**Whence**: Here is the link: Hymen then had been present at the marriage of Iphis and Ianthe. **Whence** from their marriage, or from Crete where their marriage was celebrated" (*Inde: Continuacio: ita Himeneus interfuerat nupciis Yphidis et Yantes, inde ex illis nupciis. Vel a Creta ubi fuerunt nupcie Yphidis et Yantes*; Vat. lat. 1598, fol. 100r). Likewise, internal echoes that structure individual stories are noted. At *Met.* 10.220 Ovid artificially binds the stories of the Cyprian girls (Propoetides) and Hyacinth through the common, albeit contrasting, motif of the pride of the region in its offspring, and the "Vulgate" commentator carefully notes the link: "Now we have the story of the inhabitants of Amathus who were turned into cattle. Ovid links the story so: Thus Sparta was not ashamed to have given birth to Hyacinth even though he was transformed, **but** and so on" (*Ecce de Amatunciadibus in boues. Continuacio talis est: Ita non pudet Sparten genuisse Iacinctum quamuis mutatum at etc.*; Vat. lat. 1598, fol. 103r).

The "Vulgate" commentary also gives the modern reader a window onto the world of the medieval schoolroom, for one frequently encounters the "voice" of the medieval master in the commentary. In *Met.* 1.45–46 Ovid describes the creation of the five zones of the earth and the sky, which prompts from the "Vulgate" commentator a long discussion of why some zones of the earth are torrid, while others are frigid (Coulson, *The "Vulgate" Commentary*, 59). To solve this problem, the master advances an analogy taken from daily life (Coulson, *The "Vulgate" Commentary*, 59–61):

Ad hoc potest assignari talis similitudo: terra est rotunda et sol similiter, et omne corpus rotundum magis ostendit umbram suam ad obliquum quam ad rectum. Et ubi umbra minor est, calor est maior. Et ut melius cognoscatur, talis potest induci similitudo …

(To solve this problem let us introduce a comparison: both the earth and the sun are spheres, and every sphere casts its shadow more to the side than straight ahead. And where there is less shade, there is more heat. To understand this better, let us introduce a further comparison …)

Likewise, our commentator often explains situations with terms that are anachronistic. So, for example, when Myrrha's father, after bedding his own daughter unbeknownst to him, seeks to learn the girl's identity by bringing in a light (*Met.* 10.472–473), the "Vulgate" commentator notes: "**by bringing in a light**, a burning candle" (***illato lumine*** *candela ardente*).

One aspect of the "Vulgate" commentary that appears unique to this commentator, however, is his marked interest in character portrayal.[71] In the story of Niobe from Book Six,[72] Ovid highlights the queen's pride, describing her as *alta* (6.169), *superba* (6.169) and *spectabilis* (6.165). At *Met.* 6.275, Ovid uses the adjective *resupina* with a unique meaning to describe Niobe's *hauteur*: "her head drawn back in a show of pride," and our "Vulgate" commentator astutely directs the reader back to Niobe's initial entry at *Met.* 6.165 where the adjective *spectabilis* is applied to her: "**Her head drawn back**: whence Ovid states above" (***Resupina***: *unde supra*; quoting *Met.* 6.165–166). Similarly, in the story of Tereus and Procne from Book Six, one of Tereus' telling character traits is the manner in which he uses feigned tears to gain sympathy and credence for his falsehoods. For example, when Tereus narrates the story of Philomela's supposed death to his wife, Ovid adds the detail: "and his tears lent credibility" (*et lacrimae fecere fidem*; *Met.* 6.566). The "Vulgate" commentator again draws the reader back to the scene between Tereus and his father-in-law Pandion, where feigned tears add credence to Tereus' story: "The author says that he was believed because he cried just as in the scene with his father-in-law, whence above"

---

[71] See McKinley, "The Medieval Commentary Tradition" and *Reading the Ovidian Heroine* for further discussion.

[72] The importance of the story of Niobe within the rhetorical and school traditions can be gleaned from the appearance of this story in the anthology of rhetorical poems from Glasgow, Hunterian Library, V.8.14. See *A Thirteenth-Century Anthology*, 30–32.

(*Creditum est ei dicit actor quia lacrimatus est, sicut apud socerum. Vnde supra*, quoting *Met.* 6.471). In other places, the "Vulgate" is remarkably sensitive to what might be termed Vergilian influences on Ovid's style and choice of dramatic movement. At *Met.* 8.120–121, for example, where Scylla in her concluding soliloquy vents her anger and rage against Minos, the "Vulgate" draws the close connection between this lament of Scylla and that of Dido in Book Four of the *Aeneid*: "Dido addresses Aeneas just so in the *Aeneid* when she says ..." (*Simile dicit Dido ad Eneam in Eneide ubi ait*; Vat. lat. 1598, fol. 70v; quoting *Aen.* 4.365–367).

Finally, I would like to stress the manner in which the "Vulgate" commentator underlines the influence of Ovid on the poets of the twelfth century. The "Vulgate" commentator alludes specifically to a variety of twelfth-century writers and works: Alan of Lille, Bartholomeus Anglicus, Bernard Silvester, the author of the *Pamphilus de amore*, the *Tobias* of Matthew of Vendôme, Eberhard of Bethune's *Graecismus,* and Alexander of Villa-Dei's *Doctrinale*. In addition, he makes reference to other school authors, such as the *Ecloga Theoduli,* and texts dating from the late antique period, such as Claudian's *De raptu Proserpinae*. The greatest number of references, however, is undoubtedly to the *Alexandreis* of Walter of Châtillon.

At a most basic level, the "Vulgate" commentary alludes to contemporary poets to illustrate more specifically Ovidian influence on a particular scene. For example, early in Book One, Ovid provides an elaborate description of the Milky Way along which the gods proceed to the council convened by Jupiter (*Met.* 1.168–173). The "Vulgate" commentator remarks on the similarity of presentation to be found in the *Anticlaudianus* of Alan of Lille: "**A path exists**: So master Alan of Lille uses similar language in his description...," (***Est via:*** *Magister Alanus de eodem idem sonat* ..., quoting *Anticlaudianus* 5.403–407). At other places, the close verbal parallel between a twelfth-century poet and his Ovidian model is explicitly stressed. Early in Book One, for example, Ovid describes the Golden Age as one in which men are free from toil and enjoy an endless spring, since the year has not yet been divided into the four seasons (*Met.* 1.107–110). The "Vulgate" alludes to the similarity in verbal presentation to be found in Walter of Châtillon's *Alexandreis* 2.317–318: "**They soothed**: Master Walter, wishing to impart the flavour of Ovid's language, describes similarly a charming place in which Darius addresses his troops..." (***Mulcebant:*** *Magister Galterus, uolens sapere uim uerborum Ouidii, locum delectabilem, in quo Darius ad suos loquitur, describit dicens* ... , Vat. lat. 1598, fol. 2r). Ovid concludes his enumeration of the four ages of man by describing the Age of Iron (*Met.* 1.127–131), on which the "Vulgate" commentator remarks: "**Next**: Holding in memory the words of Ovid, master Walter develops his scene similarly...," (*Protinus: Memoriter tenens uerba Ouidii, magister Galterus similia hiis dixit...*; Vat. lat. 1598, 2v; quoting *Alex.* 4.195–198). Finally, at *Met.* 1.150, Ovid comments that the goddess Astraea is the last to flee the earth with the advent of the Age of Iron. The "Vulgate" comments on the use made of this motif in Book One of the *Alexandreis*: "**Departed**: Aristotle the teacher appears to invite Alexander to recall this very goddess when he says..." (*Reliquit: Ad hanc reuocandam inuitare uidetur magister Aristotiles Alexandrum...*; Vat. lat. 1598, fol. 3r; quoting *Alex.* 1.176–177).

There are also places where the Ovidian text is reinterpreted to provide a Christian setting for the more purely classical allusion. For example, in Book Ten of the *Metamorphoses,* Orpheus goes to the Underworld in search of Eurydice and addresses his song to Pluto and Persephone: "you are Lords over these regions in which humankind is doomed to linger for the longest time" (*humani generis longissima regna tenetis, Met.* 10.35). Our commentator draws the connection between Ovid's use of the adjective *longissima* to describe the realm of Hades and Walter's description of Hell in Book Ten of the *Alexandreis*, where Satan calls an assembly of the gods of the Underworld: "**Longest** (*longissima*): refers to the punishments of the underworld which never cease. Walter speaks of this in the *Alexandreis*..." (*Longissima: Ad penas respicit infernales que nunquam defficiunt. De quibus dicit magister Galterus in Alexandreide...*; Coulson, *The "Vulgate" Commentary*, 131; quoting *Alex.* 10.119–120).

The "Vulgate" commentary thus represents the most sophisticated and detailed exposition of the *Metamorphoses* that has survived from the later medieval period. It has incorporated into the body of the commentary many of the earlier glosses, such as those of Arnulf and William of Orléans, composed at Orléans two generations earlier, while adding a layer of gloss that deals primarily with matters of contemporary literary interest. The commentary was disseminated widely in France and Italy throughout the thirteenth and fourteenth centuries in multiple copies, and may have exercised an important influence on vernacular authors. The approach that it adopts to the explanation of the text is polyvalent and encompasses virtually all the important modes of reading in the period, including the ethical, the utilitarian, and the literary mode.

Conclusion

Until recently, medieval commentators on classical texts have received what might be termed in the modern vernacular as "bad press." One editor of classical texts has gone so far as to describe medieval masters as "dunce monks," "monastic blockheads," and "cathedral builders."[73] More recent scholarship, particularly the studies of Alastair Minnis, Suzanne Reynolds, and the late Judson Boyce Allen,[74] however, has underlined the importance of the commentary genre for our understanding of reading practices and literary theory in the medieval period. I also seek to rehabilitate the reputation of these texts. I hope this study has confirmed for the reader the vital importance of finding and cataloguing new manuscripts that transmit these texts. I have tried to portray some of the varied interests of French commentators, which ranged from the more purely utilitarian, evidenced in those commentaries that sought to explicate the literal sense of the text, to the ethical, in which allegorical exposition was used to underline the moral sense of the story. Lastly, I have sought to introduce and emphasise the literary acumen of the "Vulgate" commentary, an edition of which is a scholarly desideratum I hope to fulfil.[75]

Ohio State University

---

[73] Willis, *Latin Textual Criticism*, 7, 8, 12.

[74] *Medieval Literary Theory*, ed. Minnis and Scott; *Cambridge History*, ed. Minnis and Johnson; Reynolds, *Medieval Reading*; and Allen, *The Friar as Critic* and *The Ethical Poetic*.

[75] I am most grateful to Virginia Brown, Bruno Roy, Ralph J. Hexter, Marjorie Curry Woods, Kathryn McKinley, Harald Jens Anderson, and the anonymous reader for the press, all of whom commented on and improved earlier drafts of this article. This article was written and revised while I was a visiting fellow at the Harry Ransom Humanities Research Center in Austin, Texas (April and May, 2005) and the Center for Medieval Studies at St. Louis University (September, 2005). I am most grateful to Thomas F. Staley, the Director of the Harry Ransom Humanities Research Center, and to David Murphy, Director of the Center for Medieval Studies at St. Louis University, for their many kindnesses and hospitality. I would also like to thank the staff of the Vatican Film Library and its director Gregory Pass for making my time at St. Louis so profitable.

THE GODDESS DIANA AND THE ETHICS
OF READING IN THE OVIDE MORALISÉ

MARILYNN DESMOND

In *Metamorphoses* 3, Ovid introduces the Actaeon story by eliciting his reader's judgement regarding the events he is about to narrate: "And if you looked carefully, you would find the blame of this in fortune, not in any crime, for what crime did error have?" (*at bene si quaeras, fortunae crimen in illo,* | *non scelus invenies; quod enim scelus error habebat?* 3.141–142).[1] In the course of hunting, Actaeon accidentally stumbles upon the pool where the goddess Diana is bathing with her nymphs. As a consequence of this *error*, this wandering into sacred space, Actaeon sees Diana nude and suffers a fierce penalty: he is transformed into a stag and his own hunting dogs pursue and devour him. In explicitly designating Actaeon's transgression as an *error* at the start of the Actaeon-Diana myth, Ovid uses the narrative of Diana's punishment of Actaeon to pose the ethical questions raised by the divine retribution meted out throughout the first five books of the *Metamorphoses* – the portion of the *Metamorphoses* that relates stories about the gods and goddesses. In these five books, the deities jealously and cruelly punish mortals, many of whom, such as Io, Callisto and Europa – in addition to Actaeon – do not appear to have wilfully offended the gods. At the start of Book Six, Ovid offers a brief summary of these divine atrocities in the ekphrastic depiction of the *caelestia crimina* (6.131) that Arachne weaves into her tapestry in the course of her contest with Pallas Athena. Pallas Athena, of course, does not appreciate this representation of divine activity any more than she appreciates Arachne's challenge; in an explicit example of divine injustice, she transforms Arachne into a spider.

The introductory question regarding Actaeon's *error* (*quod enim scelus error habebat?* 3.142) articulates the interpretive problem that hovers over the first five books of the *Metamorphoses*: how should a reader negotiate the ethical issues posed by this series of stories that relentlessly

---

[1] Ovid, *Metamorphoses*, ed. Anderson. Translations are my own.

depicts the vindictive and even vicious deeds of gods and goddesses?[2] *Error* denotes a wandering, particularly in the notion of wandering off course. While Actaeon strays off course and consequently sees Diana undressed, his actions lack the volition that would make his mistake a misdeed. Diana nonetheless holds him responsible for the unintended consequences of his actions, so that the cruelty of her response is suited to the impiety of a *scelus* or evil deed. Actaeon's error is thus punished as a crime. The category of *error* becomes a critical issue in Ovid's exile poetry when he cites Actaeon in pleading his own case: "Actaeon unknowingly saw Diana without clothes: he nonetheless became the prey of his own dogs" (*inscius Actaeon vidit sine veste Dianam:* | *praeda fuit canibus non minus ille suis*, Tr. 2.105–106).[3] Ovid insists that the transgression that caused his relegation was no more than an *error*: "Either timidity or an error, an error first, has injured me" (*aut timor aut error nobis, prius obfuit error*, Tr. 4.4.39). Ovid's use of the term *error* in these contexts demands an ethical judgement – on the part of Diana in the *Metamorphoses* who ignores the issue of volition when she punishes Actaeon, on the part of the reader of the *Metamorphoses* whose interpretive response could exculpate Actaeon to some degree, and on the part of Augustus who had the power to recognise Ovid's transgression as an *error* and recall him to Rome.

In the literary landscape of the *Metamorphoses*, the punishment of Actaeon for his *error* illustrates the premise developed throughout the narrative that no coherent moral system exists within which to explain divine actions; indeed, Ovid frequently depicts the gods intervening into human affairs without making judgement. Faced with such stories of divine antics, Ovid's reader has to formulate a separate ethical judgement in response to the contingencies of each story. Actaeon's lack of volition ostensibly places him in the same category as female mortals such as Io or Callisto who are raped by a god and then punished for that "transgression" by a jealous goddess, or even females such as Syrinx or Daphne who are pursued by divine predators such as Pan or Apollo and must undergo a metamorphosis as the only means of escaping sexual assault. As a mortal hunter victimised by a divine huntress, Actaeon does not fit the paradigm set by the *caelestia crimina*; his status as male victim increases the pathos generated by the encounter with the divine and throws into

---

[2] Nantet, "La faute d'Actéon"; Barkan, "Diana and Acteon."
[3] Ovid, *Tristia*; translations are my own.

relief the questions of agency posed by the sequence of stories of females raped and preyed upon by gods. While Actaeon has more agency than these female victims, his "transgression" is also more legible – he does indeed invade a sacred grove – and his masculinity renders his punishment a more extreme reversal and, by implication, a starker judgement. These issues frame the conclusion to the Actaeon/Diana story when the narrator shifts the focus from the status of Actaeon's action to the justice of Diana's response: "Rumour is undecided: to some, the goddess seems more cruel than just, others praise her and call it worthy of her harsh virginity. Both sides find some reasons" (*Rumor in ambiguo est: aliis violentior aequo | visa dea est, alii laudant dignamque severa | virginitate vocant; pars invenit utraque causas*, 3.253–255). In acknowledging that Diana might be considered cruel, Ovid's narrator questions divine prerogatives yet leaves final interpretive judgement to his readers. The rhetorical texture of the Actaeon story highlights how the reader of the *Metamorphoses* has to negotiate the moral ambiguities posed by the *caelestia crimina*. The interpretive decisions left to the reader result in a structural irony: the more the reader is left to judge divine actions, the more questionable those actions appear. Since the *Metamorphoses* concludes with the apotheosis of Augustus, the question posed regarding Diana's judgement is implicitly extended at the end of the poem to become a question regarding imperial as well as divine power.[4]

Ovid's representation of the deities in the *Metamorphoses* reflects Roman cultural assumptions towards ethics and morality: in classical Rome, ethics and morality were philosophical rather than religious issues, and Roman religion did not look to deities as figures who represented ethical ideals.[5] Such cultural attitudes towards divinity represented considerable obstacles for the medieval Christian reader situated in a culture that assumed that divinity represented ethical exemplarity. Early in the fourteenth century, an anonymous Franciscan friar undertook a French translation of Ovid's *Metamorphoses*, the *Ovide moralisé*, to which he added extensive moralising and allegorising commentaries designed to direct the reader's response to the ethical ambiguities posed by the Latin text.[6] These moralisations address the

---

[4] See Hardie, "Augustan Poets."

[5] See Liebeschuetz, *Continuity and Change*, 39–54.

[6] See Engels, *Études*, 62. For studies of the *Ovide moralisé*, see Blumenfeld-Kosinski, *Myth*, 90–135, and "Scandal"; Demats, *Fabula*, 61–177; Copeland, *Rhetoric*, 107–130; Feimer, "Medea in Ovid's *Metamorphoses* and the *Ovide moralisé*"; Simpson,

uncertainties of Ovid's text by producing didactic interpretations of Ovid's narratives, perhaps intended for preachers to use as *exempla*. Such a moralising approach to Ovid's *Metamorphoses* constitutes a vernacular version of Latin interpretive practice in regard to classical texts such as the *Metamorphoses*. The medieval appropriation of classical texts articulates the *utilitas* of pre-Christian texts, their potential to offer modes for comprehending or evaluating behaviours.[7] In medieval academic prologues, the *accessus ad auctores*, Ovid's *Metamorphoses* is classified as ethics and Ovid as an ethical poet – *Ovidius ethicus* – since, as the commentators assert, his poetry treats the topic of behaviour.[8] As a vernacular translation and commentary, the *Ovide moralisé* likewise assumes that Ovid's text should be read for its ethical applications, as the translator programmatically asserts (1.31–33) when he states his intention: "to make such verses from which all are able to take the example of doing well and despising evil" (*tel ditié faire | Ou tuit puissent prendre examplaire | De bien fere et de mal despire*).[9] The translator pursues his didactic purposes by presenting a translation of each unit of narrative – which accounts for roughly half of the 70,000 lines of the *Ovide moralisé* – to which are appended several explanations. Each book of the *Ovide moralisé* follows the narrative sequence of the *Metamorphoses*, though the translator frequently adds material from other classical texts and from Scripture, wherever applicable, so that a synopsis of *Genesis* is inserted into the pagan version of the creation myth, and Noah's flood makes its appearance alongside the story of Deucalion and Pyrrha. Likewise, the Theban material in Ovid is augmented from Statius, and excerpts from Ovid's *Heroides* are inserted at appropriate points in the narrative. After each individual story, the translator appends explanatory material that rationalises, historicises, or allegorises the "fable" as he calls his base text; much of this explanatory material is translated from medieval Latin commentary and Latin glosses found in the margins of manuscripts of Ovid's *Metamorphoses*.[10]

Fantasy, 133–190; Possamaï-Perez, "La réécriture de la métamorphose." For the reception of the *Ars amatoria* in medieval French, see Desmond, *Ovid's Art.*

[7] See Minnis, *Medieval Theory of Authorship*, 182–190.

[8] See Allen, *The Ethical Poetic*; Ginsberg, "*Ovidius Ethicus?*"

[9] *Ovide moralisé*; translations are my own.

[10] Demats, *Fabula*, 61–63; on the Latin commentary tradition, see Coulson, "The *Vulgate* Commentary," and Hexter, "Medieval Articulations"; Levine, "Exploiting Ovid"; Barkan, *Gods Made Flesh*; Born, "Ovid and Allegory."

The rational and euhemeristic readings of the *Ovide moralisé* constitute a vernacular version of Latin mythographic traditions. The format of the *Ovide moralisé* – narrative followed by commentary – isolates each story of the *Metamorphoses* as a discrete unit with a set of competing interpretations. For instance, the first explanation for Arachne states that she signifies a foolish man; the second identifies her as a figure for the devil. While the formal structure of the *Ovide moralisé* emphasises the juxtaposition of pre-Christian narrative and Christian allegory, the allegorical explanations of the *Ovide moralisé* translator cumulatively develop an ethical approach to Ovid's *Metamorphoses*. Brian Stock argues that medieval allegory has an ethical imperative; as a form of contemplative reading, allegory "clarified the role of moral, emotional and psychological forces in the individual's ethical orientation."[11] In addition, three fourteenth-century manuscripts of the *Ovide moralisé* contain extensive illustrations; since each image illustrates the text or moralisation of an individual story, the visual component in these manuscripts further contributes to the highly articulated arrangement of the *Ovide moralisé* as a sequence of short narratives.[12] The fifteen books of the *Ovide moralisé* are thus arranged as a compendium of pagan myths and heroic narratives framed by an exuberant interpretive effort – both visual and textual – designed to make Ovid's *perpetuum carmen* serve the rhetorical and iconographic purposes of Christian rhetoric.

Ovid's *Metamorphoses* nonetheless resists assimilation into a didactic Christian tract. Even the Ovidian trope of the volatility of bodies that thematically organises Ovid's text as a sequence of transformations – of bodies changed into new forms – poses a doctrinal problem: as the translator explains, since God the creator made the world, once he gave form to bodies, that form could not be changed. This doctrinal precept accounts for the frequent inclusion of rational explanations that allow each of Ovid's metamorphoses to be read descriptively. For example,

---

[11] Stock, *After Augustine*, 17.

[12] The three illustrated manuscripts are: Rouen, Bib. Mun. 04 (1315–20) which has 453 miniatures of which 90 illustrate the allegories; Arsenal 5069 (1325–50) which originally had 340 miniatures of which 34 are allegorical, and Lyon Bib. Mun., MS 742 (1390) which has 57 miniatures, of which only two are allegorical. On the Lyon manuscript, see Jung, "Ovide, texte, translateur"; on the visual tradition of *Ovide moralisé* manuscripts, see Lord, "Three Manuscripts"; Desmond and Sheingorn, *Myth, Montage, and Visuality*, 103–108; for the iconographic tradition in Latin texts of the *Metamorphoses*, see Orofino, "Ovidio nel Medioevo."

the translator states that Io was a young girl who was seduced and abandoned by Jupiter, the king of Crete, and who then became a prostitute. Phaethon was a scholar who studied astronomy; he published books on astrology which Jupiter destroyed, so Phaethon thereupon committed suicide by throwing himself from a high mountain. The translator includes these rationalistic explanations to counteract the narration of bodily deformations and transformations that occur throughout Ovid's narrative. The artists involved in producing the illustrated copies of these manuscripts nonetheless found the tales of transformation to be visually provocative and often chose to illustrate the metamorphosis itself, so that the visual programs actually emphasise the bodily transformations that are treated sceptically by the translator. For instance, the frontispiece to the Rouen manuscript (fig. 3.1) presents eight quatrefoils that frame individual examples of bodies that are half-human and half-animal; in each case the head and torso remain human while the lower half of the body is depicted as some form of animal. This frontispiece initiates a visual program that frequently depicts the precise moment in the process of corporeal change, when the human figure is aware of becoming not-human. Such a visual program is often more attuned to the Ovidian ethos that develops in the Latin text of the *Metamorphoses* than to the moralised translation it illustrates.

In addition to the problematic issue of metamorphosis itself, Ovid's text also reflects Roman sexual ethics that are completely at odds with the reproductive, heterosexual regimes of medieval Christianity. The tales of rape, incest, pederasty, and bestiality in the *Metamorphoses* require extensive *allegoresis* or moralisation to make them workable within Christian sexual ethics. The aspect of the *Metamorphoses* most resistant to medieval Christian assimilation, however, is the depiction of the pagan deities, figures whose sexual antics and gender – in the case of goddesses such as Diana – make them antithetical to a Christian ethos. In his commentaries on the stories of the *Metamorphoses*, the translator develops a range of approaches to the pagan deities. He frequently draws on the Latin mythographic tradition in order to provide euhemeristic explanations for the gods, so that Saturn and Jupiter become the kings of Crete instead of gods, and demigods are identified as nobles.[13] Throughout the visual programs in *Ovide moralisé* manuscripts, gods are

---

[13] On euhemerism, see Seznec, *Survival*; Simon, "Les Dieux antiques."

distinguished from mortals by their crowns. The translator also offers astrological explanations for deities who cannot be explained euhemeristically. In order to contrast the supposedly monotheistic theology of Christianity to the unabashedly polytheistic world depicted in Ovid's pre-Christian text, the translator has to reconcile the three persons of the Trinity with the monotheism of Christianity. He addresses the issue of polytheism in the Prologue:

> Que que li païen creüssent
> Des dieus que pluisors en fussent,
> Nous devons croire fermement
> Qu'il n'est fors uns Dieus seulement,
> Uns seulz Crierres, qui cria
> Tout, et trios personnes y a
> D'une maiesté, d'une essance,
> D'une egaulté, d'une sustance
> Et d'une pardurableté,
> Sans point de variableté:
> Peres et Filz et Esperis.   (1.107–117)

Though the pagans believed that there are many gods, we ought to believe firmly that there is only one god, a single creator, who created all, and there are three persons in one majesty, of one essence, and one nature, of one substance, and of one eternity, without any variability: Father and Son and Spirit.)

This passage initiates a long exposition on the doctrine of the Trinity (1.107–146) which is then juxtaposed to the polytheism depicted in the *Metamorphoses* so that the Trinity becomes one allegorical vehicle for assimilating Ovid's unruly deities.

While the doctrine of the Trinity allows the translator to accommodate the polytheism depicted in Ovid's text, he nonetheless has to reconcile the immoral actions of the pagan deities to a Christian purpose. As we have seen in the case of Diana and Actaeon, the pagan deities in the *Metamorphoses* do not behave as though there were moral standards by which they are held; indeed, Ovid uses Diana to question whether humans should be held accountable for their actions in the face of divine indifference, if not divine injustice. In the *Metamorphoses*, the Actaeon/Diana story becomes a case study of the nuanced relationship between volition and crime. The *Ovide moralisé* translator, by contrast, exculpates Actaeon even as he recuperates Diana. He insists from the start that Actaeon's transgression is no more than an error when he declares that he will tell the story of Actaeon's wrong turn: "I will recount to you how the young man went astray" (*Or vous raconterai commant | Meserra puis li damoisiaulz*, 3.378–379). The translator is decisive in his assertions that Actaeon's transgression results from misfortune or bad luck: "Thus while she was bathing, Actaeon, who knew nothing about it, came there by mistake, as if fortune and bad luck led him to his mortal suffering" (*Tant dis come elle se lavoit, | Acteon, qui riens n'en savoit, | Est la venus par ignorance, | Si com fortune et mescheance | Le mainent a sa mortel paine*, 3.421–425). As if in answer to Ovid's rhetorical question (*quod enim scelus error habebat?*), the *Ovide moralisé* translator emphasises Actaeon's innocence. Unlike the ethical ambivalence posed by Ovid in the *Metamorphoses*, the *Ovide moralisé* narrator offers two interpretive explanations for the Actaeon/Diana story; in the first "moralisation," he reads the Actaeon story as an *exemplum* that illustrates the dangers of the hunt. The second allegory, however, draws again on the doctrine of the Trinity: "Diana is the deity who reigns in the Trinity – Naked, without human nature – whom Actaeon saw without cover – that is the son of God, who saw purely disclosed in nudity the blessed Trinity that reigns eternally, without beginning and without end" (*Dyane, c'est la Deïté | Qui regnoit en la Trinité, | Nue, sans humaine nature, | Qu'Acteon vit sans couverture, | C'est li filz Dieu, qui purement | Vit a nu descouvertement | La beneoite Trinité, | Qui regnoit en eternité, | Sans comencement et sans fin*, 3.635–643). In contrast to his efforts throughout the text to euhemerise the pagan deities so that the gods are reductively explained away as mortals, the translator allegorically equates Diana with the Trinity and Actaeon specifically with the second person of the Trinity.[14] Unlike other deities, the goddess Diana retains a divine status in the moralisation of the *Ovide moralisé*, and she personifies the doctrinal statement he had made earlier in the Prologue that the polytheism of the ancients could be reconciled to the doctrine of the Trinity. Actaeon's mistake of stumbling into the spring where Diana is bathing becomes an allegory for the incarnation, so that Actaeon – a man who stumbles upon a goddess – signifies the reverse of the process by which god became man. If Ovid's text made ethical demands on the reader by questioning the nature of Actaeon's transgression and the justice of Diana's actions, the French text responds to that question by asserting Actaeon's innocence and bracketing the question of Diana's cruelty by

---

[14] See Casanova-Robin, *Diane et Actéon*, 115–122.

invoking the incarnation, the transformation central to Christian theology.

Despite the moralised certainties of the textual commentaries in the *Ovide moralisé* that attempt to subordinate the pagan narrative to a Christian paradigm, the visual programs in the illustrated manuscripts tend to highlight the stark contrast between the pagan and Christian codes (fig. 3.2). The Rouen illustration of the Actaeon/Diana encounter ostensibly visualises the key elements of the story; yet to visualise divinity is to embody it, and the embodied Diana is a highly gendered and sexualised figure. The illustration situates Diana standing nude in a pool of water, surrounded by her followers. She and her nymphs have set aside their signature accessories, their bows and quivers full of arrows, along with their clothes. Actaeon has already been transformed into a stag: he is no longer the mortal hunter who has wandered into sight of Diana; only his size and his enormous antlers suggest the inadvertent, male aggression that led to his punishment. Compared to the text, the image de-emphasises Actaeon's humanity and his human error; instead, the contrast between the three nude figures and the stag would appear to embody a raw confrontation between human and beast. The image suggestively depicts the homoerotic possibilities of Diana's band of chaste huntresses: one woman has her arm possessively wrapped about her nude leader and the other places both hands on her shoulder. At the visual level, Actaeon's intrusion is not that of a mortal into a sacred space, but that of an animal who has strayed into a homosocial female space. The next image (fig. 3.3) depicts the stag Actaeon suspended between two dogs: the expressive face of the stag suggests Actaeon's human awareness of his physical vulnerability as his changed form is about to be torn and devoured by his own hounds. This visual emphasis on Actaeon's physicality is developed allegorically in the second of the two illustrations that accompany the two allegorical interpretations of the story (fig. 3.4). The first illustration depicts a hunter on horseback following a hound in pursuit of a hare in order to signal the moral reading that Actaeon represents the dangers of hunting. Juxtaposed to this allegorical image, an image of the Flagellation in the next column illustrates the suffering of Christ in the second person of the Trinity. While the text of the allegory simply identifies Actaeon as a figure for the second person of the Trinity, the image of the flagellation visualises not only the embodied Christ, but the violence and humiliation to which Christ's physical body was subjected.

Although the visual program emphasises the horror of Actaeon's transformation and his corporeal suffering, it redeems that suffering through the allegory of the incarnation. Diana, by contrast, remains legible in the visual program only as a pagan deity, even though the text proposes that she represents the Trinity. Indeed, the image of Diana depicts the homoerotic significance of Diana's band of women that is suggested in Ovid's Latin text and developed in the French translation. As we have seen, Diana's vicious punishment of Actaeon in *Metamorphoses* 3 is one incident in a sequence of stories depicting divine aggression, particularly sexual aggression, towards mortals. Several of these earlier victims of divine predators – Daphne, Syrinx, and Callisto – are classified in Ovid's text as followers of Diana. Although the members of Diana's coterie are affiliated with her same-sex community through two identifications, as huntresses and as women who renounce heterosexual relations, it is specifically their resistance to the heterosexual regime in favour of chastity that identifies them as followers of Diana. The Latin text specifically identifies Daphne, Syrinx, and Callisto as followers of Diana, an identification emphasised in the *Ovide moralisé*. When Daphne pleads with her father to be allowed to remain unmarried, she states that she wishes to "follow Diana": "She said: Good father, I have no desire or need to take a husband. By God, let me live as a virgin and follow my lady Diana" (*Si dist: "Biau pere, je n'ai soing | De baron prendre ne besoing. | Pour Dieu, me lessiez vierge vivre, | Et ma dame Dyane ensivre"* (1.2845–2848). Syrinx is identified with Diana's band: "She was a virgin and she busied herself with the hunt, like Diana, she placed her attention and her study in it" (*Vierge estoit, et de chacerie | Comme Dyane s'entremist: | Sa cure et son estuide i mist*, 1.3688–3690). Callisto is described as a member of Diana's coterie: "She was a follower of Diana, the most senior and most prized of all the company" (*Elle estoit compaigne Dyane, | La plus mestresse et plus prisie | De trestoute sa compaignie*, 2.1408–1410). When Callisto is approached by Jupiter disguised as Diana, the French translation develops the idea that Callisto thinks that it is Diana who is making erotic advances towards her, and so she responds quite warmly. When Callisto becomes pregnant as a result of Jupiter's assault, Diana excludes her from her community because Callisto's pregnancy testifies to her heterosexual encounter, however unwilling. The Callisto story demonstrates that – in the libidinal economies represented in Ovid's text – Diana's followers are identified as chaste only in so far as they renounce heterosexual desire; indeed, the identity of Diana's followers as chaste maidens enables the circulation of homoerotic desire among her band of women.[15] While the metamorphosis of Syrinx and Daphne is a recognition of their dedication to the principles of "chastity" required of the followers of Diana, the exclusion of Callisto, who has been raped and impregnated by Jupiter, like the punishment of Actaeon, illustrates the vengeful means Diana employs to discipline the sexuality of her followers and maintain the homosocial integrity of her band of women.

This notion in the *Ovide moralisé* that "chaste" women were followers of Diana offers a literate version of a popular medieval belief in a "Cult of Diana." Of the entire Roman pantheon, Diana is the only deity imagined to claim a following in the Christian Middle Ages. This cult is first described as a form of witchcraft in a tenth-century legal text, the *Canon episcopi*:

> [S]ome wicked women perverted by the devil, seduced by illusions and phantasms of demons, believe and profess themselves, in the night hours, to ride upon certain beasts with Diana, the goddess of the pagans, and an innumerable multitude of women, and in the silence of the dead of night to traverse great spaces of earth, and to obey her commands as of their mistress, and to be summoned to her service on certain nights.[16]

This description of "following the goddess" is repeated in penitential texts.[17] Testimony to this notion of "following the goddess" is not limited to ecclesiastical documents; literary references appear in a variety of texts and traditions, both Latin and vernacular. For instance, Matheolus' thirteenth-century *Lamentations* (2.1476–1479) describes how sorcerers convince women that they ride in Diana's company by night; Jean le Fèvre's translation of the *Lamentations* into French refers to this goddess as Dame Habonde instead of Diana (2.2073–2082), as does Jean de Meun in the *Roman de la rose* (18397–18468). Throughout the high and late Middle Ages, the classical deity Diana remains associated, even if only indirectly, with what Carlo Ginzburg calls "a primarily female ecstatic religion, dominated by a nocturnal goddess."[18]

The *Ovide moralisé* never refers to this popular notion of Diana as a pagan goddess who summons women to follow her on certain nights.

---

[15] For a full discussion of the Callisto story in the *Ovide moralisé*, see Desmond and Sheingorn, *Myth, Montage and Visuality*, 126–128.

[16] Lea, *Materials toward a History of Witchcraft*, 1:178–179.

[17] See Russell, *Witchcraft in the Middle Ages*, 76–78.

[18] Ginzburg, *Ecstasies*, 122.

Instead, the moraliser's attitude toward the women in Ovid's text who follow Diana assimilates them into a Christian moral system: their identity as chaste followers of Diana enables the translator to characterise them by their virginity and then classify them as figures who represent the Virgin Mary. The translator allegorically equates Daphne with the Virgin (1.3215–3260). The Rouen manuscript illustrates the Daphne story with two images: the first depicts Apollo's pursuit of Daphne and his embrace of the laurel tree after her transformation (fig. 3.5).[19] This image is juxtaposed to an image of the Annunciation that illustrates the *glose* in which Daphne's desire to follow Diana is allegorically read as an allegory for the conception of Christ through the agency of the Holy Spirit (fig. 3.6). This image of the Annunciation in the Daphne story complements the image of the nativity that illustrates the *glose* to the Callisto story, where the pregnancy of Diana's follower is read as an allegory of the Virgin birth (fig. 3.7). In the visual program of the Rouen manuscript, the narrative of the spiritual conception of Christ and his virgin birth are overlaid on the stories of Diana as the virgin goddess of the pagans. The *Ovide moralisé* develops the suggestions of the *Metamorphoses* that the cult of Diana designates a female homosocial and homoerotic community from which heterosexual desire as well as masculinity are rigorously excluded. In the *Ovide moralisé*, the stories of Daphne and Syrinx are moralised so that the Roman category of chastity – which in the *Metamorphosis* appears to be renouncing heterosexual desire for same-sex desire – becomes equated with the elite Christian ideal of virginity.[20] The *Ovide moralisé* suggests that if chastity is the means by which pagan women might elect to "follow the goddess," virginity might offer similar possibilities within Christian culture.

The cult of Diana forms a thematic link between the stories of Syrinx, Daphne, Callisto, and Actaeon in the first third of Ovid's poem. The translator emphasises the thematic links between these stories in the allegories appended to each text. For the translator of the *Ovide moralisé*, the cult of Diana offers a new set of possibilities at the end of the poem. Book Fifteen brings the narrative to a close by focussing on the deification of the Caesars – mortals who achieve divine status. This final book of the *Metamorphoses* addresses the topic of divinity in a different

---

[19] For the iconographic tradition of the Daphne story, see Giraud, *La Fable de Daphné*.

[20] On the ideal of virginity, see Cooper, *The Virgin and the Bride*.

register from the first five books which thematically emphasise the *caelestia crimina*. One of the historical figures treated in this book is Numa, an ancient Roman king who, drawing on the wisdom of Pythagoras, attempted to teach the arts of peace to a warlike people. Upon his death Numa's wife, the nymph Egeria, is so inconsolable that she retreats from the city into a space dedicated to Diana. When the nymphs do not succeed in consoling her, a demi-god who identifies himself as Hippolytus tells her the story of his misfortune, his death, and his resurrection under the name Virbius. At the conclusion of this story, he states that he is now a follower of Diana. When the narrative of Hippolytus/Virbius' woes also fails to console Egeria, Diana transforms her into a fountain. At this point in the *Metamorphoses*, the male demi-god Hippolytus is not excluded from the worship of the goddess Diana. In addition, the metamorphosis of the grieving widow Egeria – who is neither huntress, nor virgin – into a fountain offers a highly redemptive transformation, particularly in the context of Book Fifteen which dedicates a long passage to the life-affirming properties of fountains. The single illustration to the Egeria story in the Rouen manuscript depicts Diana seated on a bench while Egeria and Virbius appeal to her for assistance (fig. 3.8). This image does not offer a Christian iconography for the cult of Diana; the divinity of Diana is not allegorised in text or in image in the final book of the *Ovide moralisé*. The metamorphosis of Egeria into a fountain suggests a much less vindictive Diana than the one who had expelled Callisto, and a much less violent goddess than the one who had transformed Actaeon into a stag. Likewise, the inclusion of the demi-god Virbius among Diana's followers suggests that some males – such as the victimised Hippolytus – might be included in Diana's coterie. In terms of the composition of the *Metamorphoses*, this myth represents a specific cult of Diana, here called the Orestian Diana (15.489).[21] To the medieval translator, however, such distinctions between different Roman cults mean nothing and he translates the passage to identify this goddess simply as Diana: "Diana had pity on her suffering and out of charity changed her body into a cold fountain" (*Dyane ot de son duel pitié, | Si li mua par amistié | Le cors en froide fontenele*, 15.1447–1449). The moralisations for Book Fifteen are all collected together at the end of the book; the allegory for this tale briefly identifies Numa as a figure for the early saints and Hippolytus as the early Christian

---

[21] On the Roman cult of Diana, see Gordon, "On the Origin of Diana."

martyr by the same name (15.6249– 6284). No allegorical explanation is offered for Diana.

As the Egeria story demonstrates, the moralisations in Book Fifteen of the *Ovide moralisé* are much less extensive than in earlier books. While this has led Renate Blumenfeld-Kosinki to suggest that the *Ovide moralisé* translator lost interest in the moralisations in the process of translating the text of the *Metamorphoses*, the brief allegory appended to the Egeria story suggests instead that the Pythagorean discourse at the end of the *Metamorphoses* did not require much adjustment in order to fit the classical narrative into Christian notions of divine ethics.[22] Indeed, the translator specifically identifies the benevolent Diana who takes pity on Egeria with the cult of Diana represented in the stories of Daphne, Syrinx, Callisto, and Actaeon in the first few books of the *Ovide moralisé*. In that respect, the *Ovide moralisé* translator recognises Book Fifteen as a commentary on the earlier books of the *Metamorphoses*, and the Diana of Book Fifteen works to recuperate the earlier, more problematic figure of Diana as a vengeful goddess who punishes mortals such as Actaeon or Callisto.

Ovid's *Metamorphoses* appears to allow the reader considerable latitude in navigating the implications of mythical stories such as the Actaeon/Diana encounter. Like much of the first five books of the *Metamorphoses*, the Actaeon myth depicts a terrifying deity and a horrific transformation of human into beast. Nonetheless, the narrator refuses to structure the Actaeon myth as a moral *exemplum*. Yet, if the world depicted in the *Metamorphoses* lacks a moral centre, Ovid's rhetorical framework repeatedly calls upon the reader to formulate an ethical response to this sequence of unsettling narratives. The translator of the *Ovide moralisé* develops his commentaries on the text in direct response to the rhetorical demands that Ovid's text places upon the reader. Whereas Ovid's treatment of the Diana story offered the reader a set of ethical choices, the *Ovide moralisé* translator eliminates such readerly judgement and situates its audience in a more secure space in which reading pre-Christian narratives can be framed by a coherent system. As a Christian exegete dealing with the pagan deities, the *Ovide moralisé* translator elaborates on the Christian mysteries of the Trinity and the story of the Incarnation in order to restore a notion of divine ethics to

---

[22] On the Pythagorean discourse of the *Ovide moralisé*, see Viarre, *La Survie d'Ovide*, 72–73; Hardie, "Questions of Authority."

Ovid's text. The ethical certainties of the Incarnation provide the *Ovide moralisé* translator a secure vantage point; from this perspective, the moralisation of the Actaeon/Diana story suggests that the doctrine of the Trinity could allegorically represent a homoerotic female community led by a goddess in which the Incarnation is figured as a masculine intruder in a homosocial female space. While such moralisations testify to the triumph of the medieval notion that Ovid was an ethical poet and that his *Metamorphoses* could be read for its ethical applications, it effectively recuperates Diana from her pagan identity as a cruel goddess as well as from her medieval association with witchcraft. In the process, such moralisations also imply that virginity offers the medieval Christian the option of "following the goddess" and the homoerotic possibilities that represents.[23]

BINGHAMTON UNIVERSITY

---

[23] I am grateful to Miri Rubin for her insightful reading of a draft of this essay.

METAPHOR AND METAMORPHOSIS IN THE OVIDE MORALISÉ AND CHRISTINE DE PIZAN'S MUTACION DE FORTUNE

SUZANNE CONKLIN AKBARI

Although it may seem hard to believe, there was a time when the works of Christine de Pizan were not widely read. These days, any survey of medieval literature that omits her works would be considered conspicuous and unusual. In part, of course, the awakening of interest in the writings of Christine is the result of a desire, which developed first during the early 1970s, to seek out women writers who might afford a different perspective on the familiar territory of medieval culture. Not surprisingly, the work of Christine's that is almost invariably assigned to students is the *Livre de la cité des dames*, or *Book of the City of Ladies*. This book is not only authored by a woman, but is also explicitly devoted to the effort to promote the reputation of women in world history; as a classroom text, therefore, this is what we might call "hitting two birds with one stone." When other selections from the writings of Christine de Pizan are provided, they are almost always the autobiographical passages that appear in her *Livre de la mutacion de Fortune* and in her *Avision-Christine*.[1] Once again, the life of the medieval woman – here, Christine herself – is the focus of study, rather than the broader cultural milieu in which the works were produced.

This article includes a close examination of one of these famous passages: namely, Christine's autobiographical description of how she was transformed, at the hands of Fortune, from a woman into a man. This passage will not, however, be examined in the light of comparative feminist theory, which has been overwhelmingly the norm in numerous published studies.[2] Instead, it will be explored in the context of medieval

---

[1] See, for example, the recent collections *Writings of Christine de Pizan*, ed. Willard, and *Selected Writings of Christine de Pizan*, ed. Blumenfeld-Kosinski and Brownlee.

[2] Huot, "Seduction and Sublimation"; Schibanoff, "Taking the Gold out of Egypt"; Quilligan, *Allegory of Female Authority*; Desmond, *Reading Dido*, 195; Kellogg,

understandings of change, revealing both how Christine conceptualised the process of change and how it was articulated within the framework of Ovidian metamorphosis.[3] Christine, like many medieval readers, was intimately familiar with the moralised versions of Ovid that proliferated in Latin and the vernacular: her writings repeatedly make reference to the *Ovide moralisé*, an Old French verse text in which the metamorphoses recounted by Ovid serve as the germ of extended allegorical expositions.[4] A comparative look at Christine's treatment of metamorphosis and that found in the *Ovide moralisé* will shed light not only on late medieval constructions of gender categories, but also on Christine's theory of allegory. In short, the aim of this article is to take the first steps in an exploration of the relationship between metaphor and metamorphosis in the allegories of Christine de Pizan.

Christine de Pizan is probably best known as a woman writer of the Middle Ages. She should, however, also be known as probably the most prolific writer of allegory during the whole of that period. Because Christine so self-consciously presents herself as a writer following in the tradition of earlier allegorists, especially Jean de Meun and Dante, it is tempting to read her allegories as part of a late medieval literary tradition, produced by a group of writers having shared assumptions regarding the function of figurative language.[5] It is possible to show, however, that Christine's assumptions regarding the function of figurative language differ significantly from her predecessors, and that they differ precisely on the basis of how metaphor (a term Christine uses explicitly) can be understood in terms of Ovidian metamorphosis. This essay therefore treats three incidences of the term *methafore* in the writings of Christine,

---

"Transforming Ovid"; Nephew, "Gender Reversals."

[3] On medieval expressions of the Ovidian model of change, see Bynum, *Metamorphosis and Identity*, 86–101, 166–189.

[4] Christine cites the *Ovide moralisé* frequently in her *Mutacion de Fortune*, as in her other allegories (lines 1159–1164, 3065–3072, 13913–13918); the editor of the *Mutacion de Fortune*, Suzanne Solente, argues that Christine's description of her own transformation owes a great deal to the literary models found in the *Ovide moralisé* (1: xxxiv). On Christine's use of the *Ovide moralisé*, see Campbell, *L'Epître d'Othéa*, 110–141; Brownlee, "Ovide et la moi poétique"; Blumenfeld-Kosinski, *Reading Myth*, 171–212.

[5] On the interrelation of Jean de Meun, Dante, and Christine in the late medieval writing of allegory, see Brownlee, "Discourses of the Self"; Huot, "Seduction and Sublimation"; Richards, "Christine de Pizan and Dante"; Quilligan, *Allegory of Female Authority*.

using the *Ovide moralisé* as a key to her innovative presentation of the relationship of metaphor and metamorphosis.

Curiously, the most useful place to look for a definition of figurative language in the works of Christine de Pizan is not among her many allegories, but in her biography of the French king Charles V. There, Christine uses visual terminology to characterise *poesie*, the term she uses to describe all figurative writing, including allegory. She indicates that language can express meaning *apparaument* or *clerement* (openly or clearly), or else *occultement* or *en ombre* (secretly or in shadows).[6] This dichotomy is arguably the most common trope used to define allegorical language, as understanding is described in terms of clear sight.[7] A formulation similar to that found in the biography of Charles V appears in the preface found in one of the manuscripts of her last allegory, *Avision-Christine*. There, Christine states that she, following the "poets' manner of speaking" (*maniere de parler des pouetes*), writes "under the figure of metaphor; that is to say, under covered words" (*soubz figure de methaphore, c'est a dire de parole couverte*).[8] Ordinarily, metaphor is described as a trope of language that makes the abstract concrete, by offering a visible image; in the words of Aristotle, metaphor puts the concept "before the eyes" (*pro ommaton*).[9] In other words, metaphor translates what can be seen only by the eye of the mind into a form that can be seen by the eye of the body. Paradoxically, however, in Christine's description of *methafore* as *parole couverte*, metaphor's role is instead to cover up meaning, to hide it behind the veil of figurative language. Though, as for Aristotle, the metaphor makes meaning visible or "vivid," for Christine the metaphor is also a covering. In some ways, this notion of metaphor is close to allegory, with its guiding trope of the *integument* or veil.[10] It is, however, strikingly different from conventional medieval practices of allegory in that it is fundamentally grounded in the notion of change: more specifically, it is grounded in metamorphosis.

Unlike other medieval allegorists, Christine uses the term *methafore* to describe her own mode of writing. We have seen this usage already in the prologue to *Avision-Christine*; her most striking use of the term, however,

---

[6] *Le Livre des fais et bonnes meurs du sage roy Charles V*, ed. Solente; cited by line number in the text. Translations are my own.

[7] Akbari, *Seeing through the Veil*, 3–20.

[8] Reno, "Preface to the *Avision-Christine*," 208.

[9] Arist. *Rhet.* 3.11.1–2, 1411b; cf. 3.10.7, 1411a–b: see Akbari, *Seeing Through the Veil*, 9.

[10] Jeauneau, "L'Usage de la notion d'*integumentum*." On the notion of *integumentum* in medieval vernacular literature, see Akbari, *Seeing Through the Veil*, 57–62, 102–113.

appears in the *Livre de la mutacion de Fortune*, where Christine prefaces her account of how she herself was changed from a woman into a man with two other accounts of sexual transformation. She first describes Tiresias, who was changed into a woman and then back into a man, and then Yplis (Ovid's Iphis), who was born female but raised as a male, and whose body took on a male form after Yplis appealed to the goddess Vesta (1153–1158).[11] These two metamorphoses anticipate Christine's own metamorphosis into a man and illustrate the relationship of gender to knowledge. Because he has lived both as a male and as a female, Tiresias gains special, normally hidden knowledge in two senses. First of all, his experience of living under two different genders makes him uniquely qualified to judge a dispute between the gods concerning whether men or women take greater pleasure in sex. Second, Tiresias' judgement in the case causes him to be punished by Juno with the loss of bodily sight, but rewarded by Jupiter with spiritual sight – that is, the ability to foresee the future. For Tiresias, then, androgyny enables prophecy. For Yplis (Ovid's Iphis), however, success comes not through androgyny but through being once and for all transformed into a man. Christine stresses the parallel between Yplis' transformation and her own by paraphrasing the Ovidian account of Yplis' change in the subsequent description of her own metamorphosis, suggesting that for Christine – like Yplis – success comes through taking on a masculine nature.

Because she herself has been transformed, Christine is able in the following chapters to write authoritatively on world history about the sweeping changes wrought by Fortune. In this way, Ovidian change serves as the necessary precursor that permits the narrator to recount a universal history in terms of Boethian change, as Fortune turns the wheel that raises a man to a position of power one day, and throws him down the next.[12] At the same time, the narrator's transformation, unlike the historical ones she recounts, is only figurative. Christine elides the distinction between figurative and literal transformation in her statement that the following account of her transformation is true – true, that is, insofar as it is metaphorically true:

---

[11] *Le Livre de la mutacion de Fortune*, ed. Solente; cited in the text by line number. Translations are my own.

[12] On Christine's use of Boethius, see Cropp, "Boèce et Christine de Pizan"; Semple, "Consolation of a Woman Writer"; Paupert, "Christine et Boèce."

> Or est il temps que je raconte ...
> Comment de femme homme devins ...
> Qui trop est chose merveillable
> Et si n'est mençonge, ne fable,
> A parler selon methafore,
> Qui pas ne met verité fore,
> Car Fortune a bien la puissance
> Sur ceulx de son obeissance
> Faire miracles trop greigneurs.   (1025–1037)

(Now it is time that I recount... | how I changed from a woman into a man.... | It is a very marvellous thing, | and it is not a lie or fable | to speak according to metaphor, | which does not expose the truth openly; | for Fortune certainly has the power, | over those obedient to her, | to work very great miracles.)

The denial that her figurative writing is *mençonge* or *fable* recalls the opening lines of the *Roman de la rose*, where Guillaume de Lorris refutes the belief "that in dreams there is nothing but fictions and lies" (*fables* and *mençonges*) and declares that his own dream contains a hidden truth which the reader will, in the end, perceive openly or *apertement*.[13] By repeating the truth claim found in the opening lines of the *Roman de la rose*, Christine implies that the reader of her *Mutacion de Fortune* will similarly discover the truth hidden in the metaphor through an effort to penetrate beyond the covering of figurative language.

As noted above, Christine precedes her account of her own bodily transformation in the *Mutacion de Fortune* with the story of Yplis who, like Christine, was changed from a woman into a man. Yplis is clothed as a boy in order to avoid her father's decree that any daughters of his would be killed, and remains *soubs vestement de filz* (in – literally, 'under' – the clothes of a boy) until her marriage to a woman becomes inevitable. Fearful that this ruse will be discovered on her wedding night, Yplis prays to the goddess Vesta for help. She is changed into a young man through divine intervention; curiously, however, by changing the goddess involved in the transformation from Isis (as Ovid has it) to Vesta, Christine implies that Yplis herself participates in the transformation by being dressed (*vestue*) as a male. Here, clothes literally make the man.

---

[13] Guillaume de Lorris and Jean de Meun, *Le Roman de la rose*, ed. Lecoy, lines 1–2. On the couplet, see Blumenfeld(-Kosinski), "Remarques sur *songe/mensonge*"; Akbari, *Seeing Through the Veil*, 49–51.

Yplis' transformation reveals something interesting not just about gender categories, but about the status of figurative language within Christine's system of allegory. Yplis' body must be changed in order to remove the discrepancy between the outer appearance of her clothing and the corporeal form beneath; it would seem to follow, then, that the meaning clothed by figurative language must similarly be changed to remove the discrepancy between outer appearance and inner reality. Body is to clothing as meaning is to figurative language. Just as Yplis' female body changes to correspond to her masculine clothing, so meaning must change to correspond to the veil of language that covers it. This in turn suggests that, in metaphor, the hidden meaning does not necessarily hold primacy over the beautiful covering. By likening metaphor to metamorphosis, Christine challenges the conventional primacy of meaning over the veil of language. Which is the "real" shape of the body, male or female? And which is the "real" meaning?

In order to probe more deeply into the role of embodiment and metamorphosis in Christine's use of *methafore*, it is helpful to examine Christine's other uses of the term in the *Mutacion de Fortune*, the first of which appears in the course of a description of the magnificent castle of the goddess Fortune. The gates of her castle are guarded by four figures: Richece (Riches), Poverté (Poverty), Esperance (Hope), and Atropos (one of the three Fates, associated with death and despair). These gates are organised in terms of the dichotomy of light and darkness. Richece's facade shines brightly with rich jewels and gold, while Poverté's side is surrounded by houses which are "gloomy and dark" (*obscures [et] noires*, 3437). No sun shines there (3466), which means that the place is characterised not just by lack of light but by lack of warmth, so that the half-clothed inhabitants of the region near the gate are surrounded by snow and ice. Similarly, the side presided over by Atropos, symmetrically set against that guarded by Esperance or Hope, is said to be "very black" (*tres noir*, 3506) and bitterly cold (3513). Neither sun nor moon shines there (3420), and the entire place is "gloomy and dim" (*obscur et trouble*, 3523).

The opposition symmetrically embodied in the four facades of the castle restates an opposition essential to Fortune herself. In keeping with classical and medieval conventions, she is said to have two faces, one white and smiling, the other "black, shadowy, horrible, gloomy" (*[n]oir, tenebreux, orrible, obscur*, 1933).[14] Fortune's malignant aspect is expressed

---

[14]For an overview of the tradition, see Patch, *Goddess Fortuna*.

in the facade guarded by Poverté and that guarded by Atropos, whose facade is described primarily in terms of its privation of light: "It is so horrible and dark, terrifying and so shadowy that nothing so gloomy is found in humanity" (*Tant est horrible et tenebreuse,* | *Espouantable et si umbreuse* | *Que nulle chose tant obscure* | *N'est a humaine creature,* 2743–2746). Atropos too is characterised by darkness and obscurity, not only in how she appears but in how she herself sees: she has "eyes dim and crossed, half open and turned back in her head" (*yeulx troubles et traversez* | *Demy ouvers et ranversez,* 2795–2796). As one of the three Fates, Atropos cuts the thread of life and presides over the passage from life into death. Therefore, the darkness that characterises her signifies not just ignorance, but death; correspondingly, the absent light signifies not just intellectual illumination, but life itself.

Atropos is unique among the guardians of the four gates of Fortune's castle, for while the other three guardians (Richece, Poverté, and Esperance) are personifications, Atropos is a figure of myth, one of the three Fates. Christine addresses this discrepancy directly by stating that Atropos, unlike her accompanying personifications (or *personnages*), is actually a metaphor. She writes: "The gatekeeper is named Atropos, speaking according to the manner which is appropriate to metaphor; accordingly, the poet so calls her" (*Attroppos a nom la portiere,* | *A parler selon la maniere* | *Qui a methafore compete,* | *Ainsi l'appella le poete,* 2819–2822). In her *Epistre Othéa*, written just a few years earlier, Christine identifies Atropos explicitly with death, noting that "the poets called death, Atropos" (*les poetes appellerent la mort Atropos*) and referring to "Atropos, by whom death is designated" (*Atropos, qui est nottee la mort*; 202.14, 202.23–24; ch. 34).[15] This begs the question: Why does Christine use Atropos as the guardian of the gate representing death rather than simply personifying "Death," which would have been more in keeping with the personifications guarding the other gates? A plausible answer concerns the relationship of metaphor and metamorphosis, and death's role as the agent of the final earthly metamorphosis.

Such a notion of metamorphosis would be alien to Ovid, who explicitly describes the transformation of Myrrha, for example, as a state in between death and life. Change me, Myrrha begs, so that I may offend neither the dead nor the living: "lest, surviving, I offend the living, and,

---

15 A possible source for Christine's depiction of Atropos can be found in the *Ovide moralisé*, 6.2246; noted by Solente, note to *Mutacion de Fortune*, line 2822.

dying, I offend the dead, drive me from both realms; change me and refuse me both life and death" (*sed ne violem vivosque superstes | mortuaque exstinctos, ambobus pellite regnis | mutataeque mihi vitamque necemque negate*, Ov. *Met.* 10.485–487).[16] The notion of metamorphosis in the late medieval assimilation of Ovid, however, was conceived in terms that explicitly framed death as an agent of the final metamorphosis. Like a butterfly emerging from its shell, the experience of death was understood as the gateway from the confines of post-lapsarian embodiment to the liberation of the eternal life of the soul. The extent to which Ovidian descriptions of metamorphosis served as the template for medieval imaginings of death can be seen in a brief quotation from the extended description of the process of dying recounted in the *De meditatione mortis* of Jean Gerson, chancellor of the University of Paris and ally of Christine de Pizan in the famous Querelle de la *Rose*.[17] Gerson's Latin text also survives in a Middle French version, evidence of the diverse audience, both lay and clerical, to which he addressed himself; both the French and Latin texts are quoted here:

> Les mains me (f)roidissent, la face me paslist, mes yeulx me tournent et parfondissent en la teste .... Mon pouoir commence a defaillir, la bouche me noircist, la langue me fault et mon alaine aussi. Je ne voy plus goutte.

> (My hands grow cold, my face grows pale, my eyes turn backward and are sunken in the head .... My strength grows faint, my mouth is blackened, my tongue fails and my breath also. I cannot see at all.)

> En manus incipiunt rigescere, pedes frigescere, ungues nigrescere, facies pallescere, visus obumbrari, oculi profundari, intuitus reversari, horribilis per omnia fieri.

> (The hands begin to grow stiff, the feet to grow cold, the nails to become black, the face to grow pale, the sight to become darkened, the eyes to sink inward, the gaze to turn inward, dreadful in every way.)[18]

---

16 Trans. Miller, 99.

17 On Gerson and Christine's alliance in the Querelle de la *Rose*, see *Débat*, ed. Hicks; on the relationship of their political thought, see Blumenfeld-Kosinski, "Enemies."

18 The French text survives in excerpts from the *Tresor de sapience*, and the Latin text as the *De meditatione mortis*, both ed. Ouy, *Gerson bilingue*, 119 (French) and 120 (Latin). It is important to note that the Latin quotation contains no first-person references while the French contains nine. Moreover, the Latin contains rhythmic

It is easy to recognise the extent to which these passages echo the step-by-step bodily transformations recounted in both Latin and vernacular versions of the Ovidian text.[19] Ironically, the narrator of Gerson's *De meditatione* describes the inevitability of his descent into the arms of death in terms of an *in*ability to change: "It is finished," he states, "Metamorphosis is not possible" (*Conclusum est, mutari non potest*).

The third and last appearance of the term *methafore* in the *Mutacion de Fortune* occurs, appropriately, in connection with Ovid's *Metamorphoses*. In the course of her account of Hercules, Christine writes: "The poets, who observed him [i.e., Hercules], portrayed his deeds in poetry; Ovid tells of it, he who accords with the true history, speaking metaphorically. I don't think to recount it all now" (*Les poetes, qui l'aviserent, | En poesie deviserent | Ses fais; Ovide en recorde, | Qui a la vraye histoire accorde | A parler selon methafore. | Tout ne pense a recorder ore*, 13913–13918). Here, the Ovidian text (i.e., Christine's source, the *Ovide moralisé*) is described as being an example of *poesie*, the genre Christine identifies in her biography of King Charles V as language that expresses meaning "secretly" or "in shadows" (*occultement* or *en ombre*). In her preface to *Avision-Christine*, as we have seen, Christine goes further, explicitly identifying the "poets' manner of speaking" as *methafore*. A similar association of metaphor and metamorphosis appears in the passage from the *Mutacion de Fortune* quoted above, where the *Ovide moralisé* is said to be written *selon methafore*. In identifying it in this way, using a term (*methafore*) not used in the *Ovide moralisé* itself, Christine may possibly be drawing upon the connotations of the term as used in the early fourteenth-century commentary on Fulgentius, the so-called *Fulgentius metaforalis* of John Ridewall.[20]

After this discussion of the three occasions on which the term *methafore* is used in the *Mutacion de Fortune*, it is helpful to turn to Christine's treatment of metamorphosis in order to show precisely how

---

prose in the successive cola *rigescere ... frigescere ... nigrescere* and *obumbrari ... profundari ... reversari*.

[19] Compare, for example, Ovid's description of Myrrha's immobilised body at *Met.* 10.489–494.

[20] Ridewall, *Fulgentius metaforalis*. Liebeschütz (the editor of Ridewall's text) asserts that the title is not original to the author; whether or not the title is original, it appears in several manuscripts of Ridewall's commentary within three decades of its composition. On the *Fulgentius metaforalis*, see Allen, "Commentary as Criticism"; Blumenfeld-Kosinski, *Reading Myth*, 113.

these two are related in her use of figurative language. Christine's depiction of metamorphosis is founded on that found in the *Ovide moralisé*, where metamorphosis is presented not as a change from one thing into another, but rather a change where the outside comes to resemble the inside. To put it another way, in the *Ovide moralisé*, metamorphosis is simply the process by which the outer form comes to reflect the inner form. Such a notion of metamorphosis differs significantly from that found in Ovid's own *Metamorphoses*, in ways that can be only briefly sketched out in these pages.[21] The main difference concerns the place of the metamorphosis within the unfolding of time. In Ovid's text, as Elena Theodorakopoulos has argued, metamorphosis merely "poses as creating the sense of an ending"; it is only the *apparent* "static finished state (of) both victim and story." While the person who undergoes the metamorphosis appears to have achieved a new state of being, a state in which the turmoil that had initiated the metamorphosis is resolved, in fact the suffering of the victim frequently continues. Myrrha, for example, continues to weep even after her transformation, and experiences the pains of labour even after assuming her new body. Similarly, Niobe continues to weep bitter tears for her children even after she is transformed into stone.[22] The visible suffering of these victims persists through time, almost as a memorial of the traumas that brought these changed forms into being. Time is linear, marked by reminders of past metamorphoses that accumulate like ripples on a stream.

In the *Ovide moralisé*, by contrast, the function of the metamorphosis within time is rather different. The transformation of the body is the first, almost incidental stage in a narrative that focuses primarily on the continuation of the metamorphosis; that is, what Renate Blumenfeld-Kosinski identifies as the Ovidian work of the compiler, who "metamorphoses meanings rather than creatures."[23] In the *Ovide moralisé*, each transformation serves as the seed, as it were, that gives rise to a whole series of allegorical interpretations. Repeatedly, the writer states "the fable signifies" such and such; then, he adds, "let us expound the fable differently." He goes on to add, "The fable also signifies..." such and such. In each case, the metamorphosis moves outward into a whole

---

[21] For a fuller comparison of change in Ovid and the *Ovide moralisé*, see Possamai-Perez, "Mutacions des Fables."

[22] See Theodorakopoulos, "Closure and Transformation," 149–150; quotation from p. 149.

[23] Blumenfeld-Kosinski, *Reading Myth*, 100.

constellation of allegorical significations, sometimes even significations which are contradictory, having opposite moral valences. Instead of the linearity of Ovid's narrative, nested within nodes of retold narratives, we find explosions of multiple significances growing out of each transformation. Correspondingly, instead of the linear flow of time, we find a very different temporality, marked by the invariable reference of each metamorphosis into the atemporal realm of moral certitude, based on the eternal truths dictated by God, who stands outside of time.

This aspect of the *Ovide moralisé* deserves emphasis, for it is fundamental to the assimilation of the Ovidian notion of metamorphosis into Christian salvation history. The author begins his work with a commentary on the opening lines of Ovid's text, explicating the opening lines of the *Metamorphosis*. He writes, "Now I wish to begin my material. Ovid says, 'My heart wishes to speak of the forms that were changed into new bodies'" (*Or vueil comencier ma matire. | Ovides dist: 'Mes cuers vieult dire | Les formes qui muees furent | En nouviaux cors,'* 71–74).[24] The author corrects those who interpret Ovid as referring to bodies that were changed into new forms for, he says, "There was never – nor ever will be – any body that received a new form" (*il n'iert encors | Ne ne pooit estre nul cors | Qui nove forme receüst,* 85–87). He recalls how Ovid invoked his gods for aid in beginning his poem and accordingly invokes the Christian God – who, significantly, is also presented as a god who can change his form at will. There are three persons of the Trinity who, he says, "wisely changed themselves, for the Son wished to go from the heavens to the earth, and become a real man, in order to save the lost people" (*sensiblement se muerent, | Quar li Filz vault des cieulz venir | Au monde, et vrais homs devenir, | Pour sauver les homes peris,* 120–123). Similarly, the Holy Spirit was changed into "the form of a dove" (*forme columbine,* 126). It is crucial to note, however, that these divine changes are not part of a linear motion from one state of being to another but rather representative of a divinity that can maintain more than one identity in a single essence. As the anonymous author of the *Ovide moralisé* puts it: "These three persons ... can be very well seen in three divided semblances: without dividing their unity, and without changing their divinity, they changed themselves in a moment in three guises, wisely [or, "in a way apparent to the senses"]" (*Ces trois personnes... |*

---

24 *Ovide moralisé*, ed. de Boer; cited in the text by line number. Translations are my own.

...bien porent estre avisees | En trois samblances devisees: | Sans deviser lor unité, | Et sans muer lor deïté, | Se muerent en un moment | En trois guises sensiblement, 133–140). Here, metamorphosis is far from being an end state, or a culmination; instead, it is suspended, eternally, in the paradox of Christian divinity.

This suspension is also evident in the individual transformations recounted in the *Ovide moralisé*, where the metamorphosis of the individual is extended, through allegorical interpretation, into the eternal domain of salvation history. Thus the figure of Clytie, for example, who loved the Sun so much that she betrayed her own sister Leukathoe, is changed into a flower which endlessly gazes at the sun, adoring what she cannot have. Clytie, the author of the *Ovide moralisé* informs us, signifies those who are envious; in addition, she signifies "Judaism, which always works and schemes in order to torment Holy Church, which God holds dear, and loves, and holds close" (*Judaïme, | Qui toute se font et saïme | Pour l'exaucement sainte Yglise, | Que Diex tient chiere et aime et prise*, 4.1826–1829). Here, Leukathoe appears as a figurative representation of the beloved Church, Clytie as a figure of the spurned lover Synagoga.[25] For Clytie, her inner longing for Apollo, which causes her "to constantly turn her face toward the sun, whichever way he faces" (*tout jors flec(hier) sa face | Vers le soleil, quel tour qu'il face*, 1472–1473) leads to her metamorphosis: her outer form comes to resemble her inner form, so that she becomes a flower that "always turns its face toward the sun, whichever way he goes" (*Tous jours a sa face tournee | Vers le soleil, quel part qu'il aille*, 1483–1484). Paradoxically, the *mutacion* or change reveals the truth hidden beneath the superficial appearance: as a heliotropic flower, Clytie shows her true nature far more clearly than she did as an embodied woman.

This notion of metamorphosis, where outer form comes to reflect the inner form, was taken up from the *Ovide moralisé* by Christine de Pizan, and is exemplified in the central metamorphosis of her *Mutacion de Fortune*. There, Christine describes how she was changed from a woman into a man, her outer form coming to resemble the inner form as her masculine mind served as the basis of her new body. At the same time, however, Christine explicitly states that this transformation is true

---

[25] On Ecclesia and Synagoga, see Seiferth, *Synagogue and Church*, 33–41; Schlauch, "Allegory of Church and Synagogue"; Lipton, *Images of Intolerance, passim*, esp. 84–86, 94–99, 118.

only insofar as it is *methafore*. By doing this, she defines a relationship between metamorphosis and metaphor: just as in metamorphosis a thing is transferred from one form to another, so in metaphor a word is transferred from one meaning to another. The following few paragraphs will attempt to sketch out this relationship in more detail, arguing that, in Christine's use of allegory, changes in body reveal personal essence just as changes in language (the encoding into figurative language, or *poesie*, and its subsequent decoding) reveal truth.

It is significant that the term *methafore* appears in the *Mutacion de Fortune* only three times: first, in connection with Christine's own metaphorical transformation; second, in reference to Atropos; third, in reference to the Ovidian narrative itself. The first case is special because it is through this transformation that Christine's endeavour – narrating the historical "changes" wrought by Fortune – is authorised. The second is special because Atropos presides over the final earthly transformation, a transformation which is inherently paradoxical. The paradox of Atropos is, of course, the fact that she simultaneously admits human beings both into death and into life: she opens the door not only to corporeal death, but (for the faithful) to the eternal life of the spirit. Paradox is central not only to the work of Atropos, cutting the spun thread, but to the work of the writer, spinning the thread of the tale. It is particularly central to the work of the allegorist, for allegory has at its centre "enigma"; that is, in Aristotle's definition of enigma, hidden meaning expressed through paradox.[26] In the *Mutacion de Fortune*, Christine replaces the older conception of metaphor as simply the basic element of allegory with a new conception of metaphor as metamorphosis, in which literal transformation makes manifest paradoxes that are normally invisible. This theory of allegory is clearly related to the *poesie* of the *Ovide moralisé*, in which (as Christine puts it) the allegorised text is said to correspond to *la vraye histoire* insofar as it is *methafore* (13916–13917). Christine's own declared indebtedness to the *Ovide moralisé*, along with her telling use of the term *methafore* with reference to it, suggests strongly that her elaboration of the relationship between metaphor and metamorphosis is grounded on her understanding of the process of allegoresis enacted in the *Ovide moralisé*.

I have argued elsewhere that, by the late fourteenth century, allegory had come to be much less of a privileged mode of conveying meaning than

---

[26] On paradox in allegory, see Akbari, *Seeing Through the Veil*, 9–10.

it had been during the earlier Middle Ages. The use of vision as a figurative representation of the acquisition of knowledge had largely fallen into disuse, and a number of changes in the genre of allegory had taken place. Many of these changes relate to the use of personification: they include minimisation of the difference between human narrator and superhuman personification; more frequent coining of new personifications; increased emphasis on the personality (including gender) of the personification; and combination of personifications with classical gods and even with real, historical figures.[27] Together with these very substantial changes we must include Christine's treatment of metaphor as a species of allegory. Unlike other medieval writers, Christine distinguishes between allegory and allegoresis (what is sometimes called "imposed allegory," where a figurative meaning is imposed – by force, if necessary – on a text not originally composed as an allegory). Christine consistently refers to allegoresis as *allegorie*, as in her *Epistre Othéa*.[28] Her own writing of what *we* would call allegory, however, she describes as *poesie*, that is, the writing of poets. At times, she refers to such poetic language as *methafore*, which she explicitly posits as a form of figurative writing that, like allegory, is conceived of in terms of the dichotomy of light and darkness, where light represents knowledge. This notion of metaphor, however – unlike allegory – is explicitly grounded on the notion of change, and on the phenomenon of metamorphosis.

This article marks just the first, tentative step in an effort to probe more deeply into Christine's understanding of change (focusing particularly on her depictions of alchemy in the *Avision-Christine* and her brief commentaries on Aristotle's *Metaphysics*, appearing in the *Avision* and in the biography of King Charles V) in order to understand how, for Christine, metamorphosis could serve as a theoretical model for the use of figurative language. In addition, such a study might also shed light on the use of the *Metamorphoses* by another late medieval author – Chaucer – who frequently summarises the stories from Ovid's marvellous text, but always leaves out one tiny little detail: that is, the metamorphosis itself.

UNIVERSITY OF TORONTO

---

[27] Akbari, *Seeing Through the Veil*, 237.
[28] On allegory in the *Epistre Othéa*, see Hindman, *Christine de Pizan's "Epistre Othéa."*

At the Ovidian Pool: Christine De Pizan's Fountain of Wisdom as a Locus for Vision

Patricia Zalamea

In memory of Rona Goffen,
who first encouraged me to follow this path.

In Ovid's *Metamorphoses*, pools often provide the site of transformation, a process that is repeatedly triggered by the act of looking. Ovidian pools sometimes function as reflective mirrors, allowing the figures to recognise their transformed image, as in the stories of Io and Actaeon. In other instances, pools serve as transparent display cases for beautiful ivory bodies, as in Ovid's ekphrastic descriptions of Narcissus and Hermaphroditus. Pools may also become the place of metamorphosis, as in the story of Salmacis and Hermaphroditus.[1] Indeed, these Ovidian pools are a metaphor for the act of looking, where seeing involves self-conscious realisation and contemplation, sometimes leading to a metamorphosis or as a result of it.[2] For vision is how the process of transformation initiates and culminates: with seeing, comes desire; desire leads to metamorphosis; metamorphosis invites self-reflection. As Leonard Barkan has noted, "Metamorphosis becomes a means of creating self-consciousness because it creates a tension between identity and form, and through this tension the individual is compelled to look in the mirror."[3]

---

[1] For Io's vision of herself, see *Met.* 1.639–641; for Actaeon, see *Met.* 3.200–201. For Ovid's ekphrastic description of Narcissus, see *Met.* 3.416–423, and of Hermaphroditus, see *Met.* 4.352–355.

[2] On the nature of water and its transformative qualities as a binding element in Ovid's *Metamorphoses*, see Viarre, *L'image et la pensée*, 336–347. Although Viarre does not suggest this specific metaphor, she discusses the Ovidian pool as a mirror that "represents the soul or consciousness" and allows figures to discover their transformed selves (342–343).

[3] Barkan, "Diana and Actaeon," 322.

After the twelfth century's renewed interest in the *Metamorphoses* and the subsequent development of an Ovidian poetic tradition, pools become a powerful means for investigating love and self simultaneously. The pool as mirror turns into a recurrent theme, as in the *Roman de la rose*, whose fountain of Narcissus has been described as a "poetic image for the anatomy and physiology of human vision."[4] In late medieval poetry, the Ovidian pool is slowly transformed into an elaborate fountain of love and poetic inspiration, in which vision plays an essential role in the poetic process, as in Guillaume de Machaut's *La Fonteinne amoureuse*, where the fountain serves "as a kind of emblem" for the poem itself.[5] Similarly, in late-medieval imagery, Ovid's *locus amoenus*, the original location of such pools, is reshaped by the Garden of Eden and later turned into the so-called Garden of Love, an iconographic type that includes a combination of standard motifs associated with love: a flowering garden, a marble fountain, and a series of courtly figures often dancing or playing music.[6]

This context illuminates Christine de Pizan's fountain iconography. In her representation of the Fountain of Wisdom in the *Livre du chemin de long estude* or *Book of the Path of Long Study* (1402–1403), Christine reinvented the Ovidian pool as a locus for vision and a site of poetic activity. Written immediately after the renowned literary debate in which Christine criticised the *Roman de la rose* for its misogynistic associations, the *Chemin de long estude* is an allegorical dream vision that describes the narrator-protagonist's search for knowledge and culminates in a celestial debate about the ideal values needed to govern the world. In the *Chemin*, Christine inserts her narrator-protagonist (also called Christine) into the mythological landscape of the origins of poetry, where 'Christine' and the Cumaean Sibyl, her guide along the path of study, stand at the Fountain of Wisdom and gaze at the nine Muses who bathe in it.[7]

---

[4] For the fountain as a locus for vision in the *Roman de la rose*, see Fleming, "The Garden of the Roman de la Rose," 217–219. For the relationship between love and vision in the fountain of the *Roman de la rose*, see Knoespel, *Narcissus*, 11.

[5] See Brownlee, *Poetic Identity in Guillaume de Machaut*, 198.

[6] See Watson, *The Garden of Love*, 23 and 61 for the various traditions and pictorial elements that compose the Garden of Love. For examples of the Garden of Love beginning in twelfth-century courtly poetry from Provence and other Mediterranean areas, and its later literary development, see Pearsall, "Gardens as Symbol and Setting," 239–251.

[7] For an analysis of Christine's use of autobiographical narrative as a means of constructing "her authorial persona," see Brownlee, "Literary Genealogy," 365–369.

Undeniably, the Ovidian poetic tradition provides an important reference point for the *Chemin de long estude*; mythological allusions are interspersed throughout the text, the most significant being the Fountain of Wisdom or *Fontaine de Sapience*.[8] As has been noted on a number of occasions, Dante's *Commedia* is also one of the models for Christine's journey along the path of study. Her description of Parnassus, in fact, is based both on Dante's Earthly Paradise in the *Purgatorio* and the Jardin de Deduit in the *Roman de la rose*.[9] As suggested by Kevin Brownlee, Christine's rewriting of the *Commedia* may be seen as part of her response to the *Roman de la rose*; by invoking Dante as an "authoritative counterexample," she is able to oppose the authority of the *Roman de la rose* while simultaneously validating her authorial position and differentiating herself from Dante.[10] Most significantly, in her rewriting of Dante, Christine references the authoritative figures who have stood by the same fountain and have influenced her poetic identity, one that, as we shall see, is uniquely shaped by her gender.

Since scholars have skilfully analysed the textual links between the *Commedia* and Christine's presentation of Parnassus, this article will focus on the images of the Fountain of Wisdom in the illuminated manuscripts of the *Chemin*, while discussing the verbal and visual representations of the scene as interrelated iconographic types deriving from the *Ovide moralisé*, and contextualising them within the pictorial tradition that associated fountains with poetic activity. Although the illuminations of Christine's Fountain of Wisdom do not seem to have influenced later depictions of the theme, they provide a significant alteration of traditional iconography which may be seen as part of a larger strategy present in Christine's work, in which the Ovidian poetic tradition is meaningfully reinterpreted in terms of the relationship between vision, knowledge, and the female body.

Although the narrator-protagonist of the *Chemin* is only named "Christine" towards the end of the poem (v. 6329), this article will refer to the author as Christine and to the narrator-protagonist of the text as 'Christine.'

[8] The fountain is named by the Sibyl (vv. 984–985): *Qui de Sapience est nommee | Fontaine.* All references to the French text of the *Chemin* are from C. de Pizan, *Le Chemin de longue étude*, ed. A. Tarnowski; the translations into English are by R. Blumenfeld-Kosinski and K. Brownlee in *Selected Writings*.

[9] Brownlee, "Literary Genealogy," 375.

[10] Brownlee, "Literary Genealogy," 370; 384–387.

SEEING AND KNOWING IN THE *CHEMIN DE LONG ESTUDE*

Christine's work is marked by her sensitivity towards visual experience and the didactic power of images. Various scholars have proposed that Christine participated closely in the illumination and material production of her works.[11] Questions concerning visuality are also highlighted throughout her writing; for example, in *Le livre de la mutacion de Fortune* (1403), pictures provide the inspirational source for the book's narrative. Likewise, vision plays a particularly significant role within the *Chemin de long estude*: as an allegorical dream vision, the *Chemin* is essentially a visionary experience.[12]

Throughout the *Chemin*, 'Christine' carefully conveys her road to knowledge in visual terms, making repeated references to eyesight and the power of blinding light.[13] Her first significant visual experience occurs as she observes the Fountain of Wisdom (787–882) upon entering a paradisiacal setting. The theme of vision is later developed when she reaches the sky, where she expresses her desire *to know* through her eyes, evoking an image that recalls the mythic figure of Argus, the guardian whose body was covered with eyes: "I was so desirous to know, to understand, and to perceive all the aspects of this heaven that I would have liked, if it were possible, for all my bodily parts to be transformed into eyes" (*Mais tant os desire de savoir | Et cognoistre et appercevoir | Toutes les choses de cel estre, | Que bien voulsisse, s'il peut estre, | Que tous mes membres fussent yeulx*, 1809–1813).[14] Her desire ultimately culminates in her ability to see beyond initial appearances and understand comets and eclipses as astrological signs (2179–2202). As we advance in the text, we find that the protagonist has been transformed through her experience: she has learnt to read these visual signs and has progressed to a different level of visual experience, from physical to prophetic.

In contrast to the stars and other celestial bodies visually apprehended by 'Christine' in the *Chemin*, the fountain of the Muses remains a very grounded and physical image within the text itself. Set amidst the

---

[11] For a discussion of Christine's role in the making of her manuscripts and their images, see Hindman, *Christine de Pizan's "Epistre Othéa,"* 62–99.

[12] Note how Christine is careful to differentiate between a vision and an illusion: *Que j'oz estrange vision; | Ce ne fus pas illusion* (453–454). Translated in *Selected Writings*, 66: "I had a strange vision that was not an illusion."

[13] Note the repeated use of words (1785–1817) that make reference to vision: eyes, blindness, light, etc. I thank Ana Pairet for pointing out the parallel with Argus (1813).

[14] Translated in *Selected Writings*, 83.

conventions of courtly gardens, the fountain is described in a traditional way: its clarity and profundity are highlighted (806), while the fountain's streams are compared to shining silver, endowed with a soft murmuring sound and whose waters keep the trees safe from the sun (823–852). The Muses are initially described by 'Christine' as nine unidentified ladies bathing nude in a fountain: "I therefore stopped to look at what I am about to tell you: I saw nine ladies bathing nude in the fountain; they truly seemed to have great authority, worth, and wisdom" (*Si m'arrestay pour aviser | Ce que vous m'orrés deviser: | La vi ge .ix. dames venues | Qui se baignoient toutes nues | En la fontaine; en verité | Moult sembloient d'octorité | Et de grant valour et savoir*, 811–817).[15]

The scene is later re-presented by the Sibyl, who reveals its name, location, and origins, as well as the identity of the bathing ladies:

> La montaigne que vois lassus
> Est appellee Pernasus.
> Ou mons Helicon est de moult
> Appellé ce tres beau hault mont.
> Et la fontaine que sus vois…
> Qui de Sapience est nommee…
> Et le nom te veuil enseigner
> Des dames que tu vois baigner,
> A quoy ententivement muses.
> On les appelle les .ix. muses.
> Celles gouvernent la fontaine
> Qui tant est belle, clere et saine;…
> Le cheval que tu vois qui vole,
> Jadis par lui fu celle escole
> Establie, chose est certaine;
> Car de son pié vint la fontaine   (977–1000)

(The mountain upon which you gaze is called Parnassus; or, as many people also call this noble height, Mount Helicon. The fountain that you see up there … is named the Fountain of Wisdom … And I want you to know the names of the ladies whose bathing you observe so attentively: they are called the nine Muses. They control the fountain which is so beautiful, clear, and healthy … The flying horse that you see truly constructed this school long ago, for the fountain resulted from a powerful blow of his foot).[16]

---

[15] Translated in *Selected Writings*, 70.
[16] Translated in *Selected Writings*, 72.

The Sibyl then tells 'Christine' of the various authorities who have frequented the fountain, starting with philosophers such as Aristotle, Socrates, and Plato, and following with poets such as Vergil, Homer, Ovid, and Orpheus. At the end of the list of philosophers, the Sibyl includes Christine's father, who had been a physician and astrologer at the court of King Charles V (1018–1074).[17] The Sibyl also conflates the fountain with the place where Cadmus, the legendary founder of the Greek alphabet, defeated the dragon (1075–1080), and ends by recalling Pallas, who spent considerable time at this fountain and whose presence, the Sibyl suggests, lingers at the site (1094–1096). The mention of Cadmus and Pallas, figures associated with knowledge, thus reinforces the fountain as a source of wisdom.[18] Finally, at the end of her speech, the Sibyl reveals the name of their path as that of *Lonc estude* (1103).

The site's double description – first presented in the narrator-protagonist's words and then in the Sibyl's – follows the narrative device used by Ovid to enhance and reinforce a setting or object, but reverses the original arrangement of the passage in the *Metamorphoses*, in which the *mirabile* fountain of the Muses is first recalled for its fame and only later observed. In the *Metamorphoses*, the spring's fame and origins are initially reported by Athena who journeys to Helicon, home of the Muses, to see it; Athena is then led by Urania, the Muse of astronomy, to admire the sacred waters, at which point Athena's viewing of the site is described in particularly visual terms (*Met.* 5.256–266). Thus, the spring is doubly rendered: the marvellous object is anticipated through Athena's second-hand report of its fame and origins, but its actual image takes shape through Athena's observation. This same arrangement was kept and expanded in the *Ovide moralisé* (5.1678–1699). Christine rearranges the process by placing visual experience before knowledge, thereby making a commentary on the didactic nature of imagery as well as on the process of learning through images. This emphasis is especially significant in this scene, where her protagonist-narrator is standing at the very source of knowledge in its visualised form.

---

[17] See Brownlee, "Literary genealogy," 375–376, on Christine's relationship to her father as a figure of authority.

[18] Christine seems to have inserted Cadmus by condensing two references from the *Ovide moralisé*, where the fountain of Cadmus is described in similar terms to that of the fountain of the Muses and both are named *Fontaine de Clergie* (III.v.209, V.v.1674).

Christine's reordering of the description is also significant in relation to the protagonist's overall transformation and acquisition of knowledge throughout the *Chemin*. While she stands at the Fountain of Wisdom, still at an early stage in the narrative, the protagonist's visual experience is separate from her knowledge. She intuitively sees that these nude women *sembloient d'octorité* (816), but does not recognise them.[19] Only after the Sibyl has identified the figures and the path of *Lonc estude* (1103) does 'Christine' recall that she had already frequented this site, as well as read of it in Dante, who traversed this same path with Vergil (1109–1138).[20] The implication is that she had visited it through her earlier bookish experience, one that had imaginatively allowed her to enter this site. As the narrative unfolds, we find that her visual abilities progress; 'Christine' learns to see on her own and eventually no longer needs the Sibyl to guide her vision (2179–2202). Her ability to see beyond appearances and understand astrological signs in the later part of her voyage would seem to confirm not only that she has had a taste of her father's astrological knowledge, but also that she has advanced in her path to knowledge and that her ability to learn is closely connected to (in fact, often preceded by) visual experience.

Given the development of the protagonist's experience in the *Chemin*, one might say that the connection between seeing and knowing is developed through a two-fold process, where one feeds into the other. An initial sight may provide a first impression that is later reinforced through acquired knowledge. A case in point is Christine's first sighting of the Sibyl, when she mistakes her for the goddess of knowledge, "whom Ovid teaches us is named Pallas" (480–481).[21] This encounter has significant implications, since it associates two female figures of authority while providing an insight into the later connections established at the site of the fountain, where the Sibyl recalls Pallas' presence: "Formerly this was the habitation of Pallas, and I think she is still here, for she does not change with the

---

[19] See Holderness, "In the Muses' Garden," 136–139 and 158–159, for the different types of intelligence embodied by the Muses, and for how Christine's unification of the philosophical and poetic Muses (previously separated and opposed in Boethius' *Consolation of Philosophy*) provides a significant development in Christine's acquisition of knowledge.

[20] See Brownlee, "Literary Genealogy," 377–379, on Christine's first explicit reference to Dante as her model and the source of her poem's title.

[21] For the entire passage describing Christine's initial sighting of the Sibyl, see vv. 458–485. The original quoted verses are *Dont Ovide nous fait savoir | Quë ellë est Pallas nommee* (480–481). For the translation, see *Selected Writings*, 66.

passage of time" (*Et jadis y ot son repaire | Pallas, et croy qu'elle a encore, | Car telle qu'elle fu est ore;* 1094–1096).[22]

In the case of Christine's acquired knowledge while standing at the fountain, the process becomes even more intricate: the Sibyl's *naming* of the fountain, its elements, and its history allows 'Christine' to remember something that she already knew through her readings. This prior knowledge explains her intuitive recognition of the ladies' authority without any specific visual reference that would allow her to reach this conclusion. This would then suggest that images trigger remembrance. The matter is complicated, as Christine seems to acknowledge in carefully laying out its subtleties. The complexity behind this double rendering of the Muses in their fountain is multiplied when the scene is turned into a physical image on paper, thereby complicating further the correlation between vision and knowledge.

Disrobing the Muses: An Iconographic Construction

Although the mythic foundation of the fountain of the Muses and its qualities were celebrated in ancient texts, the connection between the fountain and knowledge was not clearly established. While the Muses were acclaimed as sources of wisdom, memory, and inspiration, this was kept separate from the description of their abode, as in the *Metamorphoses*, where the Muses are not physically placed inside the spring. This is also true of the visual representations of the Muses in antiquity and in the Middle Ages before the *Ovide moralisé*.[23] Following their initial visualisation in the seventh and sixth centuries B.C.E., a tradition of representing the Muses was established, as can be seen in Hellenistic reliefs and Roman funerary sarcophagi. In such objects, the Muses are fully dressed and often placed inside an architectural structure, possibly referencing libraries as a site for knowledge.[24] The Muses were also clothed in their rare appearances throughout the medieval period and were often represented as inspirational figures appearing next to a poet or philosopher.

---

[22] Translated in *Selected Writings*, 74.

[23] See Bzdak, "Wisdom and Education," 47, for a summary of the Muses' principal meanings in antiquity, and 46–49, on the visual representations of the Muses in antiquity and their rare appearance in the Middle Ages.

[24] For the increasing depiction of the Muses in the visual arts after the classical period, in connection to their role as teachers of the written word, see Small, *Wax Tablets*, 76. See also Bzdak, "Wisdom and Education," 49; 52.

The association between inspiration, knowledge, and the feminine has roots that go back to classical antiquity. Such connections were upheld particularly by Boethius in his *Consolation of Philosophy* – another significant source for Christine – and later revived by mystical writers of the twelfth century, such as Hildegard of Bingen.[25] Although the female personification of inspirational figures such as the Muses, the liberal arts, and wisdom goes back to antiquity, the emphasis on their physical bodies is a later phenomenon. The depiction of the Muses as nine nude women hovering together in a pool seems to have been first visualised in the *Ovide moralisé* and later adopted by Christine in the *Chemin de long estude*. Despite being a short-lived form, the Muses' appearance in these late-medieval manuscripts is particularly interesting for its revelations about narrative and poetic identity.

The image of the Muses in a late fourteenth-century manuscript of the *Ovide moralisé* (BnF Ms. fr. 871 fol. 116v) has been recognised as the source for the images in a number of the surviving manuscripts with illuminations made during Christine's lifetime.[26] Interestingly, the Muses' nudity is not mentioned in the text of the *Ovide moralisé*.[27] Christine's direct source seems to be the illumination in the *Ovide moralisé* and not its text. The move from image (*Ovide moralisé*) to text (the *Chemin*) and back to image (the illuminations in the *Chemin* manuscripts) again points to the importance of images for Christine's work and to her emphasis on knowledge based on visual experience.

In contrast to the classical tradition previously noted, the image of the Muses in the *Ovide moralisé* Ms. fr. 871, itself deriving from an earlier exemplar now in Lyon (BM Ms. 742), is highly unconventional. In the image of the *Ovide moralisé* Ms. fr. 871, the Muses bathe in a stream that

---

[25] Bzdak, "Wisdom and Education," 106–111, on the role of female allegories including the Muses, the liberal arts, and philosophy in Boethius' *Consolation of Philosophy*. Also see Bzdak (chap. 4) on Hildegard of Bingen and the reconnection of knowledge and learning to the feminine in other twelfth-century authors.

[26] That Christine knew the illuminations from at least two fourteenth-century manuscripts of the *Ovide moralisé* (Ms. fr. 373 and Ms. fr. 871, now in the Bibliothèque nationale in Paris) has been demonstrated through comparison to the images used in her own manuscripts. See Hindman, *Christine de Pizan's "Epistre Othéa,"* 83 n. 69; Meiss, *The Limbourgs and their Contemporaries*, 1:24–48. For a list of the nine surviving manuscripts of the *Chemin* (of which two were made after Christine's death and two are not illustrated), see C. de Pizan, *Le Chemin*, 59–61. For the relationship amongst one another and their dating, see C. de Pizan, *Le Chemin*, 63–64.

[27] All references to the text of the *Ovide moralisé* are from de Boer's edition.

flows directly from Pegasus' foot. Apollo sits atop the stream while playing a lyre; a crowned female figure – labelled Pallas – stands on the right, separated from the Muses by the stream that runs down and across the composition. The birds on the Muses' side of the composition are a reference to the nine Pierides sisters who challenged the Muses to a musical contest. The story of this contest is the subject of Book Five of the *Metamorphoses*, where the various songs are narrated to Pallas by one of the Muses. Book Five, a typical Ovidian example of embedded narratives, is thus collapsed into a single image. The presence of the first poet, Apollo, who does not appear at the scene in the *Metamorphoses*, reinforces the idea of singing a song, or telling a tale, within a larger song. The composition of the image and gestures of the Muses, all of whom – except for one, who seems to be addressing Pallas – are looking in Apollo's direction, suggests that this is the visualisation of a competition, as sung to us by the poet/narrator (fig. 5.1).

Indeed, it has been suggested that the *Ovide moralisé* emphasises the idea of a continuous retelling of Ovid's *Metamorphoses*, as it translates the text and restructures its organisation through a series of amplifications and additive digressions, to the point that the author of the *Ovide moralisé* progressively develops into what may be seen as another of the internal narrators of Ovid's *carmen perpetuum*.[28] This is also implied at the end of the fifth book, where the author recapitulates for the third time the story of the Muses; in choosing words that specifically refer to the narration and transmission of a tale, he emphasises the theme of a story within a story and ends with an allegorical reading of the competition, one whose very subject is tale-telling: "Above I have told you the story just as the Muse told it to Pallas, when she recounted the controversy and dissonance between the nine Muses and the Pierides" (*Dessus vous ai conté le conte,* | *Si come la Muse le raconte* | *Qui a Pallas dist et recorde* | *La controverse et la discorde* | *Des neuf Muses de la montaigne* | *Et des pies,* 5.3904–3909).

While the illuminators of the *Chemin* keep the general structure of the *Ovide moralisé* image, they also introduce significant changes: Apollo and the Pierides sisters are eliminated; 'Christine' and the Sibyl replace Pallas. In each illumination, the Sibyl indicates the fountain to 'Christine.' The emphasis of the story thus changes significantly; in the various *Chemin* images, the main point is the encounter with the

---

[28] For the innovative aspects of the *Ovide moralisé* as a project of *translatio*, see Pairet, *'Les mutacions des fables,"* 102–107.

fountain, not the hearing or telling of stories. Although the Muses' nudity is kept in the *Chemin* images, the illuminations also depart in a significant way from both the image of the *Ovide moralisé* and the text of the *Chemin*. In spite of the emphasis in the text of the *Chemin* on the clarity and transparency of the fountain the lower bodies of the Muses are never seen in the *Chemin* images. This choice stands in sharp contrast to the illumination of the *Ovide moralisé*, in which the Muses' bodies are clearly visible under the water and it constitutes another careful revision of the *Ovide moralisé* (figs. 5.2–5.3).

RESHAPING THE OVIDIAN LANDSCAPE: CHRISTINE AS MUSE AND SPECTATOR

By standing at this pool, 'Christine' also places herself within the problematic landscape of the Ovidian tradition, where the woods are the larger containing structure of the pools: shady groves as sites for voyeurism, desire, and rape.[29] A particularly painful image of rape is provided in the Muses' account of the myth of Proserpine, where the nymph Cyane's pool – into which she then dissolves and which becomes a metaphor for her own self – is violently traversed by Pluto (*Met.* 5.409–437). Indeed, in Ovid, the mention of a pool within a cool and shady landscape setting – often in the middle of the day when the sun is at its highest point – is a signal of something to come. The experienced Ovidian reader learns to recognise the cue: it signals the preparation of a violent scene triggered by desire.[30] Though later merged with the Garden of Eden and turned into a flowering Garden of Love, the inherent violence of Ovid's landscapes lingers on in the misogynistic metaphors of courtly poetry.

What role does 'Christine' then play in this story of landscapes largely dominated by males, where the female body provides the source of inspiration? What does it mean for a female poet, who is seemingly conflated with the protagonist of her narrative, to be placed at this very site and to be confronted with female bodies as the direct source of knowledge, a theme traditionally associated with male inspiration? Most significantly, why emphasise the Muses' nudity, albeit halfway?

---

[29] See Hinds, "Landscape with Figures," 130–134, for a discussion of Ovid's treatment of the *locus amoenus* combined with inherent sexual violence.

[30] See Parry, "Violence in a Pastoral Setting," 268–282.

There are subtle yet significant differences amongst the various *Chemin* illuminations that point to Christine's reshaping of the Ovidian landscape by reversing traditional, gendered roles. Two of the earlier manuscripts, dating to ca. 1402–1403, depict a more extensive landscape where the different pathways – a type of crossroads – are clearly visible (Brussels BR Ms.10982 and Paris BnF Ms. fr. 1188; fig. 5.2). The images in later manuscripts such as the BnF fr. 836 (ca. 1408) and Harley 4431 (1410–1411) differ from the earlier examples; the Muses and the two witnesses are placed closer to one another and it is clear that the Muses are looking back at 'Christine' and the Sibyl (fig. 5.3). This is unlike the earlier images, where the two groups are more distanced and do not interact.[31] In addition, the Muses in the later manuscripts are not placed in a natural pool, but inside an artificial font. These changes should be considered significant, because we know that Christine revised and amplified her text as well as the illustrations for the Harley 4431 manuscript of her collected works.[32] Even in the revised image, the Muses' nudity is maintained, but their heads are redressed with contemporary headdresses like the protagonist's, a type that consistently identifies the protagonist-narrator in other works by Christine de Pizan, as in the illuminations of the *Cité des dames*.

One might speculate how the changes in the later manuscripts of the *Chemin* – the closer interaction and redressing of the Muses, so that they appear as mirror images of 'Christine' – might be connected to Christine's poetic identity. In the 1404 epistolary exchange between Christine and Eustace Deschamps, Deschamps replied with a ballad in which he addressed her as "Eloquent Muse among the nine," a reference that points to the complexity of Christine's position as a female writer.[33]

---

[31] The image in the Brussels Bibliothèque Royale Ms. 10983 fol. 13r shares characteristics of both the earlier and later manuscripts. In composition, it is closer to the later images where the focus is on the interaction between the Muses and the two witnesses, but the Muses are placed inside a natural pool, much like the earlier illuminations. The Brussels BR Ms. 10983, along with another illuminated manuscript at Chantilly, Musée Condé 493, has been dated as the earliest of the surviving manuscripts of the *Chemin* (probably late 1402 – early 1403). For the dating of the various manuscripts, see C. de Pizan, *Le Chemin*, 63–64.

[32] *Le Chemin*, 67. The Harley 4431 is the base manuscript for Tarnowski's edition. Harley 4431 was a collection of Christine's works put together for Isabeau de Bavière; BnF Ms. fr. 836 was originally part of such a collection made for the Duc de Berry.

[33] For the translation of Christine and Deschamps' exchange, see *Selected Writings*, 109–113. For an analysis of this epistolary exchange and of how Deschamps is

While holding the status of a professional writer, her female body placed her on a different plane from male writers. As suggested by the revised images of the later *Chemin* manuscripts and in Deschamps' address, Christine's body could also position her as a Muse of inspiration. While standing at the fountain of poetic inspiration – a site where, as recounted by the Sibyl, the most authoritative philosophers and poets have spent time – 'Christine' is thus confronted with her intellectual legacy (a tradition of male authors) and simultaneously with her own existence within a female body. The presence of 'Christine' at this site reinforces Christine's own position as an author, for 'Christine' (the narrator-protagonist) is also a reader, writer, and compiler in the narrative.[34] Much like her narrator-protagonist, whose female body allows her to be visualised as a counterpart to the Muses, Christine (the author) is a female writer who could be equated to a Muse, as was made explicit in Deschamps' ballad.

Concurrently, the depiction of a female spectator standing at the Fountain of Wisdom disrupts the standard pictorial tradition that showed male poets standing or reclining next to fountains; examples include panels of the Garden of Love and the illuminated manuscripts of Machaut's *La Fonteinne amoureuse* (fig. 5.4).[35] Interestingly, the pictorial association between fountains and poetic activity coincides with the period when the line between the poet-narrator and the lover-protagonist becomes blurred.[36] Unlike such male narrators, however, 'Christine' cannot embody the position of the lover-protagonist; thus, she remains detached, standing at the scene as a female voyeur who is also the poet-narrator.

Unlike her male poet-narrator counterparts, 'Christine' could embody the very object of desire; her body (and her headdress in the

---

responding to Christine's petition in her own terms, see Richards, "The Lady Wants to Talk," 109–122.

[34] The question of Christine's status as a female writer has been much discussed; for a bibliography on the subject, see Holderness, "In the Muses' Garden," 239–244; 246–255. Holderness argues that Christine does not claim the status of an *auctor* (understood in the medieval tradition as a 'figure of authority'), and instead proposes the role of 'compiler' as Christine's preferred mode of identification (255–288).

[35] For a *Garden of Love* painting, based on Boccaccio's *Amorosa visione* and which shows three poets (recognisable through their laurels) discoursing next to a fountain, see Watson, figure 1.

[36] See Brownlee, *Poetic Identity*, 9–12, on the development of the narrator in the different genres of Old French literature.

later manuscripts) suggests that she could be *like* a Muse, the embodiment of knowledge itself. So, rather than assuming the stance of the lover-protagonist, a female narrator-protagonist might reverse the traditional roles by placing herself in the position of the beloved, the carrier of inspiration. As a Muse, Christine has natural access to the Fountain of Wisdom. Indeed, Christine's wisdom was confirmed by Deschamps in the lines that followed his initial address, in which he expounded on her knowledge and its validating sources.[37] A certain degree of knowledge is transferred to Christine in her initial confrontation with the Muses. As we shall see, her emphasis on the visual aspects of the cognitive operation that leads to this acquisition of knowledge suggests that knowledge may begin as an intuitive experience.

By not including the ancient authors named by the Sibyl and by focusing instead only on the elements initially described by 'Christine,' the *Chemin* illuminations seem to depict a specific moment of the narrative (that is, the protagonist's first sight of the fountain), while complementing the Sibyl's following revelation. In their synthetic and focused presentation, the images simulate the protagonist's inadvertent initial vision, depicting only the two witnesses to the scene and the elements described by 'Christine': the nine Muses and Pegasus, initially described by 'Christine' as "a great winged horse in the air above the rock, flying over the ladies" (820–822).[38] The images force the viewer to acknowledge the unusual inclusion of two female figures standing next to a fountain – a role traditionally reserved for male poets – while gazing at nine nude female bodies. The Sibyl's naming of the Fountain of Wisdom, its inhabitants and the path reinforces the impact of the image, for it explicitly situates 'Christine' at the traditional site of philosophical and poetic authority. The step-by-step learning process of 'Christine' is duplicated in the reader's visual experience of the manuscripts, where the initial vision of the scene is also confirmed by subsequent knowledge.[39]

---

[37] See *Selected Writings*, 112–113.

[38] For the translation, see *Selected Writings,* 70. The original reads: *En l'air sus la roche ravi | Un grant cheval qui avoit eles | Et aloit volant entour elles* (820–822).

[39] In the *Chemin* manuscripts, the images are usually placed before the passage where the scene is described. Thus, the reader would encounter the image of the fountain of the Muses before the text, much like the protagonist's initial experience of the site.

The male authors do not appear in the illuminations not simply because Christine has eliminated the male figures that appear in the text, in order to reinforce a female presence.[40] The male philosophers and poets, recounted by the Sibyl in the past tense (1018–1066), are not actually at the scene; rather, they are *remembered* as having once been there. It is not so much that they have been eliminated, but that the illuminators – under the author's direction – have chosen not to add them. In these images, the focus is not on memory and tradition, but on the protagonist's experience and vision of the site. By not adding the male authors, but by concentrating instead on the nine nude females, which 'Christine' had intuitively recognised as the source of authority (*octorité*), Christine seems to be making a specific point: knowledge can be visualised by focusing directly on the source of knowledge. By ignoring the intervening tradition, Christine collapses historical time and defines her protagonist (or alter-ego) as the direct link to the Muses.

Similarly, Christine's emphasis on the Muses' nudity may be understood in different terms when connected to a pictorial convention, grounded in the classical notion of *aidos*, in which nudity symbolises truth.[41] The Muses' nudity may also be understood in terms of the medieval notion of *integumenta*, in which the truth is hidden under a veil of poetic fiction.[42] As noted by Millard Meiss, the depiction of nudity in Christine's manuscripts is rare, and is often used only in cases where the story demands it, as in the myth of Diana and Actaeon in the *Epistre Othea*.[43] Yet, as Meiss also points out, the representations of Apollo and Daphne in Christine's manuscripts of the *Epistre* are particularly innovative in their emphasis on Daphne's bodily transformation: they are amongst the first in post-classical art to show Daphne's nudity as well as the idea of metamorphosis in pictorial form (fig. 5.5).[44] It is interesting

[40] Gibbons, "Bath of the Muses," 138, notes the elimination of the male authors.

[41] See Ferrari, "Figures of Speech," on the meaning of *aidos* as a sentiment often evoked in literature; in the *Iliad*, for example, when Hector is going to war, his parents try to dissuade him by undressing before his eyes. An example in Christine's work is the female figures that disrobe themselves as a sign of truth in the *Cité des dames* (II.50 and II.52).

[42] See Holderness, "In the Muses' Garden," 150: "To undress the Muses is to lift the veil of fiction and discover the truth below – to undress the Muses is to read allegorically." See also Akbari, in thie volume, with further references.

[43] Meiss, *Limbourgs and their Contemporaries*, 29. As an example, see the illumination of the Diana and Actaeon story in the *Epistre* BnF Ms. fr. 606 fol. 32r.

[44] Meiss, *Limbourgs and their Contemporaries*, 29.

that the story of Apollo and Daphne is traditionally associated with the origins of poetry, since the fountain of the Muses, as the source of inspiration, is also linked to poetic activity. In both cases, the female body provides the source of inspiration.

In her treatment of the Fountain of Wisdom, Christine follows the Ovidian tradition that establishes the pool as an image inviting poetic self-reflection and transformation, while re-casting the relationship between the viewer and the pool. Christine's fountain thus functions in a double sense: as the source of poetry (or knowledge) and as the source of vision (or perception). This two-fold meaning seems to echo the very process of double description initially encountered in Ovid's *mise-en-scène* of the Muses' fountain, later amplified in the *Ovide moralisé*, and finally reversed in the *Chemin*, where description – an initial perception or experience – is placed before learned or acquired knowledge.

On another level, Christine's fountain is visualised as the carrier of female bodies that, as tradition would have it, represent the embodiment of knowledge and inspiration. At first sight, this might seem like a paradoxical choice, given the misogynistic associations of the female body as text and the erotic connotations of the body on a visual level.[45] In Christine's fountain iconography, the visual senses are invoked and simultaneously manipulated through written description and interpretation so that the female protagonist-narrator's confrontation with the nude body is comparable to an initiation, which must ultimately be completed through a path of learning.[46]

RUTGERS UNIVERSITY

---

[45] For the tradition of the female body as a text for *translatio*, see Dinshaw, *Chaucer's Sexual Poetics*, 134.

[46] I am very grateful to Ana Pairet for her advice in the preparation of this article, originally written for her seminar on Christine de Pizan (Rutgers University, 2004).

Lessons for a King
from Gower's Confessio Amantis 5

Kathryn McKinley

John Gower's poetry often engages subjects of a political nature: questions of kingship, the proper relation of the ruler to his realm, and the nature of the body politic. Like many of his contemporaries, Gower grew increasingly embittered by the corruptions of King Richard II's rule.[1] The *Confessio amantis* is thought to have been commissioned by Richard II,[2] and it is the last major work of Gower's, composed in the middle years of the king's reign. In the poem Gower draws liberally from Ovid's poetry, as he relates tale after tale within the larger framework of the narrator Amans' confession to his priest. As Gower proceeds through each of the seven deadly sins, he takes up many stories from Biblical and classical tradition to mediate his message about love, but especially about proper governance. The Jason and Tereus tales from Book Five, in particular, illustrate the ways in which Gower's poetic narrative can function as a type of political discourse.[3]

By 1390, when Gower is believed to have completed the *Confessio amantis*,[4] Richard II had already experienced the Rising of 1381 and his near deposition in 1387.[5] Chronicle accounts were to refer increasingly frequently to his tyrannical acts;[6] by 1399 Richard would be deposed and Henry IV would assume the throne.[7] Writing throughout Richard's reign,

---

[1] Saul, *Richard II*, 436–437.

[2] Fisher, *John Gower*, 108–109; Hines, Cohen, and Roffey, "*Iohannes Gower, armiger, poeta*," 25–26.

[3] On Gower and Richard II see the studies by Coleman, Ferster, Porter, Saul, Simpson, Watt, and Yeager in the Bibliography. See also the classic 1945 article of Coffman, "John Gower in His Most Significant Role."

[4] Fisher, *John Gower*, 108–109. Fisher suggests that the *Confessio* was begun sometime around 1386 and finished by 1390.

[5] Saul, *Richard II*, 190–191.

[6] Stow, "Richard II in Thomas Walsingham's Chronicles," 91, 93. On the authorship of the *Annales Ricardi Secundi* see Clark, "Thomas Walsingham Reconsidered," 845.

[7] The *Confessio* was revised by Gower from 1390 onward to remove passages that

Gower frequently addresses Richard's rule and projects his social and political vision through his poems. Throughout the *Confessio* Gower engages Ovid to effect an ethical metamorphosis within the understanding of his royal reader or his counsellors. The most important transformation in Gower occurs when Genius interprets the tale for Amans, and thus for the king; what results is metamorphosis in hermeneutical terms.

Recent work on the literature of Ricardian England has paid increasing attention to the ways in which authors directed oblique criticism at Richard II. Judith Ferster, in her study on the genre of the *Fürstenspiegel*, observes that medieval poets wishing to offer harsh criticism of their rulers were frequently forced to do so under a cloak of silence, often resorting to classical story-material as a type of code to veil their intentions.[8] Diane Watt, in *Amoral Gower*, discusses how the final book of the *Confessio amantis*, which focuses on the story of Apollonius, may be read as a commentary on Richard II and the dangers of tyranny.[9] Similarly, David Wallace, in *Chaucerian Polity*, addresses the ways in which the king and his realm are figured as husband and wife in late medieval English literature, sometimes in conjunction with the themes of tyranny or royal power and its limits.[10]

According to the articles of his 1399 deposition, Richard II was charged with a failure to heed counsel:

> in many great councils of the king, when the lords of the realm, the justices, and others were charged faithfully to counsel the king in matters touching the estate of himself and the realm, often the lords, justices and others when they were giving their advice according to their discretion were suddenly and sharply rebuked and censured by him, so that they did not dare to speak the truth about the state of the king and the kingdom in giving their advice.[11]

Like other medieval poets, Gower in his verse offered advice to the king; his counsel repays close scrutiny. According to Ferster:

---

praised the king and to rededicate it to Henry IV. These changes, and the addition of other passages more harshly critical of Richard II, reveal that Gower wrote the poem for two royal readers (see Fisher, *John Gower*, 9–13, 89–91, 116–127).

[8] Ferster, *Fictions of Advice*, 36–37. In England John of Salisbury had, much earlier, used this technique with his ruler, Henry II, in the *Policraticus*.

[9] Watt, *Amoral Gower*, Chapter 6.

[10] Wallace, *Chaucerian Polity*, 295–298.

[11] *English Historical Documents*, ed. Myers, 411, article 23; see also, generally, *Chronicles of the Revolution, 1397–1400*, ed. Given-Wilson.

in the late 1380s ... political discourse was probably dangerous ... Given
that the king's struggle with the Appellants was couched in terms of advice,
with their criticisms swirling around his counsellors, the years during
which Gower wrote the first draft of the *Confessio amantis* (1386–1390)
were highly charged ones in which to write a mirror for princes.[12]

In this period one alternative for those with a particularly trenchant
political message was to resort to Biblical and classical material.[13] That
Gower had the concerns of kingship in mind in writing the *Confessio* is
clear from the final lines of the work, where Genius informs Amans of
the foundations of ideal kingly rule, that is, reason and self-control:

> For conseil passeth alle thing
> To him which thenkth to ben a king;
> And every man for his partie
> A kingdom hath to justefie,
> That is to sein his oghne dom.
> If he misreule that kingdom,
> He lest himself, and that is more
> Than if he loste Schip and Ore
> And al the worldes good withal:
> For what man that in special
> Hath noght himself, he hath noght elles,
> Nomor the perles than the schelles;
> Al is to him of o value
> . . . .
> For love, which that blind was evere,
> Makth alle his servantz blinde also.
> My sone, and if thou have be so,
> Yit is it time to withdrawe,
> And set thin herte under that lawe,
> The which of reson is governed
> And noght of will. And to be lerned,
> Ensamples thou hast many on
> Of now and ek of time gon,
> That every lust is bot a while;
> And who that wole himself beguile,
> He may the rathere be deceived.   (8.2109–2121, 2130–2141)[14]

---

12 Ferster, *Fictions of Advice*, 110.

13 Ferster, *Fictions of Advice*, 38.

14 *Confessio amantis*, ed. Macaulay. All quotations from the *Confessio amantis* are
from this edition.

The most politically charged lines for a man "which thenkth to ben a king" are "And set thin herte under that lawe, | The which of reson is governed | And noght of will." For reasons which will become clearer below, the issue of ruling by will was a particularly fraught one in the course of Richard II's reign. Not only was ruling by personal will a violation of the king's coronation oath; it was the very crux of Richard's downfall.

Amans is often seen as a double for Gower, but Gower equally deftly employs the lover figure as a representative of the king. Elizabeth Porter has observed the ways in which Gower's tales can have, among many other significations, a level of meaning relevant for the monarch:

> In these first six books Gower also anticipates the instruction in the royal virtues appropriate to Amans as a surrogate for Richard II. One way in which this is achieved is by the telling of tales which can be read on more than one level. Thus, the "Tale of Mundus and Paulina" (I.761–1069), told ostensibly as a warning against hypocrisy in love, serves also as a condemnation of hypocrisy among priests ... and, in the emperor who punishes the priests and Mundus for their treachery, offers an idealised portrait of the royal virtues of reverence for justice .... The story of "The Trump of Death," told to the lover as a warning against presumption in love, has as its central character a king who, recognising his own mortality, practices the royal virtue of humility (I.2010–2253).[15]

Other Gower scholars are in agreement that a principal intended reader for the *Vox clamantis*, and especially the *Confessio amantis*, was the king.[16] For James Simpson,

> There are certainly powerful arguments to suggest that [Amans] is a figure for the monarch ... the often comically wide gap between the pathetic Amans and the 'tragic', royal figures of the narratives tends to diminish in stories of the Tarquin kind (VII.4953–5130), in which the disastrous results, both personal and political, of will's tyrannical domination of the imagination are revealed ... the *Confessio* is deeply critical of monarchical claims to absolute rule.[17]

---

[15] Porter, "Gower's Ethical Microcosm," 147.

[16] Yeager, *John Gower's Poetic*, 262, 265–268.

[17] Simpson, *Sciences and the Self*, 280, 281. On Gower's treatment of the Tarquin tale, see McKinley, "Kingship and the Body Politic"; also Simpson, *Sciences and the Self*, Chapter 7.

Gower negotiates such a position in the poem partly through his uses of Ovid. Before turning to Gower's renderings of Ovid's stories, it may be useful to consider Ovid's own tales as they are told in the *Metamorphoses*.

In Ovid, the tales of Tereus and Philomela and Jason and Medea are found nearly side-by-side in neighbouring books (*Met.* 6.401–674 and 7.1–404), although in the reverse order in which Gower presents them. In Ovid, the Tereus tale falls within the first third of the *Metamorphoses* (*Met.* 1–6), which often treats divine-human loves. In Book Six, we see many illustrations of human excess, whether of pride or desire: Arachne, who seeks to best Minerva in a weaving contest; Niobe, who displays excessive pride toward the goddess Latona (the mother of Apollo and Artemis); the Lycian peasants, who had contempt for the goddess Latona; the satyr Marsyas, whose challenge to Apollo's musical abilities resulted in his being flayed alive; and Tereus, whose brutal rape and dismemberment of his sister-in-law results in the equally repulsive revenge carried out by his wife. The final tale of *Metamorphoses* 6, which follows the Tereus story, relates the god Boreas' abduction of Orithyia; suffering from unrequited love, Boreas chooses to employ his own force to carry her to Thrace. Thus Book Six ends with two stories equally troubling for their use of force and violence toward the innocent, force carried out by mortals and gods alike. In general, throughout Book Six, every case of human impiety towards the gods is severely punished. The Tereus tale is thus somewhat anomalous in Book Six since its central relationships are between human beings (Tereus, Procne, Philomela) and the crimes are punished by humans.

Some scholars attribute Ovid's rendering of the Tereus tale to the now-fragmentary tragedy *Tereus* by Sophocles;[18] such a borrowing would explain the brooding drama that unfolds (as in Ovid's Myrrha story, indebted to Euripides' *Hippolytus*). The extreme cruelty of the tale may be explained in part by Tereus' Thracian origins and by Greek and Roman anti-Thracian sentiment: Tereus displays all the savagery expected of this warlike and "uncivilised" people; thus in some ways the tale operates to confirm Athenian assumptions of superiority.[19] Also of

---

[18]Dobrov, "The Tragic and the Comic Tereus," 189–234; Curley, "A Dialogue between Mother and Son," 320–322.

[19]Dobrov, "The Tragic and the Comic Tereus," 212–213. Dobrov also argues that there is an intentional irony in the fact that the two "cultured" Athenian women finally perpetrate crimes even more cruel than those of Tereus (213). See also

interest in the tale is the emphasis on literacy/illiteracy: Philomela, even in the fragmentary *Tereus*, uses writing, not just images, in her textile recreation of the story.[20] Since Procne is an Athenian, she will be able to read the written message in the piece of cloth whereas Tereus (Thracian, thus unable to read) will not. The detail of the writing is present in Ovid (*notas*, 6.577);[21] the *Ovide moralisé* (*escrit*, 6.3347), and Gower (*letres and ymagerie*, 5.5771); but not in Bersuire, who states only that Philomela "wove a web in which she depicted the whole series of events in purple figures" (*telam texuit in qua totius facti seriem imaginibus purpureis depinxit*).[22] Gregory Dobrov argues that Sophocles invented the glossectomy detail so as to cause "the destruction of Tereus by an act of writing (the recognition scene involving Philomela's *textum*). ... this 'lingual castration' is highly marked and serves to emphasize Tereus' singular savagery. His role as violent suppressor of language is thereby also specified."[23] Interestingly, the Arachne tale at the beginning of Book Six also explores the danger of language or art from the point of view of those in higher authority: Minerva punishes Arachne for the artistry of the web she weaves, despite its flawlessness; Ovid would later find himself relegated by Augustus to Tomis for his own art (and only a year after the *Metamorphoses* was completed). Perhaps Ovid employs the Arachne and Tereus tales to reflect the dangers an artist faces in employing art to expose the corrupt actions of the powerful. In the Tereus tale the written word triumphs over savagery, albeit temporarily: the sisters outwit Tereus through written language, although they later succumb to extreme violence.

The gods play a somewhat limited role in Ovid's version of the Tereus story. After Philomela's rape she threatens to pray to the gods for help, and Procne dresses as a Bacchante on her night time journey to find her sister. Ovid removes the detail in some accounts that as Tereus finally chases Procne and Philomela, the sisters pray to the gods to transform them into birds; in Ovid their transformation begins as soon as Tereus rises from the dinner table and no such prayer is uttered. Thus

---

Kaufhold, "Ovid's Tereus," 66–71.

[20]Dobrov, "The Tragic and the Comic Tereus," 204.

[21]s.v. *nota, A Latin Dictionary*, ed. Charlton Lewis and Charles Short (Oxford, 1975), B.1.b: *a letter, epistle, writing. Metamorphoses* 6. 577 is cited. All quotations from Ovid's *Metamorphoses* are from Miller's Loeb edition.

[22]Bersuire, *Metamorphosis Ovidiana moraliter . . . explanata*, fol. 52v.

[23]Dobrov, "The Tragic and the Comic Tereus," 222.

in general the tale seems to be told in a world in which the gods are not much present, again unlike the other tales of *Metamorphoses* 6. However, the Tereus and Boreas tales, with their emphasis on erotic desire, may prepare for the middle books of the *Metamorphoses*. They also set up the story of Jason and Medea. Tereus and Boreas are both located in Thrace, and the sons of Boreas (Zetes and Calais) will take part on the journey of the Argonauts; this itself becomes part of the transition to Book Seven.

Metamorphoses 7, however, opens with a completely different type of tale: the story of Jason and Medea, which commences the next triad of the *Metamorphoses*, an exploration of human loves. One of the great contributions of the *Metamorphoses* is Ovid's exploration of human psychology, often through extended monologues. In Books Seven to Ten of the poem, Ovid features many female characters engaging in deliberative monologues (the classical tendency was to engage the female, rather than male, character for such introspection in drama). Book Seven opens with just such a monologue, in which Medea battles inwardly over her newfound desire for Jason, the foreign prince. Some critics have argued that midway through the tale she grows increasingly absorbed in witchcraft and violent actions.[24] Ovid may depict both Jason and Medea as flawed characters, but he gives the weight of the dramatic attention to Medea. In another bid for Jason's love Medea initiates the murder of Pelias, but after this crime we hear very little of Jason or of his new marriage. Ovid makes quick work of the events, presumably already treated in his now-lost tragedy, *Medea*: "But after the new wife had been burnt by the Colchian witchcraft, and the two seas had seen the king's palace aflame, she stained her impious sword in the blood of her sons; and then, after this horrid vengeance, the mother fled Jason's sword" (*sed postquam Colchis arsit nova nupta venenis | flagrantemque domum regis mare vidit utrumque, | sanguine natorum perfunditur inpius ensis, | ultaque se male mater Iasonis effugit arma*, *Met.* 7.394–397). Although in the early phases of the story Ovid devotes considerable space to Medea's inner quandaries, it is not clear that she is, finally, an innocent victim. Yet, as Euripides (often Ovid's model) shows, Jason opportunistically traded Medea for the new king's daughter, Creusa. In Ovid Jason is never exonerated. He breaks his early oath of fidelity to Medea through his subsequent actions. Ovid's story notably lacks a final transformation; Medea simply seeks refuge with Aegeus in Athens.

---

24 Rosner-Seigel, "*Amor*, Metamorphosis and Magic," 231–243.

Gower situates these two tales in *Confessio* 5, the book devoted to the sin of avarice (under which fall perjury and oath-breaking), and uses them to educate Richard II.[25] The stories of Jason and Tereus focus mainly on the subcategory of oath-breaking; they also illustrate on various levels aspects of the "doctrine of marriage" seen in Giles of Rome, along with the breaking of marital oaths.[26] In the tale of Jason and Medea (*Confessio* 5.3247–4229), though Medea carries out many of her heinous crimes, in the end Gower emphasises the betrayal of Jason and his breaking of his oaths to her. Although there is no physical metamorphosis in Gower's tale, except possibly Medea's "translation" to Athena's heavenly court, Gower transmutes this story into a form of advice to the king. Gower draws often on Benoît de Ste. Maure's version of the tale in *Le Roman de Troie*, not on that of Guido delle Colonne. As is clear from his work in the *Vox clamantis* and elsewhere throughout the *Confessio amantis*, Gower also freely drew on the *Metamorphoses* itself.[27]

One notable difference between Gower's version of the Jason-Medea myth and many others (including Ovid, Benoît, *Ovide moralisé*, and the *Ovidius moralizatus*) is the mutuality of Jason and Medea's love. Benoît (1211–1311) follows Ovid's emphases, focusing more on Medea's newfound *amor* for Jason and minimising Jason's reactions.[28] In *Le Roman de Troie*, much of Jason and Medea's first meeting is presented through Medea's perceptions. When Jason arrives at Oëtes' palace, and Oëtes calls his daughter to meet the visitor, Medea dresses herself elegantly (1229–1238). Benoît lavishes attention on this description: when Medea makes her appearance, she is without rival in all the land for her beauty. This observation (1246–1248), however, is offered by the narrator; at this point Jason's reaction to Medea is not given. Next, Medea gazes on Jason, and we see the description of his physical features

---

[25] Gower himself was probably not aware of the classical literary tradition behind Ovid's two tales.

[26] Porter, "Gower's Ethical Microcosm," 147.

[27] *The Complete Works of John Gower*, ed. Macaulay, 1:497n. Macaulay has emphasised Gower's deep familiarity with Ovid and not just in moralised versions: "His knowledge of Ovid seems to have been pretty complete, for he borrows from almost every section of his works with the air of one who knows perfectly well where to turn for what he wants" (1.xxxiii). Gower's *Vox clamantis* alone shows ample use of Ovid: Stockton (*The Major Latin Works*) identifies 537 lines from Ovid; Mish ("The Influence of Ovid," 130) has identified 217 more. See also Simpson, *Sciences and the Self*, 149 n. 32.

[28] Benoît de Ste. Maure, *Le Roman de Troie*, ed. Constans, vol. 1.

from her point of view (1265–1266). As in Ovid, Medea's inner turmoil is at work in these scenes as she falls in love with Jason. Later, Benoît's Medea will determine within herself, however fearfully, how she will achieve her desire (1296–1297).

Gower, however, changes these emphases so that when Jason and Medea first see each other, they both fall in love:

> And Jason, which good hiede nam,
> Whan he hire sih, ayein hire goth;
> And sche, which was him nothing loth,
> Welcomede him into that lond,
> And softe tok him be the hond
> And doun thei seten bothe same.
> Sche hadde herd spoke of his name
> And of his grete worthinesse;
> Forthi sche gan hir yhe impresse
> Upon his face and his stature,
> And thoghte hou nevere creature
> Was so wel farende as was he.
> And Jason riht in such degre
> Ne mihte noght withholde his lok,
> Bot so good hiede on hire he tok,
> That him ne thoghte under the hevene
> Of beaute sawh he nevere hir evene,
> With al that fell to wommanhiede.
> Thus ech of other token hiede,
> Thogh ther no word was of record;
> Here hertes bothe of on acord
> Ben set to love, bot as tho
> Ther mihten be no wordes mo.   (5.3370–3392)

The mutual response of the lovers is a critical narrative intervention for Gower's development of Jason's later oath-breaking. If Ovid presents a relatively sympathetic retelling of Medea's misfortunes (despite her Euripidean excesses), Gower increases the audience's empathy for her. His handling of the story has much to do with the larger rubric of oath-keeping. Jason and Tereus will be presented unequivocally as kings who break the most sacred of vows in order to increase their power or to appropriate what is not theirs. It is important to recognise that in this instance Gower is writing against the grain of much medieval commentary on the Jason and Medea story. Further evidence of Gower's exoneration of Medea is that some of Gower's alterations to Benoît's version of the story make Medea's plight even more moving for the reader. Gower reduces Benoît's 1300-line tale by roughly a third; even so, he adds several passages that increase the psychological depth of the characters and weight the story in Medea's favour: he develops the episode that depicts their mutual "love at first sight"; he has Medea instruct Jason on how to undertake the labours set before him by King Oëtes; he adds a twenty-line emotional scene with the lovers in which Medea despairs over the dangers he will face. Gower also adds Medea's inner anguish as she watches Jason from the tower and her decision to send her maid to learn of his welfare.[29] Noteworthy too is Gower's situating of this story within the context of other tales dealing with marriage and the marriage bond. Gower uses the tales of Jason and Tereus tale to broach the question of another royal marriage (Richard II's to his realm) and to suggest the king's breaking of his coronation oath to his people.

In Richard II's reign the metaphor of marriage between ruler and people was positively employed in the 1392 poem by Richard Maidstone celebrating the king's reunion with the city after a quarrel. In the opening of the poem, Maidstone likens Richard's re-entry into London to that of a groom returning to his bride:

> When three times seven August dawns had lit the world,
> A pleasant rumor, London, spread throughout your bounds;
> For now you get your king again, your spouse, your lord,
> Whom Wicked Tongue had taken from you by deceit.
> Its grudging troop had roused the king to wrath at you,
> So that the groom gave up and left his marriage bed;
> But since your love is whole – your lover's face more fair
> Than even that of Paris – he can't hate for long.   (19–26)[30]

Later in the poem an alderman addresses the approaching king, again likening him to a husband:

> [the city] comes all ready to surrender to your will.
> Suffused with tears within, it earnestly entreats
> The king to enter in his room in gentleness.
> Let him not rend or tear apart his realm's fair walls,
> For they are his, and all that still remains inside.
> Let not the bridegroom hate the room he's always loved;
> No cause remains by which his love should be reduced. (141–147)

---

[29] For further comparisons, see Macaulay, 1:497n.
[30] Maidstone, *Concordia*, 19–26, trans. Rigg.

Other texts available in late medieval England also illustrated rulership through the marriage metaphor. Elizabeth Porter has argued that Giles of Rome's popular treatise on rulership, *De regimine principum*, was a key influence on Gower's concept of kingship, especially when Giles treats the subject of matrimony.[31] Giles deals with the relation between marriage and kingship in Book Two, where he outlines the connections between an individual's self-rule and that of a king. For Giles, the rule of a prince or monarch involves a series of concentric circles beginning with rule of self, then rule of household, and extending to rule of the realm; as John Trevisa translates it, "For no man is good rewlere of regne oþer in cyte but he kunne rewle wel himself and his maynye" (II.1.41–43).[32]

Gower's version of the Jason and Medea story includes the opening oath of marriage (as in Ovid; also found in Benoît) that Medea obtains from Jason in exchange for helping him obtain the Golden Fleece. After the two have fallen in love, Medea arranges a trade of sorts:

> For sikernesse of Mariage
> Sche fette forth a riche ymage,
> Which was figure of Jupiter,
> And Jason swor and seide ther,
> That also wiss god scholde him helpe,
> That if Medea dede him helpe,
> That he his pourpos myhte winne,
> Thei scholde never parte atwinne,
> Bot evere whil him lasteth lif,
> He wolde hire holde for his wif.   (5.3483–3493)

Gower then adds several scenes that increase the investment of Medea in this marriage and thereby redouble her suffering at the end. In one of these scenes Jason swears a further oath to her as she weeps over fears for the dangerous tests he must undergo. This oath does not appear in the *Ovide moralisé* or in Benoît, so it appears to be Gower's own addition. Gower notes that Medea's love for Jason had so grown that "al hir world on him sche sette" (5.3637). She takes him in her arms and kisses him, saying, "O, al mi worldes blisse, | Mi trust, mi lust, mi lif, min hele, |

---

[31] Porter, "Gower's Ethical Microcosm," 144; Simpson, *Sciences and the Self*, 221–222.

[32] Giles of Rome, *The Governance of Kings and Princes*, ed. Fowler, Briggs, and Remley.

To be thin helpe in this querele | I preie unto the goddes alle"
(3642–3645). Jason tells her, "Conforteth you, for be my trouthe | It
schal noght fallen in mi slouthe | That I ne wol thurghout fulfille |
Youre hestes at youre oghne wille" (3652–3656). He goes forth,
succeeds with her magical ointments, and returns to her.

In the first part of the Jason and Medea tale (*Confessio* 5.3247–3926)
Gower follows Benoît's main outlines (*Le Roman de Troie* lines
703–2062), but where Benoît breaks off the story – at the point of Jason's
arrival in Greece – Gower continues the story (3927–4242) as Ovid tells
it in *Met.* 7.159–293. Gower relates Medea's rejuvenation of Jason's
father. He reduces the murder of Pelias (*Met.* 7.296–349) to one line,
presenting it after a list of favours Medea had done for Jason. Benoît's
story stops short of Jason's most famous deed: his betrayal of Medea. In
contrast, Gower seems to wish to include at least some of the rest of the
story as Ovid tells it so as to cast a more sympathetic light on Medea.

Like Ovid, Gower handles the matter of Jason's remarriage rather
quickly, but again Gower offers an assessment emphasising especially
Jason's breaking of vows:

> Lo, what mihte eny man devise,
> A womman schewe in eny wise
> Mor hertly love in every stede,
> Than Medea to Jason dede?
> Ferst sche made him the flees to winne,
> And after that fro kiththe and kinne
> With gret tresor with him sche stal,
> And to his fader forth withal
> His Elde hath torned into youthe,
> Which thing non other womman couthe:
> Bot hou it was to hire aquit,
> The remembrance duelleth yit.
> King Peleus his Em was ded,
> Jason bar corone on his hed,
> Medea hath fulfild his wille:
> Bot whanne he scholde of riht fulfille
> The trouthe, which to hire afore
> He hadde in thyle of Colchos swore,
> Tho was Medea most deceived.
> For he an other hath received,
> Which dowhter was to king Creon,
> Creusa sche hihte, and thus Jason,
> As he that was to love untrewe,
> Medea lefte and tok a newe.   (4175–4198)

In his emphasis on Jason's villainy Gower seems to follow Benoît, who writes that Medea's *grant folie* (2030) was in loving Jason and giving up her family and country for him. Benoît refers to Jason's desertion of Medea: *la laissa, si fist grant honte* (2036). Elsewhere Benoît comments on Jason's breaking of laws and oaths (1636, 1637). Unlike Benoît, Gower relates the events of Jason's final betrayal. Medea takes her revenge on Creusa; then, unlike in Ovid, she slays her sons before Jason,[33] saying "O thou of every lond | The moste untrewe creature, | Lo, this schal be thi forfeture" (4212–4214). Gower draws from the *Ovide moralisé* the details of Creusa's name, the sending of the garment to Creusa, and Medea's slaying of her sons in front of Jason.[34] Jason tries to strike back, but Medea is spirited up to heaven, to the Court of Pallas Athena, where she laments her heartbreak.[35]

Gower's account is also more sympathetic to Medea than is that in the *Ovidius moralizatus*, where Medea is negatively described in successive allegorisations. For example, in Bersuire's work Jason, in taking Medea as his wife, is compared to Christ who has taken on our humanity; Medea's murder and dismemberment of Absyrtus to delay her father's pursuit of her is read as an illustration of the impiety of evil women and the ways that the ardour of their lust drives them to commit murder and fratricide; Medea is the sinful soul that fornicates sinfully with the devil Jason; Medea is the devil who under the appearance of goodness deceives man; Jason is God and Medea is a synagogue that kills Christ (Absyrtus); the just man's first wife is flesh (Medea), which falls into sin; Jason is God and Medea is the devil.[36] In the *Ovidius moralizatus* Jason decides to marry Creusa because he is horrified by Medea's killing of his uncle Pelias.[37] Gower omits Medea's killing of her brother and

---

[33] *Met.* 7.396. In Ovid Medea's brutal killing of her sons is reduced to one line, and it is unclear whether she was in Jason's presence or not. In the next line, she simply escapes Jason's wrath.

[34] The first and last details here are found also in the *Ovidius moralizatus*; Mainzer, "John Gower's Use of the 'Mediaeval Ovid'," 215–229.

[35] As Macaulay notes (500 n.4219), this is Gower's misreading. In Ovid, the words "Palladias arces" refer to Athens itself, where Medea would marry Aegeus (*Met.* 7.399).

[36] Bersuire, *Metamorphosis Ovidiana moraliter . . . explanata*, fols. 54v, 55r, 55v, 56r, 56v.

[37] Bersuire, *Metamorphosis Ovidiana moraliter . . . explanata*, fols. 55v, 56r, 56v. In Ovid Medea kills Pelias on her own initiative (7.297–349), though other classical accounts have her doing it at Jason's instigation.

minimises the murder of Pelias. Strikingly, despite the moralised versions of the tale which tend to condemn Medea much more frequently, Gower's tale, in its strong emphasis upon Jason's infidelity and his breaking of oaths, stands finally as a negative exemplum both for Amans and, by implication, for Gower's other readers, both aristocratic and royal. Genius concludes this tale to the listening Amans by emphasising the importance of keeping one's oath: "Thus miht thou se what sorwe it doth | To swere an oth which is noght soth, | In loves cause namely. | Mi sone, be wel war forthi, | And kep that thou be noght forswore" (4223–4227). Amans concludes that the person who cannot keep his "trouthe" (word) is not worthy of love (4362–4365).

The subject of the oath was particularly fraught in royal circles in the late 1380s. In 1377 Richard swore the coronation oath that had been used for his grandfather in 1327. It contained an additional phrase added in 1307 which, as Nigel Saul notes, would have been unpalatable from the point of view of Richard's counsellors,[38] but which Richard was compelled to swear: "holding and maintaining the just laws and customs of the church, and… enforcing what the people shall *justly and reasonably* have chosen and which the king shall protect and strengthen for the honour of God, according to his strength" (emphasis added).[39] By 1387, however, the Appellants brought an appeal against the "traitors" who had supported the king. The Appellants had become embittered for several years by watching their counsel regarding France ignored, to the country's peril; they were also angered by the king's excessive grants to Robert de Vere who, as they also discovered, had plotted with the king against them.[40] The lords challenged Richard in the chapel within the Tower on three aspects of his past behaviour, "first in violating his personal oath by failing to keep his promises to them, secondly in threatening to procure for themselves, in defiance of their noble condition, a death they did not deserve, and thirdly, in defending to his own undoing and the enfeeblement of the entire kingdom the falsest traitors." They further stated "that he must of necessity correct his mistakes and henceforward submit himself to the control of the lords."[41] Richard was

---

[38] Saul, *Richard II*, 25.

[39] *English Historical Documents*, 405. Translated by Myer from the Latin text found in *Foedera, conventiones, literae et cujuscunque generis acta publica*, ed. Rymer (The Hague, 1739–1745), III.iii.63.

[40] Saul, *Richard II*, 177, 182.

[41] *Westminster Chronicle*, ed. Hector and Harvey, 227–229.

required to repeat his coronation oath in 1387. Saul argues that the king may in fact have been deposed temporarily for several days.[42] At his deposition in 1399, he would again be charged with violating the oath.[43] According to Michael Wilks:

> In spite of his original absolute power as a source of authority in the community, the ruler must make himself obey the *lex terrae*: he must bind himself to keep his own law – it is, so to speak, an enforced 'voluntary' act ... the ruler's restriction of his own authority puts his power into the category of private right: and here he is on a par with his people and is therefore not only morally but also legally bound to observe the law. This voluntary abdication of absolute power thus comes to be seen as the first act of kingship. It serves in fact to explain the need for the coronation oath ... As Thomas Occleve put it at the beginning of the next century, the king's oath to observe the law is "the lock and key of the public security."[44]

Although Gower's tale of Jason and Medea would have had many different significations for medieval readers, its emphasis on oath-breaking suggests Gower's interest in the tale's value as a negative exemplum within the "curriculum" that makes up the *Confessio*. Amans is enjoined to be faithful to his lady and true to his word, but this lover/beloved fiction operates on many levels throughout the work, not least as a monarch's guide to self-rule and rule of a kingdom. As Gower puts it more directly in Book Seven:

> What king of lawe takth no kepe,
> Be lawe he mai no regne kepe.
> Do lawe awey, what is a king?
> Wher is the riht of eny thing,
> If that ther be no lawe in londe?
> This oghte a king wel understonde,
> As he which is to lawe swore,
> That if the lawe be forbore
> Withouten execucioun,
> It makth a lond torne up so doun,
> Which is unto the king a sclandre.   (3073–3083)

---

42 Saul, *Richard II*, 189–190, 195.

43 Wilks, *The Problem of Sovereignty*, 217.

44 Wilks, *The Problem of Sovereignty,* 216, 217. Occleve, *De regimine principis*, ed. Wright, 100.

It is well to remember Gower's familiarity with, if not training in, the law,[45] and thus the urgency for him of the king's observance of it (*rex sub lege*).[46]

A look at Gower's contemporary, Chaucer, reveals that he was engaging similar subject matter during Richard II's reign. David Wallace traces the themes of tyranny and absolutism throughout Chaucer's poetry, examining figures such as Walter of the Clerk's Tale, January of the Merchant's Tale, and the many kings of the Monk's Tale. Wallace observes that in the *de casibus* genre of the Monk's Tale there are many exempla of tyrannical figures – some from late fourteenth-century Italy – for Richard II to consider. He also argues that, in Chaucer, it is often to the detriment of the tyrant-figure to ignore the prudent counsel of his wife and, emphasising the marriage metaphor, he stresses Chaucer's advice to the king in the poem "Lak of Stedfastnesse" (ca. 1397–1399) to return to a wiser path of action and "wed thy folk agein to stedfast-nesse." Wallace argues that "in urging Richard to recognize the bonds of matrimony that tie him to his subjects, Chaucer imagines the 'folk' as collective bride to Richard's 'stedfastnesse,' the virtue that holds the [king's personal will] in check."[47] At stake here are the "laws of the land and the arbitrary will and pleasure of the king";[48] Richard was deposed in part because, rather than faithfully upholding his coronation oath, he acted arbitrarily: "according to the whim of his desire he wanted to do whatever appealed to his wishes"; furthermore, he had declared that "he alone could change or establish the laws of his realm."[49] As Wilks points out, "a good deal of English constitutional history centres round the perennial attempts of the magnates to force the king to swear an oath by which he should promise not to act by will. … Richard II was deposed on the basis that his claim to act absolutely by will was a contravention of his coronation oath."[50] If Gower focuses on the theme of oath-keeping in the Jason story, he treats the theme of abuses of royal power in the Tereus tale.

---

[45] Fisher, *John Gower*, 57–58.

[46] Wilks, *The Problem of Sovereignty*, 216.

[47] Wallace, *Chaucerian Polity*, 297.

[48] Wallace, *Chaucerian Polity*, 297.

[49] *Rotuli Parliamentorum* 3.416, translated in *English Historical Documents*, 410; Wallace, *Chaucerian Polity*, 297.

[50] Wilks, *The Problem of Sovereignty*, 217n.

The Tereus story (*Confessio* 5.5551–6074)[51] also falls under the rubric of avarice, or theft, and figures a king who rapes his sister-in-law. This story anticipates the tale of the rape of Lucrece in Book Seven, the book interpreted as Gower's main *speculum principis* for Richard II. Scholars such as Simpson and Ferster have seen the Lucrece tale as a warning to Richard on the dangers of a king driven by self-interest and have seen Tarquin as a figuration of a tyrant-king,[52] taking the people's will by force. In the context of "languages of advice" to a king whom chroniclers eventually likened to a tyrant, such a rape story can betoken the concept of the violation of individual will, alongside the violation of marriage oaths. As we have seen, part of Richard II's coronation oath required his voluntary submission to the will of the people and to their laws (*rex sub lege*). According to Bracton, "For he is called *rex* not from reigning but from ruling well, since he is a king as long as he rules well but a tyrant when he oppresses by violent domination the people entrusted to his care" (*Dicitur enim rex a bene regendo et non a regnando, quia rex est dum bene regit, tyrannus dum populum sibi creditum violenta opprimit dominatione*).[53]

Just prior to the Tereus story, Genius instructs Amans regarding "ravine," or robbery, and in so doing brings up the related subject of extortion and the ways in which a powerful lord may extort monies from those in his power. In the articles of Richard's deposition, we find, "He extorted large sums of money from abbots and priors for his expedition to Ireland" and "by letters under seals ... he obtained great sums of money conceded by the clergy and people of the shires, to be taken at the king's pleasure ... Thus he deceived his people, and craftily extorted their goods from them."[54] Chronicles from the year 1383 note Richard's extortion of money from "several monasteries"; in the articles of deposition and the *Annales* of 1399 he is recorded as extorting money from as many as seventeen counties.[55] Genius warns Amans:

> In the lignage of Avarice,
> Mi Sone, yit ther is a vice,
> His rihte name it is Ravine,

---

[51] In Ovid, *Met.* 6.401–675.
[52] Simpson, *Sciences and the Self*, 213–215, 280; Ferster, *Fictions of Advice*, 113–115.
[53] *De legibus*, trans. Thorne, 2.305, lines 30–31.
[54] *English Historical Documents*, 411, articles 22, 21.
[55] Stow, "Richard II in Thomas Walsingham's Chronicles," 84, 95.

Which hath a route of his covine.
Ravine among the maistres duelleth,
And with his servantz, as men telleth
Extorcion is nou withholde:
Ravine of othre mennes folde
Makth his larder and paieth noght;
For wher as evere it mai be soght,
In his hous ther schal nothing lacke,
And that fulofte abyth the packe
Of povere men that duelle aboute.
Thus stant the comun poeple in doute,
Which can do non amendement;
For whanne him faileth paiement,
Ravine makth non other skile,
Bot takth be strengthe what he wile. (5.5505–5522)[56]

Even though Genius will warn Amans not to be a "Raviner in love," it seems clear that Gower has matters of a social and political nature in mind in this passage. Gower thus prefaces his story of Tereus with reflections about abuse of power seen more generally in the political realm.

In the Tereus story Gower draws on the *Ovide moralisé* and the *Ovidius moralizatus* for some details, but often contributes additions of his own. Betrayal and the violation of the marriage bond occur at the beginning of the tale. Tereus is one of the notorious villains of Ovid's poem. With Tereus Gower begins with a king known far and wide for his "knightly" status, seemingly an ideal match for King Pandion's daughter Progne. Gower describes Tereus as "a worthi king of hih lignage, | A noble kniht eke of his hond, | So was he kid in every lond" (5566–5568). This follows Ovid's description of Tereus having an "illustrious name" (*clarum nomen*) from his past victory in defending Athens from its enemies. In Ovid Tereus is also characterised as "strong in wealth and men" (*opibusque virisque potentem, Met.* 6.426) before he marries Procne. In both Ovid and Gower Philomena condemns Tereus after the rape: she laments her loss of virginity and his abuse of his marriage bond and she promises to tell all what he has done. In an addition to Ovid, Gower uses the term *felonie* twice to describe Tereus' actions (5.5668, 5772).[57] In Ovid Tereus punishes Philomela for her

---

[56] In one Gower manuscript a marginal comment on this passage reads, "Extortion is the mother of Ravine" (*Complete Works*, ed. Macaulay, 504 n. 5511).

outburst by cutting out her tongue and later raping her repeatedly. Gower omits some of the more gruesome details, such as the tongue contorting at Philomena's feet; he also changes the story so that once Tereus has removed her tongue she is sent to a prison and there is no repeated rape. Gower adds a lament by Philomela from prison that evokes even more sympathy. After her transformation, Gower describes her plaints as mixing joy with woe (5989), evoking the tradition of the nightingale's song in medieval religious lyric as a song of both joy and pain, a mystical song uniting the singer in his devotion to Christ.[58] For her part Progne, before the transformation, is given an additional speech, a prayer to the gods in which she asks for their aid in avenging her sister. In her anger that her husband "hadde his espousaile broke" (5816), she makes a vow to avenge his crimes and reminds the gods Cupide and Venus that she has always been "trewe in mi degre" "with al mi will and al my wit" to her husband Tereus and that she has found him "most untrewe and most unkinde" (5829, 5826, 5836) Again Gower stresses the making, keeping, and breaking of vows. Progne also offers a prayer to Apollo for his help.[59]

In Ovid Tereus is twice compared to a tyrant (*Met.* 6.549, 581); Gower uses the term in different forms three times (5.5627, 5646, 5921), once in a speech which again he adds. In Gower, in the scene just before their transformations, Progne and Philomela slay Progne's son Itys, make him into a stew and feed him to the unsuspecting Tereus. Then Progne brings the head of Itys to Tereus and offers it to him with these words: "O werste of alle wicke, | Of conscience whom no pricke | Mai stere, lo, what thou hast do! | Lo, hier ben nou we Sostres tuo; | O Raviner, lo hier thi preie, | With whom so falsliche on the weie | Thou hast thi tirannye wroght" (5.5915–5921). In the later chronicles of Richard's reign, the king's tyrannical actions were increasingly documented.[60] As Porter has argued regarding the story of Lucrece's rape in *Confessio* Book Seven, "the rape of Lucrece by Aruns, like the king's abuse of the law in his desire for Virginia, are crimes against the community which are both personal and political."[61] For the final bird transformations of the Tereus story, Gower drew the details from medieval moralised versions

---

57 These details can be traced to the *Ovide moralisé* tradition.
58 The tradition of Rossignol, for example.
59 These details do not appear in the *Ovide moralisé*.
60 Stow, "Richard II in Thomas Walsingham's Chronicles," 91, 93.
61 Porter, "Gower's Ethical Microcosm," 159.

of Ovid.[62] Ovid uses *tyrannus* of Tereus in his version of the story (*Met.* 6.401–674), and Arnulf characterises the hoopoe into which Tereus is transformed as *tirannis* in one manuscript.[63] In Gower Tereus is transformed into a "lappewincke" (a crested plover) which is similar to a hoopoe because of its crest (5.6046–6047): "A lappewincke hath lore his feith | And is the brid falseste of alle." Chaucer also refers to this bird negatively in the *Parliament of Fowls*: "the false lapwynge ful of trecherye" (347).[64]

In the *Ovide moralisé*, there is a striking allegorisation of the story of Tereus and Philomela (6.3719–3781) in which the marriage of body and soul is presented. Progne is compared to the soul and Tereus to the body. The fruit of their union is Itys. All is well until Progne inquires about her sister. Tereus is sent to fetch Philomela, and en route he, as body, is overcome with desire. In the process Progne (as soul) is also to blame, and finally the body brings the soul to damnation in hell. In this version the body (Tereus) is the culprit, but Progne also shoulders the blame; furthermore, Philomela figures deceptive love, impermanent and unstable in this world (3755–3760). Unfortunately this version presents innocent female characters as prone to sin, or sinful. It is noteworthy, however, that Tereus is figured in a body-soul marriage; since Gower at times drew from the *Ovide moralisé*, it is likely that he was aware of this strategy of figuring Tereus, as ruler, on a more complex level. The *Ovidius moralizatus* for its part condemns the actions of Tereus, focusing on the sin of incest.[65] Incest is featured as the central sin in *Confessio 8*, the concluding book of the poem. Porter, Yeager, and others have drawn attention to the medieval understanding of incest as a sin figuring self-absorption,[66] one of the worst (and most dangerous) of all weaknesses in a king. After the tale, Genius warns Amans about Covine, conspiracy, and Ravine, in matters of love.

---

[62] See Mainzer, "John Gower's Use of the 'Mediaeval Ovid'," 215–229. Gower does not appear to have used any details from John of Garland's version of the Tereus story.

[63] Giovanni del Virgilio, *Allegorie*, ed. Ghisalberti, 74 n. 32. This reading is not found in Ghisalberti's edition of Arnulf.

[64] Macaulay, 506n.

[65] Bersuire, *Metamorphosis Ovidiana moraliter . . . explanata*, fol. 52v.

[66] Porter, "Gower's Ethical Microcosm," 160–161; Yeager, *John Gower's Poetic*, 217–229; *Confessio amantis*, ed. Peck, xxii–xxix.

In rendering the Jason and Tereus tales, Gower seems to follow Ovid's emphases much more strongly than those of the medieval moralising tradition. With the Jason story, in fact, Gower not only rejects the assessment of Jason and Medea in the texts that we know he used (*Ovide moralisé*, *Ovidius moralizatus*), but also goes further than Ovid in assigning blame: Jason, far from "Christ" or "god," is the oath-breaking villain; Medea, far from the "devil," is the innocent victim. If Benoît follows some of Ovid's storyline more closely, Gower shifts the focus so that he can highlight the importance of oath-keeping: Jason, sympathetic to the reader because of his love for Medea, is all the more culpable for his final betrayal of his oath to her. Ultimately, despite Gower's rewriting of the initial responses of Jason to Medea, his reading of Jason is aligned with that of Ovid; both poets make clear Jason's opportunistic change in behaviour. In the case of Tereus, Gower again seems to draw more strongly from Ovid's version than from the medieval moralised accounts: Progne and Philomela are restored to their innocent status (before their revenge) in his tale. Whether or not he was aware of it, Gower's decision to employ Tereus as a reflection on the dangers of tyranny (i.e. Richard II's increasingly tyrannical actions) approximates in interesting ways the use by Ovid and other classical authors of Tereus to represent hostile rulers (Thracian kings). Gower's political readings are finally similar to the classical uses of such characters and dissimilar to medieval moralising versions that tend to read such characters as emblematic of sinful spiritual states. By following more closely Ovid's own emphases, Gower in this section of Book Five presents negative illustrations of rulers who violate oaths of various kinds. When one considers the various versions of these stories available to Gower and examines his departures from them, one can see both the independence of his judgment and his determination to recreate a more truly "Ovidian" telling of each tale. In the *Confessio amantis*, Gower is concerned not just with the larger rubric of Amans' confession of his sins to Genius; he intends above all to employ this larger framework to mediate his own reflections on proper governance and self-rule. It is worth citing in this context Genius' words to Amans, and thus Gower's to Richard II, as found in the last book of the *Confessio*:

> Yit is it time to withdrawe,
> And set thin herte under that lawe,
> The which of reson is governed
> And noght of will. And to be lerned,
> Ensamples thou hast many on

> Of now and ek of time gon,
> That every lust is bot a while;
> And who that wole himself beguile,
> He may the rathere be deceived.   (8.2133–2141)[67]

Throughout the *Confessio* Gower employs amatory discourse to engage political questions: of key importance here is the subjection of the heart to law and reason and not to the lover's, or king's, own will. The 1380s and 1390s were treacherous times for a poet to broach these questions, and it is to Ovid that Gower turned repeatedly to offer his most serious reflections on kingship.[68]

FLORIDA INTERNATIONAL UNIVERSITY

---

[67] The final two lines may echo *Piers Plowman*, Passus 18, 361–363, where Christ addresses Lucifer: "And gile is bigiled, and in his gile fallen: / *Et cecidit in foveam quam fecit.* / Now bigynneth thi gile ageyn thee to turne." The Latin quote is Psalm 7:16: "he has fallen into the pit which he made" (*Piers Plowman*, ed. Schmidt). In 1399 Gower in the *Cronica Tripertita* uses a similar phrase to characterize Richard II's perfidies: *quos laqueos fecit in eos, sua culpa reiecit* ("his own guilt threw him back into the nooses which he had made," 3.192). Stockton, *Major Latin Works*, discusses Gower's familiarity with Langland (24).

[68] I would like to thank James Clark, Frank Coulson, Jamie Fumo, and James Simpson for their helpful comments on this article.

ARGUS' EYES, MIDAS' EARS,
AND THE WIFE OF BATH AS STORYTELLER

JAMIE C. FUMO

Res est blanda canor: discant cantare puellae.
(A persuasive thing is song: let women learn to sing.)
– Ovid, *Ars amatoria* 3.315

When Ovid turns from his male charges to "arm" women in Book
Three of the *Ars amatoria*, he memorably shapes himself as a poet of
duality, even self-contradiction. His legacy in the Middle Ages is
similarly multivalent, at times paradoxical. The medieval Ovid, as the
careful studies of Dimmick, Hexter ("Ovid in the Middle Ages"), and
Fleming ("The Best Line") have shown, served as a kind of ethical
lightning rod for conflicting understandings of erotic love at the same
time that Ovid's legacy shaped the ways in which commentators and
poets imagined the very concepts of selfhood, authority, and change:
"Ovid is the ideal guide in reclaiming, questioning and revising the
cultural authority of the ancients, precisely because he is himself already
engaged in the effort of reclamation and problematization."[1] Chaucer's
Wife of Bath, that uncanny reincarnation of Ovid's Dipsas as channelled
through the *Roman de la rose*, has won many laurels as a star pupil of
Master Naso and has been described by one of the most astute recent
students of Chaucer's Ovidianism as "the most deeply embroiled of all
Chaucer's characters not only in Ovid's texts themselves but in their
medieval manifestations and implications."[2] If the Wife of Bath stages a
battle of the sexes, however, Ovid fights on both sides – appropriately
for one who remarked: "Nor do I doubt that I shall be attacked with
my own weapons" (*Nec dubito, telis quin petar ipse meis, Ars am.* 3.590).
The same author who, in anthologised and redacted form, is included
as an antifeminist authority along with the likes of Jerome and Theo-

---

[1] Dimmick, "Ovid in the Middle Ages," 286.
[2] Calabrese, *Chaucer's Ovidian Arts*, 81.

phrastus in Jankyn's *Book of Wicked Wives*, has also taught Alison of Bath the "olde daunce" – a talent which, as readers of Ovid's didactic poetry will appreciate, has as much to do with art as it does with love. Ovid provides the Wife of Bath not merely with a repository of allusions, or even with a stock of sexual strategies, but with a model of the subversion and reappropriation of *auctoritas* through storytelling. Ovid is, indeed, the one man who is equipped to understand what the Wife really wants out of her act of narration: as Dimmick cogently observes in another context, "If Ovid is an *auctor*, he is one who reveals *auctoritas* to be a power-source, exploited and contested, rather than the stable, central authority of Scripture .... His authorship constituted a locus where discursive authority could be explored, asserted and disputed."[3]

Despite such sophisticated recent approaches to medieval Ovidianism, attentive as they are to the cultural construction and institutional framework of Ovid's transmission, too little attention has been paid to the narratological relevance of the *Metamorphoses* in particular to Chaucer's poetry. Fyler's classic study, for example, is noteworthy for downplaying the *Metamorphoses* in favour of Ovid's amatory poetry in its analysis of the structural and philosophical influence of Ovid upon Chaucer. While Fyler's excellent monograph remains foundational to contemporary explorations of Chaucer's Ovidianism, since 1979 the rapidly developing fields of intertextuality and narratology have opened considerable space for the enhancement and reorientation of the terms of Fyler's study. It would be surprising, indeed, if a poem as self-consciously concerned with the act and power of storytelling as Ovid's *Metamorphoses*[4] did not command Chaucer's attention during the writing of a story collection as poetically self-aware and polyphonic as the *Canterbury Tales*.[5] Fundamental to this polyphony is the Wife of Bath, who is, if not the centrepiece, at least the pulse of the *Canterbury Tales* as a story collection. Her Prologue and Tale are quite possibly the most acutely and self-consciously concerned of all those in the collection with what we might call, in contemporary language, the ideological power

---

[3] Dimmick, "Ovid in the Middle Ages," 266, 286.

[4] See, for example, the narratological analyses of the *Metamorphoses* by Nagle, Wheeler, Barchiesi, "Narrative Technique," and Rosati.

[5] Hoffman, *Ovid and the Canterbury Tales*, 3–20, and Pelen, "Chaucer's Wife of Midas Reconsidered," 141–160, have gone so far as to argue that the internal storytelling competitions and other contests of the *Metamorphoses* inspired Chaucer's framing concept of the Canterbury pilgrimage.

of fiction. The Wife has long been seen as the instigator of a productive literary debate about marriage within the heart of the *Canterbury Tales*. More recently, critics such as Patterson and Wallace have argued that the Wife's particular narrative idiosyncrasies invite an unparalleled glimpse into Chaucer's theoretical aims in the *Canterbury Tales* as a whole, whether these involve the interplay of subjectivity and temporality (Patterson) or the importance of wifely eloquence as an ingredient of male authority (Wallace). The force the Wife exerts is both centripetal and centrifugal: she draws other pilgrims into her tale, provoking not simply interrupters of, but collaborators in the story she unfolds; and she leaks out (rather eerily) into the tales of other pilgrims – archwife in the Clerk's Envoy, authority on marriage in the Merchant's Tale.

While much ink has been spilled over the question of whether Chaucer "empowers" the Wife of Bath or undercuts her through his vivid portrayal of her contribution to the hermeneutic wars of her day, it can be argued that we have it backwards: it is the Wife of Bath who empowers Chaucer. She empowers him as an author by opening the field to a kind of experimentation with the texture of Ovidianism and with the multivalent potentials of storytelling unprecedented in Chaucer's verse, distinguished as his dossier was by the early 1390s. The present article addresses the gap in our understanding of the narratological influence of the *Metamorphoses* upon the *Canterbury Tales* by exploring those aspects of the Wife of Bath's techniques as a storyteller and as a subverter of *auctoritas* that can be traced to Ovid. More specifically, this reading illuminates a connection between two suggestive Ovidian citations in Chaucer's Wife of Bath's Prologue and Tale: the Wife's comparison of her husbands to the blinded Argus and her infamous botching of the myth of Midas' ears. It will become clear that the Wife's strategic revisions of both Ovidian myths foreground the power – and danger – of the female voice, and, further, that the Wife's rhetorical display in her Prologue and Tale, usually understood as shaped by the discourses of confession,[6] preaching,[7] exegesis,[8] or legal argument,[9] is also substantially indebted to Ovidian techniques of storytelling. The key to this argument is the significance of the embedded Ovidian tale

---

[6] Root, "'Space to speke,'" 252–274.

[7] Patterson, "Feminine Rhetoric," 330–339; Shain, "Pulpit Rhetoric," 235–245.

[8] Robertson, *Preface to Chaucer*, 317–331; Fleming, "Sacred and Secular Exegesis," 73–90.

[9] Thomas, "What the Man of Law Can't Say," 256–271.

of Pan's pursuit of Syrinx, which Mercury narrates as a soporific to Argus, the guard of the bovine Io. The Syrinx story is structurally related to the Midas myth as well. The Ovidian tale of Syrinx offered Chaucer a means of exploring the motivation and representation of storytelling, while the narrative in which it is embedded (that of Jove and Io) forms a thematic precedent for the Wife's Tale of rape, remorse, and transformation.

★   ★   ★

In the midst of a long speech in which the Wife of Bath catalogues the multitudinous antifeminist bromides that spew from her husbands' mouths when drunk (admitting, at the end, that they did not actually say these things), the Wife responds to the accusation that women roam the streets like cats in heat by invoking the futility of Argus' watch over Io:

> Sire olde fool, what helpeth thee to spyen?
> Thogh thou preye Argus with his hundred yen
> To be my warde-cors, as he kan best,
> In feith, he shal nat kepe me but me lest;
> Yet koude I make his berd, so moot I thee!   (Prologue, 357–361)

In Ovid's version of the story in Book One of the *Metamorphoses*, Mercury's pipe-playing and, especially, storytelling lull the hundred-eyed Argus to sleep, making possible his decapitation and thus enabling Mercury (on Jupiter's command) to free Io from the oppression of the jealous Juno. Ovid's Io is simply a victim and she is silent – indeed, Ovid comically calls attention to her frustration with this silence by telling us that her pathetic attempts at speech come out as moos (even when she regains her human form at the end, she is at first afraid to speak, lest she moo). The Wife, in contrast, gives Io both will and voice, in the same turn making Argus not an agent of a jealous wife, but a stand-in for a jealous husband, and, more importantly, eliminating the role of Mercury entirely. Indeed, she *conflates* the wily Mercury with the oppressed Io, granting her vocal efficacy as a woman who, like the Wife of Bath, can outtalk her husband's attempts to control her.[10]

---

[10] Here the Wife of Bath would seem to be collapsing her own distinction (Prologue, 697–710) between the children of Mercury and Venus by showing that the "wysdam and science" of Mercury (699) can serve the "ryot and dispence" of Venus (700) through peculiarly female powers of persuasive speech. Cf. Chance,

This move is not original to Chaucer: it was ultimately inspired by a passage in Book Three of the *Ars amatoria*, in which Ovid presents the deception of Argus as a model for how a woman can deceive her guardian or husband *through speech*: "Though as many keep watch as Argus had eyes (so your purpose be but firm) you will deceive them [lit. you will give words]" (*Tot licet observent (adsit modo certa voluntas),* | *Quot fuerant Argo lumina, verba dabis,* 3.616–618). In *Amores* 3.4.19–20, Ovid uses Argus to make a similar point, again by removing the agency from Mercury. This more cynical version of the Argus myth became commonplace in medieval antifeminist and comic traditions. Its influence was extended by the speech of the Wife of Bath's Ovidian ancestress, La Vieille, in the *Roman de la rose*.[11] Even the *Gesta Romanorum*, which avoids the erotic context of the story and instead presents it as a simple exemplum about the importance of vigilance, introduces the antifeminist trope of the deceptive female voice in its moralisation, in which the cow represents the soul, Argus a prelate, Mercury the devil, and the songs Mercury sings "singing women."[12] In fact, one of the analogues of the *Gesta Romanorum* story, an anonymous Latin narrative entitled "De Mauro bubulco," tellingly complicates the tale – and reflects the complications of its medieval transmission – by giving the Mercury figure a *wife*. It is she, in this version, who perpetrates the deception upon the Argus character (who, interestingly, keeps his head).[13] Chaucer toys with this tradition of the emasculated Argus elsewhere in his poetry as well. In Book Four of *Troilus and Criseyde*, Troilus warns that Calkas, now acting as a possessive guardian, has as many tricks up his sleeve as Argus has eyes, despite Criseyde's confidence in her womanly ability to "blende" him (4.1462).[14] In the Merchant's Tale (2107–2115), the

---

Mythographic Chaucer, 219–220.

[11] Guillaume de Lorris and Jean de Meun, *Roman*, II, 14,351–14,364. On these aspects of the Argus myth, see Hoffman, *Ovid and the Canterbury Tales*, 131–133; Yager, "The End of Knowledge," 15–26; and cf. Chance, *Mythographic Chaucer*, 220–221 (who offers several possible equations of the Io/Mercury/Argus triad with the Wife, Jankyn, and her other four husbands). Broader surveys of the ways in which mythographers moralised the Argus myth are available in Hoffman and Yager. This essay departs from these critics insofar as it is concerned mainly with the narratological, rather than the moral or allegorical, dimensions of the Argus myth in its medieval Latin and vernacular incarnations.

[12] *Gesta Romanorum* CXI.

[13] The Latin text is edited by Wright in *A Selection of Latin Stories*, 1–6.

[14] See the excellent discussions of this allusion in Schibanoff, "Argus and Argyve,"

blindness of Januarie is ironically compared with the futility of Argus' hundred-eyed vision in the face of duplicity, while young love is aligned with the power of physical sight via another Ovidian allusion, to Pyramus and Thisbe, whose sharp eyes enabled them to thwart their parents' prohibition: "What sleighte is it, thogh it be long and hoot, | That Love nyl fynde it out in som manere?" (2126–2127). At the end of the tale May, like the Wife of Bath's feminised Mercury, (re)blinds her Argus, motivated by adulterous love and armed very specifically (more so than Criseyde) with the power of speech: in her long final speech, her words paradoxically blind Januarie by verbally "painting a picture" in his imaginative faculty that supersedes the shape of reality itself.

The conflation in this tradition of the roles of the silent Io and the vocal Mercury becomes still more intriguing when we consider that one of Mercury's attributes, in Bersuire's *Ovidius moralizatus*, is the power to change himself from male to female whenever he wishes: it is because of this adaptability, says Bersuire, that Mercury was able to conquer Argus.[15] Gower follows this tradition in his euhemeristic survey of Greek religion in Book Five of the *Confessio amantis*, in which it is said of Mercury: "Of Sorcerie he couthe ynowh, | That whanne he wolde himself transforme, | Fulofte time he tok the forme | Of womman and his oghne lefte; | So dede he wel the more thefte" (5.940–944).[16] It is especially interesting that Gower seems to associate this (Loathly Lady-like?) power of shape-shifting – the ability to inhabit a female form – with the rhetorical manipulation for which Mercury is also known, which follows immediately upon the preceding account: "A gret spekere in alle thinges | He was also, and of lesinges | An Auctour" (5.945–997). In these ways, then, antifeminist concerns surrounding the nature of female speech were built into the Argus story as the Wife of Bath (and Chaucer) inherited it.

The tale of Pan's attempted rape of Syrinx is equally important to an understanding of the allusive function of the myth of Argus' blinding in which it is embedded. Though the Wife of Bath makes no explicit

---

647–658, and Yager, "End of Knowledge," 23–24.

[15] Both in the *De formis figurisque deorum* (25) and the *Ovidius moralizatus* proper (*Reductorium morale*, 43). This tradition was further disseminated by the anonymous "De Deorum Imaginibus Libellus" (119). Bersuire and the *Libellus* (like Gower, as we will see shortly) discuss Mercury's shape-shifting in close proximity to his eloquence.

[16] All Gower references are from Macaulay's edition.

reference to the inset Ovidian tale of Pan and Syrinx in her allusion to Argus, it is implicitly present. We recall that in the *Metamorphoses* the tale Mercury chooses to tell Argus is a strategic one, relevant not only as an aetiology of the rustic pipes he is playing (whose origin Argus had inquired into) but as a suggestive correlative of the experience of rape to which Argus is a silent witness in guarding Io, the transformed rape victim of Jupiter. Mercury thus uses a story of female victimisation in order to collude in the victimisation of another female (he has been commissioned by Jove, after all); meanwhile, Argus, far from grasping the significance of the story, falls asleep halfway through. In the section of her Prologue in which she refers to Argus, the Wife of Bath also conspicuously uses a fiction contiguous with reality – her husbands' oppression of her – in order to "blind" her husbands verbally, though she plays on their gullibility rather than their sleepiness.[17] In a larger sense, the Wife's tactics mirror Mercury's manipulative storytelling by "rewriting" male texts – much as Mercury's tale of Syrinx rewrites the other rape narratives of Book One – in order to use these texts against males.

Before investigating the full significance of the Syrinx story to the Wife of Bath as a narrator, we must consider the Wife's manipulation of the Argus story in her Prologue in light of the most prominent Ovidian moment in her Tale: the retelling of the story of Midas, a digression in her catalogue of responses to the pressing question of what "wommen moost desiren" (Wife of Bath's Tale, 905). It is untrue that women wish to be thought able to hold a secret, claims the Wife, pointing to the precedent of Midas' wife who, upon discovering her husband's ass' ears, nearly bursts with the desire to spread the news, until she comes to a marsh and "bombleth" (booms) the secret into the water. "Redeth Ovyde," advises the Wife of Bath, if you wish to know "the remenant of the tale" (981–982). Many critics have explored the implications of the Wife's substitution of Midas' wife for the character who, in Book Eleven of the *Metamorphoses*, is his male barber, and many have noted the omission of the ending, in which reeds grow on the spot where the secret had been buried and repeat the embarrassing words when they rustle in the wind. Few would still agree with Roppolo's claim that "the remainder of the story is not pertinent; it would, in fact,

---

[17] Cf. Yager: "As Mercury frees Io with the power of his eloquence, so [the Wife] vanquishes her opponent with her verbal and rhetorical skill" ("The End of Knowledge," 23). Yager does not, however, consider the Wife's techniques of storytelling in relation to this Ovidian allusion.

constitute a real digression,"[18] for, clearly, the Wife's sudden truncation of a narrative about how women cannot keep silent is a rhetorically loaded moment. What is ironic is that the Wife, so soon after the Amazonian *tour de force* of her Prologue, has created an antifeminist spectacle where there need not be one. In so doing, she has aligned herself not only with Midas' (invented) garrulous wife, but with Midas himself, whose ass' ears, which he received as punishment for the foolish claim that Pan's music is superior to that of Apollo, find their correlative in the Wife of Bath's deafness ("but she was somdel deef, and that was scathe," General Prologue, 446), which of course is also a deafness to authority.[19] Moreover, as with her treatment of the Argus story, the Wife has again conspicuously refashioned an Ovidian narrative around the theme of female voice.

She has also, by association, inadvertently reminded us of the story of Delilah, who was both a treacherous wife and a barber, as Fleming has pointed out in two recent, penetrating analyses of the Wife's Ovidianism, and who is named by Jean de Meun's Nature in a passage that similarly expostulates the folly of trusting women to keep their word.[20] Chaucer's treatment of Sampson's tragedy in the Monk's Tale corroborates this reading: just as Midas' wife, in the Wife of Bath's Tale, discovers and reveals her husband's "conseil," or secret (966), so Delilah, in the Monk's Tale (2027–2029), "koude hym (Sampson) so plese and preye | Til she his *conseil* knew; and she, untrewe, | Unto his foos his *conseil* gan biwreye" (emphasis added). Indeed, the moral of this episode in the Monk's Tale is precisely that of the Wife of Bath's story of Midas' wife – the inability of women to keep secrets: "Beth war by this ensample oold and playn | That no men telle hir conseil til hir wyves | Of swich thyng as they wolde han secree fayn, | If that it touche hir lymes or hir

---

[18] Roppolo, "Converted Knight," 269.

[19] On this point, see Hoffman, *Ovid and the Canterbury Tales*, 147–148; Allen and Gallacher, "Alison through the Looking Glass," 99–105; Robertson, "The Wife of Bath and Midas," 1–20; Fleming, "Sacred and Secular Exegesis," 73–90. Other critics have read the Wife's treatment of the Midas story more sympathetically, as an evocation of "the real strains involved in feminine submission to, and manipulation of, masculine egos" (Leicester, *Disenchanted Self*, 145); cf. Patterson, "Feminine Rhetoric," 319, and Chance, *Mythographic Chaucer*, 226–230.

[20] Fleming, "Sacred and Secular Exegesis," 83–84; "Best Line," 73–74. The relevant passage is in Guillaume de Lorris and Jean de Meun, *Roman*, II, 16,647–16,670.

lyves" (Monk's Tale, 2091–2094).[22] To return to the Wife of Bath's Prologue and Tale, it is no coincidence that in Jankyn's *Book of Wicked Wives* − the antifeminist compendium of patristic writings as well as "Ovides Art" which the Wife's fifth husband insisted upon reading to her − Delilah appears as treacherous woman, exhibit two, immediately after Eve. As a result of Jankyn's reading of this book, which the Wife proceeds to rip to pieces, fisticuffs ensue between husband and wife in the Prologue, resulting in the Wife's Midas-like deafness in one ear. What's more, the *manner* in which the Delilah story is presented in Jankyn's book cannot help but remind us of another Ovidian episode: "Tho redde he me how Sampson loste his heres: | Slepynge, his lemman kitte it with hir sheres; | *Thurgh which treson loste he bothe his yen*" (Wife of Bath's Prologue, 721–723; emphasis added). It is impossible not to think of Argus here, whose blinding (which similarly follows upon imprudent slumber) the Wife has already presented in her Prologue in the context of female deception. Of course, in the Biblical account, Delilah does not *herself* blind Sampson; rather, the Philistines to whom she betrays her husband put out his eyes and imprison him. But Chaucer, unlike in his own treatment of the story in the Monk's Tale and the precedent for the story's narration in the *Roman de la rose*, makes Jankyn's book imply that, in effect, *Delilah herself blinded Sampson*. This unusual shaping of the Biblical narrative, then, encourages a strong connection between the Delilah and Midas stories on the one hand, and the Argus myth and the context in which the Wife appropriated it on the other.

It is important to recognise that the stories of Argus and Midas, which appear at different ends of Ovid's *Metamorphoses*, are structurally linked. This helps us further appreciate how Chaucer registered and exploited the potential for their connection.[23] Whereas the story of

---

[22]Delilah's verbal treachery was an antifeminist commonplace, found for example in Nature's condemnation of her *flaterie venimeuse* (16,648) in the *Roman de la Rose* and in Lydgate, "Examples Against Women" (Lydgate, *Minor Poems*, 442–445), who says that Delilah "cowde so well fflatter, fforge, & ffeyne" (86).

[23]It should be noted that Pelen, "Chaucer's Wife of Midas Reconsidered," 147–153, has preceded me in suggesting a connection between the Wife's references to Argus and Midas, but for reasons with which I cannot agree. Specifically, Pelen contends that the action of Midas' wife when she flees her husband's company to bellow the secret into a marsh (in Ovid, it is a hole in the ground) is modelled upon Syrinx's flight from Mercury in *Metamorphoses* 1, in which she similarly runs to the site of a body of water (here a stream). This theory is attractive, but finally too ingenious, and depends on too many details ignored by Chaucer in his adaptation of

Argus presents, through the inset tale of Pan and Syrinx, the origins of Pan's pipes (the reeds into which Syrinx is transformed), the Midas story records their effects – both in Midas' imprudent musical judgment (which favours Pan's fluting over Apollo's lyre-playing) and in the revelation of Midas' deformity through the motion of the Syrinx-like reeds.[24] But if this connection is only implicit in Ovid (and requires the reader to connect events separated by the length of ten books), it is often made explicit in medieval mythographic interpretations of Midas' story at least some of which Chaucer is likely to have known. In Fulgentius' version, for example, which is repeated by the First Vatican Mythographer, it is not the rustling of the reeds in the wind that betrays Midas' secret, but the action of a shepherd who makes a flute from the reeds: when cut, the reed reveals that Midas has ass' ears.[25] In a related version told by Bersuire, it is not the cutting of the reeds that reveals Midas' secret, but the music of the pipe itself, which the shepherd has just constructed: the only song it will play, says Bersuire, is *midas aures haberet asininas* (Midas has ass' ears).[26] These mythographic renditions, characteristically, consolidate and finesse details of Ovidian myths in order to give the story tighter cohesion, important both to facilitate reference and to create the fullest possible platform for moral and allegorical

---

Ovid. Pelen's application of this reading to an interpretation of the Wife's shortcomings as an Ovidian artist, furthermore, is not convincing.

[24] Robertson, "The Wife of Bath and Midas," 10, similarly notes the structural connection between the tales of Syrinx and of Midas' judgment. Furthermore, folklorists have demonstrated that the stories of Syrinx's transformation and of the revelation of Midas' secret are related to a common body of folk-myths, attested from Britain to Asia, in which reeds or other vegetation springing either from a corpse or from a "buried secret," emit a sound or message. See Crooke, "King Midas and His Ass's Ears," 196–197 and Frécaut, "Le Barbier de Midas," 153–154. It is worth adding here that the Wife's interpolation of the story of Midas' ass' ears into her Tale may well be a function of – among many other things – the folkloric value that it adds to the essentially folkloric tale of the enchanted hag.

[25] Fulgentius, *Fulgentius the Mythographer*, 3.9; *Mythographi Vaticani*, 1.89 (cf. 2.139).

[26] *Reductorium morale*, 158. All translations of Bersuire are from Reynolds' edition. Interestingly, the shepherds' transformation of the reeds into a pipe that "replays" the secret in these mythographers' versions of the stories is not a quirky medieval innovation, but a remnant of an earlier, more popular form of the folktale. Ovid's version of the tale is unusual in featuring wind-stirred reeds, rather than a musical instrument made out of reeds, as the agent of the king's embarrassment: see Frécaut, "Le Barbier de Midas," 156–157.

interpretation. For our purposes, however, the important point is that such mythographic elaborations encourage the medieval reader to recall the story's structural connection with the Syrinx myth. The widely recognised nature of this connection is confirmed, moreover, by its appearance in one of Dante's minor poems: "Do you not understand that the flute is made songful by virtue of a god and is similar to the reeds born of the whisper, the whisper that revealed the most shameful temples of the king who by order of Bromius (Bacchus) colored the Pactolian sands?" (*Tibia non sentis quod fit virtute canora | numinis et similis natis de murmure cannis, | murmure pandenti turpissima tempora Regis | qui iussu Bromii Pactolida tinxit arenam?*).[27]

Two other pieces of evidence flesh out this complex of associations among the blinding of Argus, the deafness of Midas, and the garrulousness of Midas' wife (and the Wife of Bath). The first is Arthurian, the second Ovidian. Readers of the Wife of Bath's Tale have unanimously indicted the extraneous nature of the Midas digression in this Arthurian tale; clearly, it is said, this digression illuminates the Wife's biases and biography rather than the tale she is in the process of telling, and it is in this sense that the digression has been enjoyed as a masterful bit of Ovidian play. To date, however, critics have overlooked an intriguing connection between the myth of Midas and the body of Arthurian legend on which the Wife draws for the substance of her Tale.[28] In a strange episode from Béroul's *Tristan* (1306–1350) a meddling dwarf, enemy of the lovers, reveals to the barons a secret only he knows: King Mark has horse's ears. He does this through an interesting variation on the typical narrative pattern associated with the Midas story: while drunk, the dwarf informs the barons that he knows a secret about Mark and cannot divulge it, but invites them to eavesdrop as he repeats the secret into a trench beneath the roots of a hawthorn. The barons overhear the secret and later mention it to Mark, who explains that the ears were the result of an earlier enchantment placed upon him by the dwarf and then beheads the dwarf in anger. Stories of kings with horse's or ass' ears whose secrets are embarrassingly revealed were popular in medieval Celtic folklore. King Mark in particular seems to have been

---

[27] Dante, *Eclogues* 4.50–53, cited in Barolini ("Arachne, Argus, and St. John," 215), who provides the English translation, and to whose discussion of this passage the reader is also referred.

[28] With the partial exception of Fleming, "Sacred and Secular Exegesis," 79, who makes note of the present congruence incidentally.

associated with horse's ears because "in Celtic *marc* (Welsh and Breton *march*) means 'horse'."[29] Celtic analogues of Béroul's story of Mark follow a more familiar pattern common to "tragic" versions of the folktale in other cultures: the king (March Amheirchion, a knight of Arthur's, in one Welsh version) murders not his dwarf but his barber(s), lest they reveal his secret; reeds grow on the grave-mound, and a pipe made from the reeds melodiously publicises the secret.[30] The possibility that Béroul's *Tristan* or a Celtic version of the tale inspired Chaucer to combine the story of an ass-eared king with that of an asinine Arthurian knight, prompting his turn to Ovid, deserves closer consideration than there is space to give it here, but it is important to note that the inevitable association of Mark with cuckoldry – and, specifically, with his wife's bottomless store of deceptive ploys – links this potential intertext, at least implicitly, with the point of the Wife's allusion to Argus in her Prologue: the blinding power of female speech.[31] It may well be for this reason that one Celtic statue, described by Crooke, depicts King March with both horse's ears and *horns* – the mark of the cuckold.[32]

The second piece of evidence that lends support to the Wife of Bath's strategic association of Argus with Midas involves another Ovidian shepherd with an affection for the Pan-pipes and an ocular point of distinction: this time, one eye rather than one hundred.[33] The story of Polyphemus' love of the nymph Galatea in Book Thirteen of the *Metamorphoses* (itself derived from Theocritus' *Idylls* 11, via Vergil's *Eclogues* and *Aeneid*) is relevant to our interests not because Chaucer specifically alludes to it in the Wife of Bath's Prologue or Tale – though Chaucer does translate the story of Polyphemus' blinding by Ulysses in *Boece* 4, m.7 – but because it demonstrates the broader narrative energies of the Argus story within the *Metamorphoses* and thus highlights some ways in which the elements of that story could metamorphose (in Ovid

---

[29] Béroul, *Romance of Tristan*, II, 160.

[30] See Crooke, "King Midas and His Ass's Ears," 186; and Mandach, "Midas et Marc," 109–113.

[31] It should be recalled that the climax of the Merchant's Tale – which contains an allusion to Argus, cites the Wife of Bath as an authority on marriage, and features an extended moment of female excuse-making worthy of Alison herself – counts among its analogues a scene in Béroul's *Tristan*, in which the lovers deceive Mark while he spies on them from up a tree.

[32] See Crooke, "King Midas and His Ass's Ears," 187.

[33] I owe to Maggie Kilgour the suggestion of Polyphemus' relevance to the Argus story.

as in later tradition) into new stories. Like the narrative of Pan and Syrinx in Book One, that of Polyphemus and Galatea in Book Thirteen is a story-within-a-story – and a bucolic one at that – and as such it also self-consciously reflects upon the act of storytelling.[34] The Cyclops Polyphemus reminds us of Argus because of his ocular deformity and his jealous watch over his beloved, but, in other respects, he invites comparison with Pan: emotionally involved, he plays a hyperbolic Pan-pipe made of a hundred (rather than nine) reeds (the same number of reeds as Argus has eyes, incidentally),[35] and he, like Pan, pursues an unwilling water-nymph.[36] Like Argus, he will be blinded (the event is alluded to in Telemus' prophecy, *Met.* 13.770–773); but, as in the medieval tradition of Argus, Ovid's Polyphemus understands this as *erotic* blinding – here that of love rather than deception – when he objects to Telemus' prophecy on the grounds that "another has already taken (that one eye)" (*altera iam rapuit (lumen unum)*, 13.775).[37] The thwarted conclusion of Polyphemus' wooing of Galatea also recalls the Pan/Syrinx story, with a difference: Galatea escapes, but her lover Acis is crushed by a boulder thrown by Polyphemus after a pursuit on foot. Springing from this scene of death is a reed: "and through the cracks there rose a living, tall reed" (*vivaque per rimas proceraque surgit harundo*, 13.891), which marks Acis' rebirth as a river deity. The word used for Syrinx's new form in *Met.* 1.707 – *harundo* (reed) – reappears here. Our acquaintance with the allusive geography of the Wife of Bath's treatment of the Midas story makes a final point of interest regarding *Metamorphoses* 13. The story of Polyphemus – an embedded tale, we recall – happens to be narrated in, of all places, a beachside barber-shop. Galatea tells her story to her confidante Scylla, who will later be transformed into the

---

[34] Cf. Nagle, "Trio of Love Triangles," 76–83.

[35] Vergil's *Eclogue* 2, which Ovid uses extensively (along with Theocritus' idyll) in his song of Polyphemus, mentions the origins of the Pan-pipes: "Pan it was who first taught man to make many reeds one with wax" (*Pan primum calamos cera coniungere pluris | instituit*, *Ecl.* 2.32–33). Servius' commentary on this passage relates the story of Pan's pursuit of Syrinx and her metamorphosis (Servius, III, *ad Buc.* 2.31).

[36] On Polyphemus' unconvincing nature as a pastoral character, see Farrell, "Dialogue of Genres," 244, 246. For other important studies of Ovid's treatment of the Polyphemus story, see Griffin, "Unrequited Love," and Tissol, "Polyphemus and his Audiences."

[37] On the combination of epic and elegiac conventions in Ovid's wordplay here, see Farrell, "Dialogue of Genres," 256–257, n. 53. Translations of the *Metamorphoses* are Hill's unless otherwise noted.

proverbial sea-monster, as she offers her hair to be combed (*Met.* 13.738). In fact, one of Ovid's most signal innovations in his reworking of Theocritus in this episode is his designation of Galatea as *narrator* – the whole story (even Polyphemus' wooing song) is told in her voice and from her biased perspective – rather than merely as the silent object of Polyphemus' love.[38] This sexually independent female storyteller, revealer of secrets to a hairdresser, and erotic blinder of her myopic admirer, illustrates how poetically elastic were the Ovidian traditions out of which the Wife of Bath's own poetic consciousness, so to speak, was shaped.

From this vantage point, it can be argued that Chaucer recognised the special rhetorical and narratological functions of the inset story of Syrinx in Book One of the *Metamorphoses* and transmuted the rhetorical strategies he found there not only to the Wife's manipulative fictions about her husbands' antifeminism, but also to her strategic retelling of the Midas story in her Tale. In order to recognise this, it is necessary first to outline Ovid's own handling of the Syrinx story in Book One, as it has been understood by classical scholars.

Mercury's tale of Syrinx is one that is both pointedly relevant to the situation in which Argus has involved himself, as we have seen, and one that is – ironically – intended to put Argus to sleep. Ovid playfully rises to the challenge of this tricky narratological scenario. As Murgatroyd and Konstan have shown in detail, Ovid causes Mercury – who, of course, is himself the god of eloquence – to begin the story of Syrinx in a dry, wordy style, full of unnecessary detail. Mercury gets only as far as Pan's first sight of Syrinx when Ovid cuts in with his own voice and tells the rest of the story, which includes the metamorphosis, in a more animated style.[39] It is only when he is finished that we learn that Mercury

---

[38] See Farrell, "Dialogue of Genres," 264–267.

[39] In addition to the studies of Konstan ("Death of Argus") and Murgatroyd ("Ovid's Syrinx"), briefer analyses of note are found in Rosati, "Narrative Techniques," 274–275; Wheeler, *A Discourse of Wonders*, 1–2, 80–81; Anderson, ed., *Ovid's Metamorphoses*, notes to 1.692–694, 1.709–710; Nagle, "Erotic Pursuit and Narrative Seduction," 33–34, and "Two Miniature Carmina Perpetua," 99–100. The tedium of the inset Syrinx narrative poses a problem not only for the disinterested Argus, but (potentially) for the reader as well, for whom such rape stories are all too familiar in Book One of the *Metamorphoses*; in fact, Ovid's complex narratological play with the Syrinx story seems in part designed to provide variety for the reader, as well as to accentuate the ways in which the Io story in which it is embedded is *not* just another typical rape narrative. On this point, see Konstan, "Death of Argus," 18, and cf. Ahl,

did not finish the story at all – when Ovid cut him off, Argus had fallen asleep, and Ovid went on to narrate for *us* what Mercury was *about* to tell Argus. Through this competition of narrative voices – Ovid vs. Mercury – Ovid disrupts and defers the action (Argus' beheading) through storytelling or, more precisely, through the displacement of storytelling from one narrator to another, each of whom has a different rhetorical aim. Even as Mercury's apparent failure as a storyteller, then, constitutes his success in the world of action (a sleeping Argus is a dead Argus), it is made good by the mercurial Ovid's repossession of the story.[40]

This is a subtle point that requires a good reader of Ovid to appreciate it. A case can be made that Chaucer *was* such a reader, but first it is useful to indicate how unusual such a recognition of the narratological complexity of this section of *Metamorphoses* seems to have been in the Middle Ages. The dominant trend in medieval mythographic interpretations of Book One of the *Metamorphoses* is to separate the Argus story from that of Syrinx, ignoring its nature and function as an embedded story. Hyginus and the First and Second Vatican Mythographer, for example, state that Mercury, at Jove's command, killed Argus, without any mention of how (and hence without mention of the Syrinx story).[41] Arnulf of Orléans (partly following pseudo-Lactantius Placidus) catalogues the metamorphoses of this section of Book One in the following sequence: Io from chastity into adultery, from adultery into a cow, and from a cow into a goddess; Mercury into a shepherd; Syrinx into reeds, and reeds into a pipe; Argus into a peacock. In the allegorisations themselves, Arnulf relates Mercury's murder of Argus separately from the metamorphosis of Syrinx, giving no hint of a connection between the two.[42] Giovanni del Virgilio follows suit.[43] Robert Holkot, in his commentary on the Book of Wisdom, moralises the story of Argus without mentioning Syrinx at all: in Holkot's telling, Mercury lulls Argus to sleep through music only, not storytelling.[44]

Metaformations, 155.

[40] On Mercury's success-in-failure, see Fredericks, "Divine Wit vs. Divine Folly," 244–249.

[41] Hyginus, *Fabulae* CXLV; *Mythographi Vaticani* 1.18, 2.7 (the Syrinx story is told separately at 1.124, 2.60).

[42] Arnulf, *Allegoriae*, 201, 203 (citations refer to page numbers in Ghisalberti's edition).

[43] Giovanni del Virgilio, *Allegorie*, 1.10–11.

Bersuire states that Mercury put Argus to sleep with words *and* song (*tum sermonibus tum cantibus*), but nevertheless fails to mention the Syrinx story here;[45] he tells her tale only later, in a separate episode, with no connection to Mercury's "words" – in fact, he introduces the episode by referring to *Ovid's* words: "Ovid says that Syrinx was a nymph whom the god called Pan loved" (*Dicit Ouidius quod syringa fuit quaedam Nympha quam amauit deus qui dicitur Pan*).[46] But perhaps most interesting is how the story is told in two late-medieval English mythographies, Thomas Walsingham's *De Archana Deorum* and William Caxton's English trans-lation of the *Metamorphoses*, the latter based on one of two redactions of the *Ovide moralisé* in prose. Walsingham, apparently departing from mythographic tradition, *does* preserve the embedded form of the Syrinx story within the Argus scene, but he differs pointedly from Ovid in giving Mercury the *whole* story of Syrinx to tell (which Walsingham has him narrate in a more to-the-point style than does Ovid).[47] In the *Metamorphoses* Ovid, after he comes to the end of *his* narration of the story, makes clear that Mercury did not in fact tell the bulk of this story by stating that he was "about to speak such words" (*talia dicturis*; my translation), Mercury had noticed that Argus was asleep and so dis-patched him before going any further (*Met.* 1.713). Walsingham changes Ovid's *talia dicturis* to *talia dicendo* (*speaking* such words) – thus avoiding Ovid's tricky deferral of narrative voice and disruption of plot by letting

---

[44]Holkot, *In librum Sapientiae*, lect. 37; quoted in Allen, "Mythology," 227–229.

[45]Bersuire, *Reductorium morale*, 43. Gower follows Bersuire's example in his narration of the Argus story as an exemplum against somnolence in the *Confessio Amantis*: Mercury, combining the tactics of "Musiqe" and "lusti tales," is shown by Gower to put Argus to sleep without reference to the content of his lullaby: "And in his pipinge evere among | He tolde him such a lusti song, | That he the fol hath broght aslepe" (4.3345–3347). On the thematic significance of the Argus exemplum in the *Confessio*, see Gallacher, *Love, the Word, and Mercury*, 72–75. Gower does not include the Syrinx story in the *Confessio*, but he does twice allude to it indirectly in two important moments near the end: first, Amans, in his Supplication (8.2238–2244), cites Pan (implicitly, in his capacity as failed lover of Syrinx) as a model for his own defeat by Love (here echoing *Mythographi Vaticani* 1.124, 2.60); and second, Pan himself pipes the melody of love to which the Companies of Lovers dance in the closing promenade (8.2474–89). Pan's music is balanced by the more somber melody of Elde described later in the promenade scene, in which "herde I no pipe there | To make noise in mannes Ere" (8.2675–2676).

[46]Bersuire, *Reductorium morale*, 46; trans. Reynolds, 148.

[47]Walsingham, *De archana deorum*, 44.

Mercury have his full say and then kill Argus.[48] Caxton handles Ovid similarly, presenting a more capable Mercury who does not need to be interrupted by Ovid and who tells the whole story despite Argus' nodding off. After the entire tale of Syrinx is told in Mercury's voice, Caxton states that "Whylis Mercuryus þus floytynge recounted & tolde this fable, Argus wexe aslepe and closed alle his eyen."[49]

In fact, as far as I have been able to determine, only two medieval commentaries retain Ovid's distinction between Mercury's and Ovid's voices, one notable for its sensitivity to Ovid's narrative techniques, and the other often maligned for its apparent lack thereof. The first, the Vulgate Commentary, is unusual in the attention it pays to literary technique, explicating such details as thematic or structural links between episodes and the presence of embedded narratives.[50] The Vulgate commentator points out that Mercury stops speaking when he sees Argus fall asleep, and explains, "Ovid as narrator supplies this story that Mercury had been about to tell if Argus had not yielded to sleep so quickly, saying *restabat plura* etc." (*Ouidius uero ex parte sua suplet hec que dicturus erat Mercurius nisi tam cito Argus sompno succumberet et dicit restabat plura etc.*).[51] The second instance is in the *Ovide moralisé*, which takes many liberties with Ovid in its dizzying array of allegorisations, but which, it should be remembered, is also (unlike most of the other commentaries we have surveyed) a full translation of the *Metamorphoses*, and as such concerned with the literal level of the text. In the *Ovide moralisé*, Mercury's in-progress story of Pan and Syrinx is interrupted by the narrator at the same point as it is in the *Metamorphoses*, and the poet finishes the story in his own voice, just as Ovid does.[52] The poet of the *Ovide moralisé*, however, reverts to medieval precedent when he goes on to allegorise the Argus/Io and Pan/Syrinx stories separately; unlike the Vulgate commentator, he has nothing to say about the function or

---

[48] Similarly, Bonsignori's *Ovidio Metamorphoseos Vulgare* gives Mercury the full story, stating at its end that "Avendo Mercurio ditte queste parole ad Argo," Mercury beheads Argus (I.xxxvii).

[49] Caxton, *Metamorphoses of Ovid*, I, 1.19.

[50] See Coulson, "The *Vulgate* Commentary," 29–61, and the Introduction to the same author's edition of the Vulgate Commentary.

[51] The Latin text is quoted from Coulson, "A Study of the 'Vulgate' Commentary," 341–342. The translation is my own. I am grateful to Professor Coulson for his help construing the Vulgate commentator's Latin.

[52] *Ovide moralisé*, 1.3702–3732. The action involving Mercury and Argus resumes at 1.3733.

motivation of Ovid's layered narrative style in this sequence. Indeed, the *Ovide moralisé*-poet's retention of this stylistic feature of Ovid may best be explained as an unreflective by-product of literal translation.[53]

The sharp contrast between these workmanlike mythographic handlings of Ovid's sequence of stories and the Wife of Bath's approach to Ovidian myth suggests that Chaucer – never a slavish follower of medieval precedent – intentionally resisted the narratological example of the mythographies in his treatment of Argus and Midas. Chaucer appears not only to have understood Ovid's use of dual narrative voices and strategies of rhetorical deferral, but to have followed his Roman master in capitalising upon these techniques. Most remarkably, Chaucer accomplishes this not through a re-translation of the Syrinx story itself, but instead by reshaping the (connected) Midas story in its rhetorical image. Crucially, in the Wife of Bath's strategic retelling of the Midas tale, the conclusion (i.e., the reeds' revelation of the secret) is deferred, and we must *read Ovid* (the Wife's explicit advice) in order to find out the rest – just as, in Book One of the *Metamorphoses*, Mercury's narration is deferred, and we must quite literally "read Ovid" – the version of the tale told in the author's voice – in order to discover what happened to Syrinx. Furthermore, both Ovid's Syrinx story and the Wife's Midas exemplum are inset stories – ostensibly digressions – within self-consciously oral narratives and both have a larger significance than the unwary (or sleepy) auditor may realise.

The apparent gap in sophistication between the mythographies and Chaucer may be filled by the poet to whom Chaucer turned for the hag's sermon on *gentilesse* in the Wife of Bath's Tale. It is indeed possible that in the matter of Argus and Midas, as elsewhere, Dante guided Chaucer's reading of Ovid. Dante's two references to Argus in the *Commedia* – both in the *Purgatorio* and both involving the distinction between fallen and visionary sight[54] – notably employ the rhetorical

---

[53] The sophistication of the *Ovide moralisé*-poet as a redactor of Ovid should not be underestimated, however. The best available analysis of the poet's hermeneutics is Blumenfeld-Kosinski, *Reading Myth*, 90–136, which argues that the Christian poet exploits the frictions inherent in his interpretive project in order to present himself as a "new Ovid."

[54] See Barolini's insightful discussion of the thematic significance of these two Dantean passages, in "Arachne, Argus, and St. John," 216–221, and *Undivine Comedy*, 155–165. Barolini does not comment upon Dante's Ovidian strategies of deferral in these passages, however; nor does she observe the connection to Chaucer outlined

strategy of deferral in a way that is similar to the Ovidian and Chaucerian passages under examination. In *Purgatorio* 32, the song that accompanies the pageant of revelation induces slumber in Dante in terms that recall the sleep of Argus: "The hymn that company then chanted | is not sung on earth nor could I make it out, | nor bear to hear that music to its end" (*Io non lo 'ntesi, né qui non si canta | l'inno che quella gente allor cantaro, | né la nota soffersi tutta quanta*, 61–63). Dante then explicitly invokes the story of Argus in an elaborate *occupatio* (64–69) in which he denies the ability to describe how Argus' eyes closed as he listened to the story of Syrinx, just as the poet is unable to describe his own sleep at this crucial moment. The unfulfilled description is then deferred – like Ovid's story of Syrinx itself – to a more capable storyteller: "But let him, who can do it, portray his nodding off" (*ma qual vuol sia che l'assonnar ben finga*, 69). In *Purgatorio* 29, which describes an earlier part of the same pageant, the eyes that cover the wings of the four beasts are likened to the eyes of Argus (which Juno placed on her peacock after the guard's death); again, as in *Purgatorio* 32, the description is deferred to a fitter authority: "To describe their forms, reader, I do not spend | more rhymes, for other outlay so constrains me | I cannot deal more lavishly in this. | Go read Ezechiel" (*A descriver lor forme più non spargo | rime, lettor; ch'altra spesa mi strigne | tanto ch'a questa non posso esser largo; | ma leggi Ezechïel*, *Purg*. 29.97–100). This last line especially seems to anticipate the Wife of Bath's directive in her Tale: "The remenant of the tale if ye wol heere, | Redeth Ovyde, and ther ye may it leere" (981–982).

Dante may have functioned as a mediator for Chaucer's reading of Ovid, then, but there is no doubt that Chaucer's narratological experimentation in the Wife of Bath's Prologue and Tale resulted from a direct engagement with Ovid's *Metamorphoses*. The performance value of the stories in question reveals another link between the concerns of the English and the Roman authors. Like Ovid, who plays upon the notion of a dual audience, the Wife too, in both her Prologue and her Tale, adapts her rhetorical strategies to dual ends: first, to refute what she sees as the groundless authority of her past husbands and all they represent, and second, to convince, and even perhaps seduce, her immediate audience, the Canterbury pilgrims. (She freely acknowledges, after all, that she is actively seeking husband number six and that pilgrimages are as good a setting as any for "wandrynge by the weye"; General Prologue, 467).[55]

above.

These two aims, indeed, are mutually implicated in a way that strikingly anticipates Chambers' characterisation, in his study of nineteenth-century fiction, of the erotic dimensions of storytelling (which, to Chambers, by its very nature dramatises a struggle for authority): "seduction, producing authority where there is no power, is a means of converting (historical) weakness into (discursive) strength."[56]

In this broader narratological sense what the Wife of Bath has learned from Book One of Ovid's *Metamorphoses* resonates beyond her particular manipulation of the Midas story. The Wife's Prologue and, to a lesser extent, her Tale, rest centrally upon strategies of deferral or, to borrow a term from Patterson and Parker, dilation. Whereas Patterson traces the rhetorical precedent of dilation to La Vieille's speech in the *Roman de la rose*, there is an equally compelling precedent for this in the *Metamorphoses*.[57] The length of the Wife's preamble, the interruptions of fellow pilgrims as well as her own non-sequiturs and self-interrup-

---

[55] Indeed, the Wife of Bath employs seduction as a rhetorical strategy in a way that is thoroughly Ovidian in resonance, echoing both Ovid's Dipsas and the *magister* of the *Ars amatoria*. Sharrock's characterisation of the *Ars amatoria*'s techniques of narrative seduction could be applied just as aptly to the Wife of Bath's Prologue and Tale: "it holds on to us, controls us, keeps us spellbound, embraces us with the erotics of its text. The poem inflames our poetic and erotic interest by its delay: it holds us back to hold on to us" (*Seduction and Repetition*, 24). See further Sharrock, 21–86, and on the connection between Dipsas and the *Ars amatoria*, 84–86. Nagle's studies of the techniques of narrative and erotic seduction in the embedded narratives of the *Metamorphoses* are also pertinent ("Erotic Pursuit and Narrative Seduction," 32–51; "A Trio of Love Triangles," 75–98). Cf. Patterson's description of the effect of feminine rhetoric on the shape of the *Roman de la rose* (and, by extension, the Wife of Bath's Prologue and Tale): "(Jean de Meun) manages to translate the central Ovidian principle of amorous delay into stylistic terms and to show with impressive specificity how rhetorical structure can bear erotic value" ("Feminine Rhetoric," 329).

[56] Chambers, *Story and Situation*, 212; further, 205–223.

[57] Patterson does briefly suggest a correlation between the Wife's deferred Midas story and the larger rhetorical pattern of her Prologue, with its "delayed narrative moment(s)" ("Feminine Rhetoric," 334). My reading differs from his, however, in reading the Argus sequence of *Metamorphoses* 1 as the real heart of this phenomenon. Pelen, "Chaucer's Wife of Midas Reconsidered," 141–160, argues for a different kind of Ovidian narrative influence upon the Wife of Bath's Tale in particular. According to Pelen, Chaucer's implicit poetic judgment of his characters, inspired by Ovid's penchant for scenes of contest and judgment in the *Metamorphoses*, renders the multivalence of the Tale ironic. Pelen's reliance on overly abstract concepts of style and influence, however, weakens his argument.

tions, and the embedding of smaller stories within the fabric of both Prologue and Tale all serve to dilate the narrative. The argumentative style of her Prologue is notoriously associative and circular, and the rhetorical moves in her Tale are problematically jarring and unexpected.[58] All this is not accidental. Indeed, it is a facet of the tale as *performance*: applying her expertise in timing in matters of sexual deception to the narrative foreplay at hand, the Wife intentionally takes her time in making her points. The story of her fourth husband in her Prologue, for instance, strays to the extent that the Wife repeats twice, in the space of thirty lines, the intention that (452; cf. 480) "Now wol I speke of my fourthe housbonde." Similarly, the promise of the Tale itself is mentioned and deferred throughout the Prologue, appearing as early as line 193 (the Prologue swells to over 850 lines). Indeed, the Tale's status as the anticipated prize of the narrative is undermined by the Prologue's own breakdown into tales – the Wife's adventures with her five husbands – which seem, at one point, to become the *real* "tale." The potential of stories to multiply seems almost infinite, as the Wife's recollection of her fifth husband's misogyny itself burgeons into multiple stories: namely, the inset narratives of the wicked wives in Jankyn's book. In the Tale, likewise, the story of the knight's quest to save himself, sidetracked on a technicality after it has barely begun, spawns the story of Midas. The Wife disorients us through digression, confounding our preconceived expectations of what narrative *should* be, and she does so, crucially, by tapping into the unpredictable energies of Ovidian *carmen perpetuum*. The Wife is more than simply a nightmarish fulfilment of clerical fears regarding female speech,[59] for she shares with Ovid a delight in the sensuality and embeddedness of narrative, an awareness of the human attraction to stories as capsules of surprise and

---

[58] Weil, "Freedom through Association?," 27–41, proposes that the Wife's associative argumentative style dramatises the Aristotelian principle of women's inability to maintain the proper hierarchy of memory and emotion (and hence to deliberate effectively). McKinley in part anticipates the present argument when she suggests (in passing) that the surprising thematic shifts of the Wife of Bath's Tale are influenced by Ovid's employment of "dramatic juxtaposition" in the *Metamorphoses* ("The Silenced Knight," 361; on this point, cf. Dimmick, "Ovid in the Middle Ages," 270–272, and, more generally, the argument of Fyler, *Chaucer and Ovid*). I have endeavoured to show that the influence of Ovid's narratological techniques upon the Wife's Prologue and Tale are at once more extensive and more deeply situated than these studies allow.

[59] A summary of this tradition is available in Burns, *Bodytalk*, 76–79.

pleasure. She also recognises the power of stories to control and deceive, to reshape or manipulate reality. Like Ovid in his exile poetry, the Wife too is ultimately a victim of the texts that have shaped her, a page torn out of a book to which she has no further rights.[60] The Wife is, in certain respects, a bad storyteller – a Mercury who both teaches her audience something it desperately needs to know and (like the lecturing hag in her Tale, perhaps) also risks putting her audience to sleep. Her rhetorical strategies are both in and out of her control, much like the female narrators in another Ovidian text, the *Heroides*, with whom she shares a propensity for what Jacobson has called the internalisation of myth: "Seemingly objective conditions take on shades and nuances of signifi-cance that attach themselves to the events only after they have lost their independence as facts and become part of the mental and emotional world of the heroine: the past is re-created – or created – in the light of the present."[61]

The complex of rhetorical and thematic associations that surrounds the Wife's connected manipulations of the Argus and Midas myths ultimately impinges upon Chaucer's representation of storytelling itself – and its motivations – in the person of the Wife of Bath. It also helps us understand the relation between her Prologue and Tale in a new way: for in the Tale we encounter a story which, like that of Jove and Io, involves rape, remorse, and metamorphosis. The metamorphosis of the hag from ugly to beautiful, like the Wife's version of the Argus and Midas stories, pivots upon the power of female speech to persuade through rhetoric. It also carries the implication that the magical trans-formation itself may be nothing more than a trick of the eyes, in which the young knight either learns to see correctly or, to read the scene more negatively, becomes blinded (like Argus) to the "reality" of his wife.

McGILL UNIVERSITY

---

[60] The best account of the Wife's distillation of the complex potential of Ovidian *artes* is Calabrese, *Chaucer's Ovidian Arts*, 81–111. The terms of Calabrese's argument are different from mine, but largely compatible with the claims presented in this paragraph.

[61] Jacobson, *Ovid's Heroides*, 356.

The Metamorphoses of Metals: Ovid and the Alchemists

Thomas Willard

Of Ovid's many faces during the late Middle Ages and early modern era surely the strangest is that of the alchemical philosopher: the authority on metamorphosis whose words and stories can guide the aspiring adept. Perhaps it was inevitable that the poet of love and change should be quoted in texts about chemical affinities and reactions, as later generations would call them, especially when the texts were written in Latin by authors schooled on Ovid. It seemed all the more natural at a time when the seven common metals were known by the names of their presiding gods: lead and tin were Saturn and Jupiter, iron and copper were Mars and Venus, gold and silver were Apollo and Cynthia, and quicksilver was (and remains) Mercury. A story about the gods was easily construed as a chemical allegory. For example, the story of Hermaphroditus, born of the union of Mercury and Venus and joined with the nymph Salmacis,[1] was searched for clues about the Rebis: the alchemical enigma of the double natured thing (literally, *res bis*). Accompanying a seventeenth-century engraving of Hermaphroditus is a motto stating "that the Hermaphrodite is born on two mountains," which the modern editor takes to be the opposing principles of mercury and sulphur (fig. 8.1).[2]

Modern students of Ovid have marvelled at the perversity of searches like these. Eighty years ago, the Harvard classicist Edward Kennard Rand described a fifteenth-century manuscript that purports to translate tales of metamorphosis into French verse:

> Ovid's text is made a quarry for the alchemist's pick and shovel … The fable of Deucalion and Pyrrha, for instance, betokens, like the twin peaks of Parnassus, the masculine and the feminine elements among the metals, that is, gold and silver, from the union of which the philosopher's stone

---

[1] See *Met.* 4.274–388. Book and line references are to the Miller edition.

[2] Maier, *Atalanta fugiens*, ed. de Jong, 252, 254. The engraving is reproduced on p. 414.

is produced. In this fashion, the whole poem is subjected to the fatal touch of Midas; Ovid's gold is converted into the baser metal.[3]

A more recent scholar has remarked that readers of this *poème baroque* will be surprised to find Deucalion and Pyrrha alongside figures such as King Solomon and the Spanish mystic Ramon Lull.[4] One may well ask why anyone would venture what now seem such deliberate misconstructions of the *Metamorphoses*.

This is not strictly a modern question, of the sort raised during the Scientific Revolution, and an answer to it will be offered later. Even before it surfaced in attacks on alchemy, it was voiced and implied in works by serious writers on the subject. Indeed, it came up in one of the first printed books of alchemy. The *Pretiosa margarita novella* or "New Pearl of Great Price" was printed in 1546, at the famous Aldine Press in Venice, and was reprinted in several important collections. The work is usually attributed to Pietro Boni, a physician of Ferrara, though the explicit states that he simply edited the manuscript.[5] In any case, the manuscript is said to have been prepared in the 1330s, less than two centuries after the first books of alchemy were written in Latin or translated into Latin from Arabic. Set up as an academic debate and using methods taught in medieval universities like Ferrara's, it promises to determine whether alchemy "is both apparent and existent or only apparent and nonexistent," as the full title explains. It concludes, of course, that alchemy is real and that the secret procedure is "The New Pearl of Great Price" (*Pretiosa margarita novella*) for which the wise will sell all else (Matthew 13:45). It does not disclose the secret, but simply suggests ways of solving the problem and discovering the philosophers' stone.

Midway through the book there is a chapter "Of the ferment and its conditions, properties, and conversion, as performed according the philosophers of this art." The ferment is described as the *sine qua non* "without which the art of Alchemy cannot be performed and per-

---

[3] Rand, *Ovid and His Influence*, 141. Rand refers to "Le grand Olympe," a poem preserved in several manuscripts, notably Bibliothèque de l'Arsenal MS 2516 and BnF MS 14789 (3032). The author and his circle are discussed in Fulcanelli, *The Dwellings of the Philosophers*, 107–115.

[4] See *Nicolas Valois, Les cinq livres*, ed. Roger, 28; cf. 274.

[5] *Pretiosa margarita*, in *Theatrum chemicum*, 5:713. See Ferguson, *Bibliotheca chemica*, 1:115, 2:2–3. All translations are mine, unless otherwise noted.

fected," and the philosophers are said to discuss it *dupliciter* (duplicitously). On the one hand, they speak in terms of metals to explain how the work is performed, while, on the other, they use language that is "veiled" and "most occult" to hint at the secret of how the work is perfected.[6] Indeed, the discussion has to go beyond metals because the ferment is generally understood in alchemy as the process by which the soul of a substance is separated from the body and then reunited.[7] Our author gives examples of this most occult or secret language, which turns out to be very close to the language of myth. He explains that poets like Vergil and Ovid use both *historiae fictae* (made-up stories) and *fabulae mirandae* (marvellous tales) and do not write *metaphysica* (philosophy), but he asserts that their poems have a "foundation in the truth hidden in the mind of the poet, so that from poems the hidden truth regarding the wisdom of the sun [that is, of alchemical gold] can be discerned. Otherwise, indeed, neither the poems nor the images can be judged, and every poem and figure can be extended to many significations."[8] The answer to the question "Why look for answers in Ovid?" seems to be that he knew about almost everything, as Macrobius said of Vergil. And *if* the poet knew the answers, they could be found in the poetry, no matter how much he hid them.

After a series of examples from Vergil, the *Pretiosa margarita novella* gives five instances of hidden gold in Ovid (*aurum in Ovidio occultatum*).[9] The stories cited here, and summarised each in one sentence, are all immediately familiar: Phaethon and the chariot of the sun, Theseus and the Minotaur, Medea and Aeson, Jason and the Golden Fleece, Pyramus and Thisbe. Each, however, has an added twist, found in alchemical retellings but not in Ovid's poem. Phaeton enters the chariot "on a sunbeam congealed by prayer" which, for anyone schooled in the doctrine of correspondences, means on a piece of gold:

> And such is the fable of Phaethon, in the *Metamorphoses* of Ovid (2.1–400), who entered the house of the sun on a sunbeam congealed by prayer,

---

[6] *Pretiosa margarita*, in *Theatrum chemicum*, 5:607.

[7] Abraham, *A Dictionary of Alchemical Imagery*, 74.

[8] *Pretiosa margarita*, in *Theatrum chemicum*, 5:616. The abridged English translation omits this passage; for the surrounding text see *New Pearl of Great Price*, 258–259.

[9] *Pretiosa margarita*, in *Theatrum chemicum*, 5:615. The references to Vergil include wax images (*Ecl.* 8.72–81), the figure of Proteus (*Georg.* 4.422–452), the aegis of Minerva (*Aen.* 8. 407–453), and the golden bough (*Aen.* 6.136–148). Ovid refers to the last of these (*Met.* 14.113–114), as other alchemists noted.

walked about, and went up to his father; and who began to drive the chariot of the sun and its steeds, which, coming too close to the earth, were incinerated, etc.

Theseus saps the Minotaur's strength by introducing a golden substance into the labyrinth, which suggests adding sulphur to react with the poisonous form of mercury:

> And this is the same author's fable of the intricate building that is called the Labyrinth, in the isle of Crete, which once entered has one true exit and many false, in which was kept the man-eating Minotaur, and into which a large weight of gold made from animal fat and wax was thrown by Theseus, who, having enchanted the beast and sapped its strength, killed it with his weapons (8.152–182).

Medea teaches Aeson how to rejuvenate himself and helps him find an assistant to regulate the flame under her cauldron, which suggests that the alchemist must work on himself but with great care:

> And this is the same writer's fable of the old man taught by Medea, who, wanting to rejuvenate himself, severed the members of his entire anatomy and stewed them in water until it was thoroughly boiling, but no more, whereupon all the members swam into place and he was made young; however, when the watchman slept before the boiling was stopped, all the members dispersed on the surface and he did not revive, etc. (7.262–294).

Jason slays the dragon and sows "dragon's teeth," a term alchemists used for the sublimate of mercury: "And this is the hidden gold in Ovid. And this is the serpent which Jason slew, whose teeth he sowed, and from which armed men sprang."[10] Finally, the white mulberry fruit, onto which the blood of Pyramus and Thisbe falls, is first coloured black and then red, thus recalling the three stages of the alchemical process: the black work, the white work, and the red work, signifying death, life, and transformation: "And this is the fable of the mulberries, which were white at first and then were made black and red because of the

---

[10] The *Pretiosa margarita* conflates two passages from the *Argonautica*: the sowing of teeth in Book Three, where they are said to come from a serpent slain by Cadmus, and the drugging of the dragon guarding the fleece in Book Four. Ovid treats the passages separately in *Met.* 3.104–110, where Cadmus sows the teeth, and *Met.* 7.149–158, respectively.

outpouring of the blood of Pyramus, who for the love Thisbe, whom he believed slain by a wild beast, stabbed himself near a mulberry tree" (5.83–166). Only in this last example do the alchemists seem to be reading Ovid closely: Thisbe asks for the mulberry tree to bear fruit that is *pullos* (black, 4.160), but the poet calls it *pomo* (dark red, 4.165). The words *nigra* and *rubea* in the commentary correspond to the alchemists' names for the first and third stages of their work, *nigredo* and *rubedo*. In the other examples, words to the wise seem to be the details added to Ovid. This allows the author to conclude: "And, in brief, this is every strange, impossible transformation the storytellers tell."

Again, these are said to be examples from earlier treatises of alchemy. Most of them were reiterated in subsequent treatises and became closely associated with the art. The Cretan labyrinth came to represent the difficulties facing the alchemist, while Jason's ship, the Argo, represented the alchemical vessel and the Argonauts' quest the alchemical process itself. Other tales were cautionary: warnings not to overheat the chariot, as Phaeton did, and not to cook the solution too long, as happens in the alternate ending of Aeson's story. A beautiful illustration of Aeson's story, dating from the sixteenth century, shows a dove above the old man's head, as a sign that the "ferment" has succeeded and the soul is returning to the body (fig. 8.2).[11] The accompanying explanation, written by Salomon Trismosin, states:

> Ovid, the ancient poet, indicated something similar when he wrote of the wise old man who wanted to be made young again. He is said to have had himself cut up and boiled until he was perfectly cooked, and no more, then his members would unite again and be rejuvenated with great strength.[12]

A seventeenth-century version of the image shows the alchemist standing in the vessel, sword in hand, ready to do all the work himself.[13]

Trismosin seems simply to be translating the *Pretiosa margarita novella*. Other writers returned *ad fontes* and recommended comparing

---

[11] British Library, Harley MS 3469, "*Splendor solis.*" The image appears under the title "Boiling the body in the vessel" on the Alchemy Website (http://www.lev-ity.com/alchemy/ss11.html).

[12] Trismosin, *Splendor solis*, 30; cf. McLean's commentary on this emblem as "The Bath of Transformation," 91. Also cf. Roob, *Hermetic Museum*, 198.

[13] Isaacus, *Die Hand der Philosophen*, 30; reproduced in Klossowski de Rola, *The Golden Game*, [1].

the accounts of Jason's quest in the *Metamorphoses* and the *Argonautica* of Apollodorus Rhodius.[14] Gianfrancesco Pico della Mirandola, nephew of the Italian humanist Giovanni Pico della Mirandola, wrote that he compared the Latin and Greek authors and consulted a text by the Byzantine scholar Michael Psellus in order to see what was hidden "under the veils of fables and the clouds of enigmas." He concluded that "Jason sailed to Colchos on the quest of the Argonauts to seize, not the golden sheepskin of Phrygia, but a parchment of ram's membrane on which the process of making gold was described."[15] This view was popularised in a three-book epyllion on goldmaking, written by the Humanist poet Augurellus at the same time as Pico's treatise (1515).[16] Cornelius Agrippa, writing *Of the Vanitie and Vncertaintie of the Artes and Sciences*, joked about those who "thinke that the skinne of the golden fleese was a booke of Alcumie written upon a skinne after the manner of the auncients, wherein was conteined the knowledge to make golde."[17] He went on to write about the perversity of alchemists, but he showed the same reliance on Ovid in his *Three Books of Occult Philosophy*, where he quoted no other authority than the *Metamorphoses* in chapters "Of the wonderfull Natures of Water, Aire, and Winds" and "Of the occult Vertues of things."[18]

Agrippa's pronouncements on the Golden Fleece had some influence even on English literature. The Elizabethan satirist Thomas Nashe read Agrippa and noted, "Cornelius Agrippa maketh mention of some philosophers that held the skin of the sheep that bare the golden fleece to be nothing but a book of alchemy written upon it."[19] And Nashe's friend Ben Jonson had the aspiring adept in his satiric drama *The Alchemist* say: "I haue a peece of *Iason*'s fleece, too, | Which was no other, then a Booke of *Alchemie*, | Writ in large sheep-skin, a good fat Ram-Vellam."[20] Later in the play, Jonson's character is asked why he

---

[14] See Faivre, *Toison d'or et alchimie*. For a twentieth-century interpretation by a practising alchemist see Fulcanelli, *Le Mystère des cathédrales*, 155.

[15] Pico della Mirandola, *Opus aureum de auro*, in *Theatrum chemicum*, 2:324.

[16] Augurello, *Chrysopoeia*, Book Two, in *Theatrum chemicum*, 3:213–228. See Martels, "Augurello's *Chrysopoeia* (1615)."

[17] Agrippa, *The Vanitie and Vncertaintie of Arts and Sciences*, 158.

[18] Agrippa, *The Three Books of Occult Philosophy*, 11–18, 24–25 (1.6, 1.10). See Müller-Jahncke, "The Attitude of Agrippa von Nettesheim."

[19] Nash, *Nashes Lenten Stuff*, 40.

[20] Jonson, *The Alchemist*, D1v (2.1.89–91); see Abraham, 59–60.

did not try to convince another possible dupe by drawing attention to the allegorical character of the art: "Are not the choysest *Fables* of the *Poets,* | That were the Fountaines, and first Springs of *Wisedome*, | Wrapt in perplexed *Allegories*?"[21]

Francis Bacon dignified this allegorical method with the name acroamatic, meaning heard by initiates, as distinguished from the magisterial method used by schoolmasters.[22] He referred famously to the natural science in the myths of Vergil and Ovid as *The Wisdome of the Ancients.* In the book of that title, he took thirty-one figures from classical myth and interpreted each in the manner of Euhemerus, that is, in physical terms. In the twenty-ninth essay, on "Proserpina, or Spirit," he followed the legend of Proserpina as told in Book Five of the *Metamorphoses*, but he construed the goddess who cannot be kept underground as the spirit that cannot be confined in matter:

> By *Proserpina* the Auncients meant that aethereall spirite which (being separated from the vpper globe) is shut vp and detained vnder the earth (represented by *Pluto* which the Poet well expressed thus.
>
>> Siue recens tellus, seductuq; nuper ab alto
>> Aethere, cognati retinebat semina coeli.
>> Whither the youngling Tellus (that of late
>> Was from the high-reard Aether separate)
>> Did yet containe her teeming wombe within
>> The liuing seeds of Heauen, her nearest kin. (*Met.* 1.80–81)
>
> This spirit is fained to be rapted by the Earth, because nothing can with-hold it when it hath time and leasure to escape. It is therefore caught and stayed by a sudden contraction, no other wise then if a man should goe about to mixe ayre with wather, which can be done by no meanes, but by a speedy and rapid agitation, as may be seene in froth, wherein the ayre is rapted by the water.[23]

Bacon was openly sceptical of the alchemists if "in this regarde they set their *Elixar* to effect golden mountains, and the restoring of natural bodies, as it were, from the portal of Hell."[24] Nevertheless, he followed the interpretive strategies of the alchemists. "Indeed," says the Bacon

---

[21]Jonson, *The Alchemist*, E2r (2.3.205–207).

[22]*Oxford English Dictionary*, "acroamatic," *a.*; "magistral" *a.* 2; citing *The Advancement of Learning*.

[23]Bacon, *The Wisdome of the Ancients*, 158–159.

[24]Bacon, *The Wisdome of the Ancients*, 163.

scholar Charles W. Lemmi, "one is irresistibly reminded of the alchemists in reading the essay on Proserpine."[25]

It was a contemporary of Bacon, Count Michael Maier, who
elaborated the alchemical reading of Ovid to the fullest. It was Maier –
whose work Lemmi cites as a possible sign of Bacon's influence[26] – who
did the most to establish alchemy as the key to all mythologies. And it
was Maier whose many books with their gorgeous engravings helped to
define the new philosophy known as Rosicrucian. His longest book,
Symbola aureae mensae (1617), recorded the sayings (*symbola*) of sages
from twelve nations. Following speeches by representatives of Egyptian,
Hebrew, and Greek alchemy, a monk named Morienus gets up, straight
out of medieval tradition, to discourse on Roman alchemy. He names
all the great poets from Lucretius to Vergil and, in the final sentence,
Ovid: "Ovid too, with all those metamorphoses of the gods and
goddesses collected in one volume, appears to have tasted secretly of
nature and of the working of occult arts, which although not themselves
discussed, still are hidden under the wraps of fables and can easily be
discovered."[27] In a marginal note beside this last sentence Maier wrote
that "Ovid enjoys the reputation of being the father of philosophic
secrets." On the next pages, he answered the objection that gold-making
is merely a poetic fiction: "I respond to the major objection, that it is
equivocal whether 'the authors of fables truly understood the words' or
whether such things really existed in nature and the fables were made
to seem obscure and enigmatic to us, given the weakness of our
reason."[28] If the poets consciously invented nonsense stories, Maier
reasons, then the objection holds; if not, their texts are open to
interpretation. He is not far from the *if* of Pietro Boni in the *Pretiosa
margarita novella* three centuries earlier. Boni said the alchemical interpretation would be valid if hidden in the poet's mind. Maier said it was
valid unless the poet clearly thought otherwise. What seemed fabulous
might simply point up the reader's lack of reason.

Maier's own poetic practice shows that he built on the words of
Ovid, adding knowledge he had gained from many other sources.
Toward the end of his large book of *Symbola*, he included a "subtle
allegory" about the search for the mythical phoenix and its secret.[29] And

---

[25] Lemmi, *The Classic Deities in Bacon*, 77.

[26] Lemmi, *The Classic Deities in Bacon*, 144.

[27] Maier, *Symbola aureae mensae*, 181.

[28] Maier, *Symbola aureae mensae*, 185.

at the end of the allegory he wrote a pair of poems on the legend. The first was an encomium of the phoenix in which Maier described the bird's nest with the cassia bark that Ovid mentions.[30] The second was a set of elegiacs "On the Hermetic Medicine of the Phoenix," where the phoenix has both the sacred and secular dimensions that Panofsky found in Renaissance iconography associated with the bird.[31] He prefaced the poems with lines thanking Apollo for revealing the secret of the phoenix through an interpreter,[32] which could mean in the words of a poet, and followed them with a statement that sums up his scientific and literary attitudes: "If anyone will not acknowledge the force of reason, he must needs have recourse to authority."[33] Ovid is an *auctoritas*, for Maier. Those who will not accept Maier's reasoning about the bird and the panacea should bow to Ovid's authority.

Maier quoted Ovid in most of his other books, as J.B. Craven's bibliographical study of those works reveals. In what may be his best-known work, the sumptuously printed *Atalanta fugiens*, Maier elaborated on many of Ovid's tales, including that of Atalanta and Hippomenes. He offered a series of seventy-nine emblems, each with a motto, a copperplate engraving by Theodore de Bry, a poem in Latin and German, and a prose commentary. He even set the poems to music as fugues for three voices.[34] He included the account of Hermaphroditus, mentioned earlier, with such Ovidian details as the similarity of Hermaphroditus and Cupid (4.321). His learned editor H.M.E. de Jong believes Maier is closest to Ovid when reworking the story of Venus and Adonis.

In the motto above emblem 41, Maier described the scene in the engraving (fig. 8.3): "Adonis is killed by a boar and Venus, rushing up to him, painted the roses red with her blood."[35] This represents a clear departure from Ovid, where the blood is that of Adonis (10.728–733), but it is a necessary departure as Venus is to transform the dead body by

---

[29] Maier, *Symbola aureae mensae*, 561–607; reprinted in *Musaeum hermeticum*, 703–740, and translated in *Hermetic Museum*, 2:201–223.

[30] Maier, *Symbola aureae mensae*, 606; cf. *Met.* 15.398.

[31] Maier, *Symbola aureae mensae*, 607; cf. *Hermetic Museum*, 2:223, and Panofsky, *Renaissance and Renascences in Western Art*, 37.

[32] Maier, *Symbola aureae mensae*, 607.

[33] *Hermetic Museum*, 2:223.

[34] Maier, *Atalanta fugiens*, ed. Godwin.

[35] Maier, *Atalanta fugiens*, ed. de Jong, 263; the figure appears on 427.

adding something of herself. There is a further departure in the epigram beneath the engraving. After a couplet to remind us that metamorphosis runs in the family, Adonis being the son of Myrrha, who was changed into a myrrh tree (10.489–502), there are two couplets that read:

> Accurrit Venus & pede læsa cruore ruborem
>   Contulit ipsa rosæ, quæ prius alba fuit.
> Flet Dea (flent Syri, luctus communis in orbe est)
>   Illum lactucis mollibus & posuit.

> (Venus rushed up and, wounding her foot, / She herself coloured red with her blood the rose, which had been white at first. / The Goddess weeps – the Syrians weep, and the whole world is plunged into deep mourning. / And she put Adonis down under the tender lettuce.)[36]

Why lettuce instead of Ovid's anemone (10.735–739)? There is, of course, a play on the words *lactuca* (lettuce) and *luctus* (mourning), and perhaps a further play on *lac* (milk), a common synonym for quicksilver. In addition, Ovid's Venus mentions Menthe, the nymph transformed into mint, when she announces the metamorphosis of Adonis into the windflower (10.728–730). Maier may suggest the use of sympathetic magic on Venus' part: she may apply the cool moist leaves of lettuce to the object of her overheated love in order to free herself from it. In Galenic medicine, physicians prescribed the leaves and even the seeds of lettuce to subdue sexual passion and cure lovesickness. Indeed, a medical text of Maier's time told of Venus using lettuce for just this purpose.[37]

Maier insists that Adonis is the child of incest and explains that kinship is a necessity when it comes to alchemy: "For in this art nothing is achieved, if not father and daughter, or mother and son are united, and if from this union no birth results. The nearer the spouses are to each other, the more fertile they will be."[38] Maier's first modern translator, de Jong, comments:

---

[36] Maier, *Atalanta fugiens*, ed. de Jong, 263.

[37] Ferrand, *Treatise of Lovesickness*, 321. Ferrand wrote a treatise on erotomania (1610), condemned by the Parlement in Toulouse (1620) and apparently suppressed; his retelling of Ovid's story (1623) may have been influenced by Maier's (1617). Both men were physicians, and wrote principally for their peers. I owe this reference to Dr. Julia Branna Perlman.

[38] Maier, *Atalanta fugiens*, ed. de Jong, 264.

Adonis came into existence from the incestuous union between Cinyras and Myrrha, that is to say that all manifestations come from one primary matter and therefore all differentiations, which can be perceived, are related to that one starting-point. Adonis is killed by a wild animal, in other words the Lapis Philosophorum is killed in the first instance, it is the stage of the putrefactio[n]. The love of Venus and Adonis – now turning into the motif of the white roses – completes the process; the white roses are the symbols of the "whiteness," which precedes the coming into being of the "tinctura rubea"; Venus colours the white roses red.[39]

De Jong adds a black stage to the red and white of Ovid's legend, much as the author of *Pretiosa margarita novella* added a stage to the story of Pyramus and Thisbe. Another commentator follows suit:

The emblem illustrates the Dissolution (Death) of the Subject (dissolved by the marital Dissolvent), which brings about the Blackness (*nigredo*). According to Maier's text, Venus places her dead lover under tender lettuce leaves, thereby indicating the Reincrudation. Her blood colours the White Rose Red, because, beyond the long night of Death, Whiteness is eventually reached, and ultimately Whiteness is Tinged with the Redness of perfect Fixity.[40]

For all the sophistication in Maier's verse and de Bry's engraving, we have not come very far from the "hidden gold" in the Ovid of three centuries earlier. Nor would readings progress so much as they would repeat.

The title of this article, "The Metamorphosis of Metals," is taken from a Latin treatise by one Eirenaeus Philalethes, a "peaceful lover of anonymity" whose identity has been guessed but not finally established.[41] A generation after Maier, he conceded that most of his predecessors wrote "in an obscure, figurative, allegorical, and altogether perplexing style."[42] But while he claimed to speak plainly about the seed that is contained in mercury, he ended in parables, saying, "Mercury is our doorkeeper, our balm, our honey, oil, urine, may-dew, mother, egg, secret furnace, oven, true fire, venomous Dragon," and so forth.[43]

---

[39] Maier, *Atalanta fugiens*, ed. de Jong, 266.

[40] Klossowski de Rola, *The Golden Game*, 103. See *OED*, "reincrudate" *v.*, "To make crude again."

[41] See Newman, *Gennehical Fire*.

[42] Philalethes, *The Metamorphosis of Metals*, in *Hermetic Museum*, 2:233.

[43] Philalethes, *The Metamorphosis of Metals*, in *Hermetic Museum*, 2:234.

That is to say, his mercury or quicksilver was described under all these names and others, but it is still the same. Mercury is a metaphor for much that the alchemist must keep constantly in mind. Philalethes wrote in the earlier and more famous *Open Entrance* that mercury and gold were to be understood *sine ulla metaphora*, which the English translation expands to say "not metaphorically, but in a truly philosophical sense."[44] This suggests that statements about the "may-dew, mother, egg," and so forth must be taken *ad verbum* – as literal statements about an alternate reality. Like metaphors in the poetry that Maier and other alchemical authors quote, they should be taken at face value and applied only with caution to the phenomenal world.

The answer to our opening question – Why would anyone venture such deliberate misreadings of Ovid? – is that the alchemical interpretations seemed more inappropriate to some than to others, and altogether praiseworthy to a few. The different views reflected different attitudes to the classical texts and to the natural world they described. Those who were most inclined to think of alchemists as misreaders regarded the ancient poets as real people with limited knowledge of nature – limited by the learning of their times – but almost limitless powers of expression. Those who most admired the new interpretations tended to think that the poets were divinely inspired and that great poetry conveyed divine truths to interpreters of poetry, as Socrates suggests in Plato's *Ion* (536a-d). The properly inspired poet might invent lines that neither he nor his contemporaries understood, but the original inspiration could be conveyed through poetry for others to comprehend.

The same logic was applied to sacred literature. Either the Bible's account of creation was accommodated to the limited perception of fallen man, as Augustine maintained, or it concealed the secret knowledge of Moses, who was said to be "skilled in all the wisdom of the Egyptians" (Acts 7:22). In general, Roman Catholic scientists – with their more traditional, often Augustinian views of Scripture – hoped to effect a separation of science and religion that would allow each to flourish. They feared that the alchemists would go from Vergil and Ovid to the Old and New Testaments and would give experimental science a bad name. Meanwhile, to continue the generalisation, many Protestant

---

[44] *Introitus apertus, Musaeum hermeticum,* 674; *The Open Entrance,* in *Hermetic Museum,* 2:179.

chemists hoped to extend their newly won freedoms of interpretation and forge a new, millenarian harmony of religion and science. Maier was squarely on the latter side. The Rosicrucian myth that he promoted was millenarian in precisely that way.[45]

The debate is not over. Many North Americans, including certain of their leaders, remain undecided about the separation of religious and scientific education. Now that the emphasis has shifted from the creation of heaven and earth to that of animals and man, the alchemists seem in retrospect to have understood better than some writing today why an omniscient deity would have chosen to teach in parables (Mark 4:2). It may even seem refreshing to come across the old phrase of writers like Pietro Boni and Michael Maier, when a twentieth-century alchemist maintains that the stories of Noah's flood and Plato's Atlantis are not necessarily to be taken literally but should be understood "under the veil of parable."[46]

When Ovid made his famous claim, in the *Metamorphoses'* closing words, that his poetry would go wherever Roman rule and language extended, he could hardly have anticipated that his tale would be studied by a priest in Gaul professing a religion from Judea and practising a craft from Egypt and the Near East, especially one that Roman emperors like Domitian would try to suppress. That is, he could hardly have imagined readers like the priest to whom Rand drew attention in the early twentieth century. One can only guess what Ovid would have made of the alchemical metamorphoses that we have reviewed, as one can only guess what he would have thought about Shakespeare's adaptation of the Pyramus and Thisbe story in *A Midsummer Night's Dream*, or how Shakespeare might respond to "The Skinhead Hamlet" or *Caliban, the Missing Link* – interpretations offered, respectively, by a successful writer for screen and television and by the first president of University of Toronto.[47] Such claims say the most about the culture that makes them, and then pay tribute to the culture on which they draw. The claims of alchemical secrets investigated here along with the scholarly interest in such claims give evidence that Ovid, like Shakespeare, lives.

UNIVERSITY OF ARIZONA

---

[45] See Willard, "Alchemy and the Bible."
[46] Fulcanelli, *The Dwellings of the Philosophers*, 508.
[47] Curtis, "The Skinhead Hamlet"; Wilson, *Caliban, the Missing Link*.

AUTHORISING THE METAMORPHIC WITCH: OVID IN REGINALD SCOT'S DISCOVERIE OF WITCHCRAFT

CORA FOX

> I have put twenty of these witchmongers to silence
> with this one question; to wit, whether a witch that can turn
> a woman into a cat, etc., can also turn a cat into a woman?
> (Scot, *Discoverie of Witchcraft* 5.10)

The writings of late sixteenth-century England offer witness to a striking cultural confluence: the increase in literary productions influenced self-consciously by Ovid occurred at around the same time as the birth of English demonological writings. Both Ovidianism and writings on witchcraft share an interest in the metamorphic body, and particularly the female body, and yet they are rarely connected or discussed together.[1] The simultaneously increased publication of and interest in Ovidian literary texts and demonological writings occurred because these two distinct areas of representation were negotiating similar cultural interests. Both Ovidian works and works of demonology explicitly address the fear of the instability of the (usually female) body through figurations and/or analyses of metamorphosis, both share an interest in the passions of female figures, and both are particularly invested in analysing challenges to authority, whether that authority is, in literature, the epic tradition or the moral imperatives of heroic literature that accompany it or, in writings on witchcraft, the judicial, academic, or religious authorities perceived to be responsible for dealing with witches. In addition, Ovid's *Metamorphoses* was instrumental in perpetuating the literary type of the witch – mainly through the figure

---

[1] The connection between Ovidianism and witchcraft controversies is suggested by Gail Paster and Jean Howard, who include passages from Scot and Ovid to contextualise Bottom's transformation in their edition of Shakespeare's *A Midsummer Night's Dream*; see Paster and Howard, *A Midsummer Night's Dream*, 275–294.

of Medea – and in that sense this translated classical text directly influenced the constructions of English witches and their fates at the hands of religious and secular authorities.

This construction of the metamorphic witch, however, was never a matter of simple imitation or citation, but was instead the result of a complex negotiation with the authority of Ovid's literary representations. Ovid's texts are cited in writings on witchcraft as both what we would consider factual representations of experience and fictional literary imaginings or "feigning." As a number of scholars have revealed, fact and fiction were not fully recognisable categories in Elizabethan England and were indeed invented over the course of the seventeenth century.[2] Elizabeth Spiller, for example, analyses the ways in which writers and thinkers of the period describe science writing and literary writing as similar acts of "making." Her observations are particularly relevant to writings on witchcraft, although they are further complicated by the claims to fact inherent in the theological and legal discourses that informed these debates.[3] Writings on witchcraft drew upon a number of disciplinary ideas about what was truth – from theology, law, natural philosophy, and science, to name a few – and they participated in the early modern period's reassessment and refiguration of claims of proof and probability.[4] In this context, Ovid's *Metamorphoses* plays a fundamental role both in establishing and in undercutting the truth claims of stories about witches.

This article will chart Ovid's presence in Reginald Scot's *Discoverie of Witchcraft* (1584), the first demonological tract written by an Englishman. Although some excellent scholarly work has been done documenting Ovid's influence on the literary and artistic productions of Renaissance England, considering the roles Ovid's works play in nonliterary as well as imaginative texts gives us a fuller picture of English Renaissance intellectual and social life and helps us avoid the dangers of misreading early modern culture by encountering it only through a narrow representational or cultural lens.[5] While it is true that literary

---

[2] Spiller, *Science, Reading, and Renaissance Literature*, 1. See also Shapiro, *Probability and Certainty*.

[3] For an analysis of the transitions in legal discourse related to conceptualising evidence that mark witchcraft debates, see Dolan, "'Ridiculous Fictions.'"

[4] Shapiro, *Probability and Certainty*, especially Chapter 6, "Witchcraft."

[5] Recent scholarly works on English Renaissance Ovidianism include *Ovid and the Renaissance Body*, ed. Stanivukovic; Enterline, *Rhetoric of the Body*; James, *Shakespeare's Troy*; and Bate, *Shakespeare and Ovid*. See also Barkan's seminal *Gods Made Flesh*.

texts always have effects on social and cultural experience, it is rare to be able to trace the way literary constructions – in this case Ovid's metamorphic figures – influence a text that so self-consciously intervenes in social experience. In the highly charged gender context of the male-authored witchcraft debates, allusions to Ovid's texts sometimes facilitate imaginative challenges to patriarchal social evaluations of female emotion and the female body. Scot translates Ovid's text into his own and in doing so he negotiates more broadly with the transgressive, anti-authoritarian figures of metamorphosis that make up Ovid's poem.

Both discourses – what we might call "Ovidianism" and "demonism" – witnessed significant growth in the period of English history that began in what historian John Guy has called Queen Elizabeth's second reign – from roughly the defeat of the Armada in 1588 to her death in 1603.[6] As historians have shown, this was a period of heightened anxiety after many years of relative calm and prosperity. Worries about the succession and the more evident threat of Spanish invasion after the Armada combined with the instability caused by the deaths of some of Elizabeth's most important privy councillors to create unrest in governing circles. At the same time, a series of bad harvests made conditions particularly dangerous for all classes. It was, therefore, a time of heightened concern about Elizabeth's authority and her ability to lead, and under these difficult circumstances her gender must have become a more pressing issue. This political unrest combined with larger societal questioning of female authority and feminine roles within marriage to contribute to widespread interest in the status of women in both the public and private spheres. Both Ovidianism and the increased attention paid to the question of witches and witchcraft prosecutions can be read as symptoms of a cultural ethos that encouraged worry and debate about women and power, the body as a constituent of gender, and the workings of the female passions.

There is an overall consensus among scholars that the witchcraft debates and prosecutions were in some way related to cultural fantasies about actual women, although there is still much disagreement about whose fantasies they were and what were their origins.[7] While the practice of witchcraft was made a felony early in Elizabeth's reign in the

---

[6]See *Reign of Elizabeth I*, ed. Guy, and Guy, *Tudor England*.

[7]For an extensive discussion and analysis of these issues in historical studies of witchcraft, see Purkiss, *The Witch in History*.

witchcraft statute of 1563, it was rarely prosecuted and was not accompanied until this later period by what James Sharpe calls "a comprehensive model of satanic witchcraft" constructed by English writers in dialogue with continental ones in a rash of demonological tracts.[8] By a century later, witchcraft prosecutions had for the most part ended in England, although widespread belief in witchcraft probably continued into the eighteenth century, and in fact beyond.[9] Reginald Scot's *Discoverie of Witchcraft*, in addition to being the first English demonological text, was also one of only a few strongly sceptical treatises on the power of witches.[10] Stuart Clark, in fact, in *Thinking with Demons*, singles out Scot's treatise as the most famous and most radical sceptical tract of its time, while Sydney Anglo calls him an "intellectual iconoclast" because he so thoroughly disbelieves in both devilish and godly supernatural occurrences.[11] Scot's text is fundamentally anti-authoritarian in relation to a number of intellectual traditions, not just other witchcraft treatises, and it shares this characteristic with the most referenced classical author in the treatise – Ovid.

Primary among other poets, Ovid occupies a particularly ambiguous position as an authority in Scot's treatise. Citations from the Ovidian corpus, usually in Latin with a translation by Abraham Fleming, are repeatedly showcased as examples of the absurdity and untruth of metamorphosis, and at the same time as authoritative texts on witches and their behaviour. Scot's scepticism about witchcraft, therefore, is matched by a marked scepticism about classical works as records of lived experience. This doubt is cast most vehemently toward the *Metamorphoses*. The ambivalence about Ovid's metamorphic figures in the *Discoverie* reveals a larger cultural anxiety about the challenges to patriarchal structures of authority inherent in Ovid's poem, since it represents and values a feminised response to violence and other forms of oppression that complicates the emphasis on reason that is essential

---

[8]Sharpe, *Witchcraft*, 16–17. For a fuller discussion, see Sharpe, *Instruments of Darkness*.

[9]Sharpe, *Witchcraft*, 70–88.

[10]Sharpe (*Instruments of Darkness,* 50) notes "it is one of the great peculiarities of the history of witchcraft in England that the first major theoretical work on the subject published by an English writer, Reginald Scots' *Discoverie of Witchcraft* of 1584, was unrelentingly skeptical."

[11]See Clark, *Thinking with Demons*; Anglo, "Reginald Scot's Discoverie of Witchcraft," 107.

to Scot's scepticism. The metamorphic transgressions of the body accomplished by both Ovidian figures and witches, as well as their highlighted emotional states of grief and rage, represent for Scot, and presumably for others, a kind of anti-authoritarian power that is originally theorised in Ovid's epic poem. Ovid's representations contribute, in other words, to the threatening construction of witches as outsiders and powerful threats to civil, judicial, and even natural authority.

Of course, both Ovidianism and English demonism were not natively English, but were responding to movements and debates already growing on the continent. As centuries of scholarship have affirmed, Ovid's works, coming to English poetry both through the moralised tradition of the wider European Middle Ages and through a renewed humanist emphasis on the original Latin text (which was first fully translated into English in 1567 by Arthur Golding), were influential in literature ranging from the elite court poetry of the minor epics to Spenser's Ovidian epic *Faerie Queene*, to the many plays, both high- and low-brow (from Lyly to Shakespeare to Heywood), that drew primarily upon the *Metamorphoses* as an intertext. English Ovidianism connected English writings to other expressions of European interest in Ovid and was often explicitly in dialogue with continental writers strongly influenced by Ovid's works, such as Petrarch, Ariosto, and Tasso in Italy.

Demonological writings, similarly, were enmeshed in continental debates and they related witchcraft trials in England to movements across Europe. *The Discoverie* engages energetically with continental writers on witchcraft, especially Jean Bodin and the Catholic inquisitors Jacob Sprenger and Heinrich Kramer. Scot's central argument is that the witches being burned on the continent and occasionally in English villages are victims of social rather than devilish forces (*Discoverie* 1.3):

> One sort of such as are said to be witches, are women which be commonly old, lame, bleare-eyed, pale, foul, and full of wrinkles; poor, sullen, superstitious, and papists; or such as know no religion; in whose drowsy minds the devil hath gotten a fine seat; so as, what mischief, mischance, calamity, or slaughter is brought to pass, they are easily persuaded the same is done by themselves; imprinting in their minds an earnest and constant imagination thereof .... These miserable wretches are so odious unto all their neighbors, and so feared, as few dare offend them, or deny them any thing they ask: whereby they take upon them; yea, and sometimes think, that they can do such things as are beyond the abilities of human nature.[12]

---

[12] *The Discoverie of Witchcraft* is currently available in a few mostly facsimile editions.

Outraged by what he sees as blasphemous beliefs in extra-biblical occurrences and powers, Scot is one of the first writers on witchcraft to articulate a view that has dominated witchcraft scholarship into the present day: that witches are silly old women who are victims of their own and their neighbours' errors. As Diane Purkiss has pointed out, Scot's sceptical answer to the problem of witchcraft assumes no power for those women accused, even within the domestic and local spheres.[13] Scot does, however, express apparently genuine concern that these innocents are being prosecuted, tortured and killed, and that Protestants are engaged in what he considers an ungodly enterprise of witch hunting. His moral and theological outrage leads him to write a treatise that mocks the demonisers, sarcastically debunking every accusation and description of witchcraft that has authority in his period. His special targets are Sprenger and Kramer's *Malleus maleficarum* (1486) and Bodin's *De la démonomanie des sorciers* (1580), but he also rails generally against Catholics for their beliefs in what he characterises as magic, other writers on witchcraft, and, most interestingly, poets. Even granting the point made by some recent scholars of witchcraft that the tracts of the demonologists and those of their sceptics are not so radically different as was previously assumed (the demonologists share a great deal of scepticism about their topic and the sceptics often painstakingly re-inscribe an overall belief in spirits and demons), Scot's work is especially rich as a proto-anthropological account of beliefs about witchcraft, even

---

The Bodleian Library's copy is reprinted as number 299 in the series "The English Experience" published by Da Capo Press. The most accessible is the paperback Dover edition, which reprints Montague Summers' condensed edition of 1930. I have used both of these editions, but my main source for citations is a 1584 edition in the collection of St. Catharine's College, Cambridge. In the material for this essay, no serious variances among these editions were found. I have silently modernised Scot's spelling whenever an obvious modern variant was available.

[13] As Purkiss (*The Witch in History*, 64) points out, "though historians distinguish Scot sharply from demonologists like his opponent Jean Bodin, his argument has a lot in common with theirs. Both sceptics and demonologists created elaborate cosmological theses in order to deny that strange old women in villages had any real power. For demonologists, real power lay with the devils summoned by the witch, and by the beginning of the seventeenth century most argued that even the power to summon devils was illusory. While demonologists displaced the witches' power onto male demons or refused her even this much authority, Scot saw the witch as completely powerless, since in a providential universe divine power could brook no competition from demons or witches."

if not of real practices.[14] It is also a record of how Ovid's *Metamorphoses* operated outside the realm of literary writings, providing some of the fundamental stereotypical images of witches in the period and offering examples of metamorphic figures to support or refute claims that witches could produce and govern metamorphic transformations.

The published treatise opens by visually announcing in its first historiated initial (fig. 9.1) its connection to the *Metamorphoses*.[15] This woodcut has most likely been reused from an edition of the *Metamorphoses*, which would link the book paratextually to Ovid's work even if Ovid did not become one of the central authorities on magical transformations in the text itself.[16] There are only two other historiated initials in this edition, and they are both identical depictions of a naked hero (most likely Ulysses or Aeneas) riding the waves with a sea god nearby (fig. 9.2). These two ornamental initials begin the preface to the readers and the treatise itself on page one, both "T"s. Although they are most likely alluding to the traditional figure of the ship as a metaphor for narrative progression and the circulation of the text, the scene also suggests metamorphic myths, as sea gods are particularly likely to be shape-shifters in the *Metamorphoses* and most classical literature. In fact, the illustration may invoke the tale of Glaucus, a sea god, and Scylla from Books Thirteen and Fourteen of the *Metamorphoses* (and elsewhere). In this tale of magical transformations that is told during the narration of Aeneas' voyage, Glaucus goes to the witch Circe to look for love-charms to seduce Scylla. Circe instead wants Glaucus for herself and uses her magical herbs to turn her competitor, Scylla, into her more familiar form as the metamorphic monster of Homer's *Odyssey*. In addition to the connection with the witch Circe, Glaucus' tale is first alluded to in the tale of Medea in *Metamorphoses* 7, when Medea goes to find the magical herbs that will be used in this future story by her

---

[14] In this paper, I assume that sceptical writing is a sub-genre or anti-genre of demonological writing and part of the same discourse. For a discussion of how similar mainstream demonological writing can be to sceptical writing, see Clark, *Thinking with Demons*, Chapter 13: "Believers and Skeptics."

[15] Because this woodcut is a historiated initial, it is not noted in Luborsky and Ingram's entry on *The Discoverie* in *A Guide to English Illustrated Books*. The woodcuts depicting the "juggling tricks" attributed to witchcraft are described.

[16] A cursory analysis of the surviving works printed by the publishers associated with *The Discoverie*, William Brome and Henry Denham, did not reveal the origins of this initial. Although Henry Denham did publish at least two editions of the *Heroides*, neither contains such elaborately illustrated initials.

aunt, Circe. The scene of encounter between human and sea god is freighted, therefore, with complex and multiple associations with metamorphosis and witches, and it may be used here to suggest the world of magical transformations that comes into Scot's treatise through classical texts.

Even more tellingly, the first illustration in the work is quite specifically the scene of Daphne's transformation into a laurel in her flight from Apollo. That this metamorphic tale opens the dedication is partly because Scot is seeking patronage and alluding to the laurels he hopes will come with his work's success. The tale of Daphne is also, though, in many respects the paradigmatic tale in Ovid's poem of transformation as a response to rape and is therefore a compelling opening to a book asserting the impossibility of actual physical bodily changes that are not divinely sanctioned miracles. Daphne, the image implies, is shape-shifting in the same manner that witches might be. This illustration of the tale in particular captures the moment of metamorphosis as both a scene of liminal identity for Daphne and a competition between men who have different claims to Daphne's person, since it includes both Apollo and Peneus, her river-god father. In a river-god pose that in this context suggests at least potential submission to Apollo, Peneus and his daughter occupy one side of the "I" while Apollo occupies the other.[17] While Daphne, with hands that have already turned to branches and leaves, turns back toward Apollo and he reaches for her, Peneus appears defeated by his own triumph in saving Daphne from rape. The image self-consciously represents Daphne's removal from the world of masculine desire and rivalry to the realm of metamorphosis and supernatural transformation. While the homosocial competition between lover and father is downplayed in Ovid's version of the tale, its representation of a masculinised desire is a major facet of the story's history in poetry, where it becomes the source tale for poetic achievement and authority. By opening *The Discoverie* with this visual allusion to the *Metamorphoses* and this particular tale, the publisher links the debate about witches to Ovid's poem and its analyses of the body, as well as the subjection of female metamorphic figures and their

---

[17] I would like to thank the many art historians (whose names I did not record) who rushed to my assistance to identify the typical pose of a river god when I presented this illustration as a handout in my talk at the conference, *Metamorphosis: The Changing Face of Ovid in Medieval and Early Modern Europe*; University of Toronto, Canada; in March 2005.

responses to this violence. The illustration suggests the similarities between suffering Ovidian figures like Daphne and the witches who are the treatise's subject matter and, perhaps more indirectly, implies that the source of suffering may be a public realm of masculine rivalries and interests.

In addition to these visual connections to Ovid's world of female metamorphoses, the treatise repeatedly draws on Ovid's works for descriptions of witches and witchcraft practices. While Scot enlists a number of classical authors throughout his work, Ovid is often the first author citied, and he is clearly the poet most associated with poetical witchcraft throughout the work. Most notable among the Ovidian figures present in Scot's text is, of course, the witch Medea. When listing the evil deeds continental demonologists have ascribed to witches – that they can cause barrenness, kill children, pass invisibly through the air, alter the minds of judges, etc. – he lists the demonological authors under attack and then adds:

> But because I will in no wise abridge the authority of their power, you shall have also the testimonies of many other grave authors in this behalf; as followeth.
>
> And first Ovid affirmeth, that they can raise and suppress lightning and thunder, rain and hail, clouds and winds, tempests and earthquakes. Others do write that they can pull down the moon and the stars .... Some say they can transubstantiate themselves and others, and take the forms and shapes of asses, wolves, ferrets, cows, apes, horses, dogs, & c. ... (*Discoverie* 1.4)

The beginning of this list is an allusion to Medea's famous incantation in Book Seven of the *Metamorphoses,* as she gathers magical herbs at night to restore Aeson's youth. The rest of her incantation includes a number of these powers:

> ... cum volui, ripis mirantibus amnes
> in fontes rediere suos, concussaque sisto,
> stantia concutio cantu freta, nubila pello
> nubilaque induco, ventos abigoque vocoque,
> vipereas rumpo verbis et carmine fauces,
> vivaque saxa sua convulsaque robora terra
> et silvas moveo iubeoque tremescere montis
> et mugire solum manesque exire sepulcris!
> te quoque, Luna, traho, quamvis Temesaea labores
> aera tuos minuant ...   (*Met.* 7.199–208)

And in Arthur Golding's 1567 English translation:

> I have compelled streams to run clean backward to their spring.
> By charms I make the calm Seas rough, and make the rough Seas plain,
> And cover all the Sky with Clouds and chase them thence again;
> By charms I raise and lay the winds and burst the viper's jaw
> And from the bowels of the earth both stones and trees do draw.
> Whole woods and forests I remove; I make the mountains shake
> And even the earth itself to groan and fearfully to quake;
> I call up dead men from their graves; and thee, O lightsome moon,
> I darken oft, though beaten brass abate thy peril soon.[18]

Jonathan Bate has called this speech Renaissance witchcraft's "great set-piece" and points to the many imitations of it in demonological writings as well as literary productions.[19] The rest of Medea's tale in the *Metamorphoses*, in fact, has her practicing many of the habits of Scot's witches – gathering herbs and night-flying, for instance – but Medea does not herself govern over metamorphosis except in the case of Aeson from old age to youth. Metamorphosis, therefore, is an action more generally ascribed to Ovid's characters and his work, and in this sense references to Medea are references to the whole *Metamorphoses* and its most fundamental imagery and structure. The *Metamorphoses*, therefore, is implicated in Scot's treatise and in its threatening representations of witchcraft in pervasive ways. Scot implies that the witches he describes are modern Medeas and even Daphnes, aligning them with the female figures of the *Metamorphoses* in ways that ostensibly draw attention to the fictionality of witchcraft accusations, but that also more surprisingly privilege Ovid's descriptions, making them authoritative in intellectual debates on witchcraft practices. This conflation of witches with Ovid's metamorphic figures draws Ovid's works from the metaphorical realm of poetry into the realm of the everyday. The witch that might be one's neighbour becomes Medea, just as Medea becomes one's neighbour.

Later in his treatise, Scot will emphasise only one half of this equation of witches with Ovidian female figures when he sets out to prove that the practices attributed to witches are simply fictive imaginings. The use of Ovid's works as authoritative for witchcraft practices,

---

[18] Golding, *Met.* 7.268–276. I have silently modernised spelling.

[19] Bate, *Shakespeare and Ovid*, 252. Bate also cites Carroll's more extensive treatment of the translation of this passage in *The Tempest*, in *Metamorphoses of Shakespearean Comedy*.

however, suggests that the link between witches and Ovidian figures has both literary and other cultural consequences. If Scot's witches are like Ovid's metamorphic figures, they have agency beyond his characterisation of them as harmless old women. Scot's suspicion that witches are too close to Ovid's powerful female figures is further expressed in more subtle ways. When attempting to explain why those accused of witchcraft sometimes confess, he anxiously writes:

> The witch on the other side expecting her neighbor's mischances, and seeing things sometimes come to pass according to her wishes, curses, and incantations ... being called before a Justice, by due examination of the circumstances is driven to see her imprecations and desires, and her neighbor's harms and losses to concur, and as it were to take effect and so confesseth that she (as a goddess) hath brought such things to pass.
>
> (*Discoverie* 1.4)

Scot is clearly troubled that these women might think they are powerful enough to achieve the magical effects they desire. This worry is registered in his use of the term "goddess," which suggests wider connections between Renaissance witches and the goddesses of classical, and especially Ovidian, poetry.

Throughout the work and perhaps most famously, Scot also cites Ovid authoritatively to show the ineffectiveness or trickery of much behaviour associated with witches. For instance, he uses Ovid, in this case in his guise as preceptor of love, to confute the effectiveness of love potions: "And first you shall hear what Ovid saith, who wrote of the very art of love, and that so cunningly and feelingly, that he is reputed the special doctor in that science" (*Discoverie* 7.7). He goes on to cite Book Two of the *Ars amatoria* and then the *Remedia*, in both cases as evidence that love potions are ineffectual. According to Ovid, if they worked, Medea could have kept Jason and Circe could have kept Ulysses. While Scot can grant that Ovid is a "special doctor" in the "science" of love, when it comes to the *Metamorphoses* and its witches Scot is much more conflicted about how to assess the truth of Ovid's poetry.

In fact, in other places in his text Scot explicitly mocks those who take Ovid's stories for descriptions of real events. When turning his attention specifically to Jean Bodin's *De la démonomanie des sorciers*, which he finds particularly disturbing because it asserts the belief that witches can at least create the illusion of metamorphosis, he mockingly refers to Ovid as "Bodin's poet ... whose *Metamorphosis* makes so much for him" (*Discoverie* 5.5). He further rails: "But lest some poets' fables might be thought lies (whereby the witchmongers arguments should quail) he maintaineth for true the most part of Ovid's *Metamorphosis*, and the greatest absurdities and impossibilities in all that book: marry he thinketh some one tale therein may be feigned" (*Discoverie* 5.1). Scot ridicules Bodin for misreading all of Ovid's absurdities and impossibilities, but throughout the work Scot vacillates on how to value Ovid's authority. As his use of Ovid to describe witchcraft practices suggests, he is never sure that Ovid can be firmly categorised as fiction. In fact, when addressing the widespread stories of metamorphosis in Book Five, he cites Book One of the *Metamorphoses* to "overthrow" Bodin's "phantastical imagination," reminding him that Ovid states, *Os homini sublime dedit, caelumque videre | Jussit, & erectos ad sydera tollere vultus*, for which he provides Abraham Fleming's translation, "The Lord did set man's face so high | That he the heavens might behold, | And look up to the starry sky, | To see his wonders manifold" (*Discoverie* 5.5).[20] In this particular use of his pagan source, Scot allies Ovid with his Protestant belief in the great chain of being and the superiority of human beings over other creatures and then comfortably invokes Ovid as an authority on this subject.

A final and striking example of Ovid's ambiguous position as an authority in the work occurs when Scot attempts to undercut "the common fabling of lying poets," specifically Ovid and Vergil, by citing other classical authors:

> Now let any indifferent man (Christian or heathen) judge, whether the words and minds of the prophets do not directly oppunge these poets' words (I will not say minds); for that I am sure they did therein but jest and trifle, according to the common fabling of lying poets. And certainly, I can encounter them two with other two poets; namely Propertius and Horace …. For where Virgil, Ovid, etc. write that witches with their charms fetch down the moon and stars from heaven, etc.; Propertius mocks them in these words following.

After citing Propertius, he continues:

> And that you may see more certainly, that these poets did but jest and deride the credulous and timorous sort of people, I thought good to show you what Ovid says against himself, and such as have written so incredibly and ridiculously of witch's omnipotence:
>   Nec mediae magicis finduntur cantibus angues,
>   Nec redit in fontes unda supina suos.

---

[20] Reference is to *Met.* 1.85–86.

Englished by Abraham Fleming:
      Snakes in the middle are not riven
      With charms of witches' cunning,
      Nor waters to their fountains driven
      By force of backward running.   (*Discoverie* 12.15)

Unlike most citations in the work, this one is unattributed and is a rough quotation from Ovid's *Medicamina faciei femineae* (substituting *magicis* for Ovid's *Marsis*, 39–40). The fact that Scot must cite this minor poem to prove that Ovid contradicts himself registers his anxiety about poetic authority, especially Ovid's, throughout the text. Unable to search Ovid's mind to determine whether his purposes are "jesting" and "trifling" with the ignorant, Scot cannot decide whose side Ovid is on. Is he Bodin's poet or is he Scot's? At this point in his treatise, the only way to resolve this anxiety is to represent Ovid as an authority who undercuts himself.

Later in the work, Scot addresses the difficult problem of poetic authority quite explicitly in a chapter entitled, "Poetical authorities commonly alleged by witchmongers, for the proof of witches miraculous actions, and for confirmation of their supernatural power." Scot writes that he will "show what authorities are produced to defend and maintain the same [accusations of witchcraft]" (*Discoverie* 12.7). His first two examples are from Vergil's *Eclogue* 8, but he then goes on to cite Ovid three times (*Fasti* 6, and two descriptions of Medea's incantations, from *Metamorphoses* 7 and her epistle in *Heroides* 4), as well as Lucan, Horace, and a few others. Having cited these authorities, he devotes a chapter to "Poetry and popery compared in enchantments, popish witchmongers have more advantage herein than protestants," in which he writes:

You see in these verses, the poets (whether in earnest or in jest I know not), ascribe unto witches & to their charms, more than is to be found in human or diabolical power. I doubt not but the most part of the readers hereof will admit them to be fabulous; although the most learned of mine adversaries (for lack of scripture) are fain to produce these poetries for proofs, and for lack of judgment I am sure do think, that Actaeon's transformation was true. And why not? As well as the metamorphosis or transubstantiation of Ulysses his companions into swine: which S. Augustine, and so many great clarkes credit and report. (*Discoverie* 12.8)

Scot's refutation of his adversaries and their reliance on poets as witnesses is riddled with doubt. Although he begins by mocking them for believing in metamorphosis, he concludes this paragraph by acknowledging that Augustine, an authority par excellence, and "many great clarkes" do in fact credit stories of transformation.

Scot's doubt and his troubled attempt to handle the authority of the *Metamorphoses* cannot be only Scot's. What reading this tract reveals is a pervasive cultural anxiety about actual physical metamorphosis and particularly the powers it might suggest for women. This air of actual danger in Ovid's imagery can be easily overlooked if as scholars we focus too narrowly on Ovidianism in literature which we categorise anachronistically as figurative, without direct associations with the real. Scot's tract reminds us that there was not always an easy distinction made in this period between the authority granted to poets and that given to "great clarkes" – scholars, justices, or kings. Scot exposes metamorphosis as a poetic construction, while at the same time acknowledging that many in his learned community are not so sure that these constructions are not true. Debates about witchcraft, at least in this instance, are shown to be grounded in more fundamental societal speculation about what counts as fictional, and where authority lies. Scot's text also reveals that the potential for transgression – of the limits of the body, the natural, and socially accepted roles for women – that is inherent in Ovid's metamorphic figures was recognised as a very real threat in Renaissance England.

The pointed use of the *Metamorphoses* in *The Discoverie* should inform our readings of Ovidianism in literary works of this period – such as Spenser's *Faerie Queene*, which was being written as Scot's work was published, the Ovidian court plays of Lyly and others, the repeatedly Ovidian Shakespearean plays, and the whole tradition of minor epic. While Ovidianism functions in these texts in intensely literary and figurative ways, and metamorphosis is often a metaphor for exploring interior and emotional experience, its additional dangerous cultural affiliations should not be underestimated. The *Metamorphoses* and Ovid's other works were not just domesticated texts for schoolboys; they were also linked to fears of actual bodily transformation and witches themselves. The *Metamorphoses* helped construct the Renaissance witch and the poem both authorised the witch's power and allowed it to be deconstructed as "fabulous" or just a great poetic trick. Ovid's *Metamorphoses*, like the metamorphic witches authorised partly by its tales, had the potential to be both a domesticated neighbour and a terrifying Other to English citizens. Both figurative and "real," Ovid's witches, and by extension all of his metamorphic and powerful female figures, occupied a transgressive and politically central place in the Renaissance imagination.

ARIZONA STATE UNIVERSITY

A Humanist in Exile:
Ovid's Myth of Narcissus and
the Experience of Self in
Petrarch's Secretum

Gur Zak

Of the many myths assembled by Ovid in his poem of transformation, that of Narcissus has no doubt been one of the most influential and commented upon.[1] The link that Ovid created in his retelling of the story of the beautiful arrogant youth between mirroring, desire, self-awareness, and death would strongly resonate in works of writers and artists of subsequent generations, troubled by their own problematic relationship with their reflection – whether the physical one in mirrors and fountains or the textual one in language. The popularity of the myth reached a peak in the later Middle Ages, occupying a central role in works such as the *Roman de la rose* and Dante's *Commedia*. As several critics observed, it was also a clear presence in Petrarch's autobiographical corpus of writings, often blamed for a type of "narcissistic" self-idolatry.[2]

Scholars interested in probing the role of the myth of Narcissus – as that of Ovid in general – in Petrarch's writings often turn to the *Rime sparse*, the collection of poems in which Petrarch makes the most of Ovidian subtexts.[3] Nevertheless, while Ovid's Narcissus no doubt casts

---

[1] For general surveys of the fortunes of the Narcissus myth see: Golding, *The Mirror of Narcissus*, Knoespel, *Narcissus*, and Vinge, *Narcissus Theme*. For the uses of Narcissus in art, see Bann, *True Vine*.

[2] See, for example, Durling, "Introduction," in *Petrarch's Lyric Poems*, 31, Freccero, "Fig Tree and the Laurel," and Mazzotta, *Worlds of Petrarch*, 59.

[3] For discussions of Petrarch's use of the Narcissus myth in the *Rime sparse,* see Boysen, "Crucified"; Durling, "Introduction," 31–33; Enterline, "Embodied Voices," 126–127; Mazzotta, *Worlds of Petrarch*, 64–67; and Perry, *Another Reality*, 94–96. General discussions of Petrarch's use of Ovid, especially in the *Rime*, are many. In addition to the above-mentioned, see Barkan, *Gods Made Flesh*, 206–215; Calcaterra, *Nella Selva*, esp. 35–87; Greene, *Light in Troy*, esp. 127–131; Hardie, "Ovid into Laura"; Mann, "From Laurel to Fig"; Sturm-Maddox, *Petrarch's Metamorphoses*,

a long shadow over the *Rime*, it is in the *Secretum*, as Giuseppe Mazzotta pointed out, that the poet first associates himself fully with the proud youth.[4] Readers of the *Secretum* – the imaginary dialogue between himself and Augustine that Petrarch wrote and revised between the years 1347–1353[5] – mostly have refrained, however, from examining the significance of Petrarch's use of Narcissus, and of Ovid in general, in the work, focusing instead on the philosophical and rhetorical sources prevalent in it. As a result, such readings often frame the work as an inner conflict between a "medieval" ascetic world-view and a "modern" humanistic one,[6] between a desire for psychological detachment from the world and submission to the pressures of society for worldly success,[7] or as an ideological debate between an Augustinian ethics of will and faith and an Aristotelian validation of the senses and the natural sciences.[8]

This article offers a reading of the *Secretum* that focuses on Petrarch's use of the myth of Narcissus in the work, arguing that the myth serves as the focal point around which the entire dialogue revolves. Petrarch's turn to the myth is part of his search for the possible causes of and remedies for the experience of inner exile and alienation from which he suffered at the time:[9] "too long have you been an exile from your country and from your own self" (*Nimis diu iam et a patria et a te ipso exulasti*), the figure of Augustinus tells him near the end of the work.[10]

---

esp. 9–39; Vickers, "Diana Described."

[4] Mazzotta, *Worlds of Petrarch*, 64.

[5] For a summary of the debate over the dating of the *Secretum*, see Pacca, *Petrarca*, 122–24. The seminal discussions on the subject are Baron, *Petrarch's Secretum*, and Rico, *Vida*.

[6] This is the view of Baron, *Petrarch's Secretum*, 247. See also Witt, *In the Footsteps*, 250–251.

[7] Trinkaus, *Poet as Philosopher*, 70–71.

[8] This is the view of Tateo, *Dialogo interiore*, 75. Other interpretations also see in the work a division between different philosophical convictions. See, for example, Ariani, *Petrarca*, 121, and Rico, *Vida*, 55. On the conflict as a debate between two opposing attitudes towards reading and interpretation, see: Kahn, "Figure of the Reader," and Stock, *After Augustine*, 71–85.

[9] On the entry of his brother Gherardo to the Carthusian monastery at Montrieux as one of the possible immediate causes of Petrarch's crisis, see Baron, *Petrarch's Secretum*, 247.

[10] Petrarch, *Secretum,* 158. Henceforth references will be given in the text, with page numbers of the Latin quotations referring to Dotti's edition in Petrarca, *Secretum*; unless otherwise indicated, the English will be the one by Carozza and Shey. From now on I will refer to the figure of "Petrarch" in the dialogue as Franciscus, and to

In this attempt to cure his experience of exile, the dialogue is divided between two different approaches to the myth of Narcissus, suggesting ultimately two different accounts of the human condition: that of the historical Augustine, closely based on his self-portrayal in the *Confessions* as a corrected Narcissus, and the more fatalistic portrayal of Ovid's *Metamorphoses*.[11]

The aim of this article, therefore, is not so much to reject all existing interpretations of the *Secretum* – there is no doubt, for example, about the existence of a tension in the work between secular and religious aspirations – as to redefine the poles that characterise this conflict along the lines of Augustinian and Ovidian models of selfhood. The ultimate rejection of the Augustinian model in the work and the acceptance of the Ovidian one not only show the crucial role that Ovidian mythology played in Petrarch's self-understanding and self-representation – in the Latin as much as in the vernacular works – but also make manifest an experience of self that is markedly Ovidian, markedly "narcissistic": a self that is defined by the mirror-like reflection with which he identifies, and that cannot help but adhere to the uncertain reflection of his own earthly image, even while realising the necessary sense of alienation and exile that such identification entails. It is precisely this Ovidian character, this article will finally show, that both defines and undermines the modernity of Petrarch's experience of self.

THE MIRROR OF NARCISSUS

Since Petrarch's use of the myth of Narcissus in the *Secretum* is firmly based on Ovid's original text, it is necessary to start with an account of Ovid's own portrayal of the myth in the *Metamorphoses*. The following analysis will attempt to focus on the themes that were crucial for Petrarch. Among these themes, Petrarch took the emphasis on Narcissus' early state of blessedness and the close links established in the text between mirroring, desire, and selfhood especially close to heart.

In the beginning of Ovid's retelling of the myth in Book Three, the blind soothsayer Tiresias provides Narcissus' mother, the nymph Liriope, with the prophecy that her son will live to see old age only "If

---

the figure of "Augustine" as Augustinus.

[11] On Augustine's self-representation as a corrected Narcissus in the *Confessions*, see McMahon, "Autobiography as Text-Work." See also Churchill, "Inopem me copia fecit."

he ne'er know himself" (*si se non noverit, Met.* 3.348).[12] Up until the age of sixteen, the myth implies, Narcissus lived his life whole and serene. The portrayal of this "golden age" of Narcissus is provided in the text mainly through the description of the pool in which he will eventually find his death. Charles Segal has shown that landscapes in the *Metamorphoses* often serve as symbols of the character and fate of the protagonists. In the case of Narcissus, he maintains, the "clear, pure pool is, at first, a symbolical equivalent of the youth's virginity,"[13] adding later on that its sterility is also an appropriate symbol of the sterile and selfish lust from which he is to perish.[14]

While serving as a symbol of Narcissus' selfishness and sterility, the picture of the pool that Ovid paints also raises a strong sense of calmness and self-sufficiency. The pool, he emphasises, suffers no disturbance from the outside, its "smooth surface neither bird nor beast nor falling bough ever ruffled" (*quem nulla volucris | nec fera turbarat nec lapsus ab arbore ramus*; 3.409–410). In a clear image of self-sufficiency, grass grows around it in abundance, sustained by its own waters, and trees protect it from the warmth of the sun "Grass grew all around its edge, fed by the water near, and a coppice that would never suffer the sun to warm the spot" (*gramen erat circa, quod proximus umor alebat, | silvaque sole locum passura tepescere nullo*; 3.411–412). The image of the protecting shadow is an important one in descriptions of blissful pastoral existence, as in that of Tityrus' bliss in the opening lines of Vergil's first *Eclogue*: "you, Tityrus, at ease beneath the shade" (*tu, Tityre, lentus in umbra*, 1.4). The initial existence of the pool – and by extension that of Narcissus – is therefore one of blissful natural enclosure and wholeness. It is only by the intrusion of an other – ironically of Narcissus himself – that the pool's primary bliss will end, and in this sense as well it symbolises Narcissus and his fate: he will be the *other* intruding into his own primary blissful existence and leading to its demise.

While it is a time of self-sufficiency and pastoral serenity, Narcissus' primary state – as Segal and others have argued[15] – is also highly ambivalent: his self-sufficiency is, in fact, a "cold" and "hard" pride – *dura superbia* (3.354), which brings many lovers, among them the nymph

---

[12]Latin edition is the one by Anderson; translations are Miller's unless otherwise indicated.

[13]Segal, *Landscape*, 46.

[14]Segal, *Landscape*, 47.

[15]Segal, *Landscape*, 47. See also Hardie, *Ovid's Poetics*, 157, and Knoespel, *Narcissus*, 9.

Echo, to ruin. His refusal to accept the world outside himself poses a threat to society's continuity – the exogamic principle upon which society and culture are based – and hence needs to be punished.[16] As a result, following a plea made by one of the rejected lovers, the goddess Nemesis decides to punish Narcissus by making him suffer from his own sin against others –falling in love with an unattainable object of love, his own reflection in the pool: "Here the youth, worn by the chase and the heat, lies down, attracted thither by the appearance of the place and by the spring. While he seeks to slake his thirst another thirst springs up, and while he drinks he is smitten by the sight of the beautiful form he sees. He loves an unsubstantial hope and thinks that body which is only water" (*hic puer et studio venandi lassus et aestu | procubuit faciemque loci fontemque secutus, | dumque sitim sedare cupit, sitis altera crevit, | dumque bibit, visae conreptus imagine formae | spem sine corpore amat, corpus putat esse, quod unda est*, 3.413–417). Lying down to quench a natural thirst for water, Narcissus sees his image and becomes enthralled with a metaphorical thirst – desire. His own image becomes the *other* that finally manages to break down his harmful pastoral enclosure and makes him reach out of himself and fall in love. As he enters into the realm of otherness, however, he soon finds that it is also the site of his ruin.

Why is this realm of otherness a necessary source of death, according to the text? The awakening of the desire for another within Narcissus' heart will soon lead to the emergence of "self-knowledge" in him – awareness of his own self. While at first ignorant of the true identity of the reflection in the water, gradually Narcissus comes to realise that he and the image are in fact one: "I am he! I have felt it, and my image does not deceive me" (my translation of: *iste ego sum: sensi, nec me mea fallit imago*; 3.463). It is therefore through the sight of the reflection in the water and the desire that it generates that Narcissus finally comes to be aware of his own self. Mirroring, desire, and self-awareness are thus intrinsically related in the text.

Nevertheless, while providing Narcissus with self-awareness, the reflection in the water is also bound to frustrate Narcissus' desire, to lead him away from himself. The cause of this necessary frustration, the text implies, resides in the very nature of the reflection. Functioning like a linguistic metaphor – just like the metaphor *sitis* that Ovid used to describe Narcissus' infatuation (3.415) – the reflection responsible for

---

16 Barkan, *Gods Made Flesh*, 49.

self-awareness is indeterminate, both self and not-self at one and the same time. While pointing to Narcissus and allowing him to "know himself," it is also only "water" – *unda* (3.418) – and hence not truly himself. This duality in the nature of the reflection is implied in the words of Narcissus himself, when he declares that the image is simultaneously the source of his riches and his poverty: *inopem me copia fecit* (3.466).[17] The self that knows himself through the reflection is thus by necessity both present to and absent from himself, never fully one or the other.[18] Hence, as long as the source of self-awareness is also that which alienates and separates, Narcissus cannot escape the feeling of constant frustration, of inner division and exile. The ambiguous image responsible for "self-knowledge," as Tiresias prophesised, is also the source of Narcissus' inevitable ruin.

That there is, according to Ovid, no way out of the identification with the alienating reflection is evident in the text from the fact that Narcissus continues to long for the image even after he realises its emptiness and the doom that it entails: "Death is nothing to me, for in death I shall leave my troubles" (*nec mihi mors gravis est posituro morte dolores*, 3.471). Narcissus, therefore, walks to his death with open eyes, aware of his folly but unable to act otherwise – there is no other option for him but to adhere to the empty reflection. Entrapped within his all-consuming fascination with his own image, Narcissus gradually wastes away until he literally becomes his image – a lifeless shadow: "scarce does his form remain which once Echo had loved so well" (*nec corpus remanet, quondam quod amaverat Echo*, 3.493). This transformation of Narcissus into his reflection, as Leonard Barkan pointed out, is the ultimate metamorphosis in the myth, implied already at the moment of his falling in love, when the youth was described as "a statue carved from Parian marble" (*e Pario formatum marmore signum*, 3.419), lifeless just like the reflection at which he gazed.[19] The reflected image, Ovid ultimately asserts, provides us not only with alienating self-awareness,

---

[17] The duality and indeterminacy of the reflection are portrayed in the myth also through the verbal reflection that Narcissus receives from Echo. Being at the same time both his and not his, the verbal reflection is ambiguous and alienating just like the visual one (*Met.* 3.380–387). See also Knoespel, *Narcissus*, 7–8, and Gildenhard and Zissos, "Ovid's Narcissus," 142.

[18] On the ambiguous nature of mirror reflections in classical literature up to Ovid, see McCarty, "The Shape of the Mirror."

[19] Barkan, *Gods Made Flesh*, 51–52.

but also with a type of "identity" – we *become* the image with which we identify.

The relation established in the myth of Narcissus between mirroring and selfhood is prevalent in all the myths recounted in the third book of the *Metamorphoses*, "Ovid's Thebaid." Cadmus, Actaeon, Tiresias – all are plagued in some way by the mirror-like reflection at which they gaze. Nevertheless, it is the story of Narcissus that most clearly emphasises the crucial role played by desire in the formation of self-awareness and its ambiguous results: while raising self-awareness and providing the lover with a source of identification and identity, this desire also leads to a fall from a primary state of bliss into constant fluctuation and exile. These links between desire, mirroring, and inner-exile in the myth are exactly those that Petrarch will make the most of in his self-representation in the *Secretum*.

The Mirror of Laura, the Mirror of Glory

While the myth of Narcissus is explicitly mentioned in the second dialogue of the *Secretum*, it is in the third dialogue of the work that Petrarch stages his personal history in a manner that closely resembles Ovid's myth. In the beginning of the third dialogue, Augustinus informs Franciscus that he now intends to address the two major chains that bind him and lead to his current crisis: love and glory (*amor et gloria*). Turning first to the issue of love, Augustinus declares that it is the love for Laura, a mortal woman, that leads Franciscus away from truth and into the endless agitations of desire: "During those years, you endured the attacks and the flames of the most violent passion" (*his temporibus violentissime passionis flammas atque impetus pertulisti*, 124). Angered by the accusation, Franciscus insists that it is Laura who is responsible for everything that is good in him – indeed, that she made him into who he is:

> me, quantulumcunque conspicis, per illam esse; nec unquam ad hoc, siquid est, nominis aut glorie fuisse venturum, nisi virtutum tenuissimam sementem, quam pectore in hoc natura locaverat, nobilissimis hec affectibus coluisset. Illa iuvenilem animum ab omni turpitudine revocavit, uncoque, ut aiunt, retraxit, atque alta compulit espectare. Quidni enim in amatos mores transformarer? ... Et iubes illam oblivisci vel parcius amare, que me a vulgi consortio segregavit; que ... semisopitum animum excitavit? (130)

> (Whatever I am, I owe to her; and I should never have attained the modest name and glory I have, if she had not fostered, through the power of my

noble feelings for her, the feeble seeds of virtue that nature has placed in my heart. It was she who beckoned my youthful soul away from everything base and dragged me back with a hook, as they say, and forced me to have higher expectations. Why should I not be transformed into the pattern of the character that I loved? ... and now you bid me to forget or lessen my love of one who saved me from mingling with the common crowd ... and wakened to life my drowsy spirit) (translation modified)

Through love, Franciscus claims, he was transformed (*transformarer*), and this transformation was responsible for the attainment of self-awareness and an identity. The description of the effect that love had on him as the "awakening of the drowsy spirit" (*semisopitum animum*) closely resembles the accounts of the psychology of love in the "stilnovisti" tradition culminating in Dante's *Vita nuova*, in which the entry into love is associated with the birth of self-awareness. In the opening chapters of his *libello* Dante describes how the image of his glorious lady Beatrice first awakened "the vital spirit" (*lo spirito della vita*) within his heart and made him the subject of Love – a quickening that marked the beginning of his "book of memory" – the earliest trace of self-awareness in him.[20] The sight of Beatrice, therefore, awakened a desire in Dante's heart and by that generated his self-awareness, and Laura, as Franciscus describes her, affected him in a similar way. At the same time, in contrast to Dante, who ultimately regarded the awakening of the desire for the lady as the source of his desire for God, Franciscus describes his desire for the lady in the passage as the source of his longing for virtue equated with poetic and scholarly glory. Laura, he declares, is the one responsible for his "modest name and glory" (*nominis aut glorie*). As well as awakening his self-awareness, therefore, Laura is also responsible for providing him with an earthly identity as a great poet and scholar.[21]

This attainment of name and glory, as Franciscus further declares in the passage, was made possible by his adherence to the image of his beloved: "Why should I not be transformed into the pattern of the character that I loved?" (*Quidni enim in amatos mores transformarer?*). Laura thus clearly becomes a type of a mirror-reflection, fashioning the

---

[20]Dante, *Vita nuova*, 5–10. On the relation between the *Secretum* and the "stilnovisti" tradition, see Noferi, *L'esperienza poetica*, 261–266, and Santagata, *I frammenti*, 65–66. On Petrarch's use of the tradition in the *Rime*, see Sturm-Maddox, *Petrarch's Metamorphoses*, 39–64.

[21]The desire for Laura and that for earthly glory are therefore intrinsically intertwined. See also Santagata, *I frammenti*, 64–65.

desiring lover in her own image. Mirroring, desire, and selfhood are intrinsically connected in this passage in a very similar way to that of Ovid's Narcissus: in both cases, it is the desire for the image that alters the lover's internal state and makes him self-aware; moreover, in both cases, the lover, as Franciscus believes, eventually becomes like the reflection. Laura – and the desire for glory she generates – thus becomes in the third dialogue the equivalent of Narcissus' reflection in the pool, fulfilling *in bono*, in Franciscus' view, the two roles that Narcissus' reflection fulfilled in the myth.

Confronted with Franciscus' claim that love made him who he is, Augustinus argues that Laura in fact prevented him from becoming what he could have been,[22] and that because of this love he has fallen into great unhappiness, hampered by endless toils and labours: "When you say she involved you with countless labours, there you are right" (*Iam quod innumeris illam te laboribus implicuisse commemoras, hoc unum verum predicas*, 132). In order to convince Franciscus that this is indeed the case, Augustinus asks him whether he can still recall his youth (*puerilium annorum*) and how at that time he was filled with "fear of God ... thought of death ... love of the upright life" (my translation of: *timor Dei,...mortis cogitatio,... amor honestatis?* 136). Franciscus answers that his youth is perfectly alive in his memory and that he often regrets the waning of this early uprightness. Augustinus then invites him to recall when exactly that downward turn in his life took place and to compare it to the time "when he first saw the beauty of this woman" (my translation of: *quando illius tibi primum mulieris species visa est*, 138). Comparing the dates, Franciscus admits that they match perfectly – it was the emergence of his love for Laura that brought him down from his early state of bliss.

In their staging of Franciscus' personal history in the third dialogue, therefore, both Augustinus and Franciscus agree that the latter enjoyed in his early years a type of "golden age" of uprightness, a *dolce tempo* completely devoid of the pangs of desire. This golden age, however, as Franciscus is led to admit, ended exactly like in the myth of Narcissus with the intrusion of an *other*, an object of desire serving as a mirror reflection, into the early pastoral enclosure of the self.[23] Further, as in

---

[22] *O quantum in virum evadere poteras, nisi illa te forme blanditiis retraxisset!* (130: "What a great man you could have turned out to be, if that woman had not held you back by her seductive beauty!").

[23] See also the similar description in the opening lines of *Rime* 23: *Nel dolce tempo de la prima etade*.

the myth, it is the same image that is responsible for ending this golden age and leading him to endless torments of desire, that, in Franciscus' view, also provides him with self-awareness and a model according to which his own self is established. The very source of his abundance, Franciscus painfully discovers, also makes him poor.

Franciscus' very being is therefore marked, according to the third dialogue, by an essential ambiguity, a sense of presence and satisfaction that is constantly accompanied by a feeling of absence and exile.[24] According to the figure of Augustinus, there is no doubt about the source of this ambiguity: the reflection. In the same way that Narcissus' frustration, as the myth implied, stemmed from the ambiguous nature of the reflection which provided him with self-awareness – being both self and not-self at the same time – so, according to Augustinus, Franciscus' frustration essentially emanates from the imperfect nature of the image. Being subjected to time, change and ultimately death, Laura – or otherwise the name and glory that she provided him with – can never satisfy Franciscus' longings, but only frustrate them: "Do you not understand what folly it is to subject your soul to things of this world, things that kindle the flames of desire, that can give you no peace and cannot last? They offer the promise of sweetness, but torment you with constant agitation" (*O cece, necdum intelligis quanta dementia est sic animum rebus subiecisse mortalibus, que eum et desiderii flammis accendant, nec quietare noverint nec permanere valeant in finem, et crebris motibus quem demulcere pollicentur excrucient?* 126).

Book Three of the *Secretum*, therefore, establishes a close thematic parallel between the figure of Franciscus and Ovid's Narcissus: both enjoyed a golden age of bliss that ended with the entry of an ambiguous object of desire. Nevertheless, while Ovid's account of the myth made clear that there is no possible way out of the identification with the alienating image and the existential labyrinth that it entails, the figure of Augustinus constantly tries to convince Franciscus that there is a way to transcend the fate of Narcissus, to overcome the inner exile. The efforts of Augustinus to cure Franciscus' malaise in the *Secretum*, in this sense, become an attempt to alter the reflection in the mirror, to unite self and image. In these efforts, Augustine's *Confessions* and the concept of the corrected Narcissus preva-lent in them become the other main literary mirror upon which the *Secretum* is based, with the clear aim of leading Franciscus to alter – after

---

[24] On Petrarch's "ambiguous subjectivity" in the *Rime*, see Boysen, "Crucified."

the fashion of his spiritual mentor – the reflection of Laura and glory with that of the mirror of the Word of God.

The Mirror of God

The best place to start following the traces of Augustinus' attempt to alter the reflection in Franciscus' mirror and to lead him to become a corrected Narcissus is the Augustinian allusion to the myth near the beginning of the second dialogue. After establishing, by the end of the first dialogue, that what holds Franciscus back from transcending his crisis is his imperfect will and reluctance to give up his earthly passions,[25] Augustinus sets out in the second dialogue to address these passions more specifically. Going through the list of the seven deadly sins, Augustinus mentions first the sin of pride, associating it with Franciscus' passion for glory: "How many are the things that tempt your soul to perilous flights. You have great natural abilities, but they tire you out and make you forgetful of the weakness you so often experience. They crowd in and occupy your mind, until it can think of nothing else. And thus you become so proud, self-reliant, and self-satisfied that finally you hate your creator" (*Quam multa sunt que animum tuum funestis alis extollunt et sub insite nobilitatis obtentu, totiens experte fragilitatis immemorem fatigant, occupant, circumvolvunt, aliud cogitare non sinunt, superbientem fidentemque suis viribus, et usque ad Creatoris odium placentem sibi!* 54).

The pride that Franciscus takes in his own abilities, Augustinus maintains, leads him to a form of self-idolatry – loving himself more than the creator. At first, Augustinus compares this pride to that of Lucifer and his throng of rebellious angels: "consider the sin which caused those noble spirits to fall at the dawn of creation" (*unde ab initio creaturarum omnium illi nobilissimi spiritus corruerunt,* 54), but it is not long afterwards that another popular medieval exemplum of the dangers of pride is mentioned – Narcissus.[26] Addressing Franciscus' infatuation with his own bodily appearance, Augustinus declares: "Does not the story of Narcissus terrify you? And does not a manly consideration of

---

25 *Nunquam te ad salutem qua decuit aspirasse, sed tepidius remissiusque quam periculorum tantorum consideratio requirebat* (24; "You never desired salvation as you should have. Your wishes were half-hearted and feeble, considering the great peril you were in").

26 On Narcissus as an exemplum of the sin of pride in the Middle Ages, see Knoespel, *Narcissus*, 23–58. On the association of Narcissus' sin with that of the devil in Dante, see McMahon, "Satan."

the foulness of the body remind you what you are inwardly? Content with gazing only at the exterior skin, you do not extend the eyes of the mind beyond that (my translation of: *Neque te Narcissi terruit fabella, nec quid esses introrsus virilis consideratio corporee feditatis admonuit? Exterioris cutis contentus aspectu, oculos mentis ultra non porrigis*, 60).

Franciscus' fallacy, like that of Narcissus, Augustinus declares, is taking pride in the false beauty of earthly objects such as the body, rather than directing one's gaze to an eternal object such as the soul. Clinging to the body, both Franciscus and Narcissus are trapped in the shadowy world of appearances. This Neoplatonic interpretation of the myth goes back to Plotinus and was prevalent in the Middle Ages as well, for example in Alexander Neckham's *De naturis rerum*.[27] At the same time, this allusion to the myth also contains an element that is unmistakably Augustinian. The references to the body as a covering (*exterioris cutis*), and to the reluctance to "look beyond it" as the source of failure, closely echo the Augustinian hermeneutics of the Bible with its emphasis on the need to go beyond the "letter" – the "body" – to the meaning lying within – the "spirit."[28] The body is thus presented in this passage as a "sign" to be read, and Franciscus' failure as one of interpretation – failing to probe deeper into meaning. Guided by his pride to a failure of reading, therefore, the outcome for Franciscus is a literal carnality, identification with the false image of the body.

The link established in this reference to Narcissus in the *Secretum* between pride, mirroring, reading and selfhood and the use of the terminology of biblical hermeneutics closely resemble the passage from Book Three of the *Confessions* in which Augustine describes his attitude towards the Bible in his student years: "What I am now saying did not then enter my mind when I gave my attention to the *Scripture*. It seemed to me unworthy in comparison with the dignity of Cicero. My inflated conceit shunned the Bible's restraint, and *my gaze never penetrated to its inwardness (Non enim sicut modo loquor, ita sensi, cum attendi ad illam scripturam, sed visa est mihi indigna quam tullianae dignitati compararem. Tumor enim meus refugiebat modum eius et acies mea non penetrabat interiora*

---

[27] On Plotinus' use of Narcissus (Enn. I: 6–8), see Vinge, *The Narcissus Theme*, 37. On Neckham, see Vinge, *The Narcissus Theme*, 75.

[28] Augustine, *De doctrina christiana*, 3.5.9: *"Littera occidit, spiritus autem vivificat (2 Cor. 3:6)." Cum enim figurate dictum sic accipitur, tamquam proprie dictum sit, carnaliter sapitur* ("'the letter kills but the spirit gives life.' For when something meant figuratively is interpreted as if it were meant literally, it is understood in a carnal way").

eius, 3.5.9, emphasis added).[29] It is his puffed up pride, Augustine tells us in language later echoed in the *Secretum*, which left him on the level of the letter and did not allow him to penetrate the inner secrets of the Bible. The outcome of this carnality was identification with false objects – words manifesting Ciceronian eloquence such as those of the Manichees – and a constant feeling of lack and frustration: "I derived no nourishment from them but was left more exhausted than before" (*nec nutriebar eis, sed exhauriebar magis*, 3.6.10). The analysis of Augustine's attitude towards the Bible in the *Confessions* thus provides the exact same structure as that of Franciscus' and Narcissus' malaise in the *Secretum*: pride that leads to a failure of language and to identification with a false object bound to frustrate. Augustine of the *Confessions* is therefore the source lying behind Petrarch's explicit use of the Narcissus myth in Book Two, and we might assume, as a result, that in Petrarch's view Narcissus was also a dominant figure haunting Augustine in the *Confessions*. It is thus Augustine's solution to his own "narcissistic" problem in the *Confessions* that we now expect Franciscus to follow in the *Secretum*.

Indeed, this passage from the *Confessions* describing the attitude of the young Augustine to the Bible is a part of a series of similar episodes documenting the saint's journey through false linguistic identifications back to the satisfaction and certainty of the Word – the image of God residing within every human soul and accessible solely through its outward manifestation in *Scripture*.[30] Among these alienating identifications – all stemming from a failure or an abuse of language – Augustine includes the story of Dido and Aeneas with which he strongly identified and by that identification became only more absent from God (1.13.20),[31] the Manichees' teachings to which he clung due to their eloquence rather than meaning, his longing for false glory by means of his own corrupt eloquence (3.4.7),[32] and, finally, the many lovers who

---

[29] The edition of the *Confessions* is that of O'Donnell. Translations are taken from Chadwick, unless otherwise indicated.

[30] On the *Confessions* as Augustine's journey *in* language back to the Word, see Vance, "Augustine's Confessions." On the Word manifested in *Scripture* as the sole linguistic certainty that might bring us back to "ourselves" – the image of God within, see Vance, 18–25. See also Colish, *Mirror of Language*, 25–26; Freccero, "Fig Tree and Laurel," 22–25; and Stock, *Augustine the Reader*, 273–278.

[31] *Cum interea me ipsum in his a te morientem, deus, vita mea* ("in reading this, O God my life, I myself was meanwhile dying by my alienation from you").

[32] *Eminere cupiebam fine damnabili et ventoso per gaudia vanitatis humanae* ("I wanted to distinguish myself as an orator for a damnable and conceited purpose, namely

constantly reminded him of the desires of the flesh (8.7.17).[33] Serving thus as sources of false identification that keep frustrating Augustine's desires and alienating him from himself, these objects all become possible echoes of Narcissus' reflection in the pool, and the entire *Confessions*, in this sense, turns into the narrative of Augustine's journey to transcend the fate of Narcissus. This journey finally ended in the garden in Milan, when, touched by grace, Augustine was able at last to renounce all his false identifications and to cling solely to the Word of God (8.12.30).[34] This Augustinian Odyssey is closely reflected in Franciscus' own voyage in the *Secretum*, thus making the Augustinian model of a Narcissus corrected by the reflection of the Word a dominant one in the work.

Franciscus' parallel journey through false identifications stemming from linguistic failures in the *Secretum* begins right before the allusion to the Narcissus myth in Book Two, when Augustinus criticises the pride Franciscus takes in his eloquence. In this discussion, Augustinus identifies the writing of poetry as another form of Franciscus' fascination with his own empty reflection – this time the linguistic and aural one:

> Quid enim, queso, puerilius imo vero quid insanius quam, ..., verborum studio tempus impendere et lippis oculis nunquam sua probra cernentem, tantam voluptatem ex sermone percipere, quarundam avicolarum in morem, quas aiunt usque in perniciem proprii cantus dulcedine delectari. (56)

> (Tell me, what can be more childish, indeed more insane, than to be careless and lazy in all other matters, but waste time in the study of words and derive so much pleasure in speaking, while in your ignorance you never see your own reprehensible behaviour? You are like those little birds they say take so much pleasure in their own singing that they sing themselves to death.)

Franciscus' poems, according to Augustinus, are like those of birds – pleasing sounds that lack any meaning whatsoever. Failing, or unwilling,

---

delight in human vanity").

[33] *At ego adulescens miser valde, miser in exordio ipsius adulescentiae, etiam petieram a te castitatem et dixeram, "da mihi castitatem et continentiam, sed noli modo"* ("But I was an unhappy young man, wretched as at the beginning of my adolescence when I prayed for your chastity but said: 'Grant me chastity and continence, but not yet'").

[34] *Convertisti enim me ad te, ut nec uxorem quaererem nec aliquam spem saeculi huius, stans in ea regula fidei* ("The effect of your converting me to yourself was that I did not now seek a wife and had no ambition for success in this world. I stood firm upon that rule of faith").

to acknowledge their emptiness, Franciscus continues to take delight in his own vain creation, with the end result of death and ruin. The poems, in this sense, become another version of Franciscus' bodily image in the mirror, another reflection he must renounce in order to transcend the fate of Narcissus.

A very similar critique appears in the second direct reference to mirroring in the work – this time in the discussion of shame as a possible remedy for Franciscus' love in the third dialogue. Asking Franciscus whether he has looked in the mirror lately (*Vidisti ne te nuper in speculo*, 162), Augustinus then goes on to inquire whether he noticed there the grey hairs showing around his temples and, later, whether this brought about any change in his soul (*mutavit ne animum ulla ex parte corporis conspecta mutatio?* 164). Franciscus answers that while these signs no doubt "disturbed" him, they did not bring about change (*Concussit utique, sed non mutavit*; 164), and continues to explain that the cause of this was the consolation he received from several classical exempla of great men who accepted with equanimity the signs of old age. Angered by his answer, Augustinus criticises the effect of these exempla: "All they do is persuade you to neglect the passing of time and forget the day of your death" (*Quid enim aliud suadent quam lapsum etatis negligere et supremi temporis oblivisci?* 164). This passage, therefore, once again criticises Franciscus' failure to read correctly the signs in the mirror and his continuing identification with the image of the body; at the same time, it also addresses another of Franciscus' mirror reflections – the classical texts according to which he fashions his own self. Diverting him from the recognition of the truth, these texts become another link in the chain of his alienating reflections that needs to be broken.[35]

Finally, as I have shown, Augustinus turns in the third dialogue to address the two most dangerous of Franciscus' identifications – love and glory, the two final obstacles that Augustine himself had to shed on the way to the Word. Focusing at the end of the work on Franciscus' hope

---

[35] While a little later on Augustinus modifies his criticism of ancient exempla: *Laudo quicquid id est, propter quod nec adventantem metuas senectutem* (166: "I have nothing but praise for whatever causes you not to fear the onset of old age"), thus suggesting that the problem does not reside in the ancient texts themselves, but rather in the way Franciscus reads them, the fact remains that as long as Franciscus will not renounce his earthly and alienating identifications – including these misleading exempla – he will not be able to become the reader he should be. See also Kahn, "Figure of the Reader," 161.

to attain eternal glory by means of his Latin works, Augustinus explicitly describes this passion as an outcome of a failure of language: "The name of glory is known to you; but what it really is seems to be unknown to you, to judge from your actions" (*Tibi vero nomen glorie notum, res ipsa, ut ex actibus colligitur, esse videtur incognita,* 176). The glory Franciscus follows, Augustinus goes on to say, is nothing but reputation, "a kind of breath or changing breeze" (*Est igitur flatus quidam atque aura volubilis,* 176), while true glory is that which is attached to virtue, attained without even being sought. Following the false but common meaning of the word rather than the true one, Franciscus is once again adhering to the empty covering, identifying with a false reflection that is bound to lead him away from himself: "You prefer to abandon yourself rather than your little books" (*Te ipsum derelinquere mavis, quam libellos tuos,* 192).

Franciscus' bodily reflection, his poetry, the ancient texts, Laura and his glory all become in the *Secretum* echoes of Narcissus' reflection in the pool, and of the series of empty images that Augustine shed on his way back to the certainty of the Word. Petrarch's journey in the *Secretum* is thus closely modelled upon Augustine's quest in the *Confessions* to become a corrected Narcissus, returning slowly but surely to his "true self" – the Word of God residing within.

Inescapable "Narcissism"

Throughout the *Secretum,* it appears that Franciscus gradually accepts Augustinus' admonitions and agrees to give up his earthly reflections, reaching the doorstep of conversion – "because you have gotten the better of me in reasoning on many points, I will surrender before I am utterly defeated" (*quia in multis me ratione superasti, volo et hic, prius quam deiciar, arma deponere,* 112), he says at the end of Book Two following a long discussion of the dangers of his ambition and melancholy. At the end of their debate over the dangers of earthly love in Book Three Franciscus even agrees to give up his self-proclaimed noble love for Laura, and engages in a lengthy discussion on the possible *remedia amoris.*

Nevertheless, as we reach the end of the work, the parallel between the *Secretum* and the *Confessions* abruptly ends. In contrast to his saintly mentor, Franciscus declares that there is one passion – that for earthly glory – that he would not be able to leave behind, even though he is fully aware of its danger:

Adero michi ipse quantum potero, et sparsa anime fragmenta recolligam, moraborque mecum sedulo. Sane nunc, dum loquimur, multa me magnaque, quamvis adhuc mortalia, negotia expectant ... non ignarus, ut paulo ante dicebas, multo michi futurum esse securius studium hoc unum sectari et, deviis pretermissis, rectum callem salutis apprehendere. Sed desiderium frenare non valeo. (198–200)

(I shall be as true to myself as I can, collect the scattered fragments of my soul, and diligently aim at self-possession. But even as we speak, many important matters, though they are of this world, await my attention ... I am not ignorant, as you were just saying, that it would be a much safer course to tend to the care of my soul and set myself straight on the road to salvation ... but I cannot restrain my desire for study.)

At the end of the work, therefore, Franciscus rejects the arguments of Augustinus, and with that also the entire Augustinian model of the corrected Narcissus upon which the *Secretum* is based. Rather than fashioning the work – and his life – completely along the lines of the *Confessions*, in the end Petrarch maintains that he cannot help but follow in the footsteps of Ovid's Narcissus. For just as Narcissus in the myth eventually realised the vanity of the reflection and its subsequent doom but could not stop desiring it, so Franciscus in the end sees the deadly threat posed by the reflection of his own glory and consciously continues to pursue it. The end of the *Secretum* thus completes the parallel established in Book Three with Ovid's original account of the myth: the reflection of his own glory (which, as I have shown, cannot be separated from that of Laura), that provided Franciscus with self-awareness and identity while leading him away from his golden age, is bound to lead to his ruin. In contrast to the view of the historical Augustine, for Petrarch of the *Secretum*, just as for Ovid, there is no way out of the unavoidable experience of inner absence and exile, no way out of the fate of Narcissus. The insurmountable desire for the flower of glory necessarily entails the price of death.

The eventual rejection of the Augustinian model and the triumph of the Ovidian subtext in the *Secretum* are also closely reflected in the very structure of the work. In the end of the third and final dialogue, answering Franciscus' claim that he is unable to abandon his passion for glory, Augustinus declares: "we are slipping back into an old argument. You are calling the will lacking in power" (*In antiquam litem relabimur, voluntatem impotentiam vocas*, 200). This "old quarrel" regarding the impotence of the will is the same one with which the two started the work: "there is no doubt that many are unhappy and that they have no choice in the matter, though they would have it otherwise" (*Dubitari igitur meo iudicio non potest quin multi quidem inviti nolentesque sint miseri,* 12), as Franciscus maintained near the beginning of the work. After three long days of conversation, therefore, the two have come full circle and ended at their beginning.

This circularity of the *Secretum,* standing in stark contrast to the linearity of the Augustinian narrative in the *Confessions,* is therefore the mark of stasis, of Petrarch's dependence upon the same patterns of thought and the same passions without being able to break the cycle.[36] Petrarch alludes to his wish to structure such a healing narrative in his promise at the end of the work to "recollect the scattered fragments of my soul" (*sparsa anime fragmenta recolligam*), a phrase that closely echoes Augustine's description of his intention in the writing of the *Confessions:* "I intend to remind myself of my past foulness ... not because I love them but so that I may love you, my God ... so that you may be sweet to me, a sweetness touched by no deception ... *gathering me together from the state of disintegration in which I had been fruitlessly divided* (slightly modified rendition of: *Recordari volo transactas foeditates meas, ... non quod eas amem, sed ut amem te, deus meus ... ut tu dulcescas mihi, dulcedo non fallax ... et conligens me a dispersione, in qua frustatim discissus sum,* 2.1.1, emphasis added). It was therefore from the vantage point of conversion, the complete surrendering of authority over himself to God, that Augustine was able to realise the meaning underlying the fluctuations of his life and to collect the fragments into a purposeful narrative.[37] Petrarch, in contrast, steadfast in his refusal, or inability, to reach a similar vantage point – a fact that is made all the more evident by his assertion that he himself, rather than God, will be the one attempting to gather the pieces – remains entrapped just like Narcissus within the endless cycles of ever-frustrated desire.

Such an emphasis on the aimless circularity imposed by desire, as Philip Hardie has shown, is also one of the dominant aspects of the entire

---

[36] On the similar circular structure of the *Rime sparse,* see Mazzotta, *Worlds of Petrarch,* 58–59. On the relation between Petrarch's circular self-representation and his view of history, see Bernardo, "Petrarch's Autobiography," esp. 57–59.

[37] See also Kahn, "Figure of the Reader," 156–157. For other references to the "gathering of the scattered fragments" in the *Confessions,* see 10.11.18; 10.40.65; 11.29.39; 12.16.23. On Dante's analogous solution to his own "narcissistic" problem in the *Commedia,* see Akbari, *Seeing through the Veil,* 170–174, and Brownlee, "Dante and Narcissus."

Metamorphoses.[38] The same violent passion that brings Narcissus down from his primary arrogant bliss in Book Three was responsible for the fall of Apollo in Book One, and is then echoed in the story of Pygmalion in Book Ten; the myths of Book Three re-enact over and over again the entrapments of mirroring; the stories of Hyacinthus and Adonis recounted by Orpheus in Book Ten are both versions of his own personal tale of loss of love.[39] This thematic repetition in the stories of Orpheus is in turn reflected in the structure of the work: the stories of loss told by Orpheus appear as a digression within the main narrative of the *Metamorphoses* in which Ovid tells about Orpheus' own loss, thus creating a small circle of stories within the larger one – each one reflecting the other.

All these thematic and structural repetitions of the same passions in Ovid's poem, manifesting "an undeniable monotony ... experienced by every reader again and again with the feeling of 'I've heard this one before',"[40] are essentially a mark of the stasis imposed by desire, the recurring patterns of lack and longing that govern, according to Ovid, every personal life and all of human history. While nothing remains the same, as the *carmen perpetuum* sets out to show, paradoxically nothing also ever truly changes. It is therefore this Ovidian notion of circularity and stasis imposed by desire that dominates the structure as well as the theme of the *Secretum*, manifesting in the work an experience of self that is markedly Ovidian, markedly "narcissistic" – a self entrapped within the circularity of his own passions, within his inescapable fascination with his own image.

Conclusion: An Ovidian Self

In his recent treatment of the question of "Petrarch's self," Timothy Reiss has followed several previous critics in complicating the common notion that Petrarch was the first "modern man."[41] He writes: "Not for

---

38 Hardie, *Ovid's Poetics*, 65–70.

39 Hardie, *Ovid's Poetics*, 65.

40 Hardie, *Ovid's Poetics*, 65.

41 For Petrarch as the harbinger of modern selfhood, see Baron, "Petrarch: His Inner Struggles"; Scaglione, "Classical Heritage and Petrarchan Self-Consciousness"; Trinkaus, *Poet as Philosopher*. Notable challenges to this notion have been provided by Burke, "Representations of the Self"; Mazzotta, *Worlds of Petrarch*; and in certain aspects Greene, *Light in Troy*, 81–146. For a recent re-evaluation of the question of the Renaissance self in general, see Martin, *Myths of Renaissance Individualism*.

him belief in Dignity of Man pitted alone against Nature and Fortune .... Not for him even modest belief in humans as essentially characterised by distinct singular interiority."[42] Petrarch's notion of who he is, Reiss maintains, was always dependent upon the "circles of being" within which he was embedded – the social, the material, the divine: "the truly solitary life, separate from the divine, human, social and material could never be a good. Selfe was ever public."[43] The analysis of the use of the Narcissus myth in the *Secretum* shows that for Petrarch, who he is was indeed dependent upon the outside, the mirror-like reflection with which he identified and which he desired; self, for him, was never a given presence.

At the same time, it would be a mistake to disregard the fact that in Petrarch's conscious decision to reject the Augustinian solution to his crisis and to adhere to that which is earthly and fleeting about him – his name, love, and earthly glory – there is something very modern, that will no doubt play a role in the formation of the modern concept of the self as unique, autonomous and authoritative. In his rejection of the mirror of the Word for that of his own glory in the *Secretum*, Petrarch is rejecting the shared and communal reflection for the sake of his own singular one, and he is doing so even while admitting that it is "not a good," as the association of this desire with both the devil and Narcissus shows. The aspect in which Petrarch is indeed very different from later modern notions of self is precisely in his recognition – Ovidian through and through – that such a desire, such identification with his own earthly reflection, necessarily implies a type of death, an unavoidable experience of lack, absence and exile. In the *Secretum,* it is Ovid's Narcissus that serves as the model for this combination of glory and exile forming the core of Petrarch's being, and it is this Ovidian experience of self that he will ultimately bequeath to future generations of humanists.[44]

UNIVERSITY OF TORONTO

---

[42]Reiss, *Mirages of the Selfe*, 303.

[43]Reiss, *Mirages of the Selfe*, 328.

[44]I am grateful to Brian Stock, Suzanne Conklin Akbari, Lawrin Armstrong, Kenneth R. Bartlett, Wendy Greyling, Jennifer A. Harris, William Robins, Jill Ross, and David Townsend for their insightful and helpful comments on earlier versions of this article. I also wish to thank Ronald G. Witt and Timothy Kircher for kindly agreeing to read this article and challenge my thinking on Petrarch. Thanks also to the anonymous readers of this article for their constructive suggestions.

Actaeon Ego Sum:
Ovidian Dismemberment and Lyric Voice in Petrarch and Maurice Scève

Cynthia Nazarian

Literary retellings of the Diana and Actaeon story from Ovid onward have distinguished multiple Actaeons by playing on the essentially fragmentary nature of the myth. The tale can be uniquely encapsulated by its constitutive moments: each fragmentary tableau of the Actaeon sequence, like a new glimpse through the keyhole, provides a different view onto the entirety of the story. Actaeon approaching the hidden pool is the doomed innocent or hubristic suitor. At the moment of forbidden sight he is the desperate voyeur or luckless bystander. The "essence" of Actaeon is multiple; it is no coincidence that the result of his metamorphosis will be dismemberment: the disintegration of hunter and tale into their constitutive fragments.

Before fragmentation, however, comes the punishment at the hands of the virgin goddess: the transformation into a stag which reifies the divine interdiction against speech. Diana phrases her sentence as a challenge: "Now you are free to tell that you have seen me all unrobed – if you can tell" (*nunc tibi me posito visam velamine narres, | sit poteris narrare, licet*, *Met.* 3.192–193).[1] It is precisely at the moment of purest alterity and alienation that Actaeon's most tragic cry, unspeakable in his new form, proves Diana's triumph. Only the pen of the author of the *Metamorphoses* can cry out for the muted stag, hunted by his own dogs "I am Actaeon" (*Actaeon ego sum*, *Met.* 3.230).

The problem not only of being Actaeon, but of speaking Actaeon saw itself repeatedly taken up by early modern poets throughout western Europe. Shakespeare, Bruno, Wyatt, Sponde, Sidney, Ronsard, Desportes, and many others tried on the mask of the transformed hunter, finding through its mouthpiece a uniquely problematic voice, reflective of

---

[1] All translations of Ovid are taken from Frank Justus Miller's edition of the *Metamorphoses* for the Loeb Classical Library, 1977.

conflicted passion and the alienation from self. The Petrarchan tradition was most instrumental in advertising the literary fecundity of the myth, in the poetic realm and beyond. In the poetry of Petrarch and of those who followed him, a more or less apparent Actaeon can be seen, heard or inferred near every hidden pool and behind every metaphor of masculine flight. This isolated figure has provided a face for many Renaissance lovers, constituting their own poetic voices by means of his tragic moment of alienation and powerlessness, transposed so easily onto the lyric despair of the masculine Petrarchan lover before the cruel indifference of his mistress.

The focus of this article is precisely this potential within the Actaeon myth to articulate the masculine poetic I-voice, as manifested in the *Canzoniere* of Francesco Petrarca and in the *Délie* of his French self-styled successor, Maurice Scève. How does the lyric fragmentation of the Actaeon sequence enable the constitution of the Petrarchan poetic voice, at once inspired by and in opposition to this disintegration? To what degree is Scève's portrayal a re-Ovidianizing of the myth and does Scève "resolve" the fragmented Petrarchan Actaeon? This article attempts to answer these questions by exploring the crafted poetic contours of the Petrarchan and Scèvian Actaeons. By reuniting the scattered fragments of the Actaeon *leitmotif*, carefully dissected and scattered throughout the *Canzoniere* and the dizains of the *Délie*, we may arrive at a glimpse of these two poetic Selves, ironically defining and speaking themselves through carefully wrought masks of Actaeon condemned to silence.

PETRARCH'S ACTAEON

Canzone 23, which narrates the birth of the poet as a consequence of his first experience with love, is perhaps the most appropriate place to begin to examine Actaeon. It shows the carefree young man before his enslavement by love and the lady that will result in his poetic immortalization. The vantage point from which this idyllic youth is recounted is clearly one in which the poetic voice is already fully realised: in the iterative present from which the poet looks back, he is both conscious and certain of his fame and the established importance of that voice, most often heard sighing and weeping.

Nonetheless, here the poet narrates his own birth, before which lyric expression and self-awareness are a confused haze reflected in the poet's moment of questioning "Alas, what am I? what was I?" (*Lasso, che son? che fui?* 30).[2] It is no coincidence, then, that the images of metamorphosis used in describing the poet's coming into being problematise expression.[3] The sequential transformations, first into the laurel (Daphne), then Cygnus, then Battus, Byblis, Echo, and finally Actaeon all figure the cycle of the poet expressing his desire, then being punished with a metamorphosis that limits this expression, in turn causing a similar transformation of the form of expression, be it weeping or praying or writing.

In *Canzone* 23, Actaeon occupies a privileged and highly significant position in that he is the final transformation that the poet undergoes before his poetic voice is fully realised. The Actaeon that we encounter from the 147th verse onwards, however, is quite different from his Ovidian prototype. First, Petrarch overturns Ovid's defence of Actaeon's transgression. Ovid had asserted "But if you seek the truth, you will find the cause of this in fortune's fault and not in any crime of his" (*at bene si quaeras, Fortunae crimen in illo,* | *non scelus invenies; quod enim scelus error habebat, Met.* 3.141–142). In fact, Fortune seems to have very little to do with the Petrarchan Actaeon's gaze. First, the poet stipulates that he enters the woods because "I followed so far my desire" (*I' segui' tanto avanti il mio desire,* 147). Furthermore, we have a distinctly desiring narrator who looks on the naked lady: Petrarch leaves no room to question the unfortunate workings of fate; he specifies "I, who am not appeased by any other sight, stood to gaze on her" (*Io perché d'altra vista non m'appago* | *stetti a mirarla,* 152–153).

This admission of desire and the re-qualification of the accidental Ovidian gaze as a deliberate and lustful one has important repercussions when taken in conjunction with another significant Petrarchan change in the myth. In the penultimate stanza of *Canzone* 23, there are two moments in which the narration shifts from the past to the present tense. First, the poet admits, "I, who am not appeased by any other sight, stood to gaze on her" using the present conjugation *non m'appago.* Later on, in describing the end of the transformation, he concludes a stanza written in the past tense with the following shift into the present "From wood to wood quickly *I am transformed* and still *I flee* the belling of my hounds" (*di selva in selva ratto mi trasformo, et ancor de' miei can fuggo lo stormo,* 159–160; emphasis added). Reading these two present-tense segments

---

[2]The edition and translation of the *Canzoniere* used is *Petrarch's Lyric Poems,* ed. Durling. Unless otherwise noted, all translations from Scève's *Délie* are my own with the kind advice of François Rigolot.

[3]Murphy, "The Death of Actaeon," 139.

together suggests that (a) the poet was and remains desirous of the sight of the nude beloved, and (b) that he has escaped the mythic dismemberment by his own dogs. By removing any Ovidian ambiguity on the question of whether Actaeon's gaze was innocently accidental, Petrarch transforms the young hunter into an active and willing voyeur. Moreover, any remaining tragic compassion at the fate of the stag unrecognised by his dogs is removed by the omission of that dismemberment. The poet continues to escape punishment for what has now become a decidedly deliberate transgressive, violating gaze. Had the Ovidian original figured such an obvious and wilful violation of the goddess' sanctuary, the other gods would certainly not have questioned the severity of Diana's punishment (*Met.* 3.253–359).

As he appears in *Canzone* 23, Actaeon is unfinished because the final and most tragic part of his story, his slaying by his dogs, is omitted. The metamorphosis, in its punitive sense, is therefore an incomplete one: the poem effects its own metamorphosis of Actaeon as tragic figure into a kind of pseudo-Actaeon as unpunished voyeur. This Peeping-Tom Actaeon reappears in *Canzone* 52, where the poet describes:

> Non al suo amante più Diana piacque
> quando per tal ventura tutta ignuda
> la vide in mezzo de le gelide acque,
> ch'a me la pastorella alpestra et cruda
> posta a bagnar un leggiadretto velo
> ch'a l'aura il vago et biondo capel chiuda   (1–6)

(Not so much did Diana please her lover when, by a similar chance, he saw her all naked amid the icy waters, as did the cruel mountain shepherdess please me, set to wash a pretty veil that keeps her lovely blond head from the breeze).

This time, however, the poet plays much more subtly on the ambiguity inherent within the Ovidian narrative: he acknowledges that the glance was *per ventura* and provides an affirmative answer in place of Ovid's silence on the question of whether Actaeon desired Diana, having seen her. In this poem, however, the poet identifies with Actaeon only indirectly and impersonally. Gone is the "I was Actaeon" of the earlier *canzone*. This time, all that poet and hunter have to link them is an accidental gaze, directed now at two different women. The Actaeon who appears in *Canzone* 52 is once again an incomplete Actaeon, lyrically encapsulated in the single isolated moment of his glance.

Besides *Canzone* 23 and *Canzone* 52, where references to Actaeon
are clearly stated, there are a series of other poems in the *Canzoniere* in
which Actaeon can be glimpsed in splintered hints. Interestingly
enough, the process of identification and fragmentation is not limited
to the Actaeon character, but also acts on the figure of the goddess.[4] In
Canzone 126, for example, in which the poet relates his various reactions
to glimpsing Laura outdoors in a natural setting (presumably woods or a
meadow), the very first verses of the poem "Clear, fresh, sweet waters,
where she who alone seems lady to me rested her lovely body" (*Chiare
fresche et dolci acque | ove le belle membra | pose colei che sola a me par donna*,
1–3), show Laura bathing in some kind of pool or river. The phrase
"sacred bright air" (*Aere sacro sereno*, 10) adds a divine dimension to the
milieu in question. Thus, a vague outline of Diana in her sacred pool
already appears. Further in the poem, the poet calls for his reader to hear
"my sorrowful dying words" (le dolenti mie parole estreme, 13),
suggesting the imminence of his own death while speaking. At the end
of the next stanza, we find him hoping "[to] flee my labouring flesh and
my bones" (*fuggir la carne travagliate et l'ossa*, 26): masculine flight and the
awareness of the separation of flesh from essence, self from body.
Interestingly enough, Laura appears here as a wild beast (*fera*), but also
as "lovely and gentle" (*bella et mansueta*). Although the term recalls its
use in *Canzone* 23, it is only the mention of a look "[there,] where she
saw me" (*là 'v'ella mi scorse*, 126.30), that hints at a connection between
Laura here and the *fera* who noticed Actaeon's illicit gaze in that previous
canzone.

In *Canzone* 190, a deer appears, but this time it is Laura who has
become "A white doe on the green grass" (*Una candida cerva sopra l'erba*,
1). The hint of Diana-Actaeon appears with a written interdiction
around her neck "Let no one touch me" (*Nessun mi tocchi*, 9). Although
the poet is expressly forbidden to touch rather than to look, the final

---

[4]In her article, "Diana Described," Vickers sees in a "scattered" presentation of
the Diana-Actaeon story a fragmentation of the female at the hands of the male poet
in an attempt to ensure the stability of his own poetic voice. However, Vickers'
contention is thrown into question when one considers that in *Canzone* 23, the poet
identifies himself with first Daphne, and then Echo –both female – in one of the most
scattered, fragmented images of Ovidian voicelessness. Although there does appear to
be a definite process of poetic fragmentation at work here and throughout the
Canzoniere, the fragmentation is not exclusively of the female other, but of the Actaeon
motif in its entirety.

verses include a significant mention that "my eyes were tired by looking but not sated" (*gli occhi miei stanchi di mirar, non sazi*, 13), hinting once again at the guilty gaze of Actaeon, whose form has been displaced here onto the lady.

This transferral of the stag image onto the female occurs once again in *Canzone* 323, which presents itself as a kind of complement to *Canzone* 23, with its *sei visioni* that correspond to 23's six metamorphoses. The *fera* image appears once again. While its previous uses in *Canzone* 23 and 126 could immediately suggest Actaeon, here the image is completed with the inclusion of two pursuing hounds, tearing at her flanks (6–12) and thus strengthening the Actaeon reference.

As we will see, the fragmentation of the Actaeon narrative into such hints scattered throughout the *Canzoniere* neutralises the destabilising effect of the myth on the poetic I-voice resulting from the poet's identification with Ovid's character. These seeming shards of Actaeon appear again and again, but never cohere into a complete image of the tragic hunter. Instead of the scattered woman that Nancy Vickers reads in the *Canzoniere*, we find a scattered Actaeon, poetically dismembered again and again and hidden carefully among his own ruins. The disintegration of the Actaeon myth into such pregnant, suggestive fragments restores and affirms the poetic voice, functioning as a kind of antidote to that side of Actaeon that limits expression. Thus, "the physical and psychological torments so graphically described in Ovid's account of Actaeon's demise are postponed, transformed and dispersed throughout the other segments of *Canzone 23,* and, by extension, throughout the entire lyric sequence."[5] The question of expression and Actaeon, more properly put, is a problem of expression *as* Actaeon, which implies a certain intrinsic impossibility. The moment at which Actaeon becomes Actaeon – that is to say, the moment at which the young man of that name acquires his mythic immortality and becomes a *sign*, is that moment at which he is confronted in his new form by his unrecognising dogs and cannot cry out "I am Actaeon! Recognize your own master!" (*Actaeon ego sum: dominum cognoscite vestrum! Met.* 3.230). Here, the boldest Petrarchan dismemberment of the myth becomes clear: in *Canzone* 23, by telling his story as Actaeon in the past tense and including references to a present in which *he still has the capacity for expression*

---

[5] Preussner, "The Actaeon Myth," 99.

through speech or writing, Petrarch dares to say the impossible, "I *was* Actaeon."

What is a speaking, living Actaeon but a voyeur who got away, a sign emptied of its constitutive signified? The answer, to be explored further, is that he is precisely *not* Actaeon. JoAnn DellaNeva sees in the multiple metamorphoses of *Canzone* 23 an anxiety on the part of the poet about the instability of the written word which, by extension, she interprets as an anxiety about the coherence of his own poetic voice: "Transformation into a laurel no longer expresses the sublimation of the lover's desires, but now serves to furnish a portrait of the lover's instability."[6] That Actaeon should be the final metamorphosis before the birth of the poet as such thus becomes doubly significant: Actaeon is the state from which the Petrarchan poet must "recover" in order to be able to complete the poem. As we will see, Petrarch requires the Actaeon myth precisely in order to destabilise it, and constitute his poetic voice from its shards.

PETRARCH'S DIANA

The fragmentation of the Actaeon myth carried out throughout the *Canzoniere* is not exclusive to the figure of Actaeon or to the Actaeon-poet equation, but includes the association of Laura with Diana. Just as Petrarch styles himself Actaeon but not quite, Laura is never exactly Diana. As we already saw in *Canzone* 23, her appearance as a *fera* displaces part of the Actaeon imagery onto her. Similarly, in *Canzone* 190 she appears as a white doe which, as Durling's note indicates,[7] is sacred to and therefore associated with Diana, but she is not herself the virgin goddess. In *Canzone* 281, where Laura appears, as we saw earlier, as a kind of divinity, she is only "in the form of a nymph or other goddess" (*in forma di ninfa o d'altra diva*; 9), exalted but anonymous. Similarly, in the fourth verse of *Canzone* 294 we hear "she is a goddess" (*ella è diva*), but once again we do not know which one. The repeated unspecific deification of Laura is not unusual in and of itself; it is simply when the repeated assertions "Laura is a (or as a) goddess" and the even more common "Laura is chaste" are never combined to make "Laura is the chaste goddess" that Diana becomes conspicuous because of her very absence.

---

6 DellaNeva, *Song and Counter-Song*, 74.
7 *Petrarch's Lyric Poems*, ed. Durling, 336.

This absence is highlighted further by the multiple fragments of the Actaeon story scattered throughout the *Canzoniere*. Reading through the sequence, it appears that a similar process of dismemberment is carried out on the figure of Laura as Diana, who will appear as hints in fragments, but never as a whole image. In *Canzone* 159 for example, the poet asks "What nymph in a fountain, in the woods what goddess ever loosed to the breeze locks of such fine gold?" (*Qual ninfa in fonti, in selve mai qual dea | chiome d'oro sì fino a l'aura sciolse?* 5–6). The goddess image appears alongside that of a nymph. Furthermore, both a fountain and woods are mentioned, hinting strongly at a certain well-known image of goddess and nymphs bathing in a secluded pool in the woods, but the allusion is never made clear. In *Canzone* 174, the lady appears as a "cruel lady who with her eyes, and *with the bow* whom I pleased only *as a target*" (*fera donna che con gli occhi suoi | et con l'arco a cui sol per segno piacqui,* 5–6, emphasis added), but despite even this image of a cruel huntress as the object of the poet's love, Diana goes unnamed.

In fact, the name (used by Ovid) of the goddess is mentioned only once throughout the *Canzoniere*,[8] and this occurs in *Canzone* 52, which we considered earlier. Here, Vickers interprets the allusion as follows: "'I am pleased by Laura's veil as Actaeon was pleased by Diana's nakedness'; 'My fetish equals Diana's body',"[9] stating the question perhaps too simply and directly. *Canzone* 52 clearly functions with the initial negation of the Laura-Diana identification: "*Not so much* did Diana please her lover" (*Non al suo amante più Diana piacque,* 1, emphasis added). Thus, from the very first word of the poem, Laura is precisely *not* Diana but *more* than Diana, perhaps because the fragments of Actaeon scattered throughout the *Canzoniere* have shown that the poet himself must be more than Actaeon in order to ensure the stability of his poetic voice.

Part of the impetus behind Petrarch's fragmentation of the Diana image might be her association with mutability and change. As we saw earlier, some critics have seen in the *Canzoniere* a marked anxiety about the coherence of the written word and therefore of the poet's own I-voice. In a poetic world in constant mutation, as reflected by the myriad metamorphoses, partial or complete, that we witness throughout the *Canzoniere*, Petrarch will extend Laura/the laurel as the only con-

---

8 Accademia della Crusca, *Concordanze del Canzoniere di Francesco Petrarca*, 470. s.v. "Diana."

9 Vickers, "Diana Described," 272.

stant symbol: "The permanence of the laurel, which is nothing other than the permanence of Petrarch's desire for Laura, is absolute. Desire is continuous across the violent discontinuity of each metamorphosis."[10] In light of this, to liken Laura to the changeable moon-goddess would be to subvert the very symbol on which the poet anchors his own lyric self.

If the poetic voice is born out of the love for Laura/the laurel, then any fickleness on her part would threaten its destabilisation. We have already seen Laura in her most threatening guise as perpetrator of metamorphosis in *Canzone* 23. Even here, however, Laura's powers of transformation are subverted at the most fundamental level by the simple narrative fact that the poet recovers from each one in turn. Even when we are left with Actaeon, which would place her at her most cruel, the image is halted in mid-narration: Actaeon survives and, all the more shockingly, narrates. Thus, metamorphosis at the figured hands of the female is permitted only to the extent that it is narrated by the object of the metamorphosis: male poetic agency is assured and articulated by the lyric I-voice that narrates its own metamorphosis. Thus, Petrarch's pseudo-Actaeon escapes obliteration and fatal silence by usurping the role of Ovid himself.

Furthermore, Petrarch imposes a solution on whatever remains of Diana's frightening changeability. As Leonard Barkan states in his work on the Actaeon myth, "metamorphosis suggests the loss of one identity and the gaining of another. The positive side of the process emerges in the myth of Daphne. Love gives the poet his identity through transformation,"[11] and Daphne provides the perfect antidote to Diana, just as Apollo will "resolve" Actaeon. Daphne, an image of petrified power-lessness, is Diana's antithesis in that she is the object rather than the agent of metamorphosis. Where Diana cannot be caught and punishes desire with silence and death, Daphne escapes capture only in the literal sense. Poetically speaking, she is eternally captured by the poet, becoming Petrarch's emblem and aiding in the constitution of his lyric self. Durling notes in the introduction to his edition of the *Canzoniere* that, "As Petrarch saw, the myth of Actaeon is an inversion of the myth of Daphne. In one, it is the beloved who flees, in the other the lover. In one, the end result is speech: poetry and fame; in the other, silence. In

---

[10] Brenckman, "Writing, Desire, Dialectic," 16.
[11] Barkan, "Diana and Actaeon," 335–336.

one, there is evergreen eternizing; in the other, dismemberment."[12] The poet will put exactly this solution into effect: having fragmented Actaeon and Diana beyond recognition and thus neutralised the myth's silencing power, Petrarch will propose Apollo and Daphne, with himself in the male leading role, as the platform on which to base a poetic voice that posits itself as stable, eternal and tinged with the divine.

THE SCÈVIAN ACTAEON:
RESOLVING AND RE-OVIDIANISING PETRARCH

Scève's use of the myth of Actaeon appears to function along opposite lines. Unlike Petrarch, Scève never says "I am" or "I was Actaeon." In fact, aside from the *embleme* 19 that precedes *dizain* 168, the name of Actaeon is never heard in the *Délie*.[13] Nonetheless, the collection is haunted by him. In contrast to Petrarch's work of fragmentation, Scève will weave Actaeon into the very thread of his *dizains*, where the young hunter will appear, silent but always there. The Scèvian treatment of Actaeon seems to function along a division into themes rather than a fragmentation along the narrative line. Several major ideas of Actaeon including innocent victimhood, the cruelty of the lady, disembodiment and alienation, constraints on speech and constraints to speak, are developed like various parts in a fugue which, when read together, coalesce into a kind of tapestry of Actaeon. The movement is contrary to Petrarch's treatment: whereas Petrarch scatters and attempts to anonymise parts of Actaeon throughout the *Canzoniere*, by weaving Actaeon's various themes throughout the *Délie*, Scève reunites the pieces to create a much more complex and detailed vision of the whole. By the end of the sequence, Actaeon is not reduced but becomes much more than he was: he becomes the sign for the poet himself.

Dizain 159, modelled on Petrarch's *Canzone* 209, illustrates the difference between the French poet's treatment of Actaeon and that of his Italian model.

> Si de sa main ma fatale ennemye,
> Et neantmoins delices de mon Ame,
> Me touche un rien, ma pensée endormye
> Plus, que le mort soubz sa pesante lame,
> Tressaulte en moy, comme si d'ardent flamme,

---

[12] *Petrarch's Lyric Poems*, ed. Durling, 29.
[13] I have used the edition of MacFarlane, *The Délie of Maurice Scève*.

Lon me touchoit dormant profondement.
Adonc l'esprit poulsant hors roidement
La veult fuyr, & moy son plus affin,
Et en ce poinct (à parler rondement)
Fuyant ma mort, j'accelere ma fin.

(If the hand of my mortal enemy, | She, the very Soul of my delight, | Should so much as graze me, | My mind, deader than a corpse | Beneath a heavy stone, leaps awake, | My deep sleep singed by her flame. | My spirit then stiffens with resolve | To flee both her, & me, its nearest kin, | And at this point (if I may be so bold), | Fleeing my death, I hasten my end.)[14]

I dolci colli ov'io lasciai me stesso,
partendo onde partir giamai non posso,
mi vanno innanzi, et emmi ogni or a dosso
quel caro peso ch'Amor m'à commesso.
Meco di me mi meraviglio spesso
ch'i' pur vo sempre, et non son ancor mosso
dal bel giogo più volte indarno scosso,
ma com' più me n'allungo et più m'appresso.
Et qual cervo ferito di saetta
col ferro avelenato dentr' al fianco
fugge et più duolsi quanto più s'affretta,
tal io, con quello stral dal lato manco
che mi consuma et parte mi diletta,
di duol mi struggo et di fuggir mi stanco

(The sweet hills where I left myself, when I departed from the place I can never depart from, are before me as I go, and still behind me is that sweet burden Love has entrusted me. | Within myself I am often amazed at myself, for I still go and yet have not moved from the sweet yoke that I have shaken off in vain many times, but the farther I go from it the closer I come. | As a hart struck by an arrow, with the poisoned steel within its side, flees and feels more pain the faster it runs, | so I, with that arrow in my left side which destroys me and at the same time delights me, am tormented by such sorrow and weary myself with fleeing.)

We note that in Petrarch the poem begins in an idyllic setting and that the tone is languid and nostalgic. The poet marvels, in the second quatrain, at himself and at the endurance of his love for Laura, and the tone remains dreamlike in its wonder. The Scèvian model begins on a

---

[14] Translation by Sieburth, *Emblems of Desire*.

much more violent image of the *fatale ennemye*. She causes delight in the poet almost against his will, since the metaphor in verse 4 mentions *le mort soubz sa pesante lame*. The poet himself is relegated to an object of Délie's action, replacing Petrarch's active first person voice by the passive position of direct object. Délie is the uncontested actor here. The violence continues with the image of the *ardent flamme* used on the sleeping figured poet, but here it finds its counterpart in the Petrarchan sonnet. The hart, *ferito di saetta*, presumably also feels pain, but the *bel giogo* and *caro peso* of the previous verses have already established the poet's delight at being thus "afflicted." The reader, confronted now with Petrarch's image of the wounded stag, sees the transparency of the metaphor, particularly when the arrow *mi consuma* and, as expected, *et parte mi diletta*. Scève, however, has lost control of his own soul, which *poulsant hors roidement | La vault fuyr & moy son plus affin*. The poet himself, almost as a secondary actor here in contrast to Délie and his rebellious soul, appears to have little control over his own flight, which accelerates his death. In Petrarch, however, we note that the final verse reverts to the first person and, albeit reflexively, the poet himself is the agent of his own fatigue: *di duol _mi_ struggo et di fuggir _mi_ stanco* (emphasis added).

Thus, an image of the Scèvian poetic voice already emerges as the object of Délie's agency, in sharp contrast to Petrarch who, as we will discuss later, creates Laura in order to create himself. Petrarch's disarmed Diana is refitted here with much deadlier weapons; in fact Délie appears most often as a huntress. This, of course, presumably places the poet in the position of prey. His situation is often a self-conscious one. The *dizain* that we have just discussed presents the poet as both victim and agent of his fatal flight. In *Dizain* 411.10, he similarly laments "I die caught in the nets that I have cast" (*Je me meurs pris es rhetz, que j'ay tendu*). Nonetheless, the blame for his fate lies squarely with Délie. Unlike the Laura figure, who is Petrarch's creation and therefore silent or expressive according to his will, Délie is presented as an unchallenged aggressor and Scève as her perfect victim. Ironically and quite tellingly, his metaphoric face will most often be that of the stag.

Like Petrarch in *Canzone* 23, Scève also refers to an earlier idyllic time, free of the yoke of love, where the poet is unbound and unfettered. *Dizain* 225 presents such a scenario, in which "Free I go and free I return" (*Libre je vois, & retourne libre*, 1). Accompanied by Virtue, the poet is virtually immune to the doubts and fears that love brings. Interestingly enough, this virtuous freedom has him in a state "All assured like the stag on the plain" (*Tout Asseuré, comme Cerf en campaigne,* 2). This stag represents both ideal freedom and the repeated demise of such freedom at the hands of Délie/Diana (whose favoured prey is the stag). In fact, these images of the stag as victim and Délie as a cruel, divine huntress are revisited throughout the *Délie*, hinting always at Actaeon as their perfect illustration. In *Dizain* 352, the poet has been wounded by his love, "Who with her eyes makes me dead, & alive" (*Qui par ses yeulx me rend mort, & vivant,* 4); in trying to decide what to do, he compares himself to "The stag wounded by the skilled hunter" (*Le Cerf blessé par l'archier bient adroit*) for whom "The more he flees death, the more his end approaches" (*Plus fuyt la mort, & plus sa fin approche,* 7–8). In *Dizain* 359, the poet portrays his suffering as that of a wounded *adversaire*, but here he cannot flee. The imagery implies an injured animal who "Flees this way and that, and cries, and struggles" (*Fuyt çà, & là, & crye, & se debat*). His case is unique in its likeness to Actaeon:

> Mais moy navré par ce traistre combat
> De tes doulx yeux, quand moins de doubte avois,
> Cele mon mal ainsi, comme tu vois,
> Pour te monstrer a l'œil evidamment,
> Que tel se taist & de langue, & de voix,
> De qui le cœur se plaint incessament. (5–10)

(But I, wounded by the treacherous attack | Of your sweet eyes, when least expecting | Thus conceal my pains, as you see | To show you clearly before your eyes | That the tongue and the voice may be silent | Of one whose heart yet laments ceaselessly.)

The importance of this silence is reinforced by the repetition of the theme throughout the *Délie*. Often we find the poet either unable or unwilling to speak his suffering, and often showing it in other ways, written on his body. His silence is frequently a result of Délie's effect on him. In *Dizain* 381 "The voice is snuffed out in my mouth | Before the feet of your divinity" (*la voix m'est en la bouche extaincte | Devant les piedz de ta divinité,* 1–2). Délie's effect is the curtailing of speech, the repercussions of which we will explore later. These verses imply, interestingly, the *death* of speech, or rather its stillbirth at the hands of the lady. What we are hearing is the silence of the innocent stag – of Actaeon – quite literally *extaincte | Devant les piedz de ta divinité.*

The significance of this speechlessness, however, goes beyond the mere death of speech. In *Dizain* 76 the poet tells us: "I opened my mouth, and on the point of crying | "Mer-" the bright appearance of her natural smile | Stopped me from completing it with "cy" (*J'ouvris la bouche, & sur le poinct du dire | Mer, un serain de son nayf soubrire | M'entreclouit le poursuyvre du cy*, 4–6). Here, Délie's interdiction causes a literal "dismemberment" of speech, embodied by the fragmentation of the word "mercy." This fragmentation functions as an emblem of Actaeon, with whom the poet has allied himself unmistakably through the images of the wounded stag, Délie as the huntress, and the constraints upon his speech. The poetic I-voice will result directly from this fragmentation and will personify fragmentation as well, as in *Dizain* 197: "The Heart, crying through the mouth, begs you | ... | That always burns and always cries for help" (*Le Coeur criant par la bouche te prie | ... | Qui tousjours ard, tousjours a l'ayde crie*, 8–10).

With the loss of speech comes an accompanying loss of self-consciousness, which Scève explains as a direct result of the effect of Délie's beauty. It puts him in a state in which, "lulled into such contentment | I had no knowledge of you or of myself" (*assoupy d'un tel contentement, | N'avois de toy ny de moy cognoissance*, 306.5–6).[15] The destabilisation effected by this loss of self-awareness is endemic to Délie's power and can be read in her very name, the most obvious meaning of which is "dé-lier," to unlink or undo. This is precisely the effect that Scève insists most heavily on. In *Dizain* 376, which begins "You are the Body, Lady, & I your shadow" (*Tu es le Corps, Dame, & je suis ton umbre*), Délie has disembodied the poet, who is reduced to the form of a shadow. The poem is characterised by a sense of vertigo evident not only in this loss of corporality, but in the concluding verses, which lament discordant wills as well as dissociated bodies (376.9–10).

The alienation from Délie's body (which is unattainable) and from her will (which is unknowable and ever-changing) is not the only disconnection produced by the poet's relationship with her. Like the Ovidian Diana, Délie "unlinks" the poet from himself: self from will, soul from body. *Dizain* 427 poses the question of how the poet, who is divided within himself, can ever be united with Délie (9–10). In *Dizain* 353 the poet describes the dissociation of soul and body that results directly from Délie's boundless goodness. In this case the soul, which is enslaved by Délie's virtue, leaves the body behind, which shrivels and

---

[15] This "enchantment" is described in pleasurable, virtually erotic terms, which are carried further by another metaphor for Délie's effect, the eternal death: see Coleman, *An Illustrated Love Canzoniere*, 36.

dries and is finally "reduced entirely to bones" (*reduict tout en os*, 7). The spiritual overtones of the *dizain*, interestingly enough, are in sharp contrast to many other descriptions of Délie's disconnecting power, where the effect is caused by the much earthier stimulant of her gaze. Thus Délie, whose powers are presented here in clearly sacred and virtuous imagery, often embodies the two-facedness of the moon and assumes elsewhere a more malevolent aspect: that of the basilisk.

Délie's gaze, likened regularly to that of this mythic beast, appears sometimes poisonous and always powerful and dissociative. Interestingly, Scève frequently describes the gaze originating from a seemingly dissociated pair of eyes, often appearing detached from their mistress. In *Dizain* 30, which begins "From the eyes in which the sun nests" (*Des yeulx, ausquelz s'enniche le Soleil*), Délie's gaze is capable of "Piercing me to the depths | Where the soul then divides into two" (*Me penetrant jusques en celle part, | Ou l'Ame attaincte or a deux il mespart*, 4–5). The poet refers in *Dizain* 42 directly to "the venom of your eyes" (*le venin de tes yeulx*), which enslaves the poet's desire for freedom and occupies his soul, causing his blood to flee into the depths of his liver.

The disembodiment that results from the gaze of Délie recalls sharply that other gaze that transgressed and was punished with this same dissociation. Actaeon's glance is continuously punished throughout the *Délie* by the lady's deadly one, which effects the Ovidian transformation of alienation from self. The very first *dizain* of the series presents Délie's gaze as overpowering the poet's own young and unguarded one:

> L'Oeil trop ardent en mes jeunes erreurs
> Girouettoit, mal cault, a l'impourveue :
> Voicy (ô paour d'agreables terreurs)
> Mon basilisque avec sa poingnant' veue
> Perçant Corps, Cœur, & Raison despourveue,
> Vint penetrer en l'Ame de mon Ame.
> Grand fut le coup, qui sans tranchante lame
> Fait, que vivant le Corps, l'Esprit desvie,
> Piteuse hostie au conspect de toy, Dame,
> Constituée Idole de ma vie.

(The Eye, too afire with my youthful errors, | Whirled like a weathercock, without design: | When suddenly (what delight, what terror) | My Basilisk, now sharpening its sights, | Pierced Body, & Heart, put Reason to flight, | Lancing deep into the Soul of my Soul. | The blow was hard, which without whetted blade | Kills the Sprit though the Body survive,

| Pitiful victim, I, now faced with you, | Lady, appointed Idol of my life.)[16]

Here, the poet represents himself with his *œil trop ardent* calling to mind another overly passionate glance, always guilty,[17] and similarly caught *a l'impourveue*. Délie's response is to punish him with her much deadlier glance, which *Perçant Corps, Cœur, & Raison despourveue, | Vint penetrer en l'Ame de mon Ame*, causing the separation of body and spirit, which are reduced miserably to the *piteuse hostie* of her power. Actaeon's gaze is punished here by Diana's, and his transformation is ever as alienating.

In fact, Actaeon's implication in this talk of competing gazes is made explicit in the poem that accompanies his emblem, *Dizain 168*. Significantly, this emblem is the only moment in the *Délie* at which Actaeon is referred to by name. The poem that accompanies it includes themes discussed so far, linking them visually as well as conceptually to the myth of the young hunter. In this case, Actaeon's transformation is caused not by Délie's gaze, but by the use of her name, because of which "The spirit, ravished by such sweet sentiment | Passes away to another, sweeter life" (*L'esprit ravy d'un si doulx sentement, | En aultre vie, & plus doulce trespasse*, 3–4). Though the poet is carried off gently, he nevertheless experiences a dissociation of body from essence: "Then the heart, which strives for such joy | Leaves the body, ready to be enshrined | And is pulled so strongly to the soul | That from itself and from the body, it is estranged" (*Alors le Coeur, qui un tel bien compasse, | Laisse le Corps prest a estre enchassé: | Et si bien a vers l'Ame pourchassé, | Que de soymesme, & du corps il s'estrange*, 5–8). At this moment of highlighted alienation from self Actaeon makes his clearest appearance and the final verses of the poem recall the motto that accompany his emblem: "Thus he is hounded by his own | Whose luck or condition Fortune has changed" (*Ainsi celuy est des siens dechassé, | A qui Fortune, ou heur, ou estat change*, 9–10). Doranne Fenoalta concludes from this *dizain* that "The poet's heart at the thought of Délie ... submits to a violent pressure which tears it from its natural and normal relation between body and soul and sends it to the soul's domain, disrupting the proper balance of parts."[18]

---

[16] Translation from Sieburth, *Emblems of Desire*.

[17] On the culpability of the speaker's gaze in Scève see Matthieu-Castellani, *Eros baroque*, 44.

[18] Fenoalta, "Three Animal Images in the *Délie*," 424.

This disembodiment in Scève, reflective of Actaeon's transformation and his final victimhood, represents to a certain degree the genesis of the poetic I-voice. *Dizain* 82 demonstrates this; here, the poet whose "living body is already darkened dust" (*corps vif est jà poulsiere Umbreuse*, 4) laments that nothing is left of "my being, thus reduced to ash" (*mon estre, ainsi reduit en cendre*, 7), as a result of his desire for the unattainable Délie except "The eye, weeping to render you compassionate | The mouth, open to cry for mercy" (*L'oeil larmoyant pour piteuse te rendre,* | *La bouche ouverte a demander mercy*, 9–10). These two final verses present a pitiful image of Actaeon represented by his frozen glance – weeping now – and an open, soundless mouth crying for pity. Here at last we have Scève directly speaking Ovid speaking Actaeon: "'Oh, woe is me!' he tries to say; but no words come. He groans – the only speech he has – and tears course down his changeling cheeks. Only his mind remains unchanged" (*'me miserum!' dicturus erat: vox nulla secuta est!* | *ingemuit: vox illa fuit, lacrimaeque per ora* | *non sua fluxerunt; mens tantum pristina mansit, Met.* 3.201–203).

Délie/Délia

The source of all this torment, silencing and alienation, is perhaps Scève's greatest transformation of the Petrarchan model. Délie is, if anything, the antithesis of Laura – perhaps even an antidote to the silent but enduring laurel that the Italian poet has dehumanised, and with which he proudly crowns himself. As we will explore later, the female others constructed in Scève and Petrarch are highly reflective of the dissimilar principles on which they base their poetic identities. Where Laura is *not*, or, in Petrarchan terms, is *more than* Diana, Délie is the virgin goddess' very incarnation. Furthermore, the Scèvian conception of Diana goes far beyond her presence in the Actaeon narrative and her usual representation as virgin huntress to encompass her various aspects as the many-faced moon, as well as healer and sister to Apollo. These aspects are evidently absent in Petrarch, as Diana herself is only vaguely alluded to in the *Canzoniere*. The *Délie* functions to a certain degree as a poetic "working out" of the various facets of the Diana figure.

The changeability associated with Diana's aspect as moon goddess is the characteristic most often called upon when the poet laments his love for her. The association with the moon is explicitly stated, leaving no room to doubt which mythological figure Délie most closely resembles. Délie's mutability is highlighted again and again throughout the sequence. Change is not only her inclination, however, but also her effect: Délie has Diana's powers of metamorphosis. As we saw earlier, she has the power to separate body from soul and to dissociate self from form, and so Actaeon's transformation is uniquely her work. In *Dizain* 358, however, the poet writes "And when her voice pierces my ear, | I am all fire & dark smoke | There where her hand works its greatest marvel | Turning me to marble, hard and cold" (*Et quand sa voix penetre en mon oreille, | Je suis en feu, & fumée noircy, | Là où sa main par plus grande merveille | Me rend en marbre & froid, & endurcy*, 7–10), which suggests that her power to transform is not limited to transforming Actaeon.

In fact, Délie's ability to metamorphose also appears as an ability to heal the wounds of the beloved, reflecting another aspect of Diana as healer. In *Dizain* 365 Délie's "regard," like that of the moon "Calms the damp cloud of my pains | Transporting me in its joyous serene weather" (*De mes douleurs resoult la nue humide, | Me conduysant en son ioyeux serain*, 9–10). In *Dizain* 422, Scève's wounded stag persona makes another appearance, wishing "If only, out of pity, she would play | My dittany, Artemis to my Stag, | And wrench the arrow from this wound | That bathes my burning pain in blood" (*Fust elle, aumoins, par vertu pitoyable | Mon dictamnum, comme aux Cerfz Artemide, | Tirant le traict de ma playe incurable, | Qui fait mon mal ardemment estre humide*, 7–10).[19] The mention of the *Cerfz Artemide* links the poet to Délie in a single image, through the same tie that binds Diana and Actaeon.

Diana's other, darker side is equally represented in her Scèvian incarnation. The virgin goddess' fierce pride characterises Délie's frequent contempt for the poet's love, while the aggressive defence of her chastity unites Délie with Diana's aspect as virgin goddess. Délie's pride often carries much further than self-defence, however, to the point that she crosses into the realm of Hecate's cruelty. Scève repeatedly portrays his mistress as bloodthirsty and vengeful, associating her more closely with the Diana of the Actaeon story, accused of excessive vindictiveness. In *Dizain* 194, the poet demands "Are you not horrified, being on all sides | Surrounded by tombs and the dead | To see thus smoking on your altars | A hundred slaughters to appease you?" (*N'as tu horreur, estant de tous costez | Environnée & de mortz, de tombes, | De veoir ainsi fumer sur tes Aultez | Pour t'appaiser, mille & mille Hecatombes?* 6–10). Délie often embodies the ferocious side of Diana in her role as huntress also,

---

[19] Translation from Sieburth, *Emblems of Desire*.

and Scève frequently shows her dressed in hunter's garb (327.1–2). *Dizain* 131 figures both Délie and Diana, portraying the former as less violent, in fact, but more deadly. Diana (mentioned by her name Délia, which makes Délie's association with her unmistakable) is seen dressed and armed, hunting stags and other prey. While the beasts flee from Diana, the poet tells Délie that "You hunt those with your chaste looks | Who are so harried by your chase | That they all, burnt in your holy fire | Follow you, while the beasts fly from her" (*Tu vennes ceulx par tes chastes regardz, | Qui tellement de ta chasse s'ennuyent: | Qu'eulx tous estantz de toy sainctement ardz, | Te vont suyant, ou les bestes la fuyent,* 7–10). Where it would have run from Diana, the stag therefore presumably follows Délie, who is the more successful huntress. Although he is her pursuer as well as her prey, he is worn down in their constant two-sided chase and "succumbing to the fact of such power | Strength, alas, wanes from day to day" (*du pouvoir soubz tel faix succumbant | Les forces, las, de jour en jour s'abaissent,* 195.9–10).

ACTAEON, APOLLO, ORPHEUS: THE BIRTH OF THE LYRIC I-VOICE

How is it, then, that Délie will display every aspect of Diana, while Laura will only weakly echo the goddess and rather embody her objective opposite as Daphne? These questions bring us to the function of the Actaeon myth in the construction of the lyric voices of Petrarch and Scève, both of which, albeit differently, hinge on the association with the doomed stag. As we saw earlier, for Petrarch Actaeon is in fact not doomed, at least not when he is identified with the poet. The motto that accompanies Scève's Actaeon emblem, *fortune par les miens me chasse,* is precisely what is lacking from the Petrarchan version of the myth: Petrarch as Actaeon never experiences the dissociation of self from form, nor is he ever confronted with his own powerless alterity.

The question of Actaeon's voice is perhaps the most important in exploring the configurations of the Scèvian and Petrarchan poetic voices. The nuances in their presentations of speech, silence, and appearances of constraint are what will distinguish one poetic voice from the other, as well as uncover the constitutive function of Actaeon in each. As we saw in *Canzone* 23 and *Dizain* 62 and elsewhere throughout the *Délie,* both Laura and Délie possess the power to transform the poet's physical being. The women's effect on his lyric voice, however, is less clear. In Petrarch's case we know that in *Canzone* 23, although all the transformations undergone by the poet at the hands of Laura purport to curtail speech,[20] none of these have the intended effect of silencing his poetic voice. In fact, as a result of the constant constraints placed on the poet's voice by the various metamorphoses of *Canzone* 23, "the narrator suggests that the denial of speech leads him only to find a more permanent, poetic means of communication. Speech is replaced first by song and then by writing, the most durable form of expression."[21]

In fact, despite any allusions on Petrarch's part to the contrary, the primary power that Laura *doesn't have* is the ability to silence him. Despite her command "Make no word of this" (*Di ciò non far parola*, 23.74), that is exactly what he does repeatedly and in various ways throughout the poem. In *Canzone* 18 the poet, in sublime irony, states that *tacito vo*, but of course he continues "I go silent; for my dead words would make people weep, and I desire my tears to be shed in solitude" (*ché le parole morte | farina pianger la gente, et l'desio | che le lagrime mie si spargan sole*, 12–14). Similarly in *Canzone* 37, the poet apparently uses his laments to complain of not being able to turn to stone and cease lamenting (49–56). The same poet who can ask, "why can I not be silent" in the midst of his poetry is the one who can say "I was Actaeon": both statements play on an impossibility in the nature of such modes of expression. In fact, at the end of this poem, the poet points out himself that that (63) *gli occhi*, often the most vocal of his speaking parts, are "always eager to weep" (*di sempre pianger vaghi*).

In *Canzone* 73, the first two long stanzas of which are concerned with the ostensible problem of being forced to speak, the poet establishes at the outset that he speaks "Since through my destiny that flaming desire forces me to speak which has forced me to sigh always" (*Poi che per mio destino | a dir mi sforza quell'accesa voglia | che m'à sforzato a sospirar mai sempre*, 1–3). Nevertheless, destiny is supported by desire, since "At the beginning I thought to find, through speech, for my burning desire some brief repose and some truce" (*Nel cominciar credia | trovar parlando al mio ardente desire | qualche breve riposo et qualche triegua*, 16–18). In *Canzone* 325, this desire to speak becomes the impossibility of being silent; the poem begins with what may be termed the "motto" of the Petrarchan poetic I-voice, "Silent I cannot be" (*Tacer non posso*). The poet immediately follows this telling statement with a mitigating one: "and I fear that my tongue may produce an effect contrary to my heart" (*et temo non adopre | contrario effetto la mia lingua al core*, 1–2). This fear has not,

20 Vickers, "Diana Described," 278.
21 DellaNeva, "Poetry, Metamorphosis, and the Laurel," 199.

even after the death of Laura, succeeded in curtailing to any degree the poet's speech. All Petrarch's suggestions of forced silence reveal their purely rhetorical nature.

For Scève, the interdiction against speech is quite evidently one of Délie's commands, as we saw earlier. In fact, given the lady's constant association with Diana and Scève's scarcely-hidden identification with Actaeon, it is not surprising that the question of speech and constraint should be less clearly distinguishable in the *Délie*. After all, the Ovidian myth includes both an interdiction on speech – Diana's transformation of Actaeon so that he cannot tell what he has seen – and simultaneously a command to do just that, in her defiant imperative "speak, if you can." Délie incorporates both of these contrary aspects: that of constraining speech and that of forcing it. The motto of emblem 5, *La Lanterne*, is after all, "Conceal I cannot" (*Celer ne puis*). The accompanying *dizain* ends "Wishing to hide the fire that all can see | Which I cover, but cannot conceal"(*Voulant cacher le feu, que chascun void | Lequel je couvre, & celer ne le puis*, 42.9–10).

Thus, both Scève and Petrarch claim an inability to be silent, although perhaps for differing reasons. In Scève, the blame lies squarely with Délie who, as we have seen, both silences and forces the poet's speech. In light of this duality, Actaeon is a particularly crucial association, because his transgressive gaze causes Diana to do both as well. Like Ovid's doomed stag, however he "groans – the only speech he has" (*ingemuit: vox illa fuit*, *Met.* 3.202). In fact, Actaeon's demise can be said to suggest the Scèvian poet's birth pains as he comes to the lyric world forced into metamorphosis by his cruel huntress. The Actaeon emblem in the *Délie* and the two that immediately precede and follow it provide the possible key to the story of the birth of the Scèvian poet. They are: the stag, Acteon, Orpheus. This chronology functions as a kind of triptych, a tableau which reverses the Actaeon story of man to half-stag to beast and thus narrates the birth of the poet. He begins in a state of innocence as the free stag, perfect and favoured victim of Délie as Diana. Her beauty and disdain force a metamorphosis: here his gaze is transgressive only of his own initial freedom because in meeting her glance he is ensnared. As a result, the Scèvian poet is forced through the metamorphosis of half-stag/half-man, represented by the Actaeon emblem, to the final stage which is that of the poet, and specifically the doomed one: Orpheus. The motto of the Orpheus emblem explains the nature of Scèvian poetry in the *Délie*: "Pleasure to all and pain to me" (*A tous plaisir et a moy peine*). The *dizain* accompanying the Orpheus

emblem narrates the creation of Scèvian poetry – Délie's virtue, state-
liness and venerability: "Bringing such astonishment to all | Through
pleasure, and supplying the fuel | For my labours that end in weeping.
| Nevertheless such perfections as yours | Bring glory to my suffering"
(*Donnant a tous mille esbahyssementz | Avec plaisir: a moy nourrissementz |
De mes travaulx avec fin larmoyeuse. | Et toutefoys telz accomplissementz |
Rendent tousjours ma peine glorieuse*, 177.6–10). The most telling moment
of Scève as Orpheus is in *Dizain* 344, where the poet praises and directly
addresses his lute, which he says provides the ideal "voice," better indeed
than his own, with which to entreat Délie. Here the Orphic lute
becomes the ideal emblem for Scèvian poetry. Just like Orpheus' own
verses, most glorious and enchanting when he sings to regain or to
lament the woman he has lost, Scève's *dizains,* compelled by and
glorifying a capricious huntress who is equally denied him, at least *rendent
tousjours ma peine glorieuse*. In Murphy's words, "the fearful torment of
Actaeon's punishment is now a *doux martyre*; the end result of metamorphosis is preferable to the original state."[22] Orpheus, who has shared
Actaeon's fate of dismemberment, nonetheless continues to sing.

For Petrarch, the self-association with a mythological poet places
him far beyond the sad and dismembered fate of Orpheus who, though
divinely gifted, was after all human and mortal. For Petrarch, no such
association will do; his poetry, born of the inextinguishable creative
voice, allies him and itself with Apollo, of whom he posits himself as
inheritor. The poets Apollo and Petrarch, one divine and one aspiring
to divinity, share the same yoke: the love of "The heavenly breeze that
breathes in that green laurel, where Love smote Apollo in the side and
on my neck placed a sweet yoke" (*L'aura celeste che'n quel verde lauro |
spira ov' Amor ferì nel fianco Apollo | et a me pose un dolce giogo al collo*,
197.1–3). In *Canzone* 34, Petrarch is Apollo's equal and even colleague,
and calls on the divine poet, "now defend the honoured and holy leaves
where you first and then I were limed" (*difendi or l'onorata et sacra fronde
| ove tu prima et poi fu' invescato io*, 7–8) who has become "*our* lady" (*la
donna nostra*, 13, emphasis added). In perhaps his boldest move, Petrarch
relegates Apollo to the past and positions himself as his successor, poised
to take over where the god left off in failure before Daphne:

> Il figliuol di Latona avea già nove
> volte guardato dal balcon sovrano

---

[22]Murphy, "The Death of Actaeon," 144.

per quella ch'alcun tempo mosse in vano
i suoi sospiri *et or gli altrui commove* ...
E così tristo standosi in disparte,
tornar non vide il viso che laudato
sarà, *s'io vivo*, in più di mille carte.   (43.1–4, 9–11)

(The son of Latona had already looked down nine times from his high
balcony, seeking her who once in vain moved his sighs *and now moves those
of another* .... And thus sadly remaining off by himself, he did not see that
face return which shall be praised, *if I live*, on more than a thousand pages.)
(emphasis added)

Thus she is praised, on more than a thousand pages, and a poet is born
under a stolen crown of laurel leaves. In *Canzone* 23 where Petrarch
describes his own birth pains and the repeated resurgences of his unique
poetic voice despite the power of his lady to petrify and to transform
him, he makes clear that "my harsh undoing is written elsewhere so that
a thousand pens are already tired by it, and almost every valley echoes
to the sound of my heavy sighs" (*'l mio duro scempio | [e] scritto altrove, sì
che mille penne | ne son già stanche, et quasi in ogni valle | rimbombi il suon
de' miei gravi sospiri*, 10–13). With perhaps borrowed Apollonian skill,
Petrarch prefigures the truth of this prophecy.

CONCLUSION

In its scattered and diffused form, the image of Actaeon in the *Canzoniere*
is, as we have seen, an almost obsessively recurring one. Petrarch
neutralises the silencing potential of the myth by effecting a lyric
fragmentation of both the Actaeon image and myth, as well as of any
possible association of Laura with Diana. By thus reducing Actaeon to
fragments and carefully cloaking them in mixed references and hidden
allusions, Petrarch can superimpose his solution to that most terrifying
problem of Actaeon, provided by the figure of Apollo. The god, as
suggested above, is the reverse of the young hunter. Divine and
therefore never a true victim, Apollo is the lover, the aggressor rather
than the passive voyeur. Although his love is unattainable, Laura's
petrification at his poetic hands results in the creation and immortalisa-
tion of his lyric voice. Whereas Actaeon was victim of his desire and of
its consequences, Petrarch is allied with a divine counterpart by means
of which his desire, though unattainable, gives birth to him as poet.
Having lyrically dismembered Actaeon and scattered him throughout
the *Canzoniere,* the poet can create and/or transform Laura from

potential Diana into Daphne. In so doing, he initiates his own meta-morphosis from silenced Actaeon, caught just before his dismember-ment and voiceless demise, into the expression of the eternal divine poetic "I" itself: the voice of Apollo's heir. Laura therefore cannot be Diana, because Petrarch must not risk Actaeon's silence. This new divine image of Apollo and the identification with the laurel that Petrarch superimposes on Actaeon's dismembered limbs and voice is exactly that and only that which can authorise his boldest of self-constitutive statements: "I was Actaeon." He has recovered and buried the shards.

For Scève, Actaeon haunts the *dizains* throughout the *Délie*, pro-posing himself constantly as a lens through which to read the entirety of the collection. Although the poet refers to him by name only in the nineteenth emblem, the metamorphosed stag is the poet's mythological reflection, the voiceless scream in which he recognises his own aliena-tion and the simultaneous silence and weeping of his poetic voice, transformed and brought into being by the fatal glance of love. In sharp contrast to Petrarch, his Délie *must* be Diana, because Scève must be Actaeon, caught at mid-point between the images of the stag and of Orpheus: of innocent freedom unencumbered by love and fettered poetic servitude constrained to eternal speech as lament. As we have seen, we can read the birth of the Scèvian poet in this triptych of Le Cerf-Acteon-Orpheus, with Actaeon as the dominant, central image. The metamorphosed hunter as intermediary stage represents the simul-taneous birth and death of the poetic voice: the confrontation of the poet's desirous gaze and Délie's proud and unattainable one, which constrains him both to silence in addressing his desire to her and to poetry as the only outlet left for his laments. The Actaeon stage is the one in which both speech and silence are constrained and the poet must represent his desire in silent but symbolically vocal fragments, imbuing each of the pieces with all the symbolic weight of the myth. This point at which the transformation from stag to poet is half-complete, however, is the definitive one in the constitution of the Scèvian poetic I-voice. In response, perhaps, to Petrarch's recovery at the end of *Canzone* 23, the birth cry of the Scèvian poet must be read from shards. It is the soundless one, thrown in the face of alterity and unattainable love: *Actaeon ego sum.*

PRINCETON UNIVERSITY

VENUS, MYRRHA, CUPID AND/AS ADONIS: METAMORPHOSES 10 AND THE ARTISTRY OF INCEST

JULIA BRANNA PERLMAN

Ovid's *Metamorphoses* inspired countless Renaissance visual images, as an ever-expanding body of modern scholarship attests. Across crude wood-cut illustrations, luxurious maiolica, small preliminary sketches and large-scale panels, canvases, and frescoes, gods and mortals enact the bitter conflicts, passionate embraces, procreations, and corporeal trans-formations made famous by the ancient Roman poet. Yet, while some images suggest a tight and largely undisputed connection to Ovid's text, others – arguably more intriguing and more interpretively complex – respond to the spirit of Ovid's rich poetic structure and narrative content by way of the pictorial artist's own witty, highly self-reflexive verbal-to-visual metamorphoses. Such is the case with a celebrated composition of ca. 1532–1533 designed by Michelangelo Buonarroti, executed in paint by Jacopo Pontormo, and representing, in Giorgio Vasari's words, "a nude Venus with Cupid who kissed her" (*una Venere ignuda con un Cupido che la bacia*) (figs. 12.1 and 12.2).[1]

The *Venus and Cupid* unquestionably draws upon manifold threads in the pictorial and literary traditions of amatory imagery and classical mythology; the composition – and its many emulative descendents – thus can hardly be exhausted through reference to Ovidian verse alone.[2]

---

[1] Vasari, *Vite* 5: 326 Vasari, *Vite* 5: 326. An abbreviated reference to the project occurs also in Vasari's section on Bronzino, *Vite* 6: 232. The earliest, albeit brief, citation of the work is by the Anonimo Magliabechiano; see *Codice Magliabechiano, Notizie*, 114. Many scholars deem the *cartone* in the Museo Nazionale di Capodimonte, Naples (fig. 12.1) to be a copy after Michelangelo's (presumed lost) original; the panel painting in the Galleria dell'Accademia, Florence (fig. 12.2) is currently accepted as the Pontormo work referred to by Vasari. However, such attributions remain a matter of continual debate; see Nero, *Raffaello, Michelangelo, e Bottega*, 27–28; and *Venere e Amore*, ed. Falletti and Nelson. Unless otherwise stated, translations are my own.

[2] Perlman, "Taking Aim"; compare *Venere e Amore*, ed. Falletti and Nelson. My

Nevertheless, relationships between poem and picture are vital. Not only does the *Metamorphoses* – specifically the tale of Myrrha, Cinyras, Cupid, Venus, and Adonis in Book Ten – shed valuable light upon Michelangelo's *invenzione*, but Michelangelo's *invenzione*, conversely, helps to direct our attention to aspects of Ovid's verses and their textual translations across time and geography. Importantly, however, the connections transcend mere characters and plot. As we shall see, visual representation and its artifice – including the latter term's full range of meanings comprising skilful craft as well as deception – figure significantly in Ovid's carefully woven narrative.

Metamorphoses 10 beckoned to craftsmen of images as well as craftsmen of words in more ways than one. The *paragone*, or longstanding comparison and competition among the visual and verbal arts, which had drawn the attention of Plato and Horace, Petrarch and Castiglione, Lorenzo Ghiberti and Leonardo da Vinci alike, was central to Michelangelo's intellectual milieu, a fact scholarship has amply recognised.[3] Yet, this same battle was, I shall demonstrate, also crucially enacted within Ovid's construction of his tale. A (necessarily selective) exploration of the *Venus and Cupid*'s design and reception, *Metamorphoses*' verses, and a few key literary and pictorial kin reveals a complexity of text-image reverberations. This, in turn, encourages a rejection of the reductive interpretive binary of "illustration" versus "unrelated," in favour of a more nuanced understanding both of Ovid's original contribution and of his respondents' diverse creations.

Vasari reports that the *Venus and Cupid* was originally fashioned to be the centrepiece for a *camera* (arguably, the principal bed chamber)[4]

---

readings of the *Venus and Cupid* and related pictorial and literary works diverge from those of the exhibition catalogue's authors along a number of points, only a few of which shall be addressed here.

[3] Integral to the general framework of the *paragone* are the arts' respective abilities cogently to portray natural and/or divine beauty. These abilities comprise, in turn, making the absent vividly present; depicting external appearance (relatively translatable to paint) and internal character (a more elusive challenge); and arousing emotion, especially amorous desire. Adopted from the verbal-visual rivalry, these same criteria later figured in debates over the relative merits of painting versus sculpture, famously concretised by the philosopher-poet Benedetto Varchi in two lectures (the *Due Lezzioni*) before the Florentine Literary Academy in 1547. See Lee, *Ut Pictura Poesis*; Mendelsohn, *Paragoni*; Farago, *Leonardo da Vinci's Paragone*; and Ames-Lewis, *The Intellectual Life of the Early Renaissance Artist*; with additional sources noted below.

[4] As Richard Aste acknowledges, no evidence yet confirms that Pontormo's

in the Florentine home of Bartolommeo Bettini, a merchant-banker and man of letters, whose associates included Michelangelo, the poet-painter Agnolo Bronzino, the philosopher-humanist Benedetto Varchi, and other prominent literati.[5] In the intended location, the finished goddess and her son were to keep company with lunette portraits by Bronzino showing "Dante, Petrarch, and Boccaccio ... and the other poets who have, in verse and Tuscan prose, sung of love" (*Dante, Petrarca, e Boccaccio, con ... gl'altri poeti che hanno con versi e prose toscane cantato d'amore*).[6] In that context, Michelangelo's *invenzione* would have self-consciously proclaimed the classical deities as the visual synecdoche for a body of writings on *amore* celebrated by the patron, his friends, and their erudite contemporaries. As it turned out, the completed panel was instead seized from Pontormo by Duke Alessandro de' Medici, as Vasari bitterly recalls; the *cartone* (full-scale preparatory drawing) alone entered the possession of the Bettini household.[7] Yet, despite – or perhaps enhanced by – its vexed history, Michelangelo's design quickly achieved great status among artistic and patronage circles in sixteenth-century Florence, as witnessed by a multitude of copies and derivations in pencil and paint.[8] More than a decade after its creation, writers as well as

---

painting was made for Bettini's bedroom; moreover, modern demarcations of private and public domestic spaces do not translate neatly to the Renaissance home, where a decorative program in a patron's "bedchamber" could well have been designed to be flaunted to chosen visitors ("Bartolommeo Bettini e la decorazione della sua 'camera' fiorentina," *Venere e Amore*, 14–19). For the purposes of interpretation, we may presume Bettini planned his décor to serve, at least in part, an agenda of quasi-public self-fashioning.

[5] See, among a wide range of scholarship, Leporatti, "Venere, Cupido e i poeti d'amore," *Venere e Amore*, 64–89; Aste, "Bartolommeo Bettini e la decorazione della sua 'camera' fiorentina," *Venere e Amore*, 2–25; Parker, *Bronzino*; Pilliod, *Pontormo, Bronzino, Allori*; Quiviger, "Benedetto Varchi and the Visual Arts," 219–224; Cecchi, "Il Bronzino, Benedetto Varchi e l'Accademia Fiorentina," 141–163; and Mendelsohn, *Paragoni*.

[6] Vasari, *Vite* 5: 326; Nelson, "Dante Portraits."

[7] As Vasari elaborates in the "Life of Pontormo," upon its completion the panel was forcibly purchased from Pontormo by an agent of Duke Alessandro de' Medici for the Duke's own possession *per far male al Bettino* ("to hurt Bettini"), *Vite* 5: 327. The *cartone* is cited close to the end of the "Life of Michelangelo," in the context of discussing Michelangelo's generosity in bestowing gifts upon his friends, *Vite* 6: 113.

[8] Among the examples most patently indebted to Michelangelo's design are drawings by Alessandro Allori (Louvre, Paris), Agnolo Bronzino (Galleria degli Uffizi, Gabinetto Disegni e Stampe, Florence), and Pontormo (Galleria degli Uffizi,

pictorial artists continued to mark the work as an apical achievement in visual–amatory representation. Varchi, for instance, cited Michelangelo's Venus as proof of visual art's power to make men fall in love: a tribute heightened by the philosopher's explicit comparison of the painted goddess with the famously enticing Greek sculpture of the Cnidian Venus and delivered, notably, in the second public lecture on the *paragone* before the Accademia Fiorentina in 1547.[9]

Notwithstanding such immense popularity and clear influence upon later renditions of the gods (including three by Bronzino himself)[10], as well as a recent starring role in the Galleria dell'Accademia's scholarly exhibition *Venere e Amore* (2002),[11] the Michelangelo-Pontormo *Venus and Cupid* remains – like its pictorial progeny – a source of much interpretive dispute. This dispute is born of, and fuelled by, the composition's visual ambiguities and adamant resistance to any neat narrative/literary (that is, narrowly iconographic) mapping. What is happening in this striking encounter between the fleshly, divine Venus and her son Cupid, devised to serve as the visual fulcrum within a bedroom homage to love's great (literary)

Gabinetto Disegni e Stampe, Florence); and paintings by Michele di Ridolfo di Ghirlandaio (Galleria Colonna, Rome), Hendrik Van den Broecke (Museo Nazionale di Capodimonte, Naples), as well as several by Vasari himself (for example, Kensington Palace, London); all are documented in *Venere e Amore*, ed. Falletti and Nelson, 195–227, 232–236.

[9]See Varchi, *Opere* 2: 643. Notorious for eliciting from her male lover-beholder the staining proof of his amorous arousal, the Cnidian Venus was long hailed as an *exemplum* of visual art's power to arouse; see Stewart, *Art, Desire, and the Body*, 100–106; Havelock, *The Aphrodite of Knidos*, 54–67; and Barkan, *Unearthing the Past*, 309–311. The story of the statue's violation is thought to originate with Posidonius, but Cinquecento audiences were likely most familiar with recitations by Pliny, *Natural History*, 36.4.20–22; Lucian, *Essays in Portraiture*, 4; and the pseudo-Lucian *Affairs of the Heart*, 15–16, this last explored in some detail in Perlman, "Taking Aim," 45–52. On the rhetorical uses of the *Venus and Cupid* with respect to discourses of the *paragone*, compare also Mendelsohn, *Paragoni*, 120–123; Pardo, "Artifice as Seduction," 73–79; and Jacobs, "Aretino and Michelangelo," which compellingly analyses Pietro Aretino's admiration for the image. For a detailed account of the Accademia Fiorentina (of which Bettini and Michelangelo both were members), including the role of Varchi's "Due Lezzioni" in advocating for the visual arts, see Plaisance, "Culture et politique à Florence" and "Une première affirmation."

[10]Bronzino's *Allegory of Love* (National Gallery, London), *Venus, Cupid, and Jealousy* (Szépművészeti Múzeum, Budapest), and *Venus, Cupid, and a Satyr* (Galleria Colonna, Rome) are among the most significant and visually striking responses to the Michelangelo-Pontormo *Venus and Cupid*; see Perlman, "Taking Aim," 216–345.

[11]*Venere e Amore*, ed. Falletti and Nelson.

portraitists? At the centre of the composition, a single arrow with its tip concealed protrudes from Cupid's quiver, the arrow shaft passing between both his and his mother's fingers; other visibly sharp darts meanwhile threaten the goddess' right thigh. As their bodies intertwine, Cupid caresses Venus' neck and accentuates her pudendum with his foot, while she with her left hand gestures towards her own chest... or is it towards her son, or both? Who might "wound" (or has wounded, or penetrated) whom, how, and to what effect?

Textual instances of Venus and Cupid caressing at all are rare, let alone with explicit involvement of the arrow, that multivalent signifier of amatory agency and ingression throughout Renaissance and classical poetic and philosophical literatures of love.[12] Partial answers to our questions may be found, however, in Ovid's *Metamorphoses*. According to the ancient Roman poet, "while the goddess' son, wearing a quiver, was kissing his mother, he chanced unwittingly to graze her breast with a projecting arrow. The wounded goddess pushed her son away; but the scratch had gone deeper than she thought, and she herself was at first deceived" (*pharetratus dum dat puer oscula matri, | inscius exstanti destrinxit harundine pectus; | laesa manu natum dea reppulit: altius actum | vulnus erat specie primoque fefellerat ipsam*, 10.525–528).[13] The possibility of this Ovidian connection was first proposed by William Keach (1978), who characterised the *Venus and Cupid* as a compositional hybrid comprising, on the one hand, the specific wounding moment (not a particularly common pictorial subject at the time Michelangelo undertook the project),[14] and, on the other, a traditional "disarming of Cupid,"

---

12 Among the vast scholarship on the mythopoetic-physiological constructs of love's "arrow," see Donaldson-Evans' classic study *Love's Fatal Glance*; Calame, *The Poetics of Eros*; and Perlman, "Taking Aim," 26–38, with further references.

13 Except where otherwise stated, I have adopted the English translations of Frank Justus Miller, Loeb edition.

14 Dollmayr in 1890 proposed this same Ovidian connection for a well-known composition of Venus, shown touching one hand to her breast while accentuating with her other hand the poised tip of Cupid's arrow, attributed to Raphael and depicted on the badly damaged wall of Cardinal Bibbiena's celebrated bathroom [*stufetta*] in the Vatican (and known also through a number of prints, such as by Agostino Veneziano); see Dollmayr, "Lo stanzino da bagno," 279, as discussed in Clayton, *Raphael and his Circle*, catalogue entry 30, 118–120. Discussions of Michelangelo's composition (and of Bronzino's Venusian paintings) have, however, tended to give minimal attention to the Raphael work, perhaps due to a general cautiousness in interpreting the deteriorated *stufetta* image.

whereby the boy-god is deprived of his weaponry (a theme depicted in a number of Quattrocento and Cinquecento prints as well as paintings).[15] Since Keach, art historians have either rejected outright *Met.* 10.525–528 as a source, arguing that Michelangelo hardly illustrates the verses faithfully,[16] or alternatively, have cited the four verses merely as one textual example of wily Cupidian triumph.[17] With either stance, though, scholarship heretofore – including Keach's own – has curiously but consistently divorced the Venusian wounding moment from any surrounding narrative context. Herein lies the problem.

Michelangelo's *invenzione*, and by extension the *Venus and Cupid*'s painterly heirs, respond not simply and faithfully to a single four-verse event, but to Ovid's deft knitting of characters and plot across the text surrounding and including verses 525–528. The rich relevance of the *paragone* to Michelangelo's pictorial rhetoric gains significantly, moreover, from the Ovidian verses leading up to the moment of arrow-action: a point which becomes even clearer when one examines different verbal translations of the poem. To assess properly the *Venus and Cupid*'s relationship with the *Metamorphoses*, and thus the multivalent *paragoni* that would have played out in Bettini's camera (had the patron's intentions not been thwarted), we first must re-examine *Metamorphoses* 10, beginning well before Cupid takes up arms.

The wounding of Venus by Cupid is embedded within an elaborate story of incest and incestuous pregnancy. Under cloak of night, the young maiden Myrrha repeatedly seduces her own (supposedly) unwitting father Cinyras, King of Paphos, who is the grandson of the legendary sculptor Pygmalion.[18] From the first of these illicit encounters, Myrrha conceives Cinyras' child. When Cinyras at last casts light – literally, by lantern – upon his paramour's true identity, he threatens to kill her. Myrrha escapes, roves the countryside, and, like so many Ovidian damsels in distress, is conveniently transformed into a tree, albeit a very pregnant one.

---

[15] Keach, "Cupid Disarmed or Venus Wounded," 327–331. The motif of Cupid disarmed is itself often ambiguous; see Perlman, "Taking Aim," 138–146.

[16] Smith, "Jealousy, Pleasure, and Pain," particularly 257 n. 4, responding specifically to Keach's reading of Bronzino's *Allegory of Love* and applicable also to the *Venus and Cupid*; and more moderate echoes by Nelson, "La 'Venere e Cupido' Fiorentina," *Venere e Amore*, 45.

[17] Mendelsohn, "Come dipingere Amore," *Venere e Amore*, 102–103.

[18] Pygmalion famously fell in love with his own artistic creation and, through Venus' intervention, received his wish for the inert maiden to come to life; their lovemaking produced Paphos, mother of Cinyras (*Met.* 10.243–299).

In due time, the arboreal Myrrha bears the son who is also her brother, a son so beautiful, Ovid tells us, that at birth he looked just like a painted Cupid:

> arbor agit rimas et fissa cortice vivum
> reddit onus, vagitque puer; quem mollibus herbis
> naides inpositum lacrimis unxere parentis.
> laudaret faciem Livor quoque; qualia namque
> corpora nudorum tabula pinguntur Amorum,
> talis erat, sed, ne faciat discrimina cultus,
> aut huic adde leves, aut illis deme pharetras. (*Met.* 10.512–518)

(the tree cracked open, the bark was rent asunder, and it gave forth its living burden, a wailing baby boy. The naiads laid him on soft leaves and anointed him with his mother's tears. Even Envy would praise his form, for such was [the form of] the bodies of the naked loves painted on panel. But, that dress may make no distinction, you should either give him [the baby boy] a light quiver or take it away from them [the portrayed *Amorini*]).[19]

As the very next verses reveal, once this nameless, newborn mortal has matured into a handsome young man, he becomes the named object of Venus' love: a love ignited, let us now emphasise, by Cupid's supposedly "unwitting" action upon his own mother:

> Labitur occulte fallitque volatilis aetas,
> et nihil est annis velocius: ille sorore
> natus avoque suo ...
>
> ...
>
> iam iuvenis, iam vir, iam se formosior ipso est,
> iam placet et Veneri matrisque ulciscitur ignes.
> namque pharetratus dum dat puer oscula matri,
> inscius exstanti destrinxit harundine pectus;
> laesa manu natum dea reppulit: altius actum
> vulnus erat specie primoque fefellerat ipsam.
> capta viri forma non iam Cythereia curat
> litora ...
>
> ...
>
> abstinet et caelo: caelo praefertur Adonis. (*Met.* 10.519–532)

---

[19] In place of Miller's "Even Envy would praise his beauty, for he looked like one of the naked loves portrayed on canvas," my wording aims to preserve Ovid's dual emphasis on Adonis' sensual appeal and, importantly, likeness to that idealised corporeal beauty found in visual art.

(Time glides by imperceptibly and cheats us in its flight, and nothing is swifter than the years. That son of his sister and his grandfather ... is now a youth, now man, now more beautiful than his former self; he now excites even Venus' love, and avenges his mother's passion. For while the goddess' son, wearing a quiver, was kissing his [own] mother, he chanced unwittingly to graze her breast with a projecting arrow. The wounded goddess pushed her son away; but the scratch had gone deeper than she thought, and she herself was at first deceived. Now, smitten with the beauty of a mortal, she cares no more for the borders of Cythera .... She stays away even from the skies; Adonis is preferred to heaven.)[20]

As Renaissance patrons and viewers knew well, Adonis and Venus go on to enjoy an amorous affair until the foolhardy hunter, ignoring the goddess' pleas, meets his untimely, grisly death at the hands – or rather, tusks – of the hunted: the wild boar. Adonis strikes with his own arrow, but the creature retaliates triumphantly, sinking its long tusks deep into the predator's groin (*inguen*) – an inescapably fatal mutilation (*Met.* 10.715–716).[21] Bereft, Venus sublimates her grief through her power to effect metamorphosis, transforming punctured Adonis' pooled blood into the deciduous Anemone.

Ovid's explicit comparison of the infant Adonis to (pictorialised) Cupid(s) (*qualia namque | corpora nudorum tabula pinguntur Amorum, | talis erat*), in conjunction with the author's flashback to Venus' wounding (notably recited immediately upon Adonis' birth and maturation), surely grants more than a tint of incestuous connotation to the Venus-Cupid caress. Furthermore, through the notion of revenge, Ovid signals overtly the parallel between the gods' embrace and Myrrha's nefarious deed. As a direct result of Venus' encounter with her divine son, the poet tells us, Adonis comes to "avenge" his mortal mother's taboo passion for her own father. The immediate juxtaposition of verses leaves no margin for oversight; indeed, medieval and Renaissance audiences recognised Ovid's calculated correspondences.[22] Though residents of Olympus

---

[20] "Wearing a quiver" (versus Miller's "with quiver on shoulder") arguably better elucidates the degree of adherence to, or deviation from, Ovid's narration in later Renaissance verbal and visual renditions of the tale.

[21] Ovid's wording warrants attention, since the term *inguen* (groin) was a prevalent literary euphemism for male and female genitalia; see Adams, *The Latin Sexual Vocabulary*, 31–32. In *Met.* 14.640, Ovid uses the term to identify the unnamed Priapus, thus supporting the notion that in 10.715 Adonis may have sacrificed more than the flesh of his thigh.

often enjoyed a looser code of conduct than that applied to mortal counterparts, some commentators on *Metamorphoses* 10, such as the renowned Pierre Bersuire (Petrus Berchorius), chastised Venus and Cupid alongside mortal Myrrha for their analogously taboo love.[23]

It was not just these characters' amatory exploits *per se* which caught later respondents' attention, however. Crucial too was the unfolding of these exploits within paradigmatic discourses of visual dissemblance and disclosure, a point Dante Alighieri makes clear in his *Commedia* (a text close to Florentine *accademici*'s hearts).[24] For Dante, it was Myrrha's wilful misrepresentation of herself to her father that was most notable, earning her a place not among the merely libidinous, as we might expect, but among the fraudulent of *Inferno* 30. The alchemist Griffolino d'Arezzo there identifies her as "wicked Myrrha, who became dear to her father in a way beyond rightful love … [and thus] came to sin with him by *feigning herself in another's form*" (*Mirrha scellerata, che divenne | al padre fuor del dritto amore amica | … a peccar con esso così venne, | falsificando sè in altrui forma*, *Inferno* 30.38–41; emphasis added). Dante here underscores for us another key thread within Ovid's interweavings: Cinyras' deception at the hands of his

---

[22]They would have recognised, too, the irony of Cupid's disclaimers of innocence, reported to the reader at the outset of the tale (*Met.* 10.311–314): *ipse negat nocuisse tibi sua tela Cupido, | Myrrha, facesque suas a crimine vindicat isto; | stipite te Stygio tumidisque adflavit echidnis | e tribus una soror* ("Cupid himself avers that his weapons did not harm you, Myrrha, and clears his torches from that crime of yours. One of the three sisters with firebrand from the Styx and with swollen vipers blasted you"). Perhaps in acknowledgement of the hollowness of Cupid's protestation, the medieval French *Ovide moralisé* eliminates altogether reference to these verses (see 10.1117–1134), while devoting five verses to characterising Venus' passion as retribution by Adonis on behalf of Myrrha; her shameful love for Cinyras was, by the French text's account, specifically Venus' doing (10.1988–1992).

[23]In his highly influential *Ovidius moralizatus* (ca. 1340–60), Bersuire applies multiple levels of exegesis to recast the consanguine union of Myrrha and Cinyras as a union of Church and Christ; at the same time, though, he critiques Venus and Cupid for their unnatural liaison; see 152–154. Passages from Bersuire's text were perpetuated within Cinquecento mythographies and Quattrocento and Cinquecento pastiched Ovidian commentaries; see Panofsky, *Renaissance and Renascences*, 78 n. 2; Lord, "Some Ovidian Themes," 152 n. 112; "Illustrated Manuscripts," 1–11; and for a deeper analysis of Bersuire's interpretive manoeuvrings with respect to Venus and Cupid, Tinkle, *Medieval Venuses and Cupids*.

[24]Dante's various writings constituted the focus of the Accademia Fiorentina's exegetical public lectures, including several by Varchi; see Bryce, "The Oral World of the Accademia Fiorentina," 77–103; Boyde, *Passion and Perception*; and Parker, *Bronzino*.

daughter is effected through blinding darkness; the ruse is revealed, conversely, only upon his (literally) enlightened viewing of his illicit beloved. Venus' deception at the hand of her son Cupid – her underestimation of his seducing arrow's depth of penetration – becomes clear to the goddess only once she sets eyes on her fated beloved, Adonis.[25] Venus' filial deceiver and her mortal beloved are, of course, two ostensibly separate characters. But for Ovid's Cinyras and the goddess alike, wounding love and its misfortunes are intertwined inextricably with the ruses and revelations of visual-sensory experience.

Such ruses and revelations were deemed to be the very means and essence of *amore*, as Michelangelo, Bettini, and others conversant with poetic and philosophical writings on love from the Ancients onward well knew. They were, too, the domain whereby literary metaphor and physiological understanding merged as one. From Plato through Dante and the *stilnovisti* poets to Lorenzo de' Medici and the Cinquecento *trattatisti d'amore*, Love and its proverbial "arrow" entered through the vulnerable, porous eyes and wreaked havoc stealthily upon the bloodstream and the heart.[26] Yet, while erotic seduction through visual-sensory deception was the *modus operandi* common to Cupid and Myrrha, this same *modus* united these characters, in turn, with practitioners of the pictorial arts. As Varchi's laudation of the *Venus and Cupid* in the second *Lezzione* implies, and as artist-advocates throughout centuries of the *paragone* addressed, great visual artists stir the heart by first tricking – and captivating – the eye. Ovid's was a tale not merely of titillating, taboo seduction, but of manipulated vision, role play, blurred identities, and – as Dante recognised – formal deception: fertile starting ground, in short, for a Cinquecento declaration of painterly triumph through beguiling visual artifice.

The Ovidian play with identity and appearance – and their implications for Michelangelo's pictorial rhetoric – are more complex still.

---

[25] Renaissance writers and audiences would have appreciated the multivalent motifs of Truth revealed by light, sight, and time; and of clandestine Love thereby exposed and potentially ruined. See Panofsky's canonical study of these themes, "Father Time," *Studies in Iconology*, 69–93; compare Perlman, "Taking Aim," 252–255.

[26] These complex, longstanding paradigms have received extensive scholarly attention, including Donaldson-Evans, *Love's Fatal Glance*; Boyde, *Passion and Perception in Dante's Comedy*; Calame, *The Poetics of Eros*; and Dempsey, *The Portrayal of Love*, especially 145–158.

As noted at the outset, in *Met.* 10.515–523 the Roman poet himself toys intriguingly with tropes of pictorial artifice and representation, thereby planting seeds for a series of engagements with the *paragone* by all future translators and respondents. The penetrative encounter between Venus and Cupid is embedded, we recall, within the narration of Adonis' birth and maturation. Ovid's analogy between the newborn Adonis and the painted *amorini* thus rebounds with a twist: not only does Venus' mortal beloved resemble at birth her depicted son, but her "living," caressing son prefigures her adult beloved. At the same time, though, Adonis comes to *surpass* in beauty his former self, and therefore, we may extrapolate, surpass the beauty of those painted *amorini*. It is a small, logical step for the reader to surmise that Venus' mature, mortal lover may outshine even divine Cupid's beauty. Within Ovid's tightly woven verses, as gods and mortals mirror each other in looks and deeds, the demarcations – and hierarchies – among divine beauty, visual artifice, and living flesh begin to dissolve: a dissolution most apposite to this tale of Pygmalion's descendents.[27]

Medieval and Renaissance translators and commentators appreciated the ancient poet's identity games, often blurring the boundaries between Adonis and Cupid, and between art and nature, even more insistently than had Ovid himself. Raphael Regius, for example, in his influential annotated Latin *Metamorphoses*, first published in Venice in 1492 (with multiple editions through the next century), explicitly glosses *Amorum* as *Cupidinum*.[28] The gloss would have been noted in Michelangelo and Bettini's intellectual circles, for the literary equivalence between a Cupid and an Amor was a point specifically discussed by Varchi, among others.[29] More than a century before Regius, the well-known French *Ovide moralisé* had taken another intriguing step, substituting "*the* god of love" for Ovid's many, and furthermore dispensing with paint on canvas in favour of the "real" thing: "No one in seeing (Adonis) would have doubted | That he resembled the god of love | Were (Adonis) only stripped of his clothing" (*Nulz nel veist qui*

---

[27] See Leonard Barkan's exploration, along different lines, of relations among metamorphosis, art, nature, creation, and destruction within the Pygmalion-Myrrha lineage, *The Gods Made Flesh*, 75–78.

[28] See *Metamorphoseon Pub. Ovidii Nasonis* (1553), 107v. The Venetian editions of 1493, 1517, and 1586 are consistent on this point. Like Bersuire's, Regius' work continually reappears also in pastiched form within other authors' commentaries.

[29] In his lecture "Della pittura d'Amore," *Opere* 2:490–491.

ne creust | Que le dieu d'amour ressamblast | Se lor habit ne dessamblast,
10.1973–1975). Even without any telltale weaponry, Adonis might at
birth be mistaken for Cupid in the flesh.

Italian vernacular editions of the *Metamorphoses* show their own
interesting variations. Giovanni de Bonsignori's Trecento *Ovidio methamorphoseos vulgare*, first published in 1497 and reissued in multiple editions
throughout the first half of the Cinquecento,[30] offers a salient case in point,
describing an Adonis so beautiful "that ... the [usually] envious would have
praised his appearance. So much so that were one to paint Cupid the son
of Venus, one could not portray him as beautiful as was [Adonis]" (*che non
tanto li altri ma l'invidiosi haveria lodata la sua facia. Tanto che Cupido figliolo de
Venere el quale se depinge | tanto bello non se poria si bello dipingere come era
costui*, 91r). Besides reminding the reader of Cupid's specific filial bond
with Adonis' future lover, Bonsignori interestingly alters the terms of
Ovid's original *paragone*. In this vernacular author's account, even a
hypothetical painted Cupid – however idealised the artist might render him
– could never approximate Adonis' actual, living beauty.

Renaissance audiences would have relished Bonsignori's play upon
the age-old conceit of art's competition with nature and the general
problem of ineffable beauty. The traditional conceit, famously exploited
by Bonsignori's contemporary Petrarch in his two poems on Simone
Martini's painting of Laura, compares the inanimate portrait to the living
beloved.[31] The portrait is intended to represent that beloved; yet, unless
made in heaven, the inert image inevitably must fall short.[32] Evoking
this familiar frame of reference, Bonsignori's Ovidian manipulation

---

[30]Originally composed between 1375–1377, Bonsignori's work was significant
not only for being the first Italian vernacular edition of the *Metamorphoses*, but also
for setting – thanks to its woodcut images in the 1497 edition (Venice, Giunta) – the
prototype for illustrated editions of the *Metamorphoses* for the next fifty-six years. See
Lord, "Some Ovidian Themes," 61–80, Appendix III Table 1; and Guthmüller, "Bild
und Text," 69.

[31]"Per mirar Policleto a prova fiso" and "Quando giunse a Simon l'alto concetto,"
in *Petrarch's Lyric Poems*, ed. Durling, poems nos. 77, 78 on pp. 176–179.

[32]Central to Italian Renaissance discourses of poetry and visual art, the conceit
figures prominently in much current art historical scholarship, which continues to be
informed by Elizabeth Cropper's "On Beautiful Women," "The Beauty of Women:
Problems in the Rhetoric of Renaissance Portraiture," and "The Place of Beauty."
Though Petrarch's Laura provided one extremely influential locus, the problem of
representing (ineffable) beauty was hardly restricted to female beloveds/sitters and thus
is important for representations of Cupid and Adonis as well.

intimates a correspondence between Adonis and the subject of the imagined portrayal, that is, the referent, "real" heavenly Cupid. Simultaneously, though, Bonsignori deftly spins the Petrarchan trope, such that no portrayal of this heavenly Cupid could ever match the earthly, living beloved Adonis. Substitution of the future hypothetical act of painting (*se poria ... dipingere* [were one to paint]) for Ovid's extant "bodies of the naked Loves painted on panel" (*corpora nudorum tabula pinguntur Amorum*) further enhances the rhetorical effect. In Bonsignori's rewriting of *Met.* 10.515–517, visual artifice – even when applied to divine subject matter – cannot compete with nature's extraordinary creation. The avowal gains witty irony in light of Adonis' descent from Pygmalion and his statue-turned-animate-beloved at the hand of Venus.

As the foregoing examples demonstrate, although any portion of the *Metamorphoses* might offer translators and commentators the occasion to challenge and surpass Ovid's literary craftsmanship, the ancient poet's tightly woven account of Adonis' appearance (in all senses of the term) and Venus' wounding presented one particular call to arms. Venus and Cupid had long been hailed as compelling subject matter for appraising artistic skill through erotic impact upon the viewer; their Ovidian embrace and its intricate narrative context thus offered an especially inviting focus for any *paragone* competition.[33] In writing of Venus, Cupid, Adonis, loves, and beauties, natural and artificed, Medieval and Renaissance literary respondents would engage implicitly – and arguably self-reflexively – with tropes of artistic rivalry and envy not merely with respect to Ovid, but with respect to the much broader class of makers of poetic and pictorial beauties across the centuries. Refashioning the descriptions of Adonisian and Cupidian beauty in verse, each successive poet would enter the fray, manipulating the terms of the *paragone* but always coming out on top, for these Adonises and Cupids – like their fellow inhabitants of the *Metamorphoses* – owed their craftsmanship ultimately to the writer's pen.

In sum, *pace* the art historical predilection for tidy excerpting of verses 525–528, Renaissance writers and literate audiences did not experience the fateful Venus-Cupid caress as an isolated narrative moment. On the contrary, implicated within Ovid's account of mortal and divine optical-erotic deceptions and seductions were the very claims

---

33 On arousing portrayals of Venus and Cupid as indices of artistic skill, see Perlman, "Taking Aim," 45–52. Certainly, other episodes in the *Metamorphoses* also saliently engage with issues of the *paragone*, as incisively demonstrated by Barkan, *The Gods Made Flesh*.

and respective statuses of the verbal and visual arts: matters at the heart of Michelangelo and Bettini's Florence and, certainly, at the heart of the patron's *camera* program.

We thus return to Michelangelo's design of the *Venus and Cupid*, ca. 1532. As a shrewd construction of overlapping relations of licit and illicit eroticism, amatory power, and artistic parrying, *Met.* 10.525–528 offered a highly appropriate springboard for a centrepiece which, while ostensibly paying tribute to those who (to recall Vasari) "have in Tuscan verse and prose sung of love," would simultaneously instantiate, through its own material-pictorial identity, the age-old theoretical and professional *paragoni* among the arts. By portraying Cupid and his mother Venus together as visible, sensuous, embodied lovers with allusion to the wounding episode, Michelangelo and Pontormo vied with Ovid's provocative textual interweavings and vied, furthermore, with all intervening literary and pictorial renditions of the ancient tale. In this regard, the visual portrayal of Cupid not as an infant, as artists often rendered him (following the ancient *putto* type), but rather as a nude older child or adolescent, intensified the Cupidian-Adonisian conflations and taboo, titillating connotations implicit in Ovid's poem.[34] In its originally intended location, moreover, the *Venus and Cupid* would have engaged in playful dialogue with Bronzino's painted portraits of Tuscan literary giants on the *camera*'s walls, together wittily enacting for the beholder a self-conscious demonstration of the respective powers of artificed beauty, visual and verbal, to seduce and enchant.[35]

As an aspiring contender in the wars of the *paragone*, however, Michelangelo's *Venus and Cupid* clearly did not, and would not, visually "transcribe" Ovid's tale. Multiple sharp arrows escape this pictorialised Cupid's quiver to threaten – and call the beholder's attention to – the goddess' thigh, not her chest (suggesting perhaps a witty allusion to

---

[34] Even in the very few multi-episodic images in which Cupid appears alongside Myrrha, Cinryas, Venus, and Adonis, the boy-god is rendered as a small infant; Bronzino, by contrast, consistently fashions his Cupids to be even more provocatively "mature" than Michelangelo/Pontormo's figure.

[35] The lunette images also constituted a playful *paragone* in themselves, as Bronzino's painterly brush vied with the authorial pens of his portraits' subjects (i.e., Dante, Petrarch, Boccaccio, etc.). Overall, the *camera*'s completed decorative program would have operated on multiple levels of self-referentiality and signalled multiple *paragoni*, among and within the arts. Prolific poets in their own rights, Michelangelo and Bronzino especially would have relished the many forms of comparison and rivalry here evoked.

Adonis' own fatal piercing). At the same time, the single, renegade dart, notably in contact with both deities' hands, defiantly conceals its tip and therefore, the core of its power. Gesturing with her left hand towards her chest on the side of her heart and with her right towards the fallen figurine and masks (these latter signifiers, arguably, of role play and duplicity),[36] this visible Venus appears simultaneously vulnerable and vigorous, potential victim but also potential vanquisher.

By casting each deity equivocally in the roles of seducer-agent and recipient of partially-visible, partially-concealed arrows, Michelangelo adamantly denies the beholder that surety offered by Ovid's narrative outcome. In contrast to the poem, the picture is never neatly resolved; the quintessential piece of the puzzle – those semi-visible darts at the composition's centre – remain defiantly inscrutable. The viewer of the pictorial *Venus and Cupid* can never be sure which protagonist is the wilful – or unwitting – dissembler, an uncertainty heightened by the ambiguity in the two characters' gazes. Yet, as the image sustains *our* gaze through its titillating lack of resolution, by this means continuously perpetuating desire,[37] it is without doubt we who become the ongoing target of these artificed deities' – and their makers' – pleasurable collusion. With amatory and artistic bewitchments here fusing as one, the words of Dante come to echo with new tones: the twin masks suspended from Cupid's bow call to mind "feigning in another form" not simply as committed dishonourably by Myrrha, but also as flaunted gloriously by Michelangelo and Pontormo, *pittori*.

By the time Ludovico Dolce published his *Trasformationi* (1553),[38] a vernacular free-verse Ovidian translation, the *Venus and Cupid* had long

---

36 Nelson, "La 'Venere e Cupido' Fiorentina," *Venere e Amore*, 48–50; Perlman, "Taking Aim," 207–208; but compare Paoletti, who sees them as symbolic self-portraits serving to establish Michelangelo's voyeuristic presence within the work, "Michelangelo's Masks," 437–440.

37 The investment in sustaining desire by means of a perpetual deferment of fulfillment is crucial to Renaissance poetic and philosophical discourses of love; modern scholars have applied this model to the visual-pictorial realm. See Perlman, "Taking Aim," 59–95.

38 Liberally exploiting poetic license, *Le trasformationi di M. Ludovico Dolce, tratte da Ovidio* first appeared in print in 1553 (Giolito, Venice) and enjoyed significant success, superseding – in part by virtue of its more elaborate illustrations – Bonsignori's *Methamorphoseos vulgare* and generating multiple editions through the end of the sixteenth century and thereafter; see Guthmüller, "Bild und Text." My subsequent citations refer to the Sansovino (Venice) edition of 1568.

stood as a pictorial institution and engendered copies and variations by a generation of draftsmen and painters. Perhaps Dolce even had Pontormo's painting in mind when he drafted his version of Ovid's telltale verses in Book Ten: "one day Cupid, tightly clasping (Venus') beautiful neck, wounded – I do not know how (or if) by mistake – her breast with one of his arrows" (*un di Cupido il suo bel col stretto | Tenendo, non so come per errore | Con un' de' strali suoi ferille il petto*, 106r). The specific description of neck-clasping, absent from Ovid's account, calls to mind Michelangelo's design. Most intriguing is Dolce's *non so come per errore*. Open to more than one translation ("how by mistake," "if by mistake"), the phrasing at least raises the possibility that the boy-god's penetration of his mother may have been no accident after all. Striking Venus somehow with his dart, "I don't know how/if by accident," this Cupid may just be as wilfully devious as Myrrha herself. If so, Dolce has entered the *paragone* with a twist of his own: introducing into verse a hint of that same mystery, menace, and machination evoked by the Michelangelo-Pontormo panel.

The semantic intricacies of Ovid's poem and Michelangelo's picture, as well as the inventive responses they each elicited both in pen and in brush, merit ongoing study. Restoration of Ovid's verses 10.525–528 to their original narrative context, together with exploration of different translations and commentaries of the *Metamorphoses*, perhaps may open new art historical and literary doors, fostering more nuanced considerations of Bettini's intended centrepiece and of the metamorphic *paragoni* into which writers and artists entered across the centuries. Yet, in some ways the *Venus and Cupid* may lie forever beyond the bounds of verbal exposition, remaining instead visually enticing while insistently enigmatic. If so, Michelangelo shall have succeeded fully in his paragon metamorphosis: transforming the powerful gods of love into personal artistic emissaries and Ovidian verse into painterly victory.[39]

THE OPEN UNIVERSITY, LONDON

---

[39] With gratitude to Leonard Barkan, who first introduced me to Ovid, the battlefields of the *paragone*, and so many of my other great pleasures in Renaissance studies. I thank also Alison Keith and Lawrin Armstrong for making the conference and preparations of this publication intellectually invigorating and joyful in equal measures; and Patricia Simons, Megan Holmes, Celeste Brusati, Michael C. Schoenfeldt, and Mark S. Lewis for invaluable feedback on earlier treatment of this material. Whatever faults I have committed in metamorphosing such gifts into print remain wholly my own.

Transforming Phaethon:
Cervantes, Ovid,
and Sancho Panza's Wild Ride

R. John McCaw

The journey – the passage from one place to another, the progress from one stage to another – figures among the most central and dynamic themes of Miguel de Cervantes' *Don Quijote*. The process of physical travel is perhaps the most celebrated manifestation of the journey in *Don Quijote*'s plot, as the wanderings of Don Quijote and his squire, Sancho Panza, have become emblematic of the comic travel adventure in popular culture.[1] It is generally accepted that *Don Quijote* was conceived as a parody of books of chivalry; as such, it spoofs the heroic quest so central to medieval and Renaissance European romance as a whole.[2] As Don Quijote undertakes three journeys – the first by himself and the

---

[1] The perception of *Don Quijote* in popular culture has been most effectively shaped by visual media such as Dale Wasserman's *Man of La Mancha* and Pablo Picasso's famous ink drawing of Don Quijote and Sancho. In a more general sense, *Don Quijote* shows its influence when movies, television shows, and other media feature a fallible hero and a comic sidekick in an idealistic but impractical journey that is both fraught with misadventures and framed by narrative irony.

[2] In the prologue to Part One of the *Quijote*, the narrator recounts a conversation in which a friend advises him on how to write the book. The friend enjoins the narrator "to let [his] aim be steadily concentrated on overthrowing the ill-based fabric of these books of chivalry, abhorred by so many yet praised by so many more" (Cervantes, *Don Quixote of la Mancha*, 47; (*llevar la mira puesta a derribar la máquina mal fundada destos caballerescos libros, aborrecidos de tantos y alabados de muchos más*; Cervantes, *El ingenioso hidalgo don Quijote*, 58). Though Cervantes certainly parodies chivalric romance, even to the point of satirising specific texts, *Don Quijote* does not completely condemn the genre. Indeed, *Don Quijote* is more of a celebration of the pitfalls and quaintness of chivalric romance. For further reading on the history and popularity of chivalric literature before and after the publication of the *Quijote*, see Eisenberg, *Romances of Chivalry*. Henceforth, all references to the Spanish original and English translations of the *Don Quijote* will refer to the two editions cited above and will be indicated simply by the short title, *Quijote* or *Quixote* and the page references embedded in the text.

second and third with Sancho by his side – we can see the distorted legacy of the journeys of previous heroes, including those of the knights errant of chivalric romance. In Don Quijote's three sallies, each beginning and ending at home, we may also discern the traces of ancient, medieval, and Renaissance epics, as well as the traces of other heroic texts – including Byzantine novels, pastoral romances, and histories – which have directly or indirectly helped to forge Cervantes' understanding of movement, travel, and transformation.[3] In addition, the novel's deployment of Don Quijote and Sancho as worldly adventurers owes much to the anti-heroic, materialist, and satirical nature of picaresque narrative – a literary genre of classical origins that emerged in Spain with the publication in 1554 of the anonymous *Lazarillo de Tormes*.[4] Though Don Quijote and Sancho remain within the Iberian peninsula and though their excursions are punctuated with episodes and incidents that temporarily suspend the process of physical travel, the two characters nonetheless manage to cover a large swath of Spanish terrain stretching from Andalusia in the south to Aragon and Catalonia in the northeast. *Don Quijote*, in effect, maps out a geographic expanse and cultural milieu at a truly national level.

Beyond the strictly Spanish context of the place names and cultural markers of physical travel, *Don Quijote* portrays and plays with the emotional, spiritual, and intellectual journeys of its characters at a level that is unwaveringly universal in scope. In Part One, Don Quijote learns – by trial and error – how to be a reasonably successful and celebrated knight; in Part Two, Sancho gradually develops a worldview that transcends his original, material interests as a squire. The paradigms for journeys of this kind – the formative journey – come from a variety of sources in life and literature: Don Quijote's ascent as a knight mimics

---

[3] Eisenberg, *A Study of Don Quixote*, offers an excellent discussion of the chivalric romances that influenced *Don Quijote*. Finello, *Pastoral Themes and Forms in Cervantes's Fiction* provides an indispensable study of the pastoral sources of Cervantes' work. In his *Cervantes, Raphael and the Classics*, de Armas examines the impact of the works and writers of classical antiquity on the Cervantine corpus. Dudley's *Endless Text* is an excellent study of the connection between Celtic romance, chivalric fiction, and *Don Quixote*.

[4] Though Cervantes scholars have debated whether *Don Quijote* may rightly be considered a picaresque novel, many acknowledge that the narrative structure, characterisation, and other features of the novel draw significantly from picaresque traditions. See Dunn, *The Spanish Picaresque Novel*, 76–91, as well as Dunn, *Spanish Picaresque Fiction*, 203–231, for more information on the *Quijote* and the picaresque.

the emotional and spiritual agonism of Lancelot, Amadís de Gaula, and other literary forbears; Sancho's political rise and fall alludes to the popular carnivalesque theme of social mobility and class status at the behest of Fortune; both Don Quijote and Sancho experience and learn from misadventures worthy of *pícaros*; and indeed, the entire novel reflects Cervantes' own extensive wanderings and experiences on land and at sea. *Don Quijote*, in effect, engages with the human journey in ways that are largely fictive yet selectively factual.

Cervantes' masterpiece reveals, however, many more subtle layers of reflection and meaning with respect to the interrelated concepts of travel and transformation. *Don Quijote* features dozens of examples of material change – almost always as a phenomenon based on the human will to determine and believe in change, and less as a phenomenon consisting of an empirically observed transformation of material properties. The inspiration for Cervantes' worldview of material change certainly reaches well beyond the chivalric, epic, pastoral, and picaresque models indicated and perhaps even includes some acquaintance with Epicurean philosophy.[5] One inspiration for Cervantes' imaginative treatment of change is Ovid's *Metamorphoses*. Indeed, this link is clear before the novel begins, as Cervantes refers to himself as *nuestro español Ovidio* in an introductory sonnet ("Gandalín, escudero de Amadís de Gaula, a Sancho Panza, escudero de don Quijote") that celebrates Sancho's metamorphosis from common man to squire.[6] Ovid's *Metamorphoses* is mentioned many times in *Don Quijote*, and specific transformation tales are used to frame or undergird a few episodes of the novel.[7] This article will briefly discuss the function of one Ovidian tale, Phaethon's tragic ride in his father's chariot, as an intertext in Sancho Panza's short-lived social transformation from squire to ruler in Part Two of *Don Quijote*.

---

[5] In *Personajes y temas del Quijote*, Márquez Villanueva perceives a degree of Christian Epicureanism in Cervantes' ethical worldview, particularly as manifest in the character of don Diego de Miranda, the Knight of the Green Cloak (168–175). However, the connection between Cervantes, the *Quijote*, and the materialist philosophies of Democritus, Epicurus, and Lucretius awaits serious scholarly attention.

[6] Schevill, *Ovid and the Renascence in Spain*, 175–176.

[7] For example, the story of Daphne and Apollo is an intertext in I, 42, and the tale of Actaeon and Diana appears in II, 58. See Schevill, *Ovid and the Renascence in Spain*, 178–198 for further examples of references to the *Metamorphoses* in *Don Quijote*.

Cervantes' familiarity with Latin is thought to have been scanty. He nonetheless had ready access to versions of the *Metamorphoses* in Castilian by Jorge de Bustamante, Francisco de Guzmán, Antonio Pérez Sigler, and Pedro Sánchez de Viana.[8] In addition, specific stories from the *Metamorphoses* enjoyed immense popularity in Spain during the sixteenth and seventeenth centuries and, as a result, became the subject of commentaries, poems, dramatic interludes, emblems, paintings, statuary, tapestries, murals, and many other media that undoubtedly nourished Cervantes' imagination. Though Cervantes' familiarity with the tales of the *Metamorphoses* undoubtedly developed by way of a dynamic and lifelong contact with primary and secondary media, the *Metamorphoses* as a complete, narrative entity nonetheless resonates in *Don Quijote* with direct immediacy. As Cervantes constantly plays with the identity of things and people in his work, and even as he experiments with the narrative structure itself, we may wonder if *Don Quijote* aspires to be, among other things, a frame narrative of transformation tales that collectively explore the pluralistic worldview of an increasingly individualistic and secular society.

Don Quijote is, of course, the lead character of the novel, through whom we see how the multi-dimensional concepts of movement, travel, and metamorphosis play out at the levels of plot, discourse, and narration. Also important, however, is the role of Sancho Panza as a traveller, as a subject of internal transformation and as an agent of external change. Throughout most of the novel, Sancho is a reluctant companion in Don Quijote's journey, frequently urging his master not to take risks and often expressing nostalgia for his home and family. Indeed, the putative reason for Sancho's participation in Don Quijote's travels is to earn the governorship of some sort of land as a reward for his obedience. Whereas Don Quijote's objective is to wander the countryside and rectify injustices, Sancho's goal is to settle down into a better economic

---

[8]Bustamante's prose *Transformaciones* was published before 1546. Its popularity led to subsequent editions in 1551, 1595, and throughout the seventeenth century. Viana's verse translation of the *Metamorphoses*, published in 1589, was considerably less popular. Guzmán's version, published in 1578, and Pérez Sigler's translation, published in 1580, await serious scholarly attention. Rudolph Schevill, *Ovid and the Renascence in Spain*, originally published in 1913, provides a good overview of the influence of all of Ovid's works in Golden Age Spain. Schevill also provides an interesting, if dated, study of the literary style and reception of Bustamante's and Viana's translations.

position. In effect, physical travel is the core of Don Quijote's stated goal; it is not the end of Sancho's. This is not to say, however, that Sancho's role as a traveller in the *Quijote* is minimal, even though he generally demonstrates a preference for sedentary activities such as eating, drinking, talking, and sleeping. From the start of Don Quijote and Sancho's relationship, and throughout most of the rest of the novel, the two characters fulfil their functions as knight and squire, yet at times they struggle with their own and each other's functional identities. One of the linguistic markers of the knight/squire relationship is Don Quijote's frequent use of the word *hijo* ("son") to refer to Sancho. Though Don Quijote bears no true fatherly relationship to Sancho, their social relationship is symbolically one of father and son. Within the context of chivalric adventure, it is Don Quijote the knight who "filiates" his squire – he culturally brings Sancho into his mock-chivalric world. Sancho in turn maintains a subordinate role in his interactions with Don Quijote, though the promise of Sancho's ascent to the governorship of some island suggests that Sancho could someday symbolically grow out of his obligations as squire, break away from his bond with Don Quijote, and take over some or all of the symbolically paternal functions of a knight and father-figure. The Clavileño episode (*Quijote*, II, 40–41) carefully and cleverly employs the binary concepts of father/son and filiation/affiliation in order to explore the development of Sancho's autonomy and authority – the hallmarks of Sancho's political ascent in the subsequent chapters which feature his possession and rule of the Island of Barataria.

In previous chapters, Don Quijote and Sancho become acquaintances of a duke and duchess and thereafter serve as a source of entertainment for them. In the Clavileño episode, we see one of the cruellest, but also one of the most intricate, tricks that the duke and duchess play on the knight and squire. Don Quijote and Sancho are introduced to La Dolorida ("The Sorrowful One"), also known as Trifaldi, who has allegedly been dispossessed of her throne in the kingdom of Candaya by the monster Malambruno. Furthermore, as Don Quijote and Sancho learn, Malambruno has cursed La Dolorida and her maidens with beards. These female characters are, in fact, male members of the ducal staff disguised as bearded women, and their objective – as set up by and for the duke and duchess – is simply to have fun with Don Quijote and Sancho by submitting them to a series of entertaining deceptions. At the core of one of these tricks is the claim made by La Dolorida that the evil Malambruno will deliver a powerful wooden horse, guided in flight by a peg in its forehead, once she finds a worthy knight capable of confronting Malambruno and delivering her from her troubles. Though La Dolorida discusses this horse's remarkable origins, history, and flight features, Sancho – not Don Quijote – asks for more information. La Dolorida tells him that the horse will arrive there by nightfall, that it carries two people, and that its name is Clavileño ("Pegwood"). In this reply, La Dolorida also states what the horse's name is not; among the eight horses mentioned, La Dolorida includes two of the horses said to belong to Phoebus Apollo, the god of the Sun: Bootes and Pirithous. This reference sets up the Clavileño episode within the mythological context of Phaethon's fatal ride in the chariot of his father Phoebus.[9]

The story of Phaethon, as told in Ovid's *Metamorphoses*, is a tale of a young man's search for his father and, in effect, his quest for self-knowledge. The young Phaethon, not quite certain of his father's identity and taunted by Epaphus, asks his mother, Climene, for confirmation that Phoebus, the Sun, is indeed his father. When Climene does confirm this, Phaethon sets off on a journey to find his father and confirm his relationship in person. Phaethon traverses a lot of terrain, to arrive finally at Phoebus' palace in India, where his father assures him of their father-son relationship. As part of his assurance, Phoebus promises to grant Phaethon any wish he desires. Much to his father's dismay, Phaethon declares his wish to drive the chariot that spreads daylight around the world. Phoebus tries to dissuade Phaethon from doing this because death and disaster are certain, but Phaethon persists. After following the tracks of his father's route for a while, Phaethon finds himself high up in the heavens and becomes frightened by the sight of the animals that constitute the signs of the zodiac. Filled with fear, Phaethon careens through the heavens, unable to control the horses that draw the chariot. After he has caused damage and destruction to the earth below, Earth begs Jove to intervene before everything is destroyed. Jove takes a thunderbolt and strikes Phaethon off the chariot, sending

---

[9] Though he does not include the story of Phaethon or any other Ovidian tale of celestial ascent (such as that of Icarus), Franklin Brantley does provide a good account of other sources and intertexts for the Clavileño journey in "Sancho's Ascent." Brantley names the end of Plato's *Republic* and Cicero's *Somnium Scipionis* as prototypes of the celestial ascent, and mentions Lucan's *Pharsalia*, Lucian's *Icaromenippus*, Boethius' *De consolatione philosophiae*, Boccaccio's *Teseida*, and Cristóbal de Villalón's *El Crotalón* as significant texts of this tradition (40–41).

the youth to his fiery death as the horses and chariot tumble away. As Phoebus laments his son's death, Phaethon's sisters weep so much that they turn into poplars and his cousin Cycnus cries until he metamorphoses into a swan.[10]

Don Quijote and Sancho's adventure on the wooden Clavileño both reflects and distorts the Phaethon myth. Even though Don Quijote – the knight and father-figure – putatively leads this adventure, Sancho – the squire and son-figure – ends up competing with him and vies for some of his power and authority. At first, Sancho resists taking part in this adventure, even though the duke and duchess insist that he do so. In his discussion with the duchess, Sancho asks: "what have squires to do with their master's adventures? Are they to get the fame for their successes and we to bear the burden?" (*Quixote*, 810; *¿Qué tienen que ver los escuderos con las aventuras de sus señores? ¿Hanse de llevar ellos la fama de las que acaban, y hemos de llevar nosotros el trabajo? Quijote*, 342). Sancho continues to question why he should have to participate in this adventure, but Don Quijote finally intervenes:

> que Sancho hará lo que yo le mandare, ya viniese Clavileño, y ya me viese con Malambruno; que yo sé que no habría navaja que con más facilidad rapase a vuestras mercedes como mi espada raparía de los hombros la cabeza de Malambruno; que Dios sufre a los malos, pero no para siempre. (*Quijote*, 343)

> (Sancho will do what I command him. Let Clavileño come and let me find myself facing Malambruno, for I know there is no razor that could shave your graces more easily than my sword will shave Malambruno's head from his shoulders, for God suffers the wicked, but not forever) (*Quixote*, 811).

This scene plays on and against the Phaethon myth. In Ovid's tale, the father urges the son not to undertake the journey. In the *Quijote*, the fatherly Don Quijote requires the son-like Sancho to take part. Sancho's attempt to get out of participating is a direct inversion of Phaethon's insistence on riding his father's chariot.

Other interesting reminders and inversions of Ovid's tale emerge in the Clavileño episode. After nightfall, four wild men bring the wooden horse into the garden, show how to operate the steering peg, and state that

---

[10] This synopsis of the Phaethon tale is based on the Loeb Classical Library edition of Ovid's *Metamorphoses*, trans. Miller and rev. Goold.

the riders will have to be blindfolded. Sancho continues to resist participating in the adventure and worries that the journey could take so long
that the island promised to him will disappear. However, the duke assures
Sancho that the island will still be there when he returns and further
stipulates that Sancho can get the island only if he participates in this
adventure. Finally, motivated by the possibility of social ascent, Sancho
agrees to mount the horse and experience the journey. In the novel, Don
Quijote assumes the main position – the saddle position – on the horse,
while Sancho assumes a marginal position – he sits in the crupper.
Furthermore, because Sancho feels uncomfortable on the crupper, he sits
sideways – *a la mujeriega* – that is, in the style in which women often sat
when accompanying a man on a horse. This physical juxtaposition of Don
Quijote and Sancho on the horse cannot underscore the social disparity
between knight and squire any more starkly; Sancho is, once again, a comic
foil to his comic master. Sancho allows himself to assume this inferior
position so that the promise of his ascent may be fulfilled. However, in
contradistinction to the socially symbolic physical arrangement of Don
Quijote and Sancho on the horse, the ensuing contrast between Don
Quijote's travel experience and Sancho's travel experience allows Sancho
to assert verbal power and narrative authority, temporarily displacing his
master. The myth of Phaethon informs Sancho's travel narrative to the
point that the author of this narrative, Sancho, steps into the discursive domain
of his master. Let us remember Sancho's question: "what have squires to do
with their master's adventures? Are they to get the fame for their successes and
we to bear the burden?" As Sancho becomes an active participant in the
creation and narration of his travel experience, he answers this question: he
demonstrates comically that squires may indeed transcend their subordinate
role and aspire to a degree of fame usually reserved for their masters.

Once seated on Clavileño, Don Quijote and Sancho are blindfolded. The surrounding people – at once spectators and accomplices of
the prank – bid the master and squire farewell. The adventure begins as
several individuals in the crowd stage a scene that simulates a ride
through the elements: bellows are used to create the effect of wind, and
candlewicks are lit against the riders' faces in order to provide the effect
of heat. Throughout the duration of this mock flight, Don Quijote
provides Sancho with commentaries regarding their whereabouts, even
though Sancho is sceptical, anxious, and physically uncomfortable.[11]

---

[11]Don Quijote's comments explain the journey in terms of the Ptolemaic cosmol-
ogy of concentric spheres and the four elements. Brantley observes that Don Quijote's

Finally, to bring the adventure to a close, someone lights a wick attached to the wooden horse's tail, powerful firecrackers hidden inside the horse explode, and Don Quijote and Sancho find themselves thrown to the ground. Among the many allusions to classical and medieval themes embedded in this episode, an allusion to the rise and fall of Phaethon serves as its playful frame. Clavileño, a wooden horse, does not budge at all; the sense of movement experienced by Don Quijote and Sancho is a deception, as it is entirely staged. In Ovid's tale, the horses and chariot do move, and as they rise into the heavens Phaethon gradually loses control. The explosion of Clavileño and the attendant fall of Don Quijote and Sancho to the ground parallel the effect of Jove's thunderbolt and Phaethon's subsequent fiery fall to earth. After Don Quijote and Sancho recover from their fall, they are presented with a parchment on which the success of their adventure is stated. Sancho, ever curious, looks for the bearded ladies to see if they have been metamorphosed – that is, de-bearded – but those men have gone, content with the trick that was played.

Until this point, the Clavileño episode reads like yet another episode in which Don Quijote takes the lead and controls the participation of Sancho. After all, if the episode is seen as a rewriting of the Phaethon story, it appears that Don Quijote symbolically steps into the role of Phaethon as he assumes the main position on Clavileño. However, in his conversation with the duchess and Don Quijote after the ride, Sancho symbolically acquires the emotional and intellectual experience of Phaethon. Sancho asserts that while Don Quijote remained blindfolded during the adventure, he (Sancho) managed to lift up his blindfold and look around:

> mas yo, que tengo no sé qué briznas de curioso y de desear saber lo que se me estorba y impide, bonitamente y sin que nadie lo viese, por junto a las narices aparté tanto cuanto el pañizuelo que me tapaba los ojos, y por allí miré hacia la tierra, y parecióme que toda ella no era mayor que un grano de mostaza, y los hombres que andaban sobre ella, poco mayores que avellanas .... (*Quijote*, 353)

commentary has the unintended consequence of promoting Sancho's development and post-journey narrative: "Sancho, as is the custom in the novel, discerns and reports the truth of the situation to his hallucinated master ... But this time, chiefly because he is blindfolded, Sancho's empirical powers are overwhelmed by Don Quijote's fantasy so that he too comes to believe that they are ascending in the sky" (Brantley, "Sancho's Ascent," 39).

(As I have some sparks of curiosity in me and want to know what is forbidden and denied me, quietly and stealthily I pushed the handkerchief that covered my eyes just a little bit up on my nose and looked down toward the earth. And the whole of it seemed to me no bigger than a grain of mustard seed and the men walking on it no bigger than hazelnuts.) (*Quixote*, 820)

Sancho's assertion of authority as an eyewitness to the experience is, of course, comic. The duchess points out that hazelnuts are larger than mustard seeds, and therefore cannot be used to describe Sancho's vision. Among the other things that Sancho "saw" during this adventure are goats:

Y sucedió que íbamos por parte donde están las siete cabrillas, y en Dios y en mi ánima que como yo en mi niñez fui en mi tierra cabrerizo, que así como las vi, ¡me dio una gana de entretenerme con ellas un rato ...! ... Sin decir nada a nadie, ni a mi señor tampoco, bonita y pasitamente me apeé de Clavileño, y me entretuve con las cabrillas...casi tres cuartos de hora, y Clavileño no se movió de un lugar, ni pasó adelante. (*Quijote*, 353–354)

(We happened to be going by the place where the seven she-goats are, and by God, as I was a goatherd in my country when I was young, as soon as I saw them I felt a longing to play with them for a bit ... Without a word to a soul, not even my master, softly and gently I skip down from Clavileño and have a frolic with the kids ... for about three quarters of an hour, and Clavileño didn't budge from the spot nor move on.) (*Quixote*, 820)

Whereas Phaethon becomes afraid and loses control of the chariot when he sees the animals of the zodiac, Sancho's story about his calm and playful reaction to the goats is a tale about his bravery and ability to venture independently of his master. Don Quijote is particularly sceptical of Sancho's story, and after some rational evaluation of the possibilities, concludes that "either Sancho is lying or Sancho is dreaming" (*Quixote*, 821; *o Sancho miente ... o Sancho sueña*; *Quijote*, 354).[12] At this juncture, we see that Sancho's narrative authority clashes with Don Quijote's rational authority. We are presented with two versions of what has – or could have – happened: a subjective testimony from Sancho in

---

[12]In her article "Ficción y realidad en *Don Quijote*," 275–279, Mercedes Juliá conjectures that Sancho falls asleep and dreams during the Clavileño episode.

which the expectations of space, time, and movement are suspended, and an objective or rational-empirical analysis from Don Quijote that uses natural laws and the powers of deduction to undermine Sancho's claims. Aside from alluding to contemporary philosophical debates such as Aristotelianism versus Platonism, this juxtaposition of claims shows Sancho and Don Quijote locked in a competition for credibility, and thus for authority. In the episode of the cave of Montesinos just a few chapters before, a similar conflict emerges in which Don Quijote claims a fantastic story and Sancho plays the sceptic. In the Montesinos episode Don Quijote descends into a cave: from Sancho's perspective, Don Quijote spends only half an hour there; from Don Quijote's perspective, three days pass by and he meets many heroes of chivalric romance. However, in the Clavileño episode, Sancho and Don Quijote switch epistemological positions, since Sancho is the visionary and Don Quijote is the sceptic. As the Clavileño episode ends, Don Quijote whispers in Sancho's ear: "Sancho, if you want me to believe what you saw up in the sky, I wish you to accept my account of what I saw in the cave of Montesinos. I say no more" (*Quixote*, 821; *Sancho, pues vos queréis que se os crea lo que habéis visto en el cielo, yo quiero que vos me creáis a mí lo que vi en la cueva de Montesinos. Y no os digo más*; *Quijote*, 355).

Sancho's travel narrative marks an attempt to claim a greater level of power and authority, even though the episode giving rise to Sancho's story is nothing more than a deception staged by the duke and duchess. As Agustín Redondo observes, the duke and duchess have no choice but to let Sancho assert control over the details of the episode, because they cannot question the squire's story too insistently without revealing the joke they have played on him and his master. In effect, as Redondo elaborates, Sancho presides over a truly carnivalesque inversion as scripted deceptions give way to experiential truths and the tricksters find themselves tricked.[13] More importantly for the dynamic between master and squire, Don Quijote himself decides to grant Sancho narrative and experiential power and authority, instead of pursuing the exposure and defeat of Sancho's alleged experience by further scrutinising the empirical plausibility of the narrative. As Phoebus grants Phaethon the reins of the chariot, Don Quijote grants Sancho the role of eyewitness in the Clavileño adventure. And as Phaethon's ride ends in his death and in the metamorphosis of many family members, Sancho's ride – with Don

---

13 Redondo, "De don Clavijo a Clavileño," 191.

Quijote's complicity – ends in success and in Sancho's metamorphosis from mere squire into a squire with the authoritative account of his and his master's adventure. With the completion of Sancho's participation, and with Don Quijote's conditional acceptance of Sancho's interpretation of the adventure, the Duke's mock promotion of Sancho is imminent. Showing his newfound disillusionment and wisdom, Sancho now says that he would prefer to govern a segment of the sky than to rule an island. Nevertheless, the Duke grants Sancho the governorship of the island of Barataria (really a walled town, described as an island in complicity with the Duke's prank), thereby initiating Sancho's Phaethon-like career as governor.[14] Though Phaethon's crash shows his mortal and, therefore, vain attempt to prove his paternity by supplanting his father Phoebus, the mock-crash in the Clavileño episode of the *Quijote* marks the beginning of Sancho's comic displacement of his master. In his rewriting of Ovid's transformation tale of Phaethon's rise and fall, Cervantes allows Sancho Panza to assume a filial role and to displace symbolically his master and father-figure, Don Quijote. Ultimately, Cervantes uses the Clavileño episode in order to show how a particular travel paradigm – Ovid's tale of Phaethon's rise and fall through self-knowledge and paternal affirmation – frames and informs an important step in Sancho's fantastic journey from humble squire to ruler of Barataria. *Don Quijote* shows how, episode by episode, Cervantes steps into Ovid's role by creating an innovative collection of metamorphosis stories for the modern age – stories that try to explain the multiple identities of things and people, stories that reveal the creative and performative nature of language, and stories that comically try to expose the fallibility and transience of the human quest for truth and understanding.

University of Wisconsin, Milwaukee

---

[14] In the Spanish Golden Age, the Phaethon tale was often seen as an allegory of the rise and fall of princes and empires due to excessive ambition. Sancho's acquisition of the governorship of Barataria parallels Phaethon's genealogical rise and spatial ascent through his ride in his father's chariot, and Sancho's subsequent loss of the governorship alludes to Phaethon's fall, crash, and death. As a result, the Clavileño episode not only enables Sancho to compete with Don Quijote for narrative power and authority, and not only promotes Sancho's gradual ascent in moral and social terms, but also functions as an experiential model – a real-life, mock-*Ovide moralisé* – for the fall and decline of Sancho's political fortunes later in the book.

A Reflection on Greed Through Bird Imagery: An Ovidian Pre-Text in Góngora's Solitudes

Sanda Munjic

Luis de Góngora's two-part *silva*, *Soledades* (*Solitudes*), composed through several revisions between 1613 and 1626, is one of the most beautiful and most difficult poems of the Spanish baroque.[1] Despite the sonority and the visually evocative beauty of Góngora's language, and despite the intellectual challenge that the *Solitudes* present – or perhaps, exactly because of that challenge – the poem has not always elicited much appreciation from its readers. The poem has not always been well understood; even today, some four hundred years after its first circulation in manuscript at the Spanish court, we are still trying to grasp how to integrate into a single, coherent interpretation all the scenes and events depicted in its verses. Reading the *Solitudes*, moreover, did not always produce much pleasure, as we can see from the outrage of the early modern literati at a poem that, with its stylistic and generic innovations, surpassed the horizon of its readers' expectations. Thus Juan de Jáuregui, one of Góngora's most insightful, albeit hostile contemporaries, wrote a commentary in 1616 he called "an antidote against the pestilent poetry of *Solitudes*, applied to the author in order to defend him from himself" (*[a]ntídoto contra la pestilente poesía de las Soledades, aplicado a su autor, para defenderle de sí mismo*),[2] whereby he equated what, in his esteem, were the noxious effects of the poet's writing with the effects of poison. In the tenth of his *Cartas filológicas* of 1634, Francisco Cascales branded the author of these obscure, Latinate verses "the prince of darkness" (*el príncipe de las tinieblas*).[3] Thus, because of his Latinate aesthetics, Cascales associated Góngora with Lucifer, the symbolic antithesis of the Hispano-Christian nationalistic and religious ethos.

---

[1] Luis de Góngora (1561–1627) circulated the early version of the *First Solitude* in May of 1613, and the *Second Solitude* towards the end of 1614. Jammes, "Introducción," 7–21, discusses in detail the dates of composition and revisions of the poem.

[2] Martínez Arancón, *La batalla en torno a Góngora*, 155–190.

[3] Martínez Arancón, *La batalla en torno a Góngora*, 208.

Readers of Ovid's *Metamorphoses* have consistently found some of the same challenges to interpretation as those described in relation to Góngora's *Solitudes*. W.S. Anderson deemed Ovid's *Metamorphoses* "the most difficult major poem that the Graeco-Roman world has bequeathed to us."[4] Part of the obscurity in both works stems from the poets' wit, a feature of their writing that demands careful attention if the reader is to capture the nuances of allusion and meaning in their playful texts.[5] Another source of difficulty is the erudition on display in their works. The *Solitudes* has been described as a "synthesis of the erudition of its time" (*[s]íntesis de saber culto de su época*).[6] In commenting on Ovid's relationship to his poetic predecessors, Richard Tarrant describes the *Metamorphoses* as a poem that "most clearly embodies Ovid's global outlook, subsuming all major forms of Greek and Latin literature into a unique and transforming synthesis."[7] The rhetorical abundance and interpretative difficulty of both Ovid's and Góngora's style resulted in criticism of their poetry as rhetoric void of meaning.[8] In addition, both poets disconcerted their readers by experimenting with literary genres. The initial verses of the *Metamorphoses* create contradictory expectations of an epic both long and continuous (*perpetuum*) and fine-spun, shorter, and unepic in effect (*deductum*), announcing a curious blend of "two incompatible poetics."[9] Similarly, Góngora's oversized *silva*[10] has been described as "a lyrical epic, whose sublime language is put to the service of a humble subject matter" (*una épica lírica, cuyo lenguaje, sublime, está al servicio de un asunto humilde*).[11] According to this assessment, the *Solitudes* breach generic demarcations through a disre-

---

[4] Anderson, "Review," 93.

[5] On "obscurity" as not just a metaphor for "difficulty," but as an actual rhetorical concept, see Roses Lozano, *Una poética de la oscuridad*, 66–187.

[6] Vilanova, "El peregrino," 1.

[7] Tarrant, "Ovid and Ancient Literary History," 19.

[8] "Ovid ... has been criticized for his empty cleverness and wit, and for elevating form over content" (Hardie, "Ovid and Early Imperial Literature," 42). Collins comments with respect to Góngora, "some critics have considered this style synonymous with ornamental excess and semantic vacuity" (Collins, *Mask of Imagination*, 2).

[9] Kenney, "Introduction," xv.

[10] Before Góngora composed the *Solitudes*, poems in this meter would amount to some hundred verses. Góngora's two-part *silva* totalling over two thousand verses represented a dramatic reinterpretation of the possibilities of this poetic form; see Ponce Cárdenas, *Góngora y la poesía culta*, 76–77.

[11] Carreira, "La novedad," 226.

gard of linguistic decorum. In addition, the seemingly unclear theme of the poem and its un-heroic protagonist, a passive observer, perplexed readers in search of unambiguous generic indicators of either epic or lyrical style.

Given both the importance of *imitatio* in early modern writing and Góngora's unique mastery of that practice, reading the *Solitudes* in relation to one of its most richly exploited hypotexts, the *Metamorphoses*, is a productive endeavour. Pamela Waley pointed out that "[a]llusions to mythology lie thick upon the ground in the *Soledades*," but deemed that they were "intrinsic to his [Góngora's] expression rather than to his matter."[12] Marsha Collins comments that "Góngora's enthusiasm for mythology in general and his fascination bordering on obsession with Ovidian tales of metamorphosis and change in particular" are typical of the period.[13] Góngora himself provides testimony to the importance of Ovid in the *Solitudes*. In a letter written in 1615 in response to an anonymous detractor, he justifies the difficulty of his poetic style by comparing it to the style of the *Metamorphoses*. The poet insists in the letter on the utility of such poetic expression in training the intellect:

> la obscuridad y estilo entrincado de Ovidio (que en lo de Ponto y en lo de Tristibus fue tan claro como se ve, y tan obscuro en las Transforma- ciones), da causa a que, vacilando el entendimiento en fuerza de discurso, trabajándole ..., alcance lo que así en la lectura superficial de sus versos no pudo entender...[14]

> (the obscurity and intricate style of Ovid (who in the *ex Ponto* and *Tristia* was so obviously clear and so obscure in the *Metamorphoses*) causes the intellect – hesitating in the process of its thought as it strives to grasp the text . . . to reach in this way what it could not understand in a superficial reading of his verses.)

---

12 Waley, "Some Uses," 197–198.

13 Collins, *Mask of Imagination*, 157. While the erudite elites, to which Góngora belonged, read Latin, Ovid's masterpiece became more accessible to the wider early modern public with translations into vernacular. In sixteenth-century Spain two such translations were in circulation: Jorge de Bustamante's prose rendering (1545) and Pedro Sánchez de Viana's verse translation (1589). Another verse translation by Antonio Pérez Sigler was printed in 1609. Welles' *Arachne's Tapestry* and *Estudios sobre tradición clásica y mitología en el Siglo de Oro*, edited by Colón Calderón and Ponce Cárdenas, are two recent additions to Schevill's classic on the influence of Ovid and classical mythology in early modern Spain.

14 Góngora, "Carta," in Martínez Arancón, *La batalla en torno a Góngora*, 43.

In the following discussion I respect Góngora's testimony regarding the value of keeping the *Metamorphoses* in mind as we read the *Solitudes*. The focal point of this study is a close reading of bird imagery in relation to a constellation of passions – in particular envy and greed, (in)gratitude and guilt. These motifs are found in Ovid's representation of Juno's wrath, and the subsequent embedded narratives in the second book (*Met.* 2.508–832), along with the representation of Orpheus' death in the eleventh book (*Met.* 11.20–43). By analysing Góngora's rewriting of these motifs in the falconry scene towards the end of the *Second Solitude*, I will expand upon Waley's observations and demonstrate that Góngora engages in an active dialogue with the Ovidian hypotext, which consequently bears not only a stylistic, but also a thematic function in the *Solitudes*. We can observe how Góngora transforms and adapts through creative imitation the elements from the *Metamorphoses* so that they acquire meaning and ethical weight in the *Solitudes* as a critique of navigation and its cause, greed. Góngora comments upon the sea voyages – epic in form, but commercial in substance – that in the aftermath of the discovery of the "New World" displace the martial spirit. Comparing the argument of the *Solitudes* with that of Jacopo Sannazzaro's *Arcadia*, Waley insightfully comments: "both introduce a direct criticism – in Sannazzaro of war and the misery it brings, in Góngora of commerce and its causes and effects – contrasting their own time with the peace and self-sufficiency of the pastoral life and age which they are evoking."[15]

The *Solitudes* are framed by a reference to two myths of metamorphosis – Jupiter's rape of Europa at the beginning, and Pluto's rape of Persephone at the end of the poem. Between these two narrative extremes demarcated by the myths of erotic violence, the poem tells various stories of amorous fulfilment and one of amorous frustration. The narrative thread of the poem is organised around the journey of the shipwrecked protagonist, whose voyage is propelled by unrequited love. As a lyrical eye of the poet,[16] he witnesses the events of the rest of the poem. The pervasiveness of amorous themes in these events establishes love as the central theme of the *Solitudes*. It also specifies love as the essential axis of human life, whether it be violent (the rape of Europa and Persephone), marital (the peasant wedding in the *First Solitude* and the anticipated marriage of two young fishermen in the *Second Solitude*),

---

[15] Waley, "Some uses," 194.

[16] Molho, *Semántica*, 41, described the pilgrim of the *Solitudes* as *el ojo y la inteligencia del poeta* "the eye and the intelligence of the poet."

or unrequited, as in the pilgrim's case. Many episodes describe amorous pursuits, but others deal with characters who have strayed from love through error and loss of perspective. Although Góngora presents those characters with compassion, he describes their endeavours not only as pointless, but as resulting in an irreparable loss. An old refugee living among the goatherd community "with show of / more than common grief" (*con muestras de dolor extraordinarias*; I, 209–211),[17] comments on his past military career as he points at the ruins covered by vegetation of what once was a fortress. A former sea merchant tells of the loss at sea of his dearest possession – his son. The stories of these futile military and commercial quests are contrasted with the praise of a humble but satisfied existence between the extremes of opulence and poverty, an aspect of the topical opposition of court and country. These motives are complemented by a lengthy critique of navigation, another classical *topos* reproduced within the historical framework of the seventeenth-century voyages of discovery and exploration, and with a scene of an aristocratic hunting party in which hunting functions as a metaphoric substitute for the violence of the war. A cruel description of killing a crow in a falconry scene illustrates the *Solitudes'* relation to the *Metamorphoses*. The scene exemplifies, on the stylistic level, Góngora's process of creative imitation and, on the thematic level, his critique of greed and its consequence – sea voyages for the sake of commercial exploitation.

At the beginning of Book Eleven of the *Metamorphoses*, Ovid describes the death of Orpheus, the arch-poet and sorrowful lover. Vengeful, crazed women attack the poet who, after the loss of his wife, scorned the rest of womankind: "Next they turned | Their bloody hands on Orpheus, flocking like | Birds that have seen a midnight owl abroad | By day, or in the amphitheatre | Upon the morning sand a pack of hounds | Round a doomed stag" (*inde cruentatis vertuntur in Orphea dextris | et coeunt ut aves, si quando luce vagantem | noctis avem cernunt, structoque utrimque theatro | ceu matutina cervus periturus harena | praeda canum est, Met.* 11.23–27).[18] Góngora imitates this passage towards the end of the *Second Solitude*, as the protagonist sails in a boat along a river towards the sea. He observes an aristocratic hunting party, and an unusual falconry scene in which a flock of crows rises in flight and darkens the

---

[17] Translations of *Solitudes* used in this paper are by Wilson; occasional modifications of his translations are indicated in the footnotes. All other translations from Spanish are my own.

[18] I rely on Melville's translation of Ovid's *Metamorphoses*.

sky with their number. In the illusion of night created by the shadow of the crows, the owl, one among the birds of prey, rises in the air:

Más tardó en desplegar sus plumas graves
el deforme fiscal de Proserpina,
que en desatarse, al polo ya vecina,
la disonante niebla de las aves:
diez a diez se calaron, ciento a ciento,
al oro intüitivo, invidïado
deste género alado,
si como ingrato no, como avariento
que a las estrellas hoy del firmamento
se atreviera su vuelo,
en cuanto ojos del cielo.
Poca palestra la región vacía
de tanta invidia era   (II, 891–903)

(Ere the misshapen witness could succeed
Of Proserpine his great wings to unfold
Down, dissonant, from pole celestial nigh
Loosened, the mist of birds began to fly,
Who swooped in tens and hundreds to the gold
Intuitive, and envied by their breed
Not through ingratitude but avarice,
For the firmament's bright stars that day
(As those are heaven's eyes)
They'd dared direct their way.
The empty region for such envy could
But little ground display.)

As the owl takes flight, the crows that in the Western tradition are described as chatty, prophetic and greedy – the last feature being the most relevant in the context of the *Solitudes* – descend in tens and hundreds towards the owl's shining eyes that glitter like gold.[19] Two falcons isolate one crow from the throng; they play with the crow in the air as if with a tennis ball and then kill it. The dying crow "gave up, perhaps restored unto the wind, | its due inheritance, a dying caw" (*dejó al viento, si no restituido, | heredado en el último graznido*; II, 935–936). The image of the last caw or breath as restored to the larger element of the air, or more precisely of the wind (*viento* in Góngora, *uentus* in Ovid),

---

[19] See Keith, *Play of Fictions*, 12–13, on the traditional attributes of crow among the ancients.

exemplifies Góngora's debt to his source, Ovid's description of Orpheus' last breath: "breathed his last | and forth into the wind his spirit passed" (*in ventos anima exhalata recessit*, *Met.* 11.43). There may also be an additional intertextual pun contained in Góngora's use of the verb *restituir* (restore) to describe the crow's last breath or caw. In the *Metamorphoses*, the verb *reddo* (restore, give back) in association with the noun *anima* is commonly used to articulate an ability to "restore the dying to life."[20] Góngora reverses Ovid's use of the term; hence, the dying bird "restores" or gives back to the air its last breath in a caw.

As we have seen, Ovid describes the women's cruel killing of Orpheus through the simile of birds flocking towards an owl flying by day. In Góngora's treatment the scene loses its mediating quality of a comparison, since the poet presents it as an actual incident in a hunting event observed by the poem's protagonist. On another level, however, the scene offers a vivid metaphorical description of abstract quality – greed. Góngora's reflection on personified Greed in the context of the *Solitudes* is a thematic counterpart to Ovid's treatment of personified Envy in Book Two. An unravelling of a complex chain of literary associations and learned footnotes exemplifies how Góngora re-contextualises a bird simile that Ovid used to illustrate the death of Orpheus in order to expose the dangers of avarice.

Robert Ball has closely analysed Góngora's deft employment of the techniques of imitation as set out by the sixteenth-century commentator Bernardino Partenio.[21] According to the method that Partenio calls *imitatio per variationem*, a successful poet will address an authoritative "pre-text" by: (1) rearranging its elements chronologically and in different contexts (*dispositione*); (2) extending the presentation of secondary, briefly presented segments (*dilatatione*); (3) limiting the narrative of long, well-known passages (*restringimento*); (4) transforming the parts so that they acquire a new appearance (*mutatione*); (5) emphasising certain aspects by invoking their opposites (*contrario*); and (6) providing analogues or repeating the very expression used in the hypotext (*sim-*

---

[20] Keith, *Play of Fictions*, 68.

[21] Ball, "Poetic Imitation," 36. Ball's work is a fundamental study of Góngora's imitative technique. In evaluating the results of Góngora's dealing with the poetic tradition, Ball claims that the poet "did not so much eschew pastoral as reinterpret it, and in measuring his poetic mettle … in the *Polifemo* and *Soledades* against Ovid, he developed the most radical revision of pastoral to be produced in the Baroque" (Ball, "Poetic Imitation," 38).

ile).[22] Several of these techniques underlie a standard rhetorical procedure in Góngora's writing that Robert Jammes has called "mythological oxymoron." Góngora usually constructs this figure in such a way that "an adjective or a determinant contradicts what is known or accepted of the mythological term used" (*el adjetivo o el determinante contradicen lo que se sabe o se admite del término mitológico empleado*).[23] The result in Góngora of such "transforming imitation," as Ball calls it, is a concise textual allusion to an extended narrative (*restringimento*), or an expansion of a brief intertext (*dilatatione*), whose central concept becomes characterised in terms opposite to the commonly accepted ones (*contrario*) and so acquires a new meaning (*mutatione*) and the thematic function required by the context of Góngora's composition. Accordingly, through a process of creative imitation that entails a re-combining of the elements of the authoritative hypotext (*dispositione*), Góngora appropriates the motives used by Ovid to describe the death of a significant mythological character, the poet Orpheus, to describe the death of an insignificant crow. The images of the *Metamorphoses* represent women killing the poet through the simile of greedy crows destroying the eyes of an owl. In the *Solitudes*, in a reversal of terms that approximates the formation of a mythological oxymoron, one greedy crow attracted by the owl's eyes becomes a victim of its own vice and has to pay with its life.

The avian simile that Ovid applies to illustrate the violence of Orpheus' death is highly allusive; none of the birds is even explicitly named. They are introduced in the phrases as "birds" and "night bird": "flocking like | Birds that have seen a midnight owl abroad | By day" (*et coeunt ut aves, si quando luce vagantem | noctis avem cernunt*, Met. 11.24–25). The poet relies on the reader's knowledge to understand his brief allusion. Although the insertion of the missing parts is a quick process, to the point of being automatic, it involves a series of logical steps that are worked into the composition of the image:

(i)   there is a bird that does not fly during day

(ii)   that bird is an owl

(iii) the owl's eyes are shining and yellow like gold;

---

[22]Ball, "Poetic Imitation," 36–37.

[23]Jammes, "Función de la retórica," 226–227. An example of mythological oxymoron is Góngora's description of the Sphinx (*esfinge*) as *bachillera*, "chatty". Góngora's usage thus contradicts the connotation of enigmatic silence that is usually associated with this mythological character.

(iv)   some birds are attracted by owls' golden eyes

(v)   the birds that are attracted by gold are crows;

(vi)   those who are attracted by gold are greedy;

(vii)   therefore, the birds that flock into the owl's golden eyes are greedy crows.

The reader has to compensate for the silence of the text – he or she has to guess, on the basis of shared knowledge, what motivates the action, and who the agents are. By contrast, the text states explicitly what motivates women to attack the poet: "'Look!' shouted one of them, tossing her hair | That floated in the breeze, 'Look, there he is, | The man who scorns us'!" (*e quibus una leves iactato crine per auras,* | *"en," ait "en, hic est nostri contemptor!",* Met. 11.6–7). The murderous women whom Ovid compares to crows are driven by a vice of their own, envy. They are envious because they are denied the appreciation of the poet who loved only one woman, Eurydice. The frenzy of envious women attacking the poet who refuses his admiration to womankind is compared to the frenzy of greedy birds that attack owl's eyes. The conceptual association of envy with greed lies in coveting.

When using the motif of the owl and the crows in the *Solitudes*, Góngora makes explicit some of the terms that are implicit in the Ovidian motif and adds others: the owl's eyes are "gold intuitive" (*oro intuitivo*). The crows are envious of owl's possession of that gold: "the gold | intuitive, and envied by their breed" (*oro intuitivo, invidïado | deste género alado*). They covet this gold for themselves; but because they covet a material good rather than admiration (in contrast to the maddened women) they are not qualified solely as "envious," but also as "avaricious" (*avariento*). Hence, the crows are members of an avaricious breed that envies the owl's possession of its golden eyes. Góngora not only exploits the relationship between the passions of envy and greed – an association that Ovid had already suggested when comparing envious women killing Orpheus with greedy crows – but he also reproduces a play on words found in Ovid's portrayal of envy. Two words that Góngora uses to depict the crows' attack on the owl's eyes are related to the action of seeing, Lat. *videre* ("to see"). One of them is the Spanish word *invidiado* (envied) that Góngora uses not in the Romance form *envidiado* but, to stress the etymological similarity, in a Latinised form.[24]

---

[24]See *Diccionario de autoridades*: "INVIDIA. f.f. Lo mismo que Envidia."

This participle is derived from the verb *invidere* (Lat.), which means "to envy," but also "to look at askance," "regard with ill will or envy," "be jealous of." The other word, the adjective *intuitivo* (Sp.), "intuitive," that Góngora applies to owl's eyes, is related to the Latin *intueor* ("to look at," "to watch," but also "to reflect upon," to consider," "contemplate").[25] This distribution of adjectives makes the owl's eyes "a seeing gold," but also "contemplative" and, by extension, a "knowing," "in-sightful" gold, in an allusion to the owl's quality of wisdom.[26] Finally, we can conceive of an image of greedy crows flocking into the owl's golden eyes, a breed envious not only of the night bird's precious instrument of sight but, as prophetic creatures themselves, and hence possessors of a special kind of knowledge, also envious of the owl's proverbial wisdom. Góngora thus creates a multilayered conceptual play, analogous to the play on words that Ovid produced to describe a scene in which Minerva visits Envy (*Met.* 2). As A.M. Keith reminds us, Minerva, unable to look directly at the personified *Invidia*, averts her eyes from the personified creature, replicating in her action of turning away the very meaning of the verb *invidere* ("to look at askance"), from which *Invidia* derives her name.[27]

Góngora completes this nexus of conceptually associated passions by adding another passion: he ensures that the reader understands that crows launch themselves towards the owl's eyes not because they are "ungrateful," but indeed because they are "avaricious": he speaks of the breed that attacks the owl's eyes, "not through ingratitude but avarice" (*si como ingrato no, como avariento*). He thus alludes to a popular saying, *Cría cuervos, y sacarte han los ojos*[28] – and denies it in accentuating that what is at stake is not the proverbial ingratitude, but the proverbial covetousness of crows. In this short passage, then, the Spanish poet accumulates an intricate web of possible emotional motivations – the vices of greed, envy, and ingratitude – for what is overtly represented as avian, but ultimately refers to human, behaviour.

---

[25] See *Oxford Latin Dictionary*, s.v. *invidia*.

[26] Ly, "La république ailée," examines the complex symbolism of birds, especially that of the owl, in the *Soledades*.

[27] Keith, *Play of Fictions*, 126–127.

[28] Literally, "if you raise crows, they will gouge out your eyes"; the equivalent English saying states "the dog bites the hand that feeds it." Jammes reminds the readers of the proverb to which Góngora alluded in this verse, *Soledades*, 564, n. 898.

With respect to Ovid's own exploration of complicated motivations, A.M. Keith in *The Play of Fictions* identifies the motifs of indiscretion, envy, greed, and the utility or value of story-telling as a thematic complex that holds together the cluster of embedded narratives in Book Two of the *Metamorphoses*. The characters in these narratives – the crow, the raven, old Battus, and Ocyroe, a woman with prophetic abilities – all commit indiscretions in reporting true events. Since they are punished, rather than rewarded for reporting truth, Keith claims:

> Ovid and his internal narrators constantly raise the issue of the "utility" of speech by explicitly formulating the question "what is my story worth"? ... The crow has learned, however, from the outcome of the event, that her narrative was not "worth" the punishment, and she brings this knowledge to the encounter with the raven. Recognizing the implicitly economic motivation of the raven, the crow lays out the risks of telling stories for a price.[29]

In their specific incentives for truth-telling some characters are greedy,[30] others envious.[31] Thus as early as Book Two of the *Metamorphoses*, Ovid openly links the two passions – envy and greed – that later in Book Eleven he will implicitly relate to one another when he narrates Orpheus' death.

We have seen that Góngora evokes a motif of ingratitude in describing the crows. In his own study of emotions, Ovid suggests two additional factors, (in)gratitude and guilt. In the verses that precede the embedded narratives in the second book of the *Metamorphoses*, Juno shares with the sea gods Tethys and Ocean her distress over Jupiter's elevation of Callisto, one of his paramours and accordingly one of Juno's rivals, to the status of goddess by transforming her into a star. The affronted Juno rages: "Who now would hesitate to insult Juno? | Who fear to offend me, me whose punishment | Proves but preferment? Such is my success! | So vast my influence! She whom I forbade | To be a woman, made a goddess! Thus | The guilty pay! So great my sovereignty!" (*et vero quisquam Iunonem laedere nolit* | *offensamque tremat, quae prosum sola nocendo?* | *o ego quantum egi! quam vasta potentia nostra est!* | *esse hominem vetui: facta est dea! sic ego poenas* | *sontibus inpono, sic est mea magna potestas!*, *Met.* 2.518–522). This passage refers back to Juno's prior

---

29 Keith, *Play of Fictions*, 102–103.
30 Keith, *Play of Fictions*, 101.
31 Keith, *Play of Fictions*, 125.

transformation of Callisto: she was both jealous and envious of Callisto – jealous, because Jupiter had desired Callisto[32] and envious because the nymph had borne him a son.[33] The goddess took revenge against the nymph by transforming her into a bear, but Jupiter eventually metamorphosed Callisto into a star. Juno is slighted by what she interprets as Jupiter's reversal into a reward of what, in her view, was her rightful punishment of the guilty (Lat. *sons*) Callisto. Ovid, however, problematises the concepts of guilt and rightful punishment, for it is unlikely that the reader will empathise with Juno, who blames Callisto rather than Jupiter for his rape of the nymph. Now, the arbitrariness of the gods' will, manifested in a somewhat random distribution of rewards and punishments among the metamorphosed subjects, is a constant feature of the *Metamorphoses*.[34] The questioning of guilt and innocence, of fitting reward and punishment, and thus implicitly of gods' (in)gratitude, pervades the narratives of the characters in Book Two. The crow, the raven, Battus, Ocyroe and Aglauros can hardly be judged as unambiguously guilty or innocent for telling their stories or for expecting rewards, or even for succumbing to the passions of greed and envy, forces larger than any of them. In any event, these characters are no guiltier than the erratic and equally passionate gods with whom they interact and the punishment they receive is as, or more, capricious than their wished-for rewards could have been. The coincidence of the emotions explored in the analysed segments of both poems – envy, greed, (in)gratitude, and guilt – suggest that the narratives of Book Two of the *Metamorphoses* inform both Góngora's treatment of the killing of the crow and his consideration of the consequences of avarice.

---

[32] Jealousy is a kindred emotion to envy – it implies a desire for something that is perceived to be in somebody else's possession.

[33] "Juno, the Thunderer's consort, knew the truth | Long since, and had deferred until due time | Her dire revenge, and now the time was due. | Her rival bore a boy (that galled her most), | Arcas" (*Senserat hoc olim magni matrona Tonantis* | *distuleratque graves in idonea tempora poenas.* | *causa morae nulla est, et iam puer Arcas (id ipsum* | *indoluit Iuno) fuerat de paelice natus, Met. 2.466–471*).

[34] In considering Arachne's destiny, Barkan reflects on the ethical and emotional tensions produced by the ever problematic and partial solutions to the conflicts in the *Metamorphoses*: "Throughout the episode, then, metamorphosis is the key to a series of precarious balances. The vengeance of the gods is just but cruel; the amours of the gods are destructive but beautiful; the talents of the girl are sacrilegious but magnificent; the fate of the girl is degradation but also eternal life as an artist. Metamorphosis is both punishment and reward, morality and beauty" (Barkan, *Gods Made Flesh*, 5).

The proverbially greedy crow we encounter in *Metamorphoses* 2 and 11 dies in the *Second Solitude* as a result of succumbing to greed's temptation. Góngora, however, does not appear to condemn the bird for its vice. He describes the bird with the compassion that, perhaps, the characters of the second book of the *Metamorphoses* merit. The poet's use of the diminutive *avecilla* (little bird), while somewhat contemptuous, points to her "defencelessness ... in the grips of forces beyond her control" and also "indicates a level of subjective involvement, of sympathetic identification with the dying crow." "After all," suggests Collins, "humans, too, have hastened the arrival of death with reckless, sinful behavior."[35] Nowhere does Góngora state that more clearly than in commenting upon the destinies of all those nameless people who, prompted by greed, participate in commercial navigation. Oceanic travel constitutes the larger, and certainly the most impressive, historical context within which greed was displayed in Góngora's time. We are to supply the missing elements in Góngora's suggestive network of allusions and understand the comparison between the blue expanse of the sea and that of the sky. The death of the crow takes place in the empty theatre of the sky that, the poet suggests, can hardly contain the display of such envy (*poca palestra la región vacía | de tanta invidia era*; II, 902–903). Likewise, the ocean, as the arena in which human lives perish, can hardly contain the economic greed of Góngora's contemporaries. The material metonymy for the ship (I, 394), *roble* (oak), preceded by the adjective *alado* (winged), produces the metaphor of a ship as a bird of prey. In completing the analogy between the sky and the sea, the theatres of violence, Góngora remembers the islands dispersed in the far away seas that cannot escape the flight of this ship/falcon (*no hay ... | ... isla hoy a su vuelo fugitiva*; I, 395–396).[36] With this composite rhetorical sequence describing navigation across the oceans through bird imagery, Góngora associates the greed involved in commercial navigation with the greed punished in the falconry scene. Admittedly, Góngora keeps his readers alert by again reversing the terms: while falcons in the hunting party punish the greed of crows, as a metaphor for ships, falcons

---

35 Collins, *Mask of Imagination*, 81.

36 The verses, and Wilson's translation, read: "the winged oak, by the attractive worth | Of this hard faithful lover of the North, | Can double now the most tempestuous cape, | Nor island, fugitive, its track escape" (*En esta, pues, fiándose atractiva | del Norte amante dura, alado roble, | no hay tormentoso cabo que no doble, | ni isla hoy a su vuelo fugitiva*; I, 393–396).

are represented as the perpetrators of greed in the context of commercial navigation.

A lengthy diatribe in the *First Solitude* (I, 366–502) against navigation explicitly names the capitalised, and hence personified *Cudicia* (Greed), as the motive for seafaring: "Covetousness the pilot is to-day | Of wandering forests not of shifting trees" (*Piloto hoy la Cudicia, no de errantes | árboles, mas de selvas inconstantes*; I, 403–403).[37] The innumerable deaths that "Greed" reaps at sea provide a lesson insufficient to make the ill-advised turn away from its lead: "Thou, Covetousness, thou, | The second Charon of the Stygian deep, | All open graves the envying sea may keep, | Destined to hold thy bones, disdainest now" (*Tú, Cudicia, tú, pues de las profundas | estigias aguas torpe marinero, | cuantos abre sepulcros el mar fiero | a tus huesos, desdeñas*; I, 444–446).[38] Misled by avarice, people enticed by material wealth are drawn to dangers like "little bird" in the falconry scene is drawn to owl's golden eyes. However, personified Greed is represented as an external cause responsible for their actions. The problematic question of (in)gratitude in the case of the characters in Book Two of the *Metamorphoses* becomes unequivocal in the *Solitudes*: unimpressed by the dues that her followers pay in the form of their very lives, Greed is deemed ungrateful, because she disregards all the tombs that the fierce sea opens to the bones of her devotees and mercilessly lures new victims. Greed is described as a *marinero* (seaman), but what kind? It is difficult to render the suggestive adjective *torpe* with any single one of its possible translations: "clumsy," "ungainly," "stupid," "sluggish," or "lewd." Compressed in just a few verses, this formidable image of Greed as a sluggish / lewd / stupid seaman who disdains the lives she reaps and buries in the sea's "deep Stygian waters" (*profundas | estigias aguas*), rivals what is possibly one of the most memorable moments in the *Metamorphoses*, Ovid's description of personified Envy in Book Two.[39] The compelling condemnation of avarice as the cause of destruction of human lives at sea parallels the force of compassion shown towards the crow, towards the old sea merchant and the old soldier. Thus the victims of greed portrayed in the *Solitudes* are not condemned, but rather appear as pitiful victims of

---

[37] Wilson translates *cudicia* as "covetousness" rather than as "greed."

[38] Wilson's translation of *fiero mar* as "the envying sea" may be misleading in the context of the present analysis. More literally, Góngora calls the sea "fierce."

[39] For the poetic tradition on the nature of envy, see Keith, *Play of Fictions*, 125–131.

a personified passion. It would nonetheless be misleading to leave off the interpretation at the point of identifying a rhetorical concept of prosopopeia as the extent of the poet's intellectual commitment. Góngora's critique of the enterprises of navigation and the conquest is indicative of his equally significant political commitment and of his engagement with his historical circumstances. This refers in particular to the desperate economic situation of seventeenth-century Spain that John Beverley has identified as lying beneath the ambiguous pastoral idyll of the *Solitudes*.

A preoccupation with love has been the central theme of the pastoral genre, supported by the philosophical, literary, and Christian traditions that elevate this passion to a place of honour in considerations of human experience. In keeping with that tradition, through the poem's focus on the protagonist whom Antonio de Vilanova calls "the pilgrim of love" (*el peregrino de amor*), and through an extensive description of wedding and courtship rituals in the *First* and the *Second Solitude*, Góngora discreetly posits love as the thematic axis of human life and of his poem. However, the merchant's and the soldier's story, each expanded through a larger treatment in, respectively, Góngora's critique of navigation and in his description of the falconry scene, appear to digress from the poem's thematic focus on love. Each of these activities, commercial navigation and hunting, functions as a historical and metaphorical substitute for war, a thematic opposite of love as implied in the *topos* of "arms and letters."[40] Thus the discursive organisation of the poem mimics its thematic structure: the stories of straying human destinies pursuing commerce and hunting digress narratively from the central plot of the poem that tells of amorous pursuits.

Through the process of creative imitation, Góngora ably weaves a complex dialogue between the falconry scene in the *Second Solitude* and the bird imagery in the treatment of passions in Books Two and Eleven of Ovid's *Metamorphoses*. He capitalises on the remarkable unity that Ovid achieves in his long and complex poem by noticing a correspondence in the constellation of passions and metaphors – envy and greed, and (in)gratitude and guilt – in relation to the motif of birds. Góngora

---

[40] Since study, and the exercise of writing, became associated with the writing of lyrical poetry, as exemplified through the figure of the Spanish warrior-poet Garcilaso de la Vega (1501–1536), the *topos* of "arms and letters" became a metonymical extension of the dichotomy "war vs. love." See Cruz, "Arms versus Letters," 186–189, and Curtius, *European Literature*, 178–179, for their treatments of this subject.

re-writes these motifs so that the text of the *Metamorphoses* functions as a pre-text for the *Solitudes* in the sense of being a preceding text, an intertext, and hence a source, of avian imagery in his own work. Ovid's *Metamorphoses* is also a pre-text in the sense of an excuse, a justification, an explanation for Góngora's creative borrowing of bird imagery that, in his treatment, gives place to a poignant ethical reflection on greed as evidence of decaying values and as an unequivocal cause for much misfortune and disillusion in the Spanish empire facing its sunset.

UNIVERSITY OF TORONTO

CHANGING OVID

MAGGIE KILGOUR

As the essays in this volume remind us, writers and artists recurrently ransack the *Metamorphoses* in search of handy fables ready for their reworking. The chance to retell Ovid provides writers especially with an opportunity to put a new spin on an old story and thus display their own wit. Yet, as well as being a source for individual tales, the *Metamorphoses* has served as a spur to thinking about metamorphosis itself and its relation to the process of artistic revision. Ovidian stories seem irresistible to anyone interested in understanding the phenomenon of change – be it natural, supernatural, religious, cultural, political, or, especially, literary. But metamorphosis is itself a slippery subject. This article will suggest how the puzzlingly paradoxical nature of Ovidian change has challenged writers to wrestle with Ovid's Protean *corpus* in the hopes of capturing and revealing a stable truth under the apparent flux. For Milton in particular the chance to change Ovid becomes a means of re-imagining the nature of change itself.

Let me begin with a brief overview of the broad context within which Milton is working. As recent critics especially have perceived, Ovid's text presents contradictory images of change. The majority of the tales are *aitia*, which in fact show the arresting and stabilisation of change: a fleeing nymph becomes forever fixed in the form of a stone or a tree.[1] Paradoxically, change ends change. At the end of the text, however, Pythagoras' lengthy speech detailing the endless recycling of forms suggests another view of metamorphosis: change as continuous flux. As Colin Burrow notes, there seems to be a tension "between the poem's closed metamorphic tales about human beings on the one hand, and on the other the unclosed, unending, changeful universe in which they take place."[2] For some writers, therefore, Ovidian change is radical

---

[1] On the aetiological aspects of the poem see Myers, *Ovid's Causes*.

[2] Burrow, "Spenser and Classical Traditions," 230. As Burrow notes, the easy way to resolve this tension is by either reading Pythagoras' speech as the key which reveals the truth about the previous metamorphoses, a "grand metaphysical principle" (230), or by dismissing it as Ovid's little joke; see also Solodow, *World of Ovid's Metamorphoses*,

transformation, in which one thing irrevocably becomes something completely different: a man becomes his opposite, a beast. For others, however, it simply reveals an essential identity under the surface: men really are beasts![3]

This double aspect of metamorphosis is suggestive for Ovid's representation of poetry as a transformative force. Critics have noted how Ovid appears to identify the arresting of change especially with the power of art to capture and preserve the moment.[4] While the poem begins in and represents constant change, it moves towards the end and transcendence of change. The poet who writes of a world of metamorphosis ultimately rises above it, as Ovid claims at the end of the poem: "And now my work is done, which neither the wrath of Jove, nor fire, nor sword, nor the gnawing tooth of time shall ever be able to undo (*Iamque opus exegi, quod nec Iovis ira nec ignis | nec poterit ferrum nec edax abolere vetustas*, 15.871–872).[5] He imagines himself rising above the stars to become immortal in his poem: "if the prophecies of bards have any truth, through all the ages shall I live in fame" (*perque omnia saecula fama, | siquid habent veri vatum praesagia, vivam*, 15.878–879). The poet's own apotheosis is the fulfilment of change that ends change.[6]

While Ovid seems to identify the goal of his own poem with the arresting of change, metamorphosis imagined as flux also has a particular appropriateness for an aesthetic that is based on revision. Ovid's work is, after all, itself a recycling of old stories. Ovid is extremely self-conscious about this act of literary metamorphosis. While he draws on a variety of sources, he is especially concerned with rewriting the *Aeneid*.

162–168. For Burrow, neither of these solutions is adequate. Solodow's solution is to argue that what Pythagoras presents is "not really metamorphosis at all, but rather mere change" (167). As we will see, later rewriters of Ovid do not always see such a clear distinction.

[3] The latter view is succinctly put by Solodow, who argues that "A cardinal feature of Ovidian metamorphosis is continuity between the person and what he is changed into"; transformation is therefore "clarification ... a process by which characteristics of a person, essential or incidental, are given physical embodiments and so are rendered visible and manifest" (174).

[4] See for example Solodow, *World of Ovid's Metamorphoses*, 203–231.

[5] All citations of the *Metamorphoses* are from the Loeb Classical Edition, translated by Miller.

[6] See also Barkan, *Gods Made Flesh*, 78–88. On Ovid's assertion of immortality and its influence on later writers, see also Philip Hardie, *Ovid's Poetics of Illusion*, 94–97 especially.

Vergil's epic presented a model of cultural and personal change in Aeneas' transformation from a Trojan into a Roman. The poem thus seems to reflect, if not unambivalently, Augustus' vision of a "Roman revolution" that shaped change as a fixed teleology of cultural development fulfilled in Rome.[7] Ovidian flux revises and undoes this model for metamorphosis: what Vergil and Augustus stabilised, Ovid puts back in motion. Revision thus seems to offer a means of freeing previously fixed traditions and of making them dynamic once more.

Ovid's own stories have offered others the chance to participate in this process of reanimation by recreating his tales of recreation.[8] As Jamie Fumo argues, for writers such as Chaucer, Ovidian revision offers a model for the undoing of authority.[9] The image of a subversive Ovid who overturns a monolithic ideology has always been an appealing one, and has been particularly alluring, if sometimes misleading, for postmodern readers and rewriters. Yet such revision can become a version of endless flux when it turns into weak imitation or the pointless proliferation of alternative versions — as we may be painfully aware in a time when the movie business especially seems trapped in an endless cycle of appalling "remakes." If revision can be a source of inspiration, the fertile generation of new stories from old forms, it can also degenerate into a sterile sapping of creative energy. As current conservative backlashes also remind us, the repeated subversion of authority may produce in reaction a greater desire for stability and fixed meaning. For other writers, especially those working within the allegorical tradition, revision becomes instead a means of stabilising change once more, by correcting and Christianising Ovid's slippery stories.

For Christian rewriters of Ovid, literary metamorphosis is complicated by the traditional association of change with the fall. Change marks our

---

[7] On Augustus' ideological fixing of change, especially through his revision of the calendar, see Barchiesi, *Poet and the Prince*. As Barchiesi notes: "the flux of history has a culmination and conclusion in universal peace; the Roman year absorbs the transformation of Rome into its *telos*, the Restoration of the New Order that puts an end to change and disturbing memories. Augustan discourse is naturally directed toward a unifying and totalizing end" (271). Ovid's revision of the *Aeneid*, especially in the last books, has been discussed at length; see for example, Solodow, *World of Ovid's Metamorphoses*, 110–156; Hinds, *Allusion and Intertext*, 104–122.

[8] On Ovidian metamorphosis as an image for revision, see Barkan, *Gods Made Flesh*. See also Barolsky, "As in Ovid," 451–474, who notes how Renaissance artists especially drew on Ovidian models for thinking about their own art.

[9] See Fumo in this volume.

distance from God who, described also in terms that draw on the Platonic-Aristotelian tradition, is seen as unchanging, an unmoved mover.[10] For Spenser, for example, change is mutability, the force of Pythagorean flux that governs the fallen world and makes the poet, at the end of the profoundly Ovidian "Mutabilitie Cantos," yearn for a state of rest:

> when no more *Change* shall be,
> But stedfast rest of all things firmely stayd
> Vpon the pillours of Eternity,
> That is contrayr to *Mutabilitie*:
> For, all that moueth, doth in *Change* delight:
> But thence-forth all shall rest eternally
> With Him that is the God of Sabbaoth hight:
> O that great Sabbaoth God, graunt me that Sabaoths sight.
>
> (*Faerie Queene*, 7.8.2.2–9)

While the poet is first impressed by the beauty of Mutabilitie and the joyful nature of her pageant of time, by the end he appears to be exhausted and dismayed by a world which "Short *Time* shall soon cut down with his consuming sickle" (*Faerie Queene*, 7.8.1.9). He longs for a definitive transformation in which "time shall come that all shall changed bee, | And from thenceforth, none no more change shall see" (*Faerie Queene*, 7.7.59.4–5). Similarly, Petrarch represents himself as a shape shifter who is unable to hold onto any form for long: "but I have certainly been a flame lit by a lovely glance and I have been a bird that rises highest in the air raising her whom in my words I honour" (*ma fui ben fiamma ch'un bel guardo accense, | e fui l'uccel che più per l'aere poggia | alzando lei che ne' miei detti onoro*).[11] Like Spenser, he yearns for a stability that eludes his grasp: "Pray for these thoughts, I beseech you, that they may at last find stability. So long have they been idling about and, finding no firm stand, been uselessly driven through so many matters. May they now turn at last to the One, the Good, the True, the stably Abiding" (*pro quibus ora, queso, ut tandiu vagi et instabiles aliquando subsistant, et inutiliter per multa iactati, ad unum, bonum, verum, certum, stabile se convertant*).[12] The last word, *convertant*, is especially poignant. As both writers

---

[10]See for example Giamatti, *Exile and Change*, and cf. Akbari in this volume.

[11]Petrarch, *Rime sparse* 23.164–166, quoted from *Petrarch's Lyric Poems*, ed. and trans. Durling.

[12]Petrarch, *Le familiari libri I-XI*. 377. The English translation is from *Renaissance Philosophy of Man*, 46. For Petrarch's metamorphic self, see also Sturm-Maddox, *Petrarch's Metamorphoses*.

suggest, Ovidian metamorphosis is frequently identified with endless restlessness that is contrasted with Christian eternity: the vision of change presented by Pythagoras.[13] Earthly flux can be controlled and stabilised only when it is absorbed into the Pauline model of conversion, in which change is redirected towards its opposite: rest. Conversion offers a new version of metamorphosis as radical change – the transformation of one thing into another, the old man into the new – and as the fixing of what was previously unstable.[14] So Petrarch looks with envy at both Augustine and Dante, whom he imagines as having been successfully transformed through conversion from changing forms to more stable, permanent ones.[15] He experiences himself as someone who cannot convert, but simply keeps turning, obsessively revolving without hope of progression or definitive end. In contrast to the model of conversion, the Petrarchan self is a type for change as continuous flux. Art does not offer Petrarch an escape from this vicious circle, but only a perpetuation of it.

Milton strikingly departs from this tradition that identifies change generally with the consequences of the fall. In fact, for Milton the fall is a metamorphosis of the nature of change that *inhibits* real change. Fallen humans are drawn too easily towards a state of stagnation like that described in *Areopagitica* as: "a grosse conforming stupidity, a stark and dead congealment of *wood and hay and stubble* forc't and frozen together."[16] As critics have long noted, *Paradise Lost* was written to explain the failure of the English revolution to bring about permanent political change. Instead, the revolution came full circle, back to a monarchy. Revising Ovid helps Milton both to understand the reasons for this failure and also to explore the kinds of change still possible. Milton attempts to imagine a form of transformation that is neither simply endless flux nor the attainment of a state of static permanence.

---

13 See Holahan's seminal reading of Ovid's association with a classical world of endless mutability which Christianity rejects in "*Iamque opus exegi*," 244–270.

14 Ladner suggests a connection between the pagan concept of metamorphosis and Christian ideas of reform and conversion in *Idea of Reform*, 39–42.

15 On Petrarch's anxiety about his own unresolved instability, especially in contrast to the Augustinian model, see also Greene, "Flexibility of the Self in Renaissance Literature," 246–248.

16 Cited from the *Riverside Milton*, 1022 (original emphasis). All further references to Milton's works are from this edition.

Milton's fondness for and debt to Ovid generally has been long noted and studied.[17] It is often assumed, however, that Ovidian metamorphosis is associated with either fallen or at least flawed characters, whose shifty nature again suggests a sinister instability. Throughout *Paradise Lost*, Eve is recurrently compared to Ovidian figures, beginning with the description of her awakening in Book Four that draws explicitly on the subtext of Ovid's tale of Narcissus. The Ovidian subtext is often used to argue that Milton's Eve is already fallen – damned by intertextuality. Other comparisons to figures such as Proserpina seem equally ominous. Our suspicion of metamorphosis is encouraged by the fact that Satan appears the most Protean figure in the text: a shape-shifter who tries on different forms and who is identified with a number of Ovidian characters.[18]

The problem with such readings, however, is that they give the Ovidian subtexts a deterministic force and so restrict the possibility of free will upon which Milton insists. If the story is already written, then the outcome is fixed from the beginning. This is indeed the case with Milton's primary model, Genesis, which the poet is not free to rewrite and correct. The kind of superficially radical change that is evident at times in postmodernism, in which the author can simply change the ending and correct the past in one mighty pen stroke, is neither available to nor adequate for him. Milton's relation to his main source is important, especially as part of his thinking about revisionary change. Few readers would assume that Milton revises the Biblical story in order to subvert its authority. His re-creation of Genesis involves a clarification and elaboration of an already present meaning, rather than a radical metamorphosis. However, while working within the necessary limitations imposed by his material, Milton uses his appropriation and rewriting of Ovidian tales to suggest the nature of change in the fallen world.

Elsewhere I have discussed in detail Milton's revision of the Narcissus episode in relation to both Eve's story in Book Four and Adam's story in Book Eight.[19] In both these passages, Milton seems free to revise the story and give it a new ending. In Book Four, the Narcissus figure, Eve, does not die, but is successfully turned away from her watery

---

[17] See especially Harding, *Milton and the Renaissance Ovid*, and the most recent book-length study, Du Rocher, *Milton and Ovid*.

[18] On the Ovidian parallels for both Eve and Satan, see Du Rocher, *Milton and Ovid*.

[19] Kilgour, "'Thy perfect image viewing.'"

object of affection. Similarly, in the story of Adam's creation in Book Eight, the story of Narcissus is recalled and revised to reach a happy conclusion. While Ovid's Narcissus, frustrated by the paradox that he cannot *have* himself because he *is* himself, wishes in vain to be split in two, Adam is granted just such a wish when God draws Eve out of his body.

However, in the fall in Book Nine, the original subtext seems to return with an almost determining force, as Adam chooses to fall with Eve because of his over-identification with her. Adam's language suggests they are relapsing into their original narcissistic relation in which they were literally one flesh. He tells Eve that he must join her: "So forcible within my heart I feel | The Bond of Nature draw me to my owne, | My own in thee, for what thou art is mine; | Our State cannot be severd, we are one, | One Flesh; to loose thee were to loose myself" (9.955–959). It is of course important that Milton associates the fall with narcissism; it may be even more important, however, that he identifies the fall with *the failure of revision*. The poet appears unable after all to escape Ovid's plot; in the end, the subtext seems to have exerted too much pressure on the poem and curtailed Milton's possibilities. Yet the poem itself is also an explanation of *why* this is the case. For Milton, one of the primary consequences of the fall is its disastrous effects on the nature of change, as a result of which his ability to rewrite the plots of the past is severely restricted.

As the revisions of the story of Narcissus in Books Four and Eight suggest, however, such rewriting was possible before the fall. The garden is a place of perpetual revision, in which pagan stories and figures are recalled to be reformed and refigured. Eden surpasses "that faire field | Of *Enna*, where *Proserpin* gathering flours | Her self a fairer Floure by gloomie *Dis* | Was gatherd" (4.268–271) and evokes images of "*Hesperian* Fables true, | If true, here only" (4.250–251). The stories are included, but, as in the case of Narcissus, redefined. The process of re-creation is not here one of correcting in the sense of stabilising and fixing; the relationship between subtext and Milton's figures is left open and in process. Ovidian figures are brought back to life and set once more into action. This unfixing of the past is possible because Milton's Eden itself is not "perfect" in the root sense of finished and complete – it is dynamic and in motion.[20] This makes sense; it is, after all, a garden,

---

[20] See the seminal discussion of Milton's striking valuation of time and movement

whose nature is to grow. While it contains elements of the classical golden age, in which natural change is suspended in an ideal of eternal spring, time is present in Milton's garden, bringing with it the potential for development. Milton's time is not Ovid's *tempus edax rerum* which drives the pattern of eternal flux in *Met.* 15.234. Ovid's time is the enemy of the poet who must seek to conquer it through art. In Spenser's Garden of Adonis also "wicked *Time*" (*Faerie Queene* 3.6.39.3) ruthlessly "flyes about, and with his flaggy wings | Beates downe both leaues and buds without regard" (3.6.39.7–8); he troubles the happiness and perfection of Spenser's garden. Even this ideal world cannot escape change, here seen as destructive mutability. Moreover, by embodying this element, Spenser gives a rather abstract and nebulous dimension a tangible substance that adds to its corrosive power. For Milton, however, time is not a literal figure in the garden, but appears simply as the natural rhythm that structures Edenic life.[21] In his first description of the garden, Milton draws particular attention to temporal movement. He notes the coming of evening three times (4.352–355, 539–542, 598–609), and, as the couple retire for the night, Adam reminds Eve of the different parts of their day (4.610–633). The presence of time does not disturb Milton's garden, but rather increases its beauty by adding variety and change.

However, the cycles of natural rhythms and change are themselves circular, following the rising and setting of the sun. They are potentially endless, like Pythagorean flux. Milton suggests a further type of change evident in the garden, one that adds a developmental and progressive dimension. Raphael describes to Adam a cosmos that is in constant motion, descending from and then rising back up to God: "O *Adam*, one Almightie is, from whom | All things proceed, and up to him return, | If not deprav'd from good, created all | Such to perfection, one first matter all, | Indu'd with various forms various degrees | Of substance, and in things that live, of life" (5.469–474). While the elements are divided into a hierarchical chain of being that sets spirit

---

in Summers, *The Muses' Method*. As Summers eloquently writes: "Surfeited with change, we like Spenser and many other men since his time, ultimately desire the time when all the changes shall be changed, when history shall be ended, whether we perceive that ending as a static aesthetic state, a static earthly society, or a celestial heaven without change …To Milton the desire for inactive, unchanging being was only a disguise for the desire for non-being" (86).

[21] For Milton's view of time and its relation to that of other writers, see also Quinones, *Renaissance Discovery of Time*.

above matter, this chain is dynamic. The divisions are temporary, as everything is in the process of moving back towards unity with God. This includes man, as Raphael suggests:

> time may come when men
> With Angels may participate, and find
> No inconvenient Diet, nor too light Fare;
> And from these corporal nutriments perhaps
> Your bodies may at last turn all to Spirit,
> Improv'd by tract of time, and wingd ascend
> Ethereal, as wee, or may at choice
> Here in Heav'nly Paradises dwell.   (5.493–500)

Time is not the enemy of eternity, but the path to it; a world of transformation does not mark our separation from God, but rather is itself the path back up to him. Through their conversations with each other and with Raphael, Adam and Eve, like the garden, grow and develop towards this goal. Adam thanks Raphael for guiding him upwards: "Well hast thou taught the way that might direct | Our knowledge, and the scale of Nature set | From center to circumference, whereon | In contemplation of created things | By steps we may ascend to God" (5.508–512). God himself suggests the possibility of such an ascent, when he announces to the angels that he is about to create

> Another World, out of one man a Race
> Of men innumerable, there to dwell,
> Not here, till by degrees of merit rais'd
> They open to themselves at length a way
> Up hither, under long obedience tri'd,
> And Earth be chang'd to Heav'n, & Heav'n to Earth,
> One Kingdom, Joy and Union without end.   (7.155–161)

God is very clear about the differences here: he draws attention to the fact that he is making a different species – something new that did not exist before – and that this new being will live in a new place separate from Heaven. The spatial terms *here, there* reiterate the distance, and also suggest a hierarchy in which the new species occupies an inferior place. Yet, here too differences seem to foreshadow, if rather obscurely, a final unity, in which *here* will become *there*. God is giving man the opportunity to rise from here to eternity.

The natural movement of all things towards God and eternity might imply that, as writers like Spenser and Petrarch imagined, earthly change and flux will ultimately be superseded by heavenly rest and stasis.

However, Milton's Heaven is also very active. The angels dance, sing, go places (as does God himself, though ubiquity makes this easier), they fight battles, have jobs. Raphael tells Adam that they eat and have sex. Activity and change are a part of Milton's vision of the highest spiritual life. The angels normally pass time:

> In song and dance about the sacred Hill,
> Mystical dance, which yonder starrie Spheare
> Of Planets and of fixt in all her Wheeles
> Resembles nearest, mazes intricate,
> Eccentric, intervolv'd, yet regular
> Then most, when most irregular they seem,
> And in thir motions harmonie Divine
> So smooths her charming tones, that Gods own ear
> Listens delighted. Eevning now approach'd
> (For wee have also our Eevning and our Morn,
> Wee ours for change delectable, not need).   (5.619–629)

The dance of the angels is compared to the movement of the stars – the traditional means of measuring time. In Heaven, time has become a dance in which also change is "delectable": a source of pleasure. The goal of change is not rest, but a higher form of change.

For Milton, then, change is not opposed to perfection but part of its nature. It is a necessary prerequisite for free will. In contrast, as *Areopagitica* suggests, Milton associates evil with stasis and stagnation. In Book Two of *Paradise Lost*, Hell is bounded by a frozen wasteland, guarded by the petrifying force of Medusa who stands "with *Gorgonian* terror" (2.611). The devils are intermittently dragged here by the Furies, by whom they are forced temporarily "to pine | Immovable, infixt, and frozen round" (2.601–602).[22] This landscape is internalised by Satan, who displays a remarkable tenacity of spirit.[23] Ironically, despite his

---

[22] See also Rumrich, who notes how Medusa here suggests "a paralyzing power over one's destiny" which prevents the devils' "only hope of change"; *Milton Unbound*, 87.

[23] On Satanic fixity and its relation to compulsive repetition, see Schwartz, *Remembering and Repeating*; Rumrich, *Milton Unbound*, 126. Samuel notes the underlying similarity here between Milton's Satan and Dante's frozen Lucifer, a parody of the unmoved mover: "Such fixity, the ultimate opposite to the spontaneity of life, is an exact symbol for Dante's view, and Milton's, of the end of evil. As the compulsively repeated choice becomes mechanical, purposeless, and ceaseless, it becomes the whole character, and the whole character thus becomes one fixed posture" (*Dante and Milton*,

superficial Ovidian versatility, Satan refuses to change in any radical way. In his great dramatic soliloquy in Book Four, he briefly entertains, only to reject, the possibility of conversion with painful if destructive self-knowledge: "O then at last relent: is there no place | Left for Repentance, none for Pardon left? | None left but by submission; and that word | *Disdain* forbids me" (4.79–82).[24] It is striking the way he turns a part of his own character – *Disdain* – into an almost allegorical character blocking the possibility of change. Satan's rhetoric creates the impression that his choice is imposed by an independent force outside of himself.[25] He is essentially turning his own character into fate, in order to prove that he cannot change: "But say I could repent and could obtaine | By Act of Grace my former state; how soon | Would highth recal high thoughts, how soon unsay | What feign'd submission swore: ease would recant | Vows made in pain, as violent and void" (4.93–97).

Satan resists the possibility for character development and growth that we glimpse, even if briefly, in Adam and Eve. This willed rejection of change calls forth God's taste for Dantesque poetic justice in Book Ten, where Satan is punished with the eternal superimposition of change. He is forcibly turned into the serpentine form he had freely chosen, as he suddenly notices a metamorphosis first in himself and then in the other devils:

> His Visage drawn he felt to sharp and spare,
> His Armes clung to his Ribs, his Leggs entwining
> Each other, till supplanted down he fell
> A monstrous Serpent on his Belly prone,
> Reluctant, but in vaine, a greater power
> Now rul'd him, punisht in the shape he sin'd,
> According to his doom: he would have spoke,
> But hiss for hiss returned with forked tongue

---

126). Burrow notes how Spenser also associates Ovidian figures with characters who refuse progression and movement; "Spenser and Classical Traditions," 229.

24 This dramatic moment of self-knowledge which leads to a tragic decision to persist in a destructive course has itself Ovidian analogues: the speeches of Medea, Scylla, Byblis for example. Like Ovid, Milton is concerned with moments of choice, in which identity momentarily wavers and is indeterminate, but which then lead to states of permanence and fixity.

25 Whether Satan has the power to change, or whether his fate is determined by God, is perennially debated by critics. Certainly by this point, his free will, which makes change possible, is at best severely weakened by the choices he has already made.

> To forked tongue, for now were all transform'd
> Alike, to Serpents all.   (10.511–521)

The moment of transformation is highly Ovidian – Milton focuses on the horror with which Satan becomes aware of his unexpected and unwilled change, and the terror of his loss of voice. The drawn-out scene recalls Ovid's fascination with representing what Solodow describes as "in-between states," moments of extreme "indeterminacy and shapelessness." As Solodow notes, "By dwelling on movements when a figure is neither one thing nor another, when it temporarily lacks identity, Ovid sharpens our sense of the permanence which metamorphosis will bring."[26] In Milton's version, the achievement of such permanence is sinister, since it means the closing off of the freedom identified with change and indeterminacy.

The specific details in the above scene recall the metamorphosis of Cadmus in *Met.* 4.563–603 that ends Ovid's presentation of stories connected with the beginnings of Thebes. The parallel is telling: Cadmus is the founder of a nation associated with incest, patricide, and fratricide. For Dante, who also revises this scene of metamorphosis in *Inferno* 24–25, Thebes is the infernal city.[27] In Milton's poem, Ovid's

---

[26] Solodow, *World of Ovid's Metamorphoses*, 188.

[27] As Jamie Fumo has also noted, Dante is an important mediator for later careful readers of Ovid such as Chaucer. Milton also frequently draws on Dante's revision of Ovid; here he recalls *Inferno* 24–25, the circle of thieves. The reference is appropriate: Satan is a thief. Dante's canto is important also as it includes Dante's own famous claim to have dreamed up a new kind of change no one else ever imagined: "Concerning Cadmus and Arethusa let be Ovid silent; for if he, poetising, converts the one into a serpent and the other into a fountain, I envy him not; for two natures front to front he never so transmuted that both forms were prompt to exchange their substance" (*Taccia di Cadmo e d'Aretusa Ovidio:* | *ché se quello in serpente, e quella in fonte* | *converte poetando, io non lo'nvidio:* || *ché due nature mai a fronte a fronte* | *non trasmutò, sì ch'amendue le forme* | *a cambiar lor matera fosser pronte, Inf.* 25.97–102; text and translation cited from Singleton's translation of the *Commedia*). Dante's claim to be imagining a completely original form of change here is suggestive for Milton's own concern with creating new forms of change. Critics have debated the implications of Dante's claim of originality here: is he celebrating his own invention, or distancing himself from this moment of poetic pride in which he steals from the past? See Kilgour, *From Communion to Cannibalism*, 66–69, and Hawkins, "Virtuosity and Virtue," who argues that the poet is self-consciously showing the danger of his own power of *ingenium*, the faculty traditionally associated with Ovid, and his peril of losing "the sense of metamorphosis as conversion" (11). The positioning of such a claim to absolute originality in this canto suggests also the dangerous proximity between revision and mere theft.

aition of the founding of Thebes has been metamorphosed and expanded to become the story of the origins of evil in the entire world. Here Milton also comments on the nature of the *aition* itself, which as Sara Myers notes, shows the fixing of forms in a final state of being.[28] The fall is a change which brings about a radical and permanent metamorphosis. An evolving dynamic cosmos turns into its opposite: a rigid world which, like Satan, resists change.

Unlike the transformations of Ovid's characters, however, the metamorphosis of the devils is not permanent. We are told that they regain their own shapes after a time. Yet, we are also told that they are "Yearly enjoynded, some say, to undergo | This annual humbling certain number'd days" (10.574–575). This annual transformation is similar to the devil's regular return to the borders of Hell to be tormented by Medusa, in Book Two. In both cases, Milton is suggesting that we are witnessing the origin of a custom, a ritual that will be repeated through time. Ritual repetition is the form that fixity will take in the fallen world.[29] Pythagorean flux is therefore itself the means of arresting change.

The spreading of Satanic stasis to Earth is also represented in Book Ten, when Satan's children, Sin and Death, build a concrete bridge between Hell and Earth. These figures themselves are formidably inflexible; like Spenser's Time or Error, they are allegorical characters whose natures are pinned down by their names. Sin is Sin, Death is Death: there's not much room for character development or growth there! When Sin and Death fly across the universe the result is not creation but destruction, as fluid potential is locked into deadly forms: "The aggregated Soyle | Death with his Mace petrific, cold and dry, | As with a Trident smote, and fix't as firm | As *Delos* floating once; the rest his look | Bound with *Gorgonian* rigor not to move" (10.293–297). The path between Earth and *Heaven* described by Raphael and God – a spiral of ascent through time and space – is replaced with a highway set in stone, that rigidly binds Earth and *Hell*: "with Pinns of Adamant | And Chains they made all fast, too fast they made | And durable" (10.318–320).

---

28 Myers, *Ovid's Causes*, 134–135.

29 While Schwartz contrasts ritual with Satanic repetition, which she also suggests attempts to arrest time and change, the scene also suggests their dangerous proximity; see *Remembering and Repeating*.

For Milton, therefore, it is the fallen world which is perfect in the sense of finished, complete – and completely rigid. It is full of change, but change which goes nowhere, as stasis is achieved through compulsive but redundant metamorphosis. The shape of time itself is transformed into a version of Pythagorean flux. In the last two books, the archangel Michael shows Adam the future. The fact that the future can now be seen suggests its fixity.[30] Moreover, the vision of history Michael presents seems tediously repetitive, as mankind simply rewrites, in different forms, Adam and Eve's story. The consequences of the fall are relived in each generation, until God himself is "Wearied" (12.107) with the endless litany of "iniquities," and even the angelic narrator gets bored with the redundant and rather homogeneous tales of sin and corruption he is forced to tell and starts to skip bits: "the rest | Were long to tell, how many Battels fought, | How many Kings destroyed, and Kingdoms won" (12.260–262). This depiction of an endless metempsychosis of sin if not literally of souls[31] seems all too familiar and a bit pointless.

Yet of course there is a point: history has a telos, Christ, whose coming will put an end to this redundant process. Christ is the goal of Milton's plot as Augustus was of Vergil's. However, as Milton noticed, the incarnation is not itself adequate for redemption. In fact, after Christ's coming, the whole damn cycle starts up all over again with further corruption: "so shall the World goe on, | To good malignant, to bad man benigne, | Under her own waight groaning" (12.537–539). The wheel will keep on spinning until the second coming.

The endless circling of history arrests the possibility of true and permanent change. This bleak vision enables Milton to explain the transformation of the English revolution from a radical break to another turn of the wheel. Humans themselves cannot change anything. For one thing, human nature is no longer dynamic, growing, like the garden,

---

[30] In Book Ten also, the fixing of the stars, whose movement was previously left indeterminate by Raphael (Book Eight), reinforces this sense of a redefinition and limitation of time.

[31] The vision of history as a repeated fall seems to undo the distinction between devilish and human fates outlined in Book Ten. There the narrator notes of the devils: "so oft they fell | Into the same illusion" (570–571), and distinguishes this recurring punishment from "Man | Whom they triumph'd once lapst" (571–572). This suggests that man's fall only happens once; if that is true, than history is simply a longer-playing version of Book Nine.

but rather petrified by Sin. Fallen individuals do not want change – like Satan, they reject freedom for the familiar pool of stagnant conformity. While in Book Seven, God had suggested that humans by themselves had the chance to turn Earth into Paradise, now it is Christ alone who can bring about final transformation in which, as Michael explains, "the Earth | Shall all be Paradise" (12.463–464). The climactic history lesson offers hope of a distant ending of the cycles of history and gives the revolutionary a convenient explanation for the failure of the revolution. Yet, it also seems to leave us without purpose, as it makes all human action superfluous.

The essential inefficacy of human action nonetheless does not permit quietism or withdrawal; if anything, it makes action even more urgent.[32] In the last books, a second pattern emerges, associated with figures such as Enoch, Abram, and, especially, Moses. Limited as they are by the redundant revolutions of history, they still manage to bring about a radical, if provisional, revolution that momentarily stops the turning of this wheel. The point of their actions is to remind us of the final change that Christ will bring about.

This anticipatory role is played also by the narrator himself, whose self-presentation exemplifies both the need for and limits of human change in the fallen world. As already suggested, the nature of the Biblical story the poet tells in itself constrains his poetic license. In the invocations, moreover, he draws attention to further restrictions on his imagination which impede his creative energy. Some of these pressures are external – he is especially concerned with the effect of time in its different senses and the "cold | Climat" (9.44–45) of a world which, symbolically if not literally, resembles the outskirts of Hell. Moreover, the narrator's blindness cuts him off from the experience of seasonal change that so clearly inspires him with its variety and beauty (3.40–44); he sees "clouds in stead, and ever-during dark" (3.45), "a Universal blanc" (3.48). He has undergone a transformation, but one which is associated with the loss of the experience of recurrent change. Similarly in Book Nine, he points to a metamorphosis of voice and even genre, claiming with regret that he must "change | Those Notes to tragic"

---

[32] This is of course the lesson of the War in Heaven, in which the good angels are sent out to wage a war which, after three days, God reveals they had no hope of winning. The war is potentially endless; only Christ can bring it to a conclusion. While the whole set-up seems perverse, it allows the angels to make choices, and to decide for themselves which side they are on.

(9.5–6) to reflect the irrevocable change he is about to represent and which constrains his poetry. For him also, change is associated with the loss of the possibility of change.

However, while the narrator says he has been forced to undergo such negative and irreversible changes, he insists that he still sings with a voice that is "unchang'd | To hoarce or mute, though fall'n on evil dayes, | On evil dayes though fall'n, and evil tongues; | In darkness, and with dangers compast round" (7.24–27). The speaker's firm insistence that he has not allowed adversity to change him seems noble and indeed heroic. Yet the presentation of his tenacity of spirit, underscored by the stubborn repetition of the word "fallen," suggests the underlying similarity between the poet and Satan that has struck almost every reader since at least the Romantics. The parallel is so obvious that is hard to believe it is not a deliberate means of drawing attention to the narrator's Satanic side: his own inner resistance to change.[33]

Perhaps even more tellingly, the narrator's presentation of himself as dwelling "In darkness, and with dangers compast round" (7.27) echoes closely Sin's earlier description of her own situation, "With terrors and with clamors compasst round" (2.862). The terrors are the hellhounds which she endlessly generates and which just as endlessly attempt to gnaw their way back into her womb. Sin's relation to her spawn provides a perfect image for the endlessly self-destructive cycles of history. But she is especially suggestive for the poet himself.[34] Like him, Sin is a creator, but one whose creations prey upon their source. The verbal echo suggests the poet's fear that his own creation, the poem, will be equally sinful and self-destructive.

Given the relevance of Sin to Milton's own enterprise, it seems appropriate that the origin of Sin is the first *aition* in the poem. While Milton's elaborate version of the birth of Sin is highly original, it is not created *ex nihilo*, but draws on a number of classical and later sources in order to describe her nature. Her birth from Satan's head clearly aligns her with Minerva, born out of Jove's mind, and so makes her an infernal form of wisdom and knowledge. Following her rape by her father, Sin undergoes a metamorphosis which turns her into an obvious version of Ovid's Scylla and her descendent, Spenser's Error. Sin's almost ostenta-

---

[33] See also Riggs.

[34] For a different but related reading of the identification of Sin with the narrator, see Rumrich, *Milton Unbound*, 99–101.

tious recollection of these models draws attention to the fact that she is the product of revision. In Sin, however, textual change has become the sterile and incestuous recycling of past figures; as Colin Burrow notes, Sin is "the most wearisomely derivative figure in *Paradise Lost*."[35] For the poet, Sin is indeed bad, unoriginal, poetry. As Satan's "perfect image" (2.764) with which he falls in love, she is the fallen equivalent of Milton's own creative revision of Ovid's Narcissus in Books Four and Eight.

As builder of the concrete bridge that binds Hell and Earth, Sin is also the perverted form of the source of all creativity for Milton: Christ. In Milton's revision of the story of creation told in Genesis, Christ moves over chaos to shape a growing, dynamic world. Here Milton imagines an alternative *aition*: a myth of origination which does not involve fixing.[36] Christ creates a flexible world whose nature has *not* yet been rigidly defined and which will now be free to grow on its own. If Sin suggests that all revision is a futile and ultimately self-consuming recycling of old figures, Christ's creative act of origination offers the poet an alternative example of change. Such a model seems somewhat different from the forms of change imagined *in* the *Metamorphoses* itself; it might be better exemplified in the dynamic and creative reception of Ovid's epic. Literary transformation is always temporary as well as temporal; Ovidian figures are never completely fixed, but await the new forms we give them. It is fitting that *Paradise Lost* ends with a beginning, Adam and Eve's entrance into the fallen world. The final scene, and the famous line "The World was all before them" (12.646), has itself been the source of countless revisions and adaptations. By changing the *Metamorphoses*, *Paradise Lost* takes its place in the chain of revision, becoming a fruitful source for revision by other writers, from Dryden to Philip Pullman, who are concerned with keeping the possibility of change itself alive.[37]

McGILL UNIVERSITY

---

35 Burrow, *Epic Romance*, 269.

36 See also Rumrich's discussion of Milton's scene of creation as an alternative to traditional creation myths; *Milton Unbound*, 118–146.

37 I would like to thank Jamie Fumo for her astute advice on things Ovidian; her comments helped transform this article in its final revisions. Thanks also to the Social Sciences and Humanities Research Council of Canada for their generous support of the project of which this work forms a part.

BIBLIOGRAPHY

A Selection of Latin Stories, from Manuscripts of the Thirteenth and Fourteenth Centuries: A Contribution to the History of Fiction during the Middle Ages. Ed. T. Wright. Early English Poetry, Ballads, and Popular Literature of the Middle Ages 8. London: C. Richards, 1842.

Abraham, L. *A Dictionary of Alchemy Imagery.* Cambridge, UK: Cambridge University Press, 1998.

Accademia della Crusca, Opera del Vocabolario. *Concordanze del Canzoniere di Francesco Petrarca.* Florence: 1971.

Accessus ad auctores, Bernard d'Utrecht, Conrad Hirsau: dialogus super Auctores. Ed. R.B.C. Huygens. Leiden: Brill, 1970.

Adams, J.N. *The Latin Sexual Vocabulary.* London: Duckworth, 1987.

Agrippa, H.C. *The Vanitie and Vncertaintie of Arts and Sciences.* Trans. Ia. Sa. [James Sanford]. London: Henry Wykes, 1569. First published *De incertitudine & vanitate omnium scientiarum & artium* (Paris: J. Petrus, 1531).

———. *The Three Books of Occult Philosophy.* Trans. J.F. [John French]. London: Gregory Moule, 1651. First published *De occulta philosophia: libri tres* (Antwerp: Graphaeus, 1531).

Ahl, F. *Metaformations: Soundplay and Wordplay in Ovid and Other Classical Poets.* Ithaca and London: Cornell University Press, 1985.

Akbari, S.C. *Seeing Through the Veil: Optical Theory and Medieval Allegory.* Toronto: University of Toronto Press, 2004.

Alighieri, Dante – see Dante.

Allen, J.B. "Mythology in the Bible Commentaries and *Moralitates* of Robert Holkot." Ph.D. dissertation, The John Hopkins University, 1963.

———. *The Friar as Critic: Literary Attitudes in the Later Middle Ages.* Nashville: Vanderbilt University Press, 1971.

———. "Commentary as Criticism: The Text, Influence, and Literary Theory of the *Fulgentius Metaphored* of John Ridewall," pp. 25–47 in *Acta conventus neo-latini Amsteldamensis (Proceedings of the Second International Congress of Neo-Latin Studies, Amsterdam, August 19–24, 1973).* Ed. P. Tuynman, G.C. Kuiper, and E. Kessler. Munich: Wilhelm Fink, 1979.

_____. *The Ethical Poetic of the Later Middle Ages: A Decorum of Convenient Distinction.* Toronto: University of Toronto Press, 1982.

_____. "Eleven Unpublished Commentaries on Ovid's *Metamorphoses* and Two Other Texts of Mythographic Interest. Some Comments on a Bibliography," pp. 281–315 in *The Mythographic Art: Classical Fable and the Rise of the Vernacular in Early France and England.* Ed. J. Chance. Gainesville: University of Florida Press, 1990.

_____ and P. Gallacher. "Alisoun through the Looking Glass: Or Every Man his Own Midas." *Chaucer Review* 4.2 (1970): 99–105.

Alton, E.H. "The Mediaeval Commentators on Ovid's *Fasti.*" *Hermathena* 44 (1926): 119–151.

_____ and D.E.W. Wormell. "Ovid in the Mediaeval Schoolroom." *Hermathena* 94 (1960): 21–38; 95 (1961): 67–82.

Ames-Lewis, F. *The Intellectual Life of the Early Renaissance Artist.* New Haven: Yale University Press, 2000.

Anderson, W.S. "Multiple Change in the *Metamorphoses.*" *Transactions of the American Philological Association* 94 (1963): 1–27.

_____. "Review of B. Otis, *Ovid as an Epic Poet.*" *American Journal of Philology* 89 (1968): 93–104.

Anglo, S. "Reginald Scot's *Discoverie of Witchcraft*: Skepticism and Sadduceeism," pp. 106–139 in *The Damned Art: Essays in the Literature of Witchcraft.* Ed. S. Anglo. London: Routledge, 1977.

Apuleius: Cupid & Psyche. Ed. E.J. Kenney. Cambridge, UK: Cambridge University Press, 1990.

Ariani, M. *Petrarca.* Rome: Salerno, 1999.

Aristotle. *Rhetoric. The Art of Rhetoric.* Trans. J.H. Freese. Loeb Classical Library. Cambridge, MA: Harvard University Press, 1975.

Arnulf of Orléans. *Allegoriae super Ovidii Metamorphosin.* "Arnolfo d'Orléans, un cultore di Ovidio nel secolo XII." Ed. F. Ghisalberti. *Memorie del Reale Istituto Lombardo di Scienze e Lettere* 24 (1932): 157–234.

"*Arnulfi Aurelianensis glosule de Remediis amoris.*" Ed. B. Roy and H.V. Shooner. *The Journal of Medieval Latin* 6 (1996): 135–196.

Arnulfi Aurelianensis glosule Ovidii Fastorum. Ed. J.R. Rieker. Florence: SISMEL, Edizioni del Galluzzo, 2005.

Augurellus, I.A. *Chrysopoeia,* pp. 197–266 in *Theatrum chemicum.* Vol. 3. Strasbourg: Zetzner, 1659. First published Venice: Aldus, 1515.

Augustine. *Confessions.* Trans. H. Chadwick. Oxford: Oxford University Press, 1991.

_____. *Confessions*. Ed. and commentary by J.J. O'Donnell. Oxford: Clarendon Press, 1992.

_____. *De doctrina christiana*. Ed. and trans. R.P.H. Green. Oxford and New York: Clarendon Press, 1995.

Bacon, F. *The Wisdome of the Ancients*. Trans. A. George. London: John Bill, 1619. First published *De sapientia vetervm* (Londini: Robertvs Barkervs, 1609). Reprinted together. The Renaissance and the Gods, 20. New York: Garland, 1976.

Ball, R. "Poetic Imitation in Góngora's 'Romance de Angélica y Medoro.'" *Bulletin of Hispanic Studies* 57 (1980): 33–54.

Bann, S. *The True Vine: On Visual Representation and the Western Tradition*. Cambridge, UK: Cambridge University Press, 1989.

Barchiesi, A. *The Poet and the Prince: Ovid and Augustan Discourse*. Berkeley: University of California Press, 1997.

_____. "Narrative Technique and Narratology in the *Metamorphoses*," pp. 180–199 in *The Cambridge Companion to Ovid*. Ed. P. Hardie. Cambridge, UK: Cambridge University Press, 2002.

Barkan, L. "Diana and Actaeon: The Myth as Synthesis." *English Literary Renaissance* 10 (1980): 317–359.

_____. *The Gods Made Flesh: Metamorphosis and the Pursuit of Paganism*. New Haven: Yale University Press, 1986.

_____. *Unearthing the Past: Archaeology and Aesthetics in the Making of Renaissance Culture*. New Haven: Yale University Press, 1999.

Barolini, T. "Arachne, Argus, and St. John: Transgressive Art in Dante and Ovid." *Ovid in Medieval Culture*. Ed. M. Desmond. Special Issue, *Mediaevalia* 13 (1989 for 1987): 207–226.

_____. *The Undivine Comedy: Detheologizing Dante*. Princeton: Princeton University Press, 1992.

Barolsky, P. "As in Ovid, So in Renaissance Art." *Renaissance Quarterly* 51 (1998): 451–474.

Baron, H. "Petrarch: His Inner Struggles and the Humanistic Discovery of Man's Nature," pp. 18–51 in *Florilegium historiale; Essays Presented to Wallace K. Ferguson*. Ed. J.G. Rowe and W.H. Stockdale. Toronto: University of Toronto Press in association with the University of Western Ontario, 1971.

_____. *Petrarch's Secretum: Its Making and Its Meaning*. Cambridge, MA: Harvard University Press, 1985.

Bate, J. *Shakespeare and Ovid*. Oxford: Oxford University Press, 1993.

Battista, C. and A. Giovanni. *Dizionario etimologico italiano.* Florence: G. Barbèra, 1952.

Benoît de Sainte-Maure. *Le Roman de Troie.* Ed. L. Constans. 6 vols. Paris: Société des Anciens Textes Français, 1904–1912.

Bernardo, A.S. "Petrarch's Autobiography: Circularity Revisited." *Annali d'italianistica* 4 (1986): 45–72.

Béroul. *The Romance of Tristran by Beroul.* 2 vols. Ed. A. Ewert. Oxford: Blackwell, 1939–1970.

Bersuire, Pierre. *De formis figurisque deorum. Reductorium morale, liber XV: Ovidius moralizatus, cap. i.* Ed. J. Engels. Utrecht: Institut voor Laat Latijn der Rijksuniversiteit, 1966.

———. *Reductorium morale, liber XV, cap. ii-xv: Ovidius Moralizatus.* Ed. J. Engels. Utrecht: Institut voor Laat Latijn der Rijksuniversiteit, 1962.

———. *Metamorphosis Ovidiana moraliter . . . explanata.* Ed. S. Orgel. Paris: 1509; New York: Garland, 1979.

———. "The *Ovidius moralizatus* of Petrus Berchorius: An Introduction and Translation." Trans. W.D. Reynolds. Ph.D. dissertation, University of Illinois at Urbana-Champaign, 1971.

Beverley, J. *Aspects of Góngora's Soledades.* Purdue University Monographs in Romance Languages 1. Amsterdam: John Benjamins, 1980.

Blumenfeld[-Kosinski], R. "Remarques sur *songe/mensonge.*" *Romania* 101 (1980): 385–390.

Blumenfeld-Kosinski, R. "The Scandal of Pasiphae: Narration and Interpretation in the *Ovide moralisé.*" *Modern Philology* 93 (1996): 307–326.

———. *Reading Myth: Classical Mythology and Its Interpretations in Medieval French Literature.* Stanford: Stanford University Press, 1997.

———. "'Enemies Within / Enemies Without': Threats to the Body Politic in Christine de Pizan." *Mediaevalia et humanistica* 26 (1999): 1–15.

Boas, M. "De librorum Catonianorum historia atque compositione." *Mnemosyne* 42 (1914): 27–46.

Bonsignori, G. *Ovidio Metamorphoseos vulgare.* Ed. E. Ardissino. Bologna: Commissione per i testi di lingua, 2001.

Bonus, P. (attrib.). *Pretiosa margarita, novella de thesauro,* pp. 527–713 in *Theatrum chemicum.* Vol. 5. Strasbourg: Zetzner, 1660. First published Venice: Aldus, 1546.

_____. *The New Pearl of Great Price*. [Ed. A.E. Waite.] London: James Elliott, 1894.

Born, L.K. "The Manuscripts of the *Integumenta* on the *Metamorphoses* of Ovid by John of Garland." *Transactions and Proceedings of the American Philological Association* 60 (1929): 179–199.

_____. "Ovid and Allegory." *Speculum* 9 (1934): 362–379.

Boyde, P. *Passion and Perception in Dante's Comedy*. Cambridge, UK: Cambridge University Press, 1993.

Boysen, B. "Crucified in the Mirror of Love: On Petrarch's Ambivalent Conception of Love in Rerum vulgarium fragmenta." *Orbis Literarum 58* (2003): 163–188.

Bracton, Henry de. *De legibus et consuetudines Angliae*. Trans. S. Thorne. Cambridge, MA: Harvard University Press, 1968; rpt. Buffalo: Hein, 1997.

Brantley, F.O. "Sancho's Ascent Into the Spheres." *Hispania* 53 (1970): 37–45.

Brenckman, J. "Writing, Desire, Dialectic in Petrarch's *Rime 23*." *Pacific Coast Philology* 9 (1974): 12–19.

Brown, N.O. "Metamorphoses II: Actaeon." *American Poetry Review* (Nov-Dec 1972): 38–40.

Brownlee, K. "Dante and Narcissus (Purg. XXX, 76–99)." *Dante Studies* 96 (1978): 201–206.

_____. *Poetic Identity in Guillaume de Machaut*. Madison: University of Wisconsin Press, 1984.

_____. "Discourses of the Self: Christine de Pizan and the *Rose*." *Romanic Review* 59 (1988): 199–221.

_____. "Ovide et la moi poétique 'moderne' à la fin du moyen âge: Jean Froissart et Christine de Pizan," pp. 153–173 in *Modernité au moyen âge: Le défi du passé*. Ed. B. Cazelles and C. Méla. Recherches et Rencontres 1. Geneva: Droz, 1990.

_____. "Literary Genealogy and the Problem of the Father: Christine de Pizan and Dante." *Journal of Medieval and Renaissance Studies* 23.3 (1993): 365–387.

Bryce, J. "The Oral World of the Accademia Fiorentina." *Renaissance Studies* 9.1 (1995): 77–103.

Burke, P. "Representations of the Self from Petrarch to Descartes," pp. 17–28 in *Rewriting the Self: Histories from the Renaissance to the Present*. Ed. R. Porter. London: Routledge, 1996.

Burns, E.J. *Bodytalk: When Women Speak in Old French Literature.* Philadelphia: University of Pennsylvania Press, 1993.

Burrow, C. *Epic Romance: Homer to Milton.* Oxford: Clarendon Press, 1993.

———. "Spenser and Classical Traditions," pp. 217–236 in *The Cambridge Companion to Spenser.* Ed. A. Hadfield. Cambridge, UK: Cambridge University Press, 2001.

Bynum, C.W. *Metamorphosis and Identity.* New York: Zone, 2001.

Bzdak, M. "Wisdom and Education in the Middle Ages: Images and Tradition." Ph.D. dissertation, Rutgers University, 2001.

Calabrese, M.A. *Chaucer's Ovidian Arts of Love.* Gainesville: University Press of Florida, 1994.

Calame, C. *The Poetics of Eros in Ancient Greece.* Trans. J. Lloyd. Princeton: Princeton University Press, 1999.

Calcaterra, C. *Nella selva del Petrarca.* Bologna: L. Cappelli, 1942.

Cambridge History of Literary Criticism, The. Volume 2: The Middle Ages. Ed. A.J. Minnis and I. Johnson. Cambridge, UK: Cambridge University Press, 2005.

Cameron, A. *Greek Mythography in the Roman World.* Oxford: Oxford University Press, 2004.

Campbell, P.G.C. *L'Epître d'Othéa: Etude sur les sources de Christine de Pizan.* Paris: Champion, 1924.

Carreira, A. "La novedad de las *Soledades*" pp. 225–237 in *Gongoremas.* Ed. A. Carreira. Barcelona: Península, 1998.

Carroll, W. *The Metamorphoses of Shakespearean Comedy.* Princeton, NJ: Princeton University Press, 1985.

Casanova-Robin, H. *Diane et Actéon: Éclats et reflets d'un mythe à la Renaissance et à l'âge baroque.* Paris: Champion, 2003.

Castiglioni, L. "Spogli riccardiani." *Bollettino di filologia classica* 27 (1920): 162–166.

A Catalogue of Books Printed in the XVth Century Now in the British Museum: Part IX: Holland, Belgium. London: Trustees of the British Museum, 1967.

Catalogus translationum et commentariorum: Mediaeval and Renaissance Latin Translations and Commentaries. Ed. E. Cranz, V. Brown, and P.O. Kristeller. 8 vols. Washington, DC: Catholic University Press, 1960-present.

Cecchi, A. "Il Bronzino, Benedetto Varchi e l'Accademia Fiorentina: Ritratti di poeti, letterati e personaggi illustri della corte Medicea." *Antichità viva* 30.1–2 (1991): 17–28.

Cerquiglini-Toulet, J. "Cadmus ou Carmenta: Réflexion sur le concept d'invention à la fin du Moyen Age," pp. 211–230 in *What is Literature? France 1100–1600*. Ed. F. Cornilliat, U. Langer, and D. Kelly. Kentucky: French Forum, 1993.

Cervantes, M. de. *Don Quixote of La Mancha*. Trans. W. Starkie. New York: Signet, 1979.

_____. *El ingenioso hidalgo don Quijote de la Mancha*. Ed. L.A. Murillo. Madrid: Castalia, 1987.

Chambers, R. *Story and Situation: Narrative Seduction and the Power of Fiction*. Minneapolis: University of Minnesota Press, 1984.

Chance, J. *The Mythographic Chaucer: The Fabulation of Sexual Politics*. Minneapolis and London: University of Minnesota Press, 1995.

Chaucer, G. *The Riverside Chaucer*. Ed. L.D. Benson. Boston: Houghton Mifflin, 1987.

Christine de Pizan. *Le Livre des fais et bonnes meurs du sage roy Charles V*. Ed. S. Solente. 2 vols. Societé de l'Histoire de France 437 and 444. Paris: Champion, 1936–1940.

_____. *Le Livre de la Mutacion de Fortune*. Ed. S. Solente. 4 vols. SATF. Paris: Picard, 1959–1966.

_____. *The Writings of Christine de Pizan*. Ed. C.C. Willard. New York: Persea, 1994.

_____. *The Selected Writings of Christine de Pizan*. Ed. R. Blumenfeld-Kosinski and K. Brownlee. New York: W.W. Norton, 1997.

_____. *Le Chemin de longue étude: Édition critique du ms. Harley 4431*. Ed. and trans. A. Tarnoswki. Paris: Librairie Générale Française, 2000.

Chronicles of the Revolution, 1397–1400. Ed. C. Given-Wilson. Boston: St. Martins, 1993.

Churchill, L. "Inopem me copia fecit: Signs of Narcissus in Augustine's Confessions." *Classical and Modern Literature* 10.4 (1990): 373–379.

Clark, J.G. "Thomas Walsingham Reconsidered: Books and Learning at Late-Medieval St. Albans." *Speculum* 77 (2002): 832–860.

Clark, S. *Thinking with Demons: The Idea of Witchcraft in Early Modern Europe*. Oxford: Oxford University Press, 1997.

Clayton, M. *Raphael and His Circle: Drawings from Windsor Castle*. London: Royal Collection Enterprises, Ltd., 1999.

Il Codice Magliabechiano cl. XVII. 17: Contenente notizie sopra l'arte degli antichi e quella de' fiorentini da Cimabue a Michelangelo Buonarroti, scritte da anonimo fiorentino. Ed. and intro. K. Frey. Berlin: Grote, 1892. Rept. Farnborough: Gregg, 1969.

Coffman, G.R. "John Gower in His Most Significant Role," pp. 40–48 in *Gower's "Confessio Amantis": A Critical Anthology*. Ed. P. Nicholson. Cambridge, UK: Cambridge University Press, 1991.

Coleman, D.G. *Maurice Scève, Poet of Love: Tradition and Originality*. Cambridge, UK: Cambridge University Press, 1975.

_____. *An Illustrated Love Canzoniere: The Délie of Maurice Scève*. Geneva: Editions Slatkine, 1981.

Coleman, J. *Medieval Readers and Writers, 1350–1400*. New York: Columbia University Press, 1981.

Colish, M.L. *The Mirror of Language: A Study in the Medieval Theory of Knowledge*. Lincoln: University of Nebraska Press, 1983.

Collins, M. *The Soledades: Góngora's Mask of Imagination*. Columbia: University of Missouri Press, 2002.

Cooper, K. *The Virgin and the Bride: Idealized Womanhood in Late Antiquity*. Cambridge, MA: Harvard University Press, 1996.

Copeland, R. *Rhetoric, Hermeneutics, and Translation in the Middle Ages: Academic Traditions and Vernacular Texts*. Cambridge, UK: Cambridge University Press, 1991.

Coulson, F.T. "A Study of the '*Vulgate*' Commentary on Ovid's *Metamorphoses* and a Critical Edition of the Glosses to Book One." Ph.D. dissertation, University of Toronto, 1982.

_____. "MSS. of the '*Vulgate*' Commentary on Ovid's *Metamorphoses*: A Checklist." *Scriptorium* 39 (1985): 118–129.

_____. "New Manuscript Evidence for Sources of the *Accessus* of Arnoul d'Orléans to the *Metamorphoses* of Ovid." *Manuscripta* 30 (1986): 103–107.

_____. "Hitherto Unedited Medieval and Renaissance Lives of Ovid (I)." *Mediaeval Studies* 49 (1987): 152–207.

_____. "MSS. of the '*Vulgate*' Commentary on Ovid's *Metamorphoses*: Addendum." *Scriptorium* 41 (1987): 263–264.

_____. "The *Vulgate* Commentary on Ovid's *Metamorphoses*." *Ovid in Medieval Culture*. Ed. M. Desmond. Special Issue, *Mediaevalia* 13 (1989 for 1987): 29–61.

_____. "An Update to Munari's Catalogue of the Manuscripts of Ovid's *Metamorphoses*." *Scriptorium* 42 (1988): 111–112.

_____. "New Manuscripts of the Medieval Interpretations of Ovid's *Metamorphoses*." *Scriptorium* 44 (1990): 272–275.

_____. *The "Vulgate" Commentary on Ovid's Metamorphoses: The Creation Myth and the Story of Orpheus*. Toronto Medieval Latin Texts 20. Toronto: Pontifical Institute of Mediaeval Studies for the Centre for Medieval Studies, 1991.

_____. "Newly Discovered Manuscripts of Ovid's *Metamorphoses* in the Libraries of Florence and Milan." *Scriptorium* 46 (1992): 285–288.

_____. "A Bibliographical Update and *corrigenda minora* to Munari's Catalogues of the Manuscripts of Ovid's *Metamorphoses*." *Manuscripta* 38 (1994): 3–22.

_____. "Addenda to Munari's Catalogues of the Manuscripts of Ovid's *Metamorphoses*." *Revue d'histoire des textes* 25 (1995): 91–127.

_____. "A Newly Discovered Copy of the '*Vulgate*' Commentary on Ovid's *Metamorphoses* in an *Incunabulum* in the British Library." *Studi medievali* 36 (1995): 321–322.

_____. "Giovanni Francesco Picenardi and the Ovidian Commentary on the *Metamorphoses* in Modena (Bibl. Estense, Lat. 306)." *Revue d'histoire des textes* 26 (1996): 251–252.

_____. "Hitherto Unedited Medieval and Renaissance Lives of Ovid (II): Humanistic Lives." *Mediaeval Studies* 59 (1997): 111–153.

_____. "A Checklist of Newly Discovered Manuscripts of Pierre Bersuire's *Ovidius moralizatus*." *Scriptorium* 51 (1997): 164–186.

_____. "Addenda and Corrigenda to *Incipitarium Ovidianum*." *The Journal of Medieval Latin* 12 (2002): 154–180.

_____. "Hitherto Unedited Medieval and Renaissance Lives of Ovid (III): The Earliest *Accessus*" (forthcoming).

_____ and K. Nawotka. "The Rediscovery of Arnulf of Orléans' Glosses to Ovid's Creation Myth." *Classica et Mediaevalia* 44 (1993): 267–299.

_____ and B. Roy. *Incipitarium Ovidianum: A Finding Guide for Texts in Latin Related to the Study of Ovid in the Middle Ages and Renaissance*. Turnhout: Brepols, 2000.

Craven, J.B. *Count Michael Maier, Doctor of Philosophy and of Medicine, Alchemist, Rosicrucian, Mystic, 1568–1622, Life and Writings*. Kirkwall: Peace & Son, 1910. Rept. London: Dawsons, 1968.

Crooke, W. "King Midas and His Ass's Ears." *Folklore* 22.2 (1911): 183–202.

Cropp, G. "Boèce et Christine de Pizan." *Moyen Age* 87 (1981): 387–417.

Cropper, E. "On Beautiful Women, Parmigianino, *Petrarchismo*, and the Vernacular Style." *Art Bulletin* 58.3 (1976): 374–394.

―――. "The Beauty of Women: Problems in the Rhetoric of Renaissance Portraiture," pp. 175–190 in *Rewriting the Renaissance: The Discourses of Sexual Difference in Early Modern Europe*. Ed. M.W. Ferguson, M. Quilligan, and N.J. Vickers. Chicago: University of Chicago Press, 1986.

―――. "The Place of Beauty in the High Renaissance and Its Displacement in the History of Art," pp. 159–205 in *Place and Displacement in the Renaissance*. Ed. A. Vos. Medieval and Renaissance Texts and Studies Series 132. Binghamton, NY: Center for Medieval and Renaissance Studies, 1995.

Cruz, A.J. "Arms versus Letters: The Poetics of War and the Career of the Poet in Early Modern Spain," pp. 186–205 in *European Literary Careers: The Author from Antiquity to the Renaissance*. Ed. P. Cheney and F.A. de Armas. Toronto: University of Toronto Press, 2002.

Cuissard, C. "Les professeurs orléanais Foulque, Arnoul et Hugues le Primat." *Bulletin de la Société archéologique et historique de l'orléanais* 10 (1871): 417–433.

Curley, D. "Ovid, *Met.* 6.640: A Dialogue between Mother and Son." *Classical Quarterly* 47 (1997): 320–322.

Curtis, R. "The Skinhead Hamlet," pp. 316–20 in *The Faber Book of Travesties*. Ed. S. Brett. London: Faber, 1990.

Curtius, E.R. *European Literature and the Latin Middle Ages*. Trans. W.R. Trask. Princeton: Princeton University Press, 1953.

Dante. *The Divine Comedy*. 6 vols. Trans. and commentary by C. Singleton. Princeton: Bollingen, 1970.

―――. *Purgatorio*. Trans. J. and R. Hollander. New York: Doubleday, 2003.

―――. *Vita nuova*. Ed. L.C. Rossi. Milan: Oscar Mondadori, 1999.

Le Débat sur le 'Roman de la Rose.' Ed. and trans. E. Hicks. Paris: Champion, 1977.

De Armas, F.A. *Cervantes, Raphael and the Classics*. Cambridge, UK: Cambridge University Press, 1998.

"De deorum imaginibus libellus," pp. 117–128 in *Fulgentius Metaforalis: Ein Beitrag zur Geschichte der antiken Mythologie im Mittelalter*. Ed. H. Liebeschütz. Leipzig and Berlin: B.G. Teubner, 1926.

Delisle, L. "Les écoles d'Orléans au douzième et au treizième siècle." *Annuaire-Bulletin de la Société de l'Histoire de France* 7 (1869): 139–154.

DellaNeva, J. "Poetry, Metamorphosis and the Laurel: Ovid, Petrarch and Scève." *French Forum* 7 (1982): 197–209.

_____. *Song and Countersong*. Lexington: French Forum, 1983.

Demats, P. *Fabula: Trois études de mythographie antique et médiévale*. Geneva: Droz, 1973.

Dempsey, C. *The Portrayal of Love: Botticelli's Primavera and Humanist Culture at the Time of Lorenzo the Magnificent*. Princeton: Princeton University Press, 1992.

Desmond, M. *Reading Dido: Gender, Textuality, and the Medieval Aeneid*. Minneapolis: University of Minnesota Press, 1994.

_____. *Ovid's Art and the Wife of Bath: The Ethics of Erotic Violence*. Ithaca: Cornell University Press, 2006.

_____ and P. Sheingorn. *Myth, Montage, and Visuality in Late Medieval Manuscript Culture: Christine de Pizan's Epistre Othea*. Ann Arbor: University of Michigan Press, 2003.

Dewar, M. "*Siquid habent ueri uatum praesagia*: Ovid in the 1st-5th centuries A.D.," pp. 383–412 in *Brill's Companion to Ovid*. Ed. B.W. Boyd. Leiden: Brill, 2002.

Dimmick, J. "Ovid in the Middle Ages: Authority and Poetry," pp. 264–287 in *The Cambridge Companion to Ovid*. Ed. P. Hardie. Cambridge, UK: Cambridge University Press, 2002

Dinshaw, C. *Chaucer's Sexual Poetics*. Madison: University of Wisconsin Press, 1989.

Dobrov, G. "The Tragic and the Comic Tereus." *American Journal of Philology* 114 (1993): 189–234.

Dolan, F. "'Ridiculous Fictions': Making Distinctions in the Discourse of Witchcraft." *Differences: A Journal of Feminist Cultural Studies* 7 (1995): 82–110.

Dolce, L. *Le transformationi di M. Ludovico Dolce, tratte da Ovidio*. Venice: Gabriello Giolito, 1553. Venice: Sansovino, 1568.

Dollmayr, H. "Lo stanzino da bagno del Cardinal Bibbiena." *Archivio storico dell'arte* 3 (1890): 272–280.

Dominik, W.J. *The Mythic Voice of Statius: Power and Politics in the Thebaid*. Leiden: Brill, 1994.

Donaldson-Evans, L.K. "Love's Fatal Glance: Eye Imagery and Maurice Scève's Délie." *Neophilologus* 62 (1978): 202–211.

_____. *Love's Fatal Glance: A Study of Eye Imagery in the Ecole Lyonnaise*. Oxford, MS: University of Mississippi Press, 1980.

Du Rocher, R. *Milton and Ovid*. Ithaca and London: Cornell University Press, 1985.

Dudley, E. *The Endless Text: Don Quixote and the Hermeneutics of Romance*. Albany, NY: SUNY, 1997.

Dunn, Peter. *The Spanish Picaresque Novel*. Boston: Twayne, 1979.

———. *Spanish Picaresque Fiction: A New Literary History*. Ithaca and London: Cornell University Press, 1993.

Eisenberg, D. *Romances of Chivalry in the Spanish Golden Age*. Newark, DE: Juan de la Cuesta, 1982.

———. *A Study of Don Quixote*. Newark, DE: Juan de la Cuesta, 2001.

Engelbrecht, W. *Filologie in de Dertiende eeuw: De Bursarii super Ovidios van Magister Willem van Orléans (fl. 1200 AD)*. Olomouc: Palacký Universiteit te Olomouc, 2003.

Engels, J. *Études sur l'Ovide moralisé*. Groningen: J.B. Wolters, 1945.

English Historical Documents, IV: 1327–1485. Ed. A.R. Myers. London: Eyre & Spottiswoode, 1969.

Enterline, L. "Embodied Voices: Petrarch Reading (Himself Reading) Ovid," pp. 120–145 in *Desire in the Renaissance: Psychoanalysis and Literature*. Ed. V. Finucci and R. Schwartz. Princeton, NJ: Princeton University Press, 1994.

———. *The Rhetoric of the Body from Ovid to Shakespeare*. Cambridge, UK: Cambridge University Press, 2000.

Estudios sobre tradición clásica y mitología en el Siglo de Oro. Ed. I. Colón Calderón and J. Ponce Cárdenas. Madrid: Ediciones Clásicas, 2000.

Faivre, A. *Toison d'or et alchimie*. Milan: Archè Edidit, 1990.

Farago, C.J. *Leonardo da Vinci's Paragone: A Critical Interpretation with a New Edition of the Text in the Codex Urbinas*. Leiden: Brill, 1991.

Farrell, J. "Dialogue of Genres in Ovid's 'Lovesong of Polyphemus' (*Metamorphoses* 13.719–897)." *The American Journal of Philology* 113.2 (1992): 235–268.

Feimer, J.N. "Medea in Ovid's *Metamorphoses* and the *Ovide moralisé*: Translation as Transmission." *Florilegium* 8 (1986): 40–55.

Fenoalta, D. "Three Animal Images in the *Délie*: New Perspectives on Scève's use of Petrarch's *Rime*." *Bibliothèque d'Humanisme et Renaissance* 34 (1972): 413–426.

———. "Establishing Contrasts: An Aspect of Scève's Use of Petrarch's Poetry in the 'Délie.'" *Studi Francesi* 55 (1975): 17–33.

Ferguson, J. *Bibliotheca Chemica*. 2 vols. Glasgow: Maclehose, 1906.

Ferrand, J. *A Treatise on Lovesickness*. Trans. D. Beecher and M. Clavolella. Syracuse: Syracuse University Press, 1990. First published *De la maladie d'amour, ou, Melancholie erotique*. Paris: Denis Moreau, 1623.

Ferrari, G. "Figures of Speech: The Picture of Aidos." *Metis* 5 (1990): 185–200.

Ferster, J. *Fictions of Advice: The Literature and Politics of Counsel in Late Medieval England*. Philadelphia: University of Pennsylvania Press, 1996.

Finello, D. *Pastoral Themes and Forms in Cervantes's Fiction*. Lewisburg: Bucknell University Press, 1994.

Fisher, J. *John Gower: Moral Philosopher and Friend of Chaucer*. New York: New York University Press, 1964.

Fleming, J.V. "The Garden of the Roman de la Rose: Vision of Landscape or Landscape of Vision?" *Dumbarton Oaks Colloquium on the History of Landscape Architecture* 9 (1986): 201–234.

————. "Sacred and Secular Exegesis in the Wyf of Bath's Tale," pp. 73–90 in *Retelling Tales: Essays in Honor of Russell Peck*. Ed. T. Hahn and A. Lupack. Woodbridge, UK / Rochester, NY: D.S. Brewer, 1997.

————. "The Best Line in Ovid and the Worst," pp. 51–74 in *New Readings of Chaucer's Poetry*. Ed. R.G. Benson and S.J. Ridyard. Woodbridge, UK / Rochester, NY : D.S. Brewer, 2003.

Foedera, conventiones, litterae et cujuscunque generis acta publica. Ed. T. Rymer. 4 vols. London: George Eyre and Andrew Strahan, 1816–1869.

Foster, K. "Beatrice or Medusa," pp. 42–56 in *Italian Studies Presented to E.R. Vincent*. Ed. C. P. Brand, K. Foster, and U. Limentani. Cambridge, UK: W. Heffer & Sons Ltd., 1962.

Foulques de Villaret, A. de. "L'enseignement des lettres et des sciences dans l'Orléanais depuis les premiers siècles du Christianisme jusqu'à la fondation de l'Université d'Orléans." *Mémoires de la société archéologique et historique de l'orléanais* 14 (1875): 299–440.

Frécaut, J.M. "'Le Barbier de Midas' ou 'Le Vent Instrumentiste' (Ovide, *Métamorphoses*, XI, 180–193)," pp. 147–162 in *Hommages à Henry Bardon*. Ed. M. Renard and P. Laurens. Collection Latomus 187. Brussels: Latomus, 1985.

Freccero, J. "The Fig Tree and the Laurel: Petrarch's Poetics." *Diacritics* 5 (1975): 34–40.

Fredericks, B.R. "Divine Wit vs. Divine Folly: Mercury and Apollo in *Metamorphoses* 1–2." *Classical Journal* 72.3 (1977): 244–249.

Fulcanelli (pseud.). *Le Mystère des cathédrales*. Trans. M. Sworder. London: Neville Spearman, 1971. Originally published Paris: Jean Schmeit, 1926.

———. *The Dwellings of the Philosophers*. Trans. B. Donvez and L. Perrin. Boulder: Archive, 1999. Originally published as *Les Demeures philosophales et le symbolisme hermétique dans ses rapports avec l'art sacré et l'ésotérisme du grand œuvre*. Paris: Jean Schémit, 1930.

Fulgentius. *Fulgentius the Mythographer*. Trans. L.G. Whitbread. Columbus: Ohio State University Press, 1971.

Fyler, J.M. *Chaucer and Ovid*. New Haven and London: Yale University Press, 1979.

Galinsky, K. *Augustan Culture*. Princeton: Princeton University Press, 1996.

Gallacher, P.J. *Love, the Word, and Mercury: A Reading of John Gower's Confessio Amantis*. Albuquerque: University of New Mexico Press, 1975.

Gerson, J. *Gerson Bilingue: Les deux rédactions, latine et française, de quelques oeuvres du chancelier parisien*. Ed. G.H. Ouy. Paris: Champion, 1988.

Gesta Romanorum: Entertaining Stories. Trans. C. Swan. London and New York, 1887.

Ghisalberti, F. "Giovanni del Virgilio, espositore delle *Metamorfosi*." *Giornale dantesco* 34 (1933): 1–110.

———. "Arnolfo d'Orléans: un cultore di Ovidio nel secolo XII." *Memorie del Reale Istituto Lombardo di Scienze e Lettere* 24 (1932): 157–234.

———. "Mediaeval Biographies of Ovid." *Journal of the Warburg and Courtauld Institutes* 9 (1946): 10–59.

———. "Il commentario medioevale all'*Ovidius maior* consultato da Dante." *Rendiconti dell'Istituto Lombardo, Classe di Lettere e Scienze Morali e Storiche* 100 (1966): 267–275.

Giamatti, A.B. *Exile and Change in Renaissance Literature*. New Haven and London: Yale University Press, 1984.

Gibbons, M.W. "The Bath of the Muses and the Visual Allegory in the *Chemin de long estude*," pp.128–145 in *Christine de Pizan and the Categories of Difference*. Ed. M. Desmond. Minneapolis: University of Minnesota Press, 1998.

Gildenhard, I. and A. Zissos. "Ovid's Narcissus (*Met.* 3.339–510): Echoes of Oedipus." *American Journal of Philology* 121 (2000): 129–147.

Giles of Rome. *The Governance of Kings and Princes*. Trans. J. Trevisa. Ed. D.C. Fowler, C.F. Briggs, and P.G. Remley. New York: Garland, 1997.

Ginsberg, W. "*Ovidius Ethicus*? Ovid and the Medieval Commentary Tradition," pp. 62–71 in *Desiring Discourse: The Literature of Love, Ovid through Chaucer*. Ed. J.J. Paxson and C.A. Gravlee, Selingsgrove, Penn.: Susquehanna University Press, 1998.

Ginzburg, C. *Ecstasies: Deciphering the Witches' Sabbath*. Trans. R. Rosenthal. New York: Penguin, 1991.

Giovanni del Virgilio. *Allegorie librorum Ovidii Metamorphoseos*. In F. Ghisalberti, "Giovanni del Virgilio espositore delle 'Metamorfosi.'" *Giornale dantesco* 34 (1933): 43–110.

Giovanni di Garlandia. Integumenta Ovidii, poemetto inedito del secolo XIII. Ed. F. Ghisalberti. Messina-Milan: Casa Editrice Giuseppe Principato, 1933.

Giraud, Y.F.-A. *La Fable de Daphné: Essai sur un type de métamorphose végétale dans la littérature et dans les arts jusqu'à la fin du XVIIe siècle.* Geneva: Droz, 1968.

Golding, F. *The Mirror of Narcissus in the Courtly Love Lyric*. Ithaca: Cornell University Press, 1967.

Góngora, Luis de. *Soledades*. Ed. R. Jammes. Madrid: Clásicos Castalia, 1994.

_____. *Solitudes*. Trans. E.M. Wilson. Cambridge, UK: Cambridge University Press, 1965.

Gordon, A.E. "On the Origin of Diana." *Transactions of the American Philological Association* 63 (1932): 177–192.

Gower, J. *Confessio Amantis. The Complete Works of John Gower*. Ed. G.C. Macaulay. 4 vols. Oxford: Clarendon, 1902–1906.

_____. *The Major Latin Works of John Gower*. Trans. E.W. Stockton. Seattle: University of Washington Press, 1962.

_____. *Confessio Amantis*. Ed. R. Peck. Toronto: MART/University of Toronto Press, 1980.

Greene, T.M. *The Light in Troy: Imitation and Discovery in Renaissance Poetry*. New Haven: Yale University Press, 1982.

_____. "The Flexibility of the Self in Renaissance Literature," pp. 241–268 in *The Disciplines of Criticism: Essays in Literary Theory, Interpretation and History*. Ed. P. Demetz et al. New Haven: Yale University Press, 1976.

Griffin, A.H.F. "Unrequited Love: Polyphemus and Galatea in Ovid's 'Metamorphoses.'" *Greece & Rome*, 2nd ser. 30.2 (1983): 190–197.

Gualteri de Castellione Alexandreis. Ed. M.L. Colker. Padua: Antenore, 1978.

Guillaume de Lorris and Jean de Meun. *Le Roman de la Rose.* Ed. F. Lecoy. 3 vols. Paris: Champion, 1965–1970.

Guthmüller, B. *Ovidio Metamorphoseos vulgare: Formen und Funktionen der volkssprachlichen Widergabe klassischer Dichtung in der italienischen Renaissance.* Boppart am Rhein: Harald Boldt Verlag, 1981.

_____. "Bild und Text in Lodovico Dolces *Trasformationi*," pp. 58–77 in *The Aphrodite of Knidos and Her Successors: A Historical Review of the Female Nude in Greek Art.* Ed. C.M. Havelock. Ann Arbor: University of Michigan Press, 1995.

Guy, J. *Tudor England.* Oxford: Oxford University Press, 1988.

Hardie, P. "Augustan Poets and the Mutability of Rome," pp. 59–82 in *Roman Poetry and Propaganda in the Age of Augustus.* Ed. A. Powell. Bristol: Bristol Classical Press, 1992.

_____. "Questions of Authority: The Invention of Tradition in Ovid's *Metamorphoses* 15," pp. 182–198 in *The Roman Cultural Revolution.* Ed. T.N. Habinek and A.Schiesaro. Cambridge, UK: Cambridge University Press, 1997.

_____. "Ovid into Laura: Absent Presences in the *Metamorphoses* and Petrarch's *Rime sparse*," pp. 254–270 in *Ovidian Transformations: Essays on Ovid's Metamorphoses and its Reception.* Ed. P. Hardie, A. Barchiesi, and S. Hinds. Cambridge Philological Society Supplementary Vol. 23. Cambridge, UK: Cambridge Philological Society, 1999.

_____. "Ovid and Early Imperial Literature," pp. 34–45 in *The Cambridge Companion to Ovid.* Ed. P. Hardie. Cambridge, UK: Cambridge University Press, 2002.

_____. *Ovid's Poetics of Illusion.* Cambridge, UK: Cambridge University Press, 2002.

Harding, D.P. *Milton and the Renaissance Ovid.* Urbana: University of Illinois Press, 1968.

Harvey, R.A. *A Commentary on Persius.* Leiden: E.J. Brill, 1981.

Haskins, C.H. *The Renaissance of the Twelfth Century.* Cambridge, MA: Harvard University Press, 1933.

Havelock, C.M. *The Aphrodite of Knidos and Her Successors: A Historical Review of the Female Nude in Greek Art.* Ann Arbor: University of Michigan Press, 1995.

Hawkins, P. "Virtuosity and Virtue: Poetic Self-Reflection in the *Commedia*." *Dante Studies* 98 (1980): 1–18.

The Hermetic Museum Restored and Enlarged. 2 vols. Introduction by A.E. Waite. London: James Elliott, 1893.

Herren, M. "Manegold of Lautenbach's Scholia on the *Metamorphoses* – Are There More?" *Notes and Queries* n.s. 5 (2004): 218–222.

Hexter, R.J. *Ovid and Medieval Schooling. Studies in Medieval School Commentaries on Ovid's Ars amatoria, Epistulae ex Ponto, and Epistulae heroidum*. Munich: Arbeo-Gesellschaft, 1986.

_____. "Medieval Articulations of Ovid's *Metamorphoses*: From Lactantian Segmentation to Arnulfian Allegory." *Ovid in Medieval Culture*. Ed. M. Desmond. Special Issue, *Mediaevalia* 13 (1989 for 1987): 63–82.

_____. "The *Allegari* of Pierre Bersuire: Interpretation and the *Reductorium morale*." *Allegorica* 10 (1989): 51–84.

_____. "Ovid in the Middle Ages: Exile, Mythographer, and Lover," pp. 413–442 in *Brill's Companion to Ovid*. Ed. B.W. Boyd. Leiden: Brill, 2002.

Hindman, S. *Christine de Pizan's "Epistre Othéa": Painting and Politics at the Court of Charles VI*. Toronto: Pontifical Institute of Mediaeval Studies, 1986.

Hines, J., N. Cohen, and S. Roffey. "*Iohannes Gower, armiger, poeta*: Records and Memorials of his Life and Death," pp. 23–41 in *A Companion to Gower*. Ed. S. Echard. Cambridge, UK / Rochester, NY: D.S. Brewer, 2004.

Hinds, S. *Allusion and Intertext: Dynamics of Appropriation in Roman Poetry*. Cambridge, UK: Cambridge University Press, 1998.

_____. "Landscape with Figures: Aesthetics of Place in the *Metamorphoses* and its Tradition," pp. 122–149 in *The Cambridge Companion to Ovid*. Ed. P. Hardie. Cambridge, UK: Cambridge University Press, 2002.

Hoffman, R.L. *Ovid and the Canterbury Tales*. Philadelphia: University of Pennsylvania Press, 1966.

Holahan, M. "*Iamque opus exegi*: Ovid's Changes and Spenser's Brief Epic of Mutability." *English Literary Renaissance* 6 (1976): 244–270.

Holderness, J.S. "In the Muses' Garden: Reminiscence and Consolation in the Early Works of Christine de Pizan." Ph.D. dissertation, Johns Hopkins University, 1999.

Hollis, A.S. "Traces of Ancient Commentaries on Ovid's *Metamorphoses*," *Papers of the Leeds International Latin Seminar* 9 (1996): 159–174.

Huot, S. "Seduction and Sublimation: Christine de Pizan, Jean de Meun, and Dante." *Romance Notes* 25 (1985): 361–373.

Hyginus. *Fabulae.* Ed. P.K. Marshall. München and Leipzig: K.G. Saur Verlag, 2002.

Isaacus, I. *Die Hand der Philosophen, mit ihren verborgenen Zeichen.* Frankfurt: Thomas Matthias Götzen, 1667.

Jacobs, F.H. "Aretino and Michelangelo, Dolce and Titian: Femmina, Masculo, Grazia." *Art Bulletin* 82.1 (2000): 51–67.

Jacobson, H. *Ovid's Heroides.* Princeton: Princeton University Press, 1974.

James, H. *Shakespeare's Troy: Drama, Politics and the Translation of Empire.* Cambridge, UK: Cambridge University Press, 1997.

Jammes, R. "Función de la retórica en las *Soledades*," pp. 213–233 in *La silva.* Ed. B. López Bueno. Sevilla: Universidad de Sevilla, 1991.

————. "Introducción," pp. 7–180 in *Soledades.* Madrid: Clásicos Castalia, 1994.

Jeauneau, E. "L'Usage de la notion d'*integumentum* à travers les gloses de Guillaume de Conches." *Archives d'histoire doctrinale et littéraire du moyen âge* 24 (1957): 35–100. Rpt. in E. Jeauneau, *"Lectio philosophorum": Recherches sur l'Ecole de Chartres,* 125–192. Amsterdam: Adolf Hakkert, 1973.

John of Garland. "The *Integumenta* on the *Metamorphoses* of Ovid by John of Garland – First Edited with Introduction and Translation." Ed. and trans. L.K. Born. Ph.D. dissertation, University of Chicago, 1929.

Jonson, B. *The Alchemist.* London: John Stepneth, 1612.

Juliá, M. "Ficción y realidad en *Don Quijote.* (Los episodios de la cueva de Montesinos y el caballo Clavileño)," pp. 275–279 in *Actas del Tercer Coloquio Internacional de la Asociación de Cervantistas. Alcalá de Henares, 12–16 nov. 1990.* Barcelona: Anthropos; Madrid: Dirección General de Relaciones Culturales y Científicas, Ministerio de Asuntos Exteriores, 1993.

Jung, M.-R. "Ovide, texte, translateur et gloses dans les manuscrits de *l'Ovide moralisé*," pp. 75–98 in *The Medieval Opus: Imitation, Rewriting and Transmission in the French Tradition. Proceedings of the Symposium Held at the Institute for the Research in the Humanities. October*

5–7, 1995, University of Wisconsin-Madison. Ed. D. Kelly. Amsterdam: Rodopi, 1996.

Kahn, V. "The Figure of the Reader in Petrarch's Secretum." *PMLA* 100 (1985): 154–166.

Kaufhold, S. "Ovid's Tereus: Fire, Birds, and the Reification of Figurative Language." *Classical Philology* 92 (1997): 66–71.

Keach, W. "Cupid Disarmed or Venus Wounded: An Ovidian Source for Michelangelo and Bronzino." *Journal of the Warburg and Courtauld Institutes* 41 (1978): 327–331.

Keith, A.M. *The Play of Fictions: Studies in Ovid's Metamorphoses Book 2.* Ann Arbor: The University of Michigan Press, 1992.

_____. "Ovidian Personae in Statius' *Thebaid*," *Arethusa* 35 (2002): 381–402.

_____. "Ovid's Theban Narrative (*Met.* 3.1–4.605) in Statius' *Thebaid*," *Hermathena* (2004–2005): 177–202.

_____. "Imperial Building Projects and Architectural Ecphrases in Ovid's *Metamorphoses* and Statius' *Thebaid*." Forthcoming in *Museion*.

Kenney, E.J. "Introduction," pp. xiii–xxix in Ovid, *Metamorphoses*. Oxford: Oxford University Press, 1986.

Kilgour, M. *From Communion to Cannibalism: An Anatomy of Metaphors of Incorporation*. Princeton: Princeton University Press, 1990.

_____."'Thy Perfect Image Viewing': Poetic Creation and Ovid's Narcissus in *Paradise Lost*." *Studies in Philology* 102 (2005): 307–339.

Klossowski de Rola, S. *The Golden Game: Alchemical Engravings of the Seventeenth Century*. London: Thames & Hudson, 1988.

Knoespel, K.J. *Narcissus and the Invention of Personal History*. New York: Garland, 1985.

Konstan, D. "The Death of Argus, or What Stories Do: Audience Response in Ancient Fiction and Theory." *Helios* 18.1 (1991): 15–30.

Ladner, G.B. *The Idea of Reform: Its Impact on Christian Thought and Action in the Age of the Fathers*. Cambridge, MA: Harvard University Press, 1959.

Langland, W. *The Vision of Piers Plowman*. Ed. A.V.C. Schmidt. 2nd ed. London: J. M. Dent, 1995.

Lea, H.C. *Materials toward a History of Witchcraft*. Ed. A.C. Howland. 3 vols. Philadelphia: University of Pennsylvania Press, 1939.

Leach, E.W. *The Rhetoric of Space: Literary and Artistic Representations of Landscape in Republican and Augustan Rome*. Princeton: Princeton University Press, 1988.

Lectures d'Ovide: Publiées à la mémoire de Jean-Pierre Néraudau. Ed. E. Bury and M. Néraudau. Paris: Les Belles Lettres, 2002.

Lee, R.W. *"Ut pictura poesis": The Humanistic Theory of Painting*. New York: sNorton, 1967.

Leicester, H.M., Jr. *The Disenchanted Self: Representing the Subject in the Canterbury Tales*. Berkeley: University of California Press, 1990.

Lemmi, C.W. *The Classic Deities in Bacon: A Study in Mythological Symbolism*. 1933. Rept. Folcroft, PA: Folcroft Press, 1969.

Leumann, M., J.B. Hofmann, and A. Szantyr. *Lateinische Grammatik*. 2 vols. Munich: C.H. Beck, 1963–1965.

Levine, R. "Exploiting Ovid: Medieval Allegorizations of the *Metamorphoses*." *Medioevo Romanzo* 14 (1989): 197–213.

Liebeschuetz, J.H.W.G. *Continuity and Change in Roman Religion*. Oxford: Clarendon Press, 1979.

Lipton, S. *Images of Intolerance: The Representation of Jews and Judaism in the Bible moralisée*. Berkeley: University of California Press, 1999.

Lord, C.[G.] "Three Manuscripts of the *Ovide moralisé*." *Art Bulletin* 57 (1975): 161–175.

Lord, C.G. "Some Ovidian Themes in Italian Renaissance Art," Ph.D. dissertation, Columbia University, 1968.

———. "Illustrated Manuscripts of Berchorius before the Age of Printing," pp. 1–11 in *Die Rezeption der Metamorphosen des Ovid in der Neuzeit: Der antike Mythos in Text und Bild*. Ed. H. Walter and H-J. Horn. Berlin: Mann, 1995.

Luborsky, R.S. and E.M. Ingram. *A Guide to English Illustrated Books: 1563–1603*. Tempe, AZ: Medieval and Renaissance Texts and Studies, 1998.

Lucian. "Essays in Portraiture." *Lucian in Eight Volumes*. Vol. 4. Trans. A.M. Harmon. Loeb Classical Library. Cambridge, MA: Harvard University Press, 1969.

Ly, N. "La république aileé dans les *Solitudes*," pp. 141–177 in *Crépusculos pisando: Once estudios sobre las Soledades de Luis de Góngora*. Perpignan: Presses Universitaires de Perpignan, 1995.

Lydgate, J. *The Minor Poems of John Lydgate*. Ed. H.N. MacCracken. EETS o.s. 192. London: Oxford University Press, 1934.

Maidstone, R. *Concordia (The Reconciliation of Richard II with London).* Trans. A.G. Rigg. Kalamazoo: Medieval Institute Publications, 2003.

Maier, M. *Symbola aureae mensae duodecim nationum.* Frankfurt: Jennis, 1617.

_____. *Atalanta fugiens: An Edition of the Emblems, Fugues and Epigrams.* Trans. and ed. J. Godwin. Magnum Opus Hermetic Sourceworks 22. Grand Rapids, MI: Phanes, 1989. First printed Edinburgh: Magnum Opus Hermetic Sourceworks, 1987.

_____. *Atalanta fugiens: Sources of an Alchemical Emblem Book.* Trans. and ed. H.M.E. de Jong. York Beach, ME: Nicholas-Hays, 2002. First printed Leiden: Brill, 1969.

Mainzer, C. "John Gower's Use of the 'Mediaeval Ovid' in the *Confessio amantis.*" *Medium Aevum* 41(1972): 215–229.

Mandach, A. de. "Midas et Marc: Le Mythe de deux souverains aux oreilles inavouables," pp. 104–126 in *Tristan et Iseut, mythe europeen et mondial: Actes du colloque des 10, 11 et 12 janvier 1986.* Ed. D. Buschinger. Göppingen, Kümmerle Verlag, 1987.

Mann, N. "From Laurel to Fig: Petrarch and the Structures of the Self." *Proceedings of the British Academy* 105 (1999): 17–42.

Márquez Villanueva, F. *Personajes y temas del Quijote.* Madrid: Taurus, 1975.

Martels, Z. von. "Augurello's *Chrysopoeia* (1515): A Turning Point in the Literary Tradition of Alchemical Texts." *Early Science and Medicine* 5.2 (2000): 178–195.

Martin, J.J. *Myths of Renaissance Individualism.* New York: Palgrave Macmillan, 2004.

Martínez Arancón, A. *La batalla en torno a Góngora.* Barcelona: Bosch, 1978.

Matheolus. *Les Lamentations de Matheolus et le Livre de leesce de Jehan Le Fèvre de Resson.* Ed. A.-G. van Hamel. Bibliothèque de l'école des hautes études. Paris: É. Bouillon, 1892–1905.

Matthieu-Castellani, G. *Eros baroque.* Paris: Union générale d'éditions, 1979.

Mazzotta, G. *The Worlds of Petrarch.* Durham, NC: Duke University Press, 1993.

McCarty, W. "The Shape of the Mirror: Metaphorical Catoptrics in Classical Literature." *Arethusa* 22 (1989): 161–195.

McKinley, K.L. "Kingship and the Body Politic: Classical *Ecphrasis* and *Confessio amantis* VII." *Mediaevalia* 21 (1996): 167–193.

———. "The Medieval Commentary Tradition 1100–1500 on *Metamorphoses* 10." *Viator* 27 (1996): 117–149.

———. "The Silenced Knight: Questions of Power and Reciprocity in the Wife of Bath's Tale." *Chaucer Review* 30.4 (1996): 359–378.

———. "Manuscripts of Ovid in England 1100 to 1500." *English Manuscript Studies* 7 (1998): 41–85.

———. *Reading the Ovidian Heroine: Metamorphoses Commentaries, 1100–1618.* Leiden: Brill, 2001.

McLean, A. "Splendor Solis Images." *The Alchemy Web Site*, ttp://www.levity.com/alchemy/ splensol.html. 22 Feb. 2005.

McMahon, R. "Autobiography as Text-Work: Augustine's Refiguring of Genesis 3 and Ovid's 'Narcissus' in His Conversion Account." *Exemplaria* 1.2 (1989): 337–366.

———. "Satan as Infernal Narcissus: Interpretive Translation in the *Commedia*," pp. 65–86 in *Dante and Ovid: Essays in Intertextuality*. Ed. M.U. Sowell. Binghamton, NY: Medieval and Renaissance Texts and Studies, 1991.

Medieval Literary Theory and Criticism c. 1100-c. 1375. Ed. A.J. Minnis and A.B. Scott. Rev. ed. Oxford: Clarendon, 1998.

Meiser, C. "Über einen Commentar zu den *Metamorphosen* des Ovid," pp. 47–89 in *Sitzungsberichte der königlichen bayerischen Akademie der Wissenschaften, philosophisch-philologische Klasse*. Munich: Im K. Central-Schulbücher Verlage, 1885.

Meiss, M. *The Limbourgs and their Contemporaries. French Painting in the Time of Jean de Berry.* New York: Braziller, 1974.

Mendelsohn, L. *Paragoni: Benedetto Varchi's Due Lezzioni and Cinquecento Art Theory.* Ann Arbor: UMI Research Press, 1982.

Milton, J. *The Riverside Milton.* Ed. R. Flannagan. Boston: Houghton Mifflin, 1998.

Minnis, A.J. *Medieval Theory of Authorship: Scholastic Literary Attitudes in the Later Middle Ages.* London: Scolar Press, 1984.

———. *Medieval Theory of Authorship: Scholastic Literary Attitudes in the Later Middle Ages.* 2nd ed. Philadelphia: University of Pennsylvania Press, 1988.

Mish, F. "The Influence of Ovid on John Gower's *Vox clamantis*." Ph.D. dissertation, University of Minnesota, 1973.

Molho, M. *Semántica y poética.* Barcelona: Crítica, 1977.

Müller-Jahncke, W.D. "The Attitude of Agrippa von Nettesheim (1486–1535) towards Alchemy." *Ambix: Journal of the Society for the History of Alchemy and Chemistry* 22 (1975): 134–50.

Munari, F. *Catalogue of the Mss of Ovid's Metamorphoses.* Bulletin Supplement 4. London: University of London Institute of Classical Studies in Conjunction with the Warburg Institute, 1957.

_____. "Supplemento al catalogo dei manoscritti delle *Metamorfosi* ovidiane." *Rivista di filologia e di istruzione classica* 93 (1965): 288–297.

_____. "Secondo supplemento al catalogo dei manoscritti delle *Metamorfosi* ovidiane," pp. 275–280 in *Studia florentina Alexandro Ronconi sexagenario oblata.* Rome: Edizioni dell'Ateneo, 1970.

Munk Olsen, B. *I Classici nel canone scolastico altomedievale.* Spoleto: Centro italiano di studi sull'alto Medioevo, 1991.

Murgatroyd, P. "Ovid's Syrinx." *Classical Quarterly* n.s. 51.2 (2001): 620–623.

Murphy, S. "The Death of Actaeon as Petrarchist Topos." *Comparative Literature Studies* 28.2 (1991): 137–155.

Musaeum hermeticum reformatum et amplificatum. Frankfurt: Hermannum à Sande, 1677–1678.

Myers, S. *Ovid's Causes: Cosmogony and Aetiology in the Metamorphoses.* Ann Arbor: University of Michigan Press, 1994.

Mythographi Vaticani I et II. Ed. P. Kulcsár. CCSL 91c. Turnholt: Brepols, 1987.

Nagle, B.R. "Erotic Pursuit and Narrative Seduction in Ovid's Metamorphoses." *Ramus* 17.1 (1988): 32–51.

_____. "A Trio of Love-Triangles in Ovid's *Metamorphoses.*" *Arethusa* 21.1 (1988): 75–98.

_____. "Two Miniature Carmina Perpetua in the Metamorphoses: Calliope and Orpheus." *Grazer Beiträge* 15 (1988): 99–125.

Nantet, M.-V. "La faute d'Actéon dans la balance de la littérature," pp. 547–557 in *Lectures d'Ovide: Publiées à la mémoire de Jean-Pierre Néraudau.* Ed. E. Bury and M. Néraudau. Paris: Les Belles Lettres, 2003.

Nash, T. *Nashes Lenten Stuff.* London, 1599.

Nelson, J. "Dante Portraits in Sixteenth-Century Florence." *Gazette des beaux-arts* 6.120 (1992): 59–77.

Nephew, J.A. "Gender Reversals and Intellectual Gender in the Works of Christine de Pizan," pp. 517–532 in *Au champ des escriptures: IIIe*

Colloque international sur Christine de Pizan, Lausanne, 18–22 juillet 1998. Ed. E. Hicks, D. Gondalez, and P. Simon. Etudes christiniennes 6. Paris: Champion, 2000.

Nero, A. *Raffaello, Michelangelo, e bottega: I cartoni farnesiani restaurati.* Naples: Soprintendenza per i beni artistici e storici di Napoli and Electa, 1993.

Newman, W.R. *Gehennical Fire: The Lives of George Starkey, an American Alchemist in the Scientific Revolution.* Cambridge, MA: Harvard University Press, 1994.

Noferi, A. *L'esperienza poetica del Petrarca.* Florence: F. Le Monnier, 1962.

Occleve, T. *De regimine principis.* Ed. T. Wright. London: J.B. Nichols and Sons, 1860.

Ormerod, B. "Scève's 'Délie' and the Mythographer's Diana." *Studi Francesi* 67 (1979): 86–93.

Orofino, G. "Ovidio nel Medioevo: L'iconografia delle metamorfosi," pp. 189–208 in *Aetates Ovidianae: Lettori di Ovidio dall'antichità al Rinascimento.* Ed. I. Gallo and L. Nicastri. Naples: Pubblicazioni dell'Università degli Studi di Salerno, 43, 1995.

Otis, B. "The Argumenta of the So-Called Lactantius," *Harvard Studies in Classical Philology* 47 (1936): 131–163.

Ovid. *Ovidio methamorphoseos vulgare / Giovanni Bonsignori di Castello.* Venice: Giunta, 1497.

———. *Metamorphoseon Pub. Ovidii Nasonis Sulmonensis libri XV / Raphaelis Regii Volterrani luculentissima explanatio, cum novis Iacobi Miculli, viri eruditissimi, additionibus; Lactantii Placidi in singulas fabulas argumenta; allegoriae quibus singularum fabularum sensa declarantur ita ut facile cognoscere possimus* Venice: Hieronymum Scotus, 1553.

———. *Ovidii Nasonis Metamorphoseon libri XV Raphaelis Regii volaterrani luculentissima explanatio.* Venice: Moretus, 1586.

———. *Tristia.* Ed. S.G. Owen. Oxford: Oxford University Press, 1955.

———. *The Metamorphoses of Ovid.* Trans. W. Caxton. 2 vols. New York: George Braziller, 1968.

———. *The Metamorphoses.* Ed. and trans. F.J. Miller. Rev. G.P. Goold. Loeb Classical Library. 2 vols. Cambridge, MA: Harvard University Press, 1977.

———. *Metamorphoses.* Ed. W.S. Anderson. Leipzig: Teubner, 1978.

_____. *The Art of Love, and Other Poems*. Trans. J.H. Mozley. Rev. G.P. Gould. 2nd ed. Loeb Classical Library. Cambridge, MA: Harvard University Press, 1979.

_____. *Metamorphoses I-IV*. Ed. and trans. D.E. Hill. Warminster: Aris & Phillips, 1985.

_____. *Metamorphoses*. Trans. A.D. Melville. Oxford: Oxford University Press, 1987.

_____. *Ovid's Metamorphoses: Books 1–5*. Ed. W. S. Anderson. Norman, OK and London: University of Oklahoma Press, 1997.

_____. *Metamorphoses XIII-XV*. Ed. and trans. D.E. Hill. Warminster: Aris & Phillips, 2000.

_____. *Ovid's Metamorphoses: The Arthur Golding Translation, 1567*. Ed. J.F. Nims. Philadelphia: Paul Dry Books, 2000.

_____. *Metamorphoses*. Ed. R.J. Tarrant. Oxford: Oxford University Press, 2004.

Ovid and the Renaissance Body. Ed. G. Stanivukovic. Toronto: University of Toronto Press, 2001.

Ovide moralisé. Ed. C. de Boer, M.G. de Boer, and J.Th.M. van't Sant. *Verhandelingen der Koninklijke Nederlandsche Akademie van Wetenschappen: Afdeeling Letterkunde*. Vols. 15, 21, 30, 36–7, 43. Amsterdam: Johannes Müller, 1915–1938.

The Oxford English Dictionary. 2nd ed. Oxford: Oxford University Press, 1989.

Pacca, V. *Petrarca*. Bari: Laterza, 1998.

Pairet, A. *'Les mutacions des fables': Figures de la métamorphose dans la littérature française du Moyen Âge*. Paris: Champion, 2002.

Panofsky, E. *Studies in Iconology: Humanistic Themes in the Art of the Renaissance*. Oxford: Oxford University Press, 1939. Rept. New York: Harper and Row, 1962.

_____. *Renaissance and Renascences in Western Art*. New York: Harper & Row, 1969.

Paoletti, J. "Michelangelo's Masks." *Art Bulletin* 74.3 (1992): 423–440.

Pardo, M. "Artifice as Seduction in Titian," pp. 55–89 in *Sexuality and Gender in Early Modern Europe*. Ed. J.G. Turner. New York: Cambridge University Press, 1993.

Parker, D. *Bronzino: Renaissance Painter as Poet*. New York: Cambridge University Press, 2001.

Parker, P. *Literary Fat Ladies: Rhetoric, Gender, Property*. London and New York: Methuen, 1987.

Parry, H. "Violence in a Pastoral Setting." *Transactions of the American Philological Association* 95 (1964): 268–282.

Patch, H.R. *The Goddess Fortuna in Mediaeval Literature.* Cambridge, MA: Harvard University Press, 1927. Rpt. New York: Octagon, 1974.

Patterson, L. "Feminine Rhetoric and the Politics of Subjectivity: La Vieille and the Wife of Bath," pp. 316–358 in *Rethinking the Romance of the Rose: Text, Image, Reception.* Ed. K. Brownlee and S. Huot. Philadelphia: University of Pennsylvania Press, 1992.

Paupert, A. "Christine et Boèce: De la lecture à l'écriture, de la réécriture à l'écriture du moi," pp. 645–662 in *Contexts and Continuities: Proceedings of the IVth International Colloquium on Christine de Pizan (Glasgow 21–27 July 2000).* Ed. A.J. Kennedy et al. Glasgow: Glasgow University Press, 2002.

Pearsall, D. "Gardens as Symbol and Setting." *Dumbarton Oaks Colloquium on the History of Landscape Architecture* 9 (1986): 237–251.

Peebles, B.M. "The *Ad Maronis mausoleum*: Petrarch's Virgil and Two Fifteenth-Century Manuscripts," pp. 169–198 in *Classical, Mediaeval and Renaissance Studies in Honor of Berthold Louis Ullman.* Vol. 2. Ed. C. Henderson. Rome: Edizioni di storia e letteratura, 1964.

Pelen, M.M. "Chaucer's Wife of Midas Reconsidered: Oppositions and Poetic Judgment in the *Wife of Bath's Tale*." *Florilegium* 13 (1994): 141–160.

Pellegrin, E. "Les *Remedia amoris* d'Ovide, texte scolaire médiéval." *Bibliothèque de l'École des Chartes* 115 (1957): 172–179. Rept. pp. 409–416 in *Bibliothèques retrouvées: Manuscrits, bibliothèques et bibliophiles du moyen âge et de la renaissance: Recueil d'études publiées de 1938 à 1985.* Paris: Editions du Centre nationale de la recherche scientifique, 1988.

Perlman, J.B. "Taking Aim at Amore: Michelangelo, Bronzino, and the Lexicon of Pictorial Ambiguity in Representations of Venus and Cupid." Ph.D. dissertation, University of Michigan, 2004.

Perry, K.A. *Another Reality: Metamorphosis and the Imagination in the Poetry of Ovid, Petrarch and Ronsard.* New York: Peter Lang, 1990.

Petrarch, F. "The Ascent of Mont Ventoux." Trans. H. Nachod. *The Renaissance Philosophy of Man.* Ed. E. Cassirer et al. Chicago and London: University of Chicago Press, 1948.

———. *Le Familiari, libri I-XI.* Introduction by U. Dotti. Urbino: Argalìa, 1974.

_____. *Petrarch's Lyric Poems: The Rime sparse and Other Lyrics*. Ed. and trans. R. Durling. Cambridge, MA: Harvard University Press, 1976.

_____. *Petrarch's Secretum, with Introduction, Notes and Critical Anthology*. Trans. D.A. Carozza and H.J. Shey. New York: Peter Lang, 1989.

_____. *Secretum*. Intro., trans. and notes by U. Dotti. Rome: Archivio Guido Izzi, 1993.

Philalethes, E. *Introitus apertus ad occlusum regis palatium*, pp. 651–699 in *Musaeum hermeticum reformatum et amplificatum*. Frankfurt: Hermannum à Sande, 1677–1678.

_____. *Metallorum Metamorphosis*, pp. 743–774 in *Musaeum hermeticum reformatum et amplificatum*. Frankfurt: Hermannum à Sande, 1677–1678.

_____. *The Metamorphosis of Metals*, pp. 227–245 in *The Hermetic Museum Restored and Enlarged*. Vol. 2. London: James Elliott, 1893.

_____. *An Open Entrance to the Closed Palace of the King*, pp. 159–198 in *The Hermetic Museum Restored and Enlarged*. Vol. 2. London: James Elliott, 1893.

Pico della Mirandola, I. *Opus aureum de auro*, pp. 312–377 in *Theatrum chemicum*. Vol. 2. Strasbourg: Zetzner, 1659. First published Venice: Baptista Somascho, 1586.

Pilliod, E. *Pontormo, Bronzino, Allori: A Genealogy of Florentine Art*. New Haven: Yale University Press, 2001.

Pitcher, R.A. "Martial's Debt to Ovid," pp. 59–76 in *Toto notus in orbe: Perspektiven der Martial-Interpretation* (= *Palingenesia LXV*). Ed. F. Grewing. Stuttgart: Franz Steiner Verlag, 1998.

Plaisance, M. "Une première affirmation de la politique culturelle de Côme Ier: La transformation de l'Académie des 'Humidi' en Académie Florentine 1540–1542," pp. 360–438 in *Les écrivains et le pouvoir en Italie a l'époque de la Renaissance*. Ed. A. Rochon. Paris: Université de la Sorbonne, 1973.

_____. "Culture et politique à Florence de 1542 à 1551: Lasca et les 'Humidi' aux prises avec L'Académie Florentine," pp. 149–242 in *Les écrivains et le pouvoir en Italie à l'époque de la Renaissance*. Ed. A. Rochon. Paris: Université de la Sorbonne, 1974.

Pliny. *Natural History in Ten Volumes*. Trans. D.E. Eichholz. Loeb Classical Library. Cambridge, MA: Harvard University Press, 1989.

Ponce Cárdenas, J. *Góngora y la poesía culta del siglo XVII*. Madrid: Ediciones del Laberinto, 2001.

Porter, E. "Gower's Ethical Microcosm and Political Macrocosm," pp. 135–162 in *Gower's Confessio amantis: Responses and Reassessments*. Ed. A.J. Minnis. Cambridge, UK: Brewer, 1983.

Possamaï-Perez, M. "Les 'Mutacions des Fables': Illusion et tromperie dans l'*Ovide moralisé*," pp. 469–489 in *Magie et illusion au moyen âge*. Sénéfiance 42. Aix-en-Provence: Université de Provence, 1999.

———. "La réécriture de la métamorphose dans l'*Ovide moralisé*," pp. 149–163 in *Lectures d'Ovide: Publiées à la mémoire de Jean-Pierre Néraudau*. Ed. E. Bury and M. Néraudau. Paris: Les Belles Lettres, 2003.

Preussner, A. "The Actaeon Myth in Ovid, Petrarch, Wyatt and Sidney." *Bestia: Yearbook of the Beast Fable Society* 5 (1993): 95–108.

Przychocki, G. *Accessus Ovidiani*. Kraków: Nakladem Akademii Umiejetnosci, 1911.

Pseudo-Lucian. "Affairs of the Heart." *Lucian in Eight Volumes*. Vol. 8. Trans. M.D. Macleod. Loeb Classical Library. Cambridge, MA: Harvard University Press, 1967.

Purkiss, D. *The Witch in History: Early Modern and Twentieth Century Representations*. London: Routledge, 1996.

Quilligan, M. *The Allegory of Female Authority: Christine de Pizan's Cité des dames*. Ithaca: Cornell University Press, 1991.

Quinones, R.J. *The Renaissance Discovery of Time*. Cambridge, MA: Harvard University Press, 1972.

Quiviger, F. "Benedetto Varchi and the Visual Arts." *Journal of the Warburg and Courtauld Institutes* 50 (1987): 219–224.

Rand, E.K. *Ovid and His Influence*. Boston: Marshall Jones, 1925.

Redondo, A. "De don Clavijo a Clavileño: algunos aspectos de la tradición carnavalesca y cazurra en el *Quijote* (II, 38–41)." *Edad de Oro* 3 (1984): 181–199.

The Reign of Elizabeth I: Court and Culture in the Last Decade. Ed. J. Guy. Cambridge, UK: Cambridge University Press, 1995.

Reiss, T.J. *Mirages of the Selfe: Patterns of Personhood in Ancient and Early Modern Europe*. Stanford: Stanford University Press, 2003.

Reno, C. "The Preface to the *Avision-Christine* in ex-Phillipps 128," pp. 207–227 in *Reinterpreting Christine de Pizan*. Ed. E.J. Richards et al. Athens: University of Georgia Press, 1992.

Reynolds, S. *Medieval Reading: Grammar, Rhetoric and the Classical Text*. Cambridge, UK: Cambridge University Press, 1996.

Richards, E.J. "Christine de Pizan and Dante: A Re-Examination." *Archiv für das Studium der Neueren Sprachen und Literaturen* 222 (1985): 100–111.

_____. "The Lady Wants to Talk: Christine de Pizan's *Epistre a Eustace Mourel*," pp. 109–122 in *Eustace Deschamps French Courtier-Poet*. Ed. D.M. Sinnreich-Levi. New York: AMS Press, 1998.

Rico, F. *Vida u obra de Petrarca, Vol. 1, Lectura del Secretum*. Chapel Hill: University of North Carolina, Department of Romance Languages, 1974.

Ridewall, J. *Fulgentius metaforalis*. Ed. H. Liebeschütz. Leipzig and Berlin: Warburg Institute, 1926.

Riggs, W.G. "The Poet and Satan in *Paradise Lost*." *Milton Studies* 2 (1970): 59–82.

Robertson, D.W. *A Preface to Chaucer: Studies in Medieval Perspectives*. Princeton: Princeton University Press, 1962.

_____. "The Wife of Bath and Midas." *Studies in the Age of Chaucer* 6 (1984): 1–20.

Rodriguez, J. *Bursario*. Ed. P. Saquero Suárez-Somonte and T. González Rolán. Madrid: Universidad Complutense, 1984.

Roman, L. "The Representation of Literary Materiality in Martial's *Epigrams*," *Journal of Roman Studies* 91 (2001): 113–145.

Roob, A. *The Hermetic Museum: Alchemy and Mysticism*. Trans. S. Whiteside. Cologne: Taschen, 1997.

Root, J. "'Space to speke': The Wife of Bath and the Discourse of Confession." *Chaucer Review* 28 (1994): 252–274.

Roppolo, J.P. "The Converted Knight in Chaucer's 'Wife of Bath's Tale.'" *College English* 12 (1951): 263–269.

Rosati, G. "Narrative Techniques and Narrative Structures in the *Metamorphoses*," pp. 271–304 in *Brill's Companion to Ovid*. Ed. B.W. Boyd. Leiden: Brill, 2002.

Roses Lozano, J. *Una poética de la oscuridad: La recepción crítica de las Soledades en el siglo XVII*. Madrid: Támesis, 1994.

Rosner-Seigel, J. "*Amor*, Metamorphosis and Magic: Ovid's Medea, *Metamorphoses* 7.1–424." *Classical Journal* 77 (1982): 231–243.

Rossi, A. "Ricognizioni sulla tradizione manoscritta delle Metamorphoses di Ovidio: Tipologie materiali, grafiche e testuali di argumenta e tituli pseudo-lattanziani dal IX al XV secolo." Ph.D. dissertation, Università di Bari, 2001.

Rotondi, G. "Ovidio nel Medioevo." *Convivium. Rivista di lettere, filosofia e storia* 6 (1934): 262–269.

Roy, B. and H.V. Shooner. "Querelles de maîtres au XIIᵉ siècle: Arnoul d'Orléans et son milieu." *Sandalion* 8–9 (1985–86): 315–341. Rept. B. Roy, pp. 141–163 in *Une culture de l'équivoque*. Montréal-Paris: Presses de l'Université de Montréal; Champion-Slatkine, 1992.

Rumrich, J. *Milton Unbound: Controversy and Reinterpretation*. Cambridge, UK: Cambridge University Press, 1996.

Russell, J.B. *Witchcraft in the Middle Ages*. Ithaca: Cornell University Press, 1972.

Samuel, I. *Dante and Milton: The Commedia and Paradise Lost*. Ithaca: Cornell University Press, 1966.

Santagata, M. *I frammenti dell'anima: Storia e racconto nel Canzoniere di Petrarca*. Bologna: Il Mulino, 1992.

Saul, N. *Richard II*. New Haven: Yale University Press, 1997.

Scaglione, A. "Classical Heritage and Petrarchan Self-Consciousness in the Literary Emergence of the Interior 'I,'" pp. 125–137 in *Petrarch*. Ed. H. Bloom. New York: Chelsea House, 1988.

Scève, Maurice. *The Délie of Maurice Scève*. Ed. I.D. MacFarlane. Cambridge, UK: Cambridge University Press, 1966.

Schevill, R. *Ovid and the Renascence in Spain*. Berkeley: University of California Press, 1913. Rept. New York and Hildesheim: Georg Olms, 1971.

Schibanoff, S. "Argus and Argyve: Etymology and Characterization in Chaucer's *Troilus*." *Speculum* 51 (1976): 647–658.

———. "Taking the Gold out of Egypt: The Art of Reading as a Woman," pp. 83–106 in *Gender and Reading: Essays on Readers, Texts, and Contexts*. Ed. E.A. Flynn and P.P. Schweikart. Baltimore: Johns Hopkins University Press, 1986.

Schlauch, M. "The Allegory of Church and Synagogue." *Speculum* 14 (1939): 448–464.

Schwartz, R. *Remembering and Repeating: On Milton's Theology and Poetics*. 2nd ed. Chicago and London: University of Chicago Press, 1993.

Scot, R. *The Discouerie of Witchcraft wherein the Lewde Dealing of Witches and Witchmongers is Notablie Detected . . .* London: William Brome, 1584.

———. *The Discoverie of Witchcraft*. "The English Experience." Amsterdam: Da Capo P, 1971. Facsimile of Bodleian Library, Shelfmarks: Douce S.216 and 4_.S.53Th.

_____. *The Discoverie of Witchcraft*. Ed. M. Summers. 1930. Mineola, NY: Dover Publications, 1972.

Scotti, M. "Il proemio delle *Metamorfosi* tra Ovidio ed Apuleio," *Giornale Italiano di Filologia* 34 (1982): 43–65.

Segal, C. *Landscape in Ovid's Metamorphoses: A Study in the Transformation of a Literary Symbol*. Hermes Zeitschrift 23. Wiesbaden: F. Steiner, 1969.

Seiferth, W.S. *Synagogue and Church in the Middle Ages: Two Symbols in Art and Literature*. Trans. L. Chadeayne and P. Gottwald. New York: Frederick Unger, 1970.

Semple, B. "The Consolation of a Woman Writer: Christine de Pizan's Use of Boethius in *L'Avision-Christine*," pp. 39–48 in *Women, the Book, and the Worldly: Selected Proceedings of the St. Hilda's Conference, 1993*. Ed. L. Smith and J.H.M. Taylor. Woodbridge: D.S. Brewer, 1995.

Servius Grammaticus. *Servii Grammatici qui feruntur in Vergilii Carmina Commentarii*. Ed. G. Thilo and H. Hagen. 3 vols. 1878–1902. Hildesheim: G. Olms, 1961.

Seznec, J. *The Survival of the Pagan Gods: The Mythological Tradition and its Place in Renaissance Humanism and Art*. Trans. B.F. Sessions. Princeton: Princeton University Press, 1953.

Shain, C.E. "Pulpit Rhetoric in Three Canterbury Tales." *Modern Language Notes* 70 (1955): 235–245.

Shakespeare, W. *A Midsummer Night's Dream: Texts and Contexts*. Ed. G.K. Paster and S. Howard. Boston: Bedford/St. Martin's, 1999.

Shapiro, B.J. *Probability and Certainty in Seventeenth-Century England: A Study of the Relationships Between Natural Science, Religion, History, Law, and Literature*. Princeton, NJ: Princeton University Press, 1983.

Sharpe, J. *Instruments of Darkness: Witchcraft in England 1550–1750*. London: Hamish Hamilton, 1996.

_____. *Witchcraft in Early Modern England*. Harlow: Pearson Education, 2001.

Sharrock, A. *Seduction and Repetition in Ovid's Ars amatoria 2*. Oxford: Clarendon Press, 1994.

Shooner, H.V. "Les *Bursarii Ovidianorum* de Guillaume d'Orléans." *Mediaeval Studies* 43 (1981): 405–424.

Sieburth, R. *Emblems of Desire: Selections from the "Délie" of Maurice Scève*. Philadelphia: University of Pennsylvania Press, 2003.

Simon, M. "Les Dieux antiques dans la pensée chrétienne." *Zeitschrift für Religions-und Geistesgeschichte* 6 (1954): 97–114.

Simpson, J. *Sciences and the Self in Medieval Poetry: Alan of Lille's Anticlaudianus and John Gower's Confessio amantis.* Cambridge, UK: Cambridge University Press, 1995.

Simpson, J.R. *Fantasy, Identity and Misrecognition in Medieval French Narrative.* Oxford: Peter Lang, 2000.

Small, J.P. *Wax Tablets of the Mind: Cognitive Studies of Memory and Literacy in Classical Antiquity.* New York: Routledge, 1997.

Smith, G. "Jealousy, Pleasure, and Pain in Agnolo Bronzino's *Allegory of Venus and Cupid.*" *Pantheon* 39 (1981): 250–258.

Solodow, J.B. *The World of Ovid's Metamorphoses.* Chapel Hill and London: University of North Carolina Press, 1988.

Spenser, E. *The Faerie Queene.* Ed. A.C. Hamilton. New York: Longman, 1977.

Spiller, E. *Science, Reading, and Renaissance Literature: The Art of Making Knowledge, 1580–1670.* Cambridge, UK: Cambridge University Press, 2004.

Stewart, A. *Art, Desire, and the Body in Ancient Greece.* New York: Cambridge University Press, 1997.

Stock, B. *Augustine the Reader: Meditation, Self-Knowledge and the Ethics of Interpretation.* Cambridge, MA: Harvard University Press, 1996.

———. *After Augustine: The Meditative Reader and the Text.* Philadelphia: University of Pennsylvania Press, 2001.

Stow, G.B. "Richard II in Thomas Walsingham's Chronicles." *Speculum* 59 (1984): 68–102.

Sturm-Maddox, S. *Petrarch's Metamorphoses: Text and Subtext in the Rime sparse.* Columbia, MO: University of Missouri Press, 1985.

Sullivan, J.P. *Literature and Politics in the Age of Nero.* Ithaca and London: Cornell University Press, 1985.

Summers, J. *The Muses' Method: An Introduction to Paradise Lost.* Cambridge, MA: Harvard University Press, 1962.

Tarrant, R.J. "Ovid," pp. 257–84 in *Texts and Transmission.* Ed. L.D. Reynolds. Oxford: Clarendon Press, 1983.

———. *Seneca's Thyestes.* Atlanta: American Philological Association, 1985.

———. "The *Narrationes* of 'Lactantius' and the Transmission of Ovid's *Metamorphoses*," pp. 83–115 in *Formative Stages of Classical Traditions: Latin Texts from Antiquity to the Renaissance: Proceedings of a Conference Held at Erice, 16–22 October 1993.* Ed. O. Pecere and

M.D. Reeve. Spoleto: Centro italiano di studi sull'Alto medioevo, 1995.

_____. "Ovid and Ancient Literary History," pp. 13–33 in *The Cambridge Companion to Ovid*. Ed. P. Hardie. Cambridge, UK: Cambridge University Press, 2002.

Tateo, F. *Dialogo interiore e polemica ideologica nel Secretum del Petrarca*. Florence: Le Monnier, 1965.

Theatrum chemicum. 6 vols. Strasbourg: Zetzner, 1659–1661. Vols. 1–4 first printed Ursel: Zetzner, 1602.

Theodorakopoulos, E. "Closure and Transformation in Ovid's *Metamorphoses*," pp. 142–161 in *Ovidian Transformations: Essays on Ovid's Metamorphoses and its Reception*. Ed. P. Hardie, A. Barchiesi, and S. Hinds. Cambridge Philological Society Supplementary Vol. 23. Cambridge, UK: Cambridge Philological Society, 1999.

Thirteenth-Century Anthology of Rhetorical Poems. Glasgow MS Hunterian V.8.14, A. Ed. B. Harbert. Toronto: Pontifical Institute of Mediaeval Studies for the Centre for Medieval Studies, 1975.

Thomas, S.S. "What the Man of Law Can't Say: The Buried Legal Argument of the Wife of Bath's Prologue." *Chaucer Review* 31 (1997): 256–71.

Tinkle, T. *Medieval Venuses and Cupids: Sexuality, Hermeneutics, and English Poetry*. Stanford: Stanford University Press, 1996.

Tissol, G. "Polyphemus and his Audiences: Narrative and Power in Ovid's *Metamorphoses*." *Syllecta Classica* 2 (1990): 45–58.

Trinkaus, C. *The Poet as Philosopher: Petrarch and the Formation of Renaissance Consciousness*. New Haven: Yale University Press, 1979.

Trismosin, S. *Splendor solis*. Trans. J. Godwin with commentary by A. McLean. Edinburgh: Magnum Opus Hermetic Sourceworks, 1981.

Nicolas Valois, "Les cinq livres ou la clef du secret des secrets" précédé de Nicolas Grosparmy "Le trésor des trésors." Ed. B. Roger. Paris: Retz, 1975.

Vance, E. "Augustine's Confessions and the Grammar of Selfhood." *Genre* 6 (1973): 1–28.

Varchi, B. *Opere*. 2 vols. Trieste: Sezione Letterario-Artistico del Lloyd Austriaco, 1858–1859.

Vasari, G. *Le vite de' più eccellenti pittori, scultori, e architettori nella redazioni del 1550 e 1568*. 6 vols. Ed. R. Bettarini and P. Barocchi. Florence: Studio per Edizioni Scelte, 1966.

Venere e Amore: Michelangelo e la nuova bellezza ideale. Venus and Love Michelangelo and the New Ideal of Beauty. Ed. F. Falletti and J. Katz Nelson. Florence: Giunti, 2002.

Vergil. *Eclogues, Georgics, Aeneid, 1–6*. Trans. H.R. Fairclough. Rev. ed. 1935. Loeb Classical Library. Cambridge, MA: Harvard University Press, 1967.

———. *Eclogues*. Trans. H. Rushton Fairclough, rev. G.P. Goold. Loeb Classical Library. Cambridge, MA: Harvard University Press, 1999.

Viarre, S. *L'image et la pensée dans les "Métamorphoses" d'Ovide*. Paris: Presses Universitaires de France, 1964.

———. *La Survie d'Ovide dans la littérature scientifique des XIIe et XIIIe siècles*. Poitiers: Université de Poitiers, 1966.

Vickers, N. "Diana Described: Scattered Woman and Scattered Rhyme." *Critical Inquiry* 8 (1981): 265–279.

Vilanova, A. "El peregrino de amor en las *Soledades* de Góngora," pp. 421–460 in *Estudios dedicados a Menéndez Pidal*. Vol. 3. Madrid: CSIC, 1952.

Vinge, L. *The Narcissus Theme in Western European Literature up to the Early Nineteenth Century*. Trans. R. Dewsnap, L. Gronlund, N. Reeves, and I. Soderberg-Reeves. Lund: Gleerups, 1967.

Waley, P. "Some Uses of Classical Mythology in the *Soledades* of Góngora." *Bulletin of Hispanic Studies* 36 (1959): 193–209.

Wallace, D. *Chaucerian Polity: Absolutist Lineages and Associational Forms in England and Italy*. Stanford: Stanford University Press, 1997.

Walsingham, T. *De archana deorum*. Ed. R.A. van Kluyve. Durham, NC: Duke University Press, 1968.

Ward, J.O. "From Marginal Gloss to Catena Commentary: The Eleventh-Century Origins of a Rhetorical Teaching Tradition in the Medieval West." *Parergon* 13 (1996): 109–120.

———. "The Catena Commentaries on the Rhetoric of Cicero and their Implications for Development of a Teaching Tradition in Rhetoric." *Studies in Medieval and Renaissance Teaching* 6 (1998): 79–95.

Watson, P. *The Garden of Love in Tuscan Art of the Early Renaissance*. Philadelphia: Art Alliance Press, 1979.

Watt, D. *Amoral Gower: Language, Sex, and Politics*. Minneapolis: University of Minnesota Press, 2003.

Weil, S. "Freedom Through Association? Chaucer's Psychology of Argumentation in *The Wife of Bath's Prologue*." *Pacific Coast Philology* 30.1 (1995): 27–41.

Welles, M. *Arachne's Tapestry: The Transformation of Myth in Seventeenth-Century Spain.* San Antonio, TX: Trinity University Press, 1986.

———. *Persephone's Girdle: Narratives of Rape in Seventeenth-Century Spanish Literature.* Nashville: Vanderbilt University Press, 2000.

Westminster Chronicle 1381–94. Ed. and trans. L.C. Hector and B.F. Harvey. Oxford: Clarendon Press, 1982.

Wheeler, S.M. *A Discourse of Wonders: Audience and Performance in Ovid's Metamorphoses.* Philadelphia: University of Pennsylvania Press, 1999.

Wieland, G.R. *The Latin Glosses on Arator and Prudentius in Cambridge University Library MS Gg.5.35.* Toronto: Pontifical Institute of Mediaeval Studies, 1983.

———. "Interpreting the Interpretation: The Polysemy of the Latin Gloss." *Journal of Medieval Latin* 8 (1998): 59–71.

Wilks, M. *The Problem of Sovereignty in the Later Middle Ages.* Cambridge, UK: Cambridge University Press, 1964.

Willard, T. "Alchemy and the Bible," pp. 115–127 in *Centre and Labyrinth: Essays in Honour of Northrop Frye.* Ed. E. Cook et al. Toronto: University of Toronto Press, 1982.

Willis, J. *Latin Textual Criticism.* Urbana: University of Illinois Press, 1972.

Wilson, Sir D. *Caliban, the Missing Link.* London: Macmillan, 1873.

Witt, R.G. *In the Footsteps of the Ancients: The Origins of Humanism from Lovato to Bruni.* Leiden: Brill, 2000.

Yager, S. "The End of Knowledge: The Argus Legend and Chaucer." *Essays in Medieval Studies* 10 (1994): 15–26.

Yeager, R.F. *John Gower's Poetic: The Search for a New Arion.* Cambridge, UK: Brewer, 1990.

INDEX

Figure 3.1 Frontispiece, *Ovide moralisé*, Rouen Bib. Mun. 04, fol. 16r. Collections de la Bibliothèque municipale de Rouen. Clichés: Thierry Ascencio-Parvy.

Figure 3.2 Actaeon as a stag looks at Diana bathing with her nymphs. *Ovide moralisé*, Rouen Bib. Mun. 04, fol. 74v. Collections de la Bibliothèque municipale de Rouen. Clichés: Thierry Ascencio- Parvy.

Figure 3.3   Actaeon devoured by his hunting dogs. *Ovide moralisé*, Rouen Bib. Mun. 04, fol. 75r. Collections de la Bibliothèque municipale de Rouen. Clichés: Thierry Ascencio-Parvy

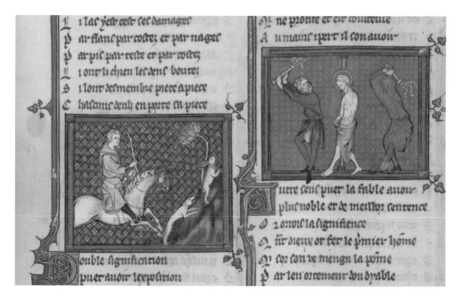

Figure 3.4 Two allegories for the Actaeon story: left, a hunter on horseback with a dog and a hare; right, the flagellation of Christ. *Ovide moralisé*, Rouen Bib. Mun. 04, fol. 76r. Collections de la Bibliothèque municipale de Rouen. Clichés: Thierry Ascencio-Parvy.

Figure 3.5   Apollo purses Daphne; Apollo embraces Daphne who has been transformed into a tree. *Ovide moralisé*, Rouen Bib. Mun. 04, fol. 33v. Collections de la Bibliothèque municipale de Rouen. Clichés: Thierry Ascencio-Parvy.

Figure 3.6 The Annunciation as an allegory for the Daphne story. *Ovide moralisé*, Rouen Bib. Mun. 04, fol. 35r. Collections de la Bibliothèque municipale de Rouen. Clichés: Thierry Ascencio-Parvy.

Figure 3.7 The nativity of Christ as an allegory for the Callisto story. *Ovide moralisé*, Rouen Bib. Mun. 04, fol. 53r. Collections de la Bibliothèque municipale de Rouen. Clichés: Thierry Ascencio-Parvy.

Figure 3.8 Diana, Virbius, and Egeria. *Ovide moralisé*, Rouen Bib. Mun. 04, fol. 396r. Collections de la Bibliothèque municipale de Rouen. Clichés: Thierry Ascencio-Parvy.

Figure 5.1 The fountain of wisdom. *Ovide moralisé* (ca. 1400), Paris, BnF
Ms. fr. 871 fol. 116v.

Figure 5.2 The fountain of wisdom. *Chemin de long estude* (ca. 1403), Paris, BnF Ms. fr. 1188 fol. 14.

Figure 5.3 The fountain of wisdom. *Chemin de long estude* (ca. 1408), Paris, BnF Ms. fr. 836 fol. 5v.

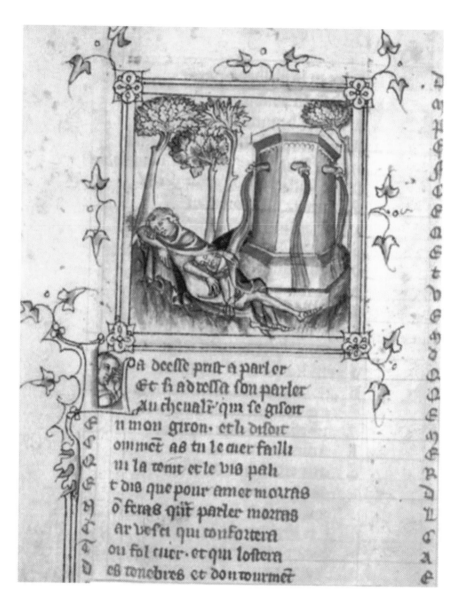

Figure 5.4 The poet and lover asleep next to the fountain. *La Fonteinne amoureuse* (ca. 1377), Paris, BnF Ms. fr. 1584 fol. 165v.

Figure 5.5 Apollo and Daphne. *Epistre Othea* (1408), Paris, BnF Ms. fr. 606 fol. 40v.

EMBLEMA XXXVIII. *De fecretis Naturæ.*

Rebis, ut Hermaphroditus, nafcitur ex duobus montibus, Mercurii & Veneris.

EPIGRAMMA XXXVIII.

R Em geminam *REBIS* veteres dixére, quod uno
　Corpore fit mas hæc fœminaque, Androgyna.
Natus enim binis in montibus HERMAPHRODITUS
　Dicitur, Hermeti quem tulit alma Venus.
Ancipitem fexum ne fpernas, nam tibi Regem
　• *Mas idem, mulierque una eademque dabit.*

Figure 8.1 Mercury, Venus, and Hermaphroditus. Michael Maier, *Symbola aureae mensae* (1617).

Figure 8.2 Boiling the body from Solomon Trismosin, *Splendor solis* (1582).

EMBLEMA XLI. *De secretis Naturæ.*

Adonis ab apro occiditur, cui Venus accurrens tinxit Rosas sanguine.

EPIGRAMMA XLI.

EX patre, *Myrrha suo pulchrum suscepit Adonim:*
    Delitias Cypriæ, quem nece stravit aper.
Accurrit Venus & pede læsa cruore ruborem
    Contulit ipsa rosæ, quæ prius alba fuit.
Flet Dea (flent Syri, luctus communis in orbe est)
    illum lactucis mollibus & posuit.
                            Q

Figure 8.3 Venus and Adonis. Michael Maier, *Atalanta fugiens* (1617).

To the Honorable,mine especiall good
Lord, Sir Roger Manwood Knight,Lord
cheefe Baron of hir Maiesties Court
of the Eschequer.

N SOMVCH
as I know that your
Lordſhip is by na-
ture whollie incli-
ned,and in purpoſe
earneſtly bent to re-
leeue the poore,and
that not onlie with
hoſpitalitie and al-
mes, but by diuerſe
other deuiſes and
waies tending to
their comfort, ha-
uing(as it were) fra-
med and ſet your ſelfe to the helpe and maintenance
of their eſtate; as appeareth by your charge and trauell in
that behalfe. Whereas alſo you haue a ſpeciall care for
the ſupporting of their right, and redreſſing of their
wrongs,as neither deſpiſing their calamitie, nor yet for-
getting their complaint, ſeeking all meanes for their a-
mendement, and for the reformation of their diſorders,
euen as a verie father to the poore. Finallie,for that I am a
poore member of that common wealth wherevour Lord

Figure 9.1 Reginald Scot, *The Discoverie of Witchcraft*. London: William
Brome (Henry Denham), 1584. With special thanks to the Masters and
Fellows of St. Catharine's College, Cambridge.

To the Readers.

O you that are wi
& difcreete few wor
may fuffice : for fu
a one iudgeth not
the firft fight, nor
prooueth by herefa
but patientlie heare
and thereby incr
feth in vnderftandin
which patience brit
eth foorth experier
whereby true iud
ment is directed
fhall not need the
fore to make anie

ther fute to you, but that it would pleafe you to read my bo
without the preiudice of time, or former conceipt : and hat
obteined this at your hands, I fubmit my felfe vnto your cenf
But to make a folemne fute to you that are parciall readers, c
ring you to fet afide parcialitie, to take in good part my writ
and with indifferent eies to looke vpon my booke, were lat
loft, and time ill imploied. For I fhould no more preuaile hei
than if a hundred yeares fince I fhould haue intreated your
deceffors to beleeue, that Robin goodfellowe, that great anc
cient bulbegger, had beene but a coufening merchant, an
diuell indeed.

If I fhould go to a papift, and faie; I praie you beleeue my
tings, wherein I will prooue all popifh charmes, coniurations

Figure 9.2 Second historiated initial from *The Discoverie*.

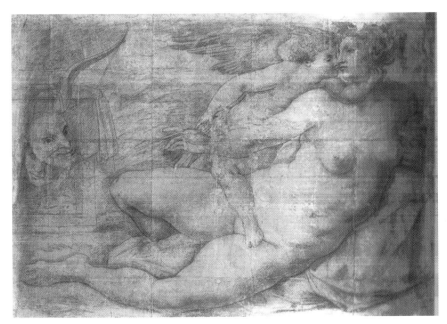

Figure 12.1 Unidentified sixteenth-century artist, after Michelangelo Buonarroti, *Venus and Cupid*, ca. 1533–1540, charcoal, 127.7 x 183.3 cm, Naples, Museo Nazionale di Capodimonte, Inv. 86654. Reproduced with the kind permission of the Fototeca della Soprintendenza per il Polo Museale Napoletano.

Figure 12.2 Jacopo Carracci, called Pontormo, following a cartoon by Michelangelo Buonarroti, *Venus and Cupid,* ca. 1533, oil on panel, 128.5 x 193 cm, Florence, Galleria dell'Accademia, Inv. 1890/1570. Reproduced with the kind permission of the Ministero per i Beni e le Attività Culturali, and may not be further reproduced or copied in any manner.

Publications of the
Centre for Reformation and Renaissance Studies

ISBN information is for paperback edition unless otherwise specified

Barnabe Riche Society Publications

Lodge, Thomas. *A Margarite of America*. Ed. by Henry Janzen and intro. by Don Beecher (2005), pp. 205. ISBN 978-0-7727-2027-6

Essays and Studies

Estes, James M. *Christian Magistrate and Territorial Church: Johannes Brenz and the German Reformation*. (2007), pp. 243. ISBN 978-0-7727-2034-4

French Ceremonial Entries in the Sixteenth Century: Event, Image, Text. Ed. by Nicolas Russell and Hélène Visentin (2007), pp. 276. ISBN 978-0-7727-2033-7

Reformation Sources: The Letters of Wolfgang Capito and his Fellow Reformers in Alsace and Switzerland. Ed. by Erika Rummel and Milton Kooista (2007), pp. 252. ISBN 978-0-7727-2032-0

Lanaro, Paola. *At the Centre of the Old World: Trade and Manufacturing in Venice and on the Venetian Mainland, 1400—1800*. (2006), pp. 416. ISBN 978-0-7727-2031-3

Connell, William J. and Giles Constable. *Sacrilege and Redemption in Renaissance Florence: The Case of Antonio Rinaldeschi*. (2005), pp. 125. ISBN 978-0-7727-2030-6

Sins of the Flesh: Responding to Sexual Disease in Early Modern Europe. Ed. by Kevin Siena (2005), pp. 296. ISBN 978-0-7727-2029-0

Zirpolo, Lilian. *Ave Papa, Ave Papabile: The Sacchetti Family, Their Art Patronage, and Political Aspirations*. (2005), pp. 252. ISBN 978-0-7727-2028-3

Fantasies of Troy: Classical Tales and the Social Imaginary in Medieval and Early Modern Europe. Ed. by Alan Shepard and Stephen D. Powell (2004), pp. 306. ISBN 978-0-7727-2025-2

Shell Games: Studies in Scams, Frauds, and Deceits (1300-1650) Ed. by Mark Crane, Richard Raiswell and Margaret Reeves (2004), pp.334. ISBN 978-0-7727-2023-8

A Renaissance of Conflicts: Visions and Revisions of Law and Society in Italy and Spain. Ed. by John Marino and Thomas Kuehn (2004), pp. 456. ISBN 978-0-7727-2022-1

The Renaissance in the Nineteenth Century / Le XIX^c siècle renaissant. Ed. by Yannick Portebois and Nicolas Terpstra (2003), pp. 302. ISBN 978-0-7727-2019-1

The Premodern Teenager: Youth in Society 1150-1650. Ed. by Konrad Eisenbichler (2002), pp. 349. ISBN 978-0-7727-2018-4

Occasional Publications

Estes, James M. *The First Forty Years: A Brief History of the Centre for Reformation and Renaissance Studies.* (2004), pp. 106. ISBN 978-0-7727-2026-9

Annotated Catalogue of Editions of Erasmus at the Centre for Reformation and Renaissance Studies, Toronto. Comp. by Jacqueline Glomski and Erika Rummel (1994), pp. 153. ISBN 978-0-9697512-1-2

Register of Sermons Preached at St. Paul's Cross (1534-1642). Comp. by Millar MacLure and revised by Peter Pauls and Jackson Campbell Boswell (1989), pp. 152. ISBN 978-0-919473-48-5

Language and Literature. Early Printed Books at the CRRS. Comp. by Willian R. Bowen and Konrad Eisenbichler (1986), pp. 112. ISBN 978-0-7727-2009-2

Published Books (1499-1700) on Science, Medicine and Natural History at the CRRS Comp. by William R. Bowen and Konrad Eisenbichler (1986), pp. 37. ISBN 978-0-7727-2005-4

Bibles, Theological Treatises and Other Religious Literature, 1492-1700, at the CRRS. Comp. by Konrad Eisenbichler, Gay MacDonald and Robert Sweetman (1981), pp. 94. ISBN 978-0-7727-2002-3

Humanist Editions of Statutes and Histories at the CRRS. Comp. by Konrad Eisenbichler, Gay MacDonald and C. Turner (1980), pp. 63. ISBN 978-0-7727-2001-6

Humanist Editions of the Classics at the CRRS. Comp. by N.L. Anderson, Kenneth R. Bartlett, Konrad Eisenbichler, and Janis Svilpis (1979), pp. 71. ISBN 978-0-7727-2000-9

Renaissance and Reformation Texts in Translation

Du Bellay, Ronsard, Sébillet. *Poetry and Language in 16th-Century France.* Trans. and intro. by Laura Willett (2004), pp.116. ISBN 978-0-7727-2021-4

Girolamo Savonarola. *A Guide to Righteous Living and Other Works.* Trans. and intro. by Konrad Eisenbichler (2003), pp. 243. ISBN 978-0-7727-2020-7

Godly Magistrates and Church Order: Johannes Brenz and the Establishment of the Lutheran Territorial Church in Germany, 1524-1559. Trans. and ed. by James M. Estes (2001), pp. 219. ISBN 978-0-7727-2017-7

Giovanni Della Casa. *Galateo: A Renaissance Treatise on Manners*. Trans. by Konrad Eisenbichler and Kenneth R. Bartlett. 3rd ed. (2001), pp. 98. ISBN 978-0-9697512-2-9

Romeo and Juliet Before Shakespeare: Four Stories of Star-Crossed Love. Trans. by Nicole Prunster (2000), pp. 127. ISBN 978-0-7727-2015-3

Jean Bodin. *On the Demon-Mania of Witches*. Abridged, trans. and ed. Randy A. Scott and Jonathan L. Pearl (1995), pp. 219. ISBN 978-0-9697512-5-0

Whether Secular Government Has the Right to Wield the Sword in Matters of Faith: A Controversy in Nürnberg in 1530. Trans. and ed. by James M. Estes (1994), pp. 118. ISBN 978-0-9697512-4-3

Lorenzo Valla. *'The Profession of the Religious' and Selections from 'The Falsely-Believed and Forged Donation of Constantine'*. Trans. and ed. Olga Z. Pugliese. 2nd ed. (1994), pp. 114. ISBN 978-0-9697512-3-6

A. Karlstadt, H. Emser, J. Eck. *A Reformation Debate: Karlstadt, Emser and Eck on Sacred Images*. Trans. and ed. Brian Mangrum and Giuseppe Scavizzi. 2nd edition (1991), pp. 112. ISBN 978-0-9697512-7-4

Nicholas of Cusa. *The Layman on Wisdom and the Mind*. Trans. by Mark L. Feuhrer (1989), pp. 112. ISBN 978-0-919473-56-0

Bernardino Ochino. *Seven Dialogues*. Trans. and ed. by Rita Belladonna (1988), pp. 96. ISBN 978-0-919473-63-8

Tudor and Stuart Texts

The Queen's Majesty's Passage and Related Documents. Ed. and intro by Germaine Warkentin. (2004), pp. 158. ISBN 978-0-7727-2024-5

Early Stuart Pastoral: 'The Shepherd's Pipe' by William Browne and others, and *'The Shepherd's Hunting' by George Wither*. Ed. and intro by James Doelman (1999), pp. 196. ISBN 978-0-9697512-9-8

The Trial of Nicholas Throckmorton. Ed. and intro by Annabel Patterson (1998), pp. 108. 978-0-9697512-8-1

James I. *The True Law of Free Monarchies* and *Basilikon Doron*. Ed. and intro by Daniel Fischlin and Mark Fortier (1996), pp. 181. ISBN 978-0-9697512-6-7

To order books, and for additional information, contact:

CRRS Publications, Victoria University
71 Queen's Park, Toronto ON, M5S 1K7, CANADA
tel: (416) 585-4465 / fax: (416) 585-4430
e-mail: crrs.publications@utoronto.ca / web: <www.crrs.ca>

DATE DUE